Lecture Notes in Artificial Intelligence   1621

Subseries of Lecture Notes in Computer Science
Edited by J. G. Carbonell and J. Siekmann

Lecture Notes in Computer Science

Edited by G. Goos, J. Hartmanis and J. van Leeuwen

T0217359

Springer

Berlin
Heidelberg
New York
Barcelona
Hong Kong
London
Milan
Paris
Singapore
Tokyo

Dieter Fensel   Rudi Studer (Eds.)

Knowledge Acquisition, Modeling and Management

11th European Workshop, EKAW '99
Dagstuhl Castle, Germany, May 26-29, 1999
Proceedings

Springer

Series Editors

Jaime G. Carbonell, Carnegie Mellon University, Pittsburgh, PA, USA
Jörg Siekmann, University of Saarland, Saarbrücken, Germany

Volume Editors

Dieter Fensel
Rudi Studer
University of Karlsruhe, AIFB
Institute for Applied Computer Science and Formal Description Methods
D-76128 Karlsruhe, Germany
E-mail: {dieter.fensel, studer}@aifb.uni-karlsruhe.de

Cataloging-in-Publication data applied for

Die Deutsche Bibliothek - CIP-Einheitsaufnahme

Knowledge acquisition, modeling and management : 11th
European workshop ; proceedings / EKAW '99, Dagstuhl Castle,
Germany, May 26 - 29, 1999. Dieter Fensel ; Rudi Studer (ed.). -
Berlin ; Heidelberg ; New York ; Barcelona ; Hong Kong ; London ;
Milan ; Paris ; Singapore ; Tokyo : Springer, 1999
   (Lecture notes in computer science ; Vol. 1621 : Lecture notes in
   artificial intelligence)
   ISBN 3-540-66044-5

CR Subject Classification (1998): I.2

ISBN 3-540-66044-5 Springer-Verlag Berlin Heidelberg New York

© Springer-Verlag Berlin Heidelberg 1999
Printed in Germany

Typesetting: Camera-ready by author
SPIN 10705262   06/3142 – 5 4 3 2 1 0   Printed on acid-free paper

Preface

Past, Present, and Future of Knowledge Acquisition

This book contains the proceedings of the 11th European Workshop on Knowledge Acquisition, Modeling, and Management (EKAW '99), held at Dagstuhl Castle (Germany) in May of 1999. This continuity and the high number of submissions reflect the mature status of the knowledge acquisition community.

Knowledge Acquisition started as an attempt to solve the main bottleneck in developing expert systems (now called knowledge-based systems): Acquiring knowledge from a human expert. Various methods and tools have been developed to improve this process. These approaches significantly reduced the cost of developing knowledge-based systems. However, these systems often only partially fulfilled the task they were developed for and maintenance remained an unsolved problem. This required a paradigm shift that views the development process of knowledge-based systems as a modeling activity. Instead of simply transferring human knowledge into machine-readable code, building a knowledge-based system is now viewed as a modeling activity. A so-called knowledge model is constructed in interaction with users and experts. This model need not necessarily reflect the already available human expertise. Instead it should provide a knowledge level characterization of the knowledge that is required by the system to solve the application task. Economy and quality in system development and maintainability are achieved by reusable problem-solving methods and ontologies. The former describe the reasoning process of the knowledge-based system (i.e., the algorithms it uses) and the latter describe the knowledge structures it uses (i.e., the data structures). Both abstract from specific application and domain specific circumstances to enable knowledge reuse. Various methods and tools have been developed in the meantime that support this (knowledge-level) modeling process. A rather new insight (and here we are in the third phase of the development process of the knowledge acquisition area) is that these methods have a much broader application area than the original purpose they were designed for. They cannot only be used to model knowledge-based systems in the sense of implemented computer programs. Individuals, organizations, and combinations of human and artificial agents are knowledgable systems that solve certain tasks by using their knowledge. Knowledge Management is concerned with acquiring, organizing, representing, and distributing the knowledge of such entities. It is not very surprising that methods and techniques developed for modeling knowledge-based systems can be applied to support such activities. Currently, it looks likely that this application scenario will become even more important for knowledge acquisition methods than their original application area.

The contributions to the workshop reflect the three purposes of research on knowledge acquisition issues. Some of them aim at further improving knowledge elicitation (i.e., support the process of extracting and creating knowledge), some of them deal with knowledge-level modeling of knowledge-based systems, and some of them discuss possible ways to apply and redefine this work in a knowledge management context.

Acknowledgments

The editors wish to thank the members of the program committee and additional reviewers who freely gave their time and dedicated attention to the review process.

Program Committee

Stuart AITKEN
Hans AKKERMANS
Nathalie AUSSENAC-GILLES
Richard BENJAMINS
Guy BOY
Joost BREUKER
B. CHANDRASEKARAN
Rose DIENG
Brian GAINES
Jean-Gabriel GANASCIA
Yolanda GIL
Asunción GOMEZ-PEREZ
Nicola GUARINO
Udo HAHN
Knut HINKELMANN
Philippe LAUBLET
Martin MOLINA
Enrico MOTTA
Mark MUSEN

Kieron O'HARA
Enric PLAZA
Frank PUPPE
Ulrich REIMER
Francois ROUSSELOT
Marie-Christine ROUSSET
Franz SCHMALHOFER
Guus SCHREIBER
Nigel SHADBOLT
Derek SLEEMAN
Annette TEN TEIJE
Jan TREUR
Andre VALENTE
Walther VAN DE VELDE
Frank VAN HARMELEN
Gertjan VAN HEIJST
Thomas WETTER
Bob WIELINGA
Takahira YAMAGUCHI

Additional Reviewers

Klaus-Dieter ALTHOFF
Franz BAADER
Pascal BEYS
Brigitte BIEBOW
Andreas BIRK
Tri M. CAO
Paul COMPTON
Olivier CORBY
Marco COSTA
Stefan DECKER
Jörg DESEL
John DOMINGUE
Robert ENGELS
Michael ERDMANN

David FAURE
Francois GOASDOUE
Rix GROENBOOM
Björn HÖFLING
Achim HOFFMANN
Machiel JANSEN
Diego JAVIER
Nicholas KUSHMERICK
Michel LIQUIERE
Rodrigo MARTINEZ-BEJAR
Claire NEDELLEC
Thibault PARMENTIER
Päivikki PARPOLA
José PATON

Rainer PERKUHN
Thomas PFISTERER
Alun PREECE
Christoph RANZE
Chantal REYNAUD
Orlando SOUSA
Steffen STAAB
Heiner STUCKENSCHMIDT
Gerd STUMME

Dagmar SURMANN
Sylvie SZULMAN
Le-Gia THONG
Maarten VAN SOMEREN
Svatek VOJTECH
Holger WACHE
Simon WHITE
Niek WIJNGAARDS
Randy P. WOLF

We would also like to thank Eddie Mönch, Yvonne Maierhofer and Gisela Schillinger for their excellent organizational support. We gratefully acknowledge the support for EKAW '99 by the European Network of Excellence in Machine Learning (MLnet-II).

March 1999

Dieter Fensel
Rudi Studer

Table of Contents

Short Papers

Reengineering and Knowledge Management

Daniel E. O'Leary

University of Southern California, 3660 Trousdale Parkway,
Los Angeles, CA 90089-1421
oleary@rcf.usc.edu

Abstract. This paper investigates some of the relationships between reengineering and knowledge management, with particular emphasis on sequencing relationships between reengineering and knowledge management. This is done using four basic approaches. First the paper explores how some knowledge management computing artifacts can be reengineered. Second, the paper traces the interaction between reengineering and knowledge management in typical organizational projects, illustrating the importance of sequence, and extending the results with a real world example. Third, the impact of reengineering on ontologies and knowledge bases is briefly reviewed. Fourth, issues that differentiate reengineering knowledge management systems and typical transaction processing flows are analyzed. Finally, simultaneous reengineering and knowledge management are investigated.

1 Introduction

The purpose of this paper is to investigate some of the issues in the relationship between reengineering and knowledge management. Both reengineering and knowledge management are seen as basic processes being used to manage a particular environment in order to improve processes and create value from the processes. Much of the focus of knowledge management has been to develop knowledge management artifacts and processes around an existing set of processes, in order to support further value creation from those processes. However, reengineering is concerned with changing processes to exploit the available technology. As a result, there are inevitable interactions between reengineering and knowledge management.

Unfortunately, knowledge management and reengineering are not often used in the same settings, either simultaneously or sequentially. This paper argues that greater improvement and value creation could occur if original artifacts and processes were reengineered and then knowledge management artifacts and processes were developed, or if both were done simultaneously.

2 Reengineering

Reengineering has been defined (Hammer 1990, p. 104) as using "...the power of modern information technology to radically redesign our business processes in order to achieve dramatic improvements in their performance." There are two basic approaches to reengineering, the obliteration approach and the best practices approach. Consistent with Hammer, the obliteration approach seeks to start from ground zero and build the right processes. The best practices approach has taken the view that a library of best practices be developed and maintained. Then firms would choose a portfolio of best practices as a way of building the reengineered organization.

Hammer elicited seven basic principles of reengineering that are useful in analyzing how reengineered systems differ from their predecessors:

- Organize around outcomes, not tasks
- Have those who use the output perform the process
- Subsume information processing work into the real work that produces the information
- Capture information once and at the source
- Put the decision point where the work is performed
- Treat geographically dispersed resources as though they were centralized
- Link parallel activities instead of integrating their results

Other authors (e.g., Davenport 1993 and Hammer and Champy 1993) have developed alternative and additional principles. However, in each case these principles suggest that reengineered systems are fundamentally different than the previous system.

Ultimately, as firms do reengineering, organizations, processes and people change. Rather than being task oriented, jobs become outcome oriented. Tasks are shifted to different persons to accommodate reengineering. Portfolios of tasks performed by particular individuals change. Reengineering leads to changes in who performs a given process with those using the output performing the process. In reengineered processes, there are fewer accountants talking to accountants. Instead, information activities are gathered while the work is being done. For example, loading dock personnel can wand bar coded goods to gather input for a centralized database. As a result, of that shift, information is gathered a single time and decisions in reengineered systems can be made where the work is performed. The dock worker gets information as to whether or not the goods were ordered, and decides how to proceed based on that information. Reengineered systems are likely to treat geographically dispersed resources as centralized, in order to generate economies of scale. Finally, rather than producing components in parallel and then assembling, the processes are linked. Too often in non-reengineered systems, parallel results did not assemble effectively. Throughout, processes are changed to exploit new technologies.

3 Reengineer Knowledge Management Computing Artifacts [1]

Recently, Brown (1999) made the case for "calm computing." One of the primary tenets of that speech was that current systems lead to information "underload" since they limit context and periphery. Brown asked the listener to imagine trying the "toilet tube" phenomena: put on the equivalent of toilet tube glasses and see your periphery disappear. Brown noted that experience was similar to what a computer user would experience in today's systems. After noting the problem of information underload, Brown addressed the issue of how computing could be changed to accommodate broadening across three dimensions to generate context: center vs. periphery focus; explicit vs. the implicit; and attending vs. attuning.

Part of that intriguing speech was concerned with generating "Knowledge Management Computing Artifacts," (KMCA) designed to mitigate the underload problem. KMCA would include the many efforts to develop maps of knowledge, such as Inxight, developments in personal digital assistants (PDA's) and other computing artifacts. In particular, Brown (1999) discussed a number of KMCA, including audio icons and some "squeezy interfaces." Since the choice of the nature of these icons and interfaces is based in process and designed using technology, they are a potential subject for reengineering.

Audio icons that make noise when objects are trashed are one such artifact. As noted by Brown, one way in which audio icons can be used is to have the noise, made based on the size of the file that is being trashed. This is analogous to other phenomena, for example, when a rock falls and hits the ground the bigger the rock, the bigger the sound. As a result, the audio icon captures some of the context in a manner that is consistent with broad reaching human experience. A big noise when the expectation is for a small noise (or conversely) creates an awareness of a potential problem.

With squeezy interfaces computing artifacts are established so that when a user interacts with an artifact the right thing happens. For example, a tilt-sensitive personal digital assistant (PDA) was developed that mimicked the movement of a Rolodex set of cards.

A physical Rolodex includes a card for each relevant person or organization. As a result, a Rolodex captures information about names, addresses, phone numbers and email addresses. A tour of organizations will find that many secretaries and some managers have rolodexes on their desks. Rolodexes can take many different forms, as can be seen in an office supply order book, each with their own look and feel.

Overtime, Rolodex's percentage of the address listing business has decreased and will continue to decrease. Increasingly, physical rolodexes are being replaced with computer-based rolodexes. Further, with the increasing use of "hoteling" in some organizations, physical rolodexes are disappearing as manager's desks disappear.

As a result, the Rolodex probably is not based in as broad reaching human experience as say the noise of a file being trashed. Many have probably never used a Rolodex. (The author has no intuition for a Rolodex.) Accordingly, a PDA that duplicates such a dated technology may be directing KMCA efforts in the wrong direction. Instead as with reengineering, squeezy interfaces for KMCA should focus

4

on experiences with broader-based human experience, or resident in more contemporary technology.

Another dated technology proposed for knowledge management is the "smart paper staple." The notion of a smart staple derives from a staple placed in a cow's ear to keep track of information about the cow. Smart paper staples have an http address stored in them so that addition or confirmatory information can be stored in an alternative form. However, the basic notion is that a paper copy is the primary version. An old technology is driving the KMCA.

In both the case of the Rolodex PDA and the smart paper staple, knowledge management was applied to an existing process without reengineering and the result is KMCA that is based in limited experience and/or old technology.

4 Stages of Interaction Between Reengineering and Knowledge Management

Reengineering and knowledge management inevitably interact with each other. In addition, typically they are sequentially used to make processes more valuable and efficient. Some of the relationships are summarized in figure 1.

Stages of Interaction Between Reengineering and Knowledge Management

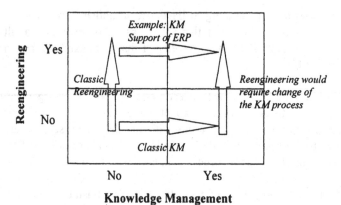

Fig. 1. The interaction of reengineering and knowledge management and their sequencing.

4.1 Classic Reengineering

In a classic reengineering process there is little attention given to knowledge management per se. The primarily concern is making sure that the processes are changed to exploit technology. As part of this change, systems are likely to be changed based on the seven principles of reengineering, discussed above.

Developing systems based on those principles gets different portfolio's of tasks to different people than in the original system. In addition, those principles often reduce the number of employees. All of these changes resulting in substantially different systems.

4.2 Classic Knowledge Management

Classic knowledge management starts with an existing process and then builds a knowledge management system to support the process. In order to assure that knowledge is gathered, updated, distributed and used, knowledge management "bakes" it into the process, i.e., the knowledge management is embedded in the process. Perhaps the clearest example of baking knowledge management into a process is in the case of a help desk. At the help desk, representatives serve customers. Each transaction between representative and customer is captured building up a history of relationships and knowledge about the customer and the representative, in addition to the product. That knowledge base can be used to provide knowledge about customer service.

4.3 Knowledge Management Support of a Reengineered Process

Increasingly, knowledge management systems and artifacts are being set up to support reengineered processes. For example, substantial reengineering is going into the development and implementation of enterprise resource planning (ERP) systems, such as SAP. Increasingly, knowledge management systems are being developed to support use and development of those ERP systems. For example, reports from ERP databases are being developed and put on Intranets as a means of distributing information. In addition, firms are building FAQ's to help users answer questions that they may have about how to use the system and other issues.

4.4 Reengineering and Knowledge Management: Which one first?

If a knowledge management system is developed for a process it will be designed to provide information to the existing process. If the system is reengineered then, as noted above, that can change who does what tasks and needs what information. If the knowledge management system is baked into the process then if the process changes so must the knowledge management system. Accordingly, reengineering will change the requirements of the knowledge management system, requiring redesign. As a result, generally, reengineering is first, followed by knowledge management.

5 Case Study: Texas Instruments' Capital Budgeting Process

This section provides a case study of Texas Instruments' knowledge management efforts in the area of capital budgeting. In this case study, a department in Texas Instruments built a knowledge management system without reengineering the underlying process. Ultimately, this bottom-up approach, without reengineering cements the existing capital budgeting process. Unfortunately, there are some limitations in the existing process that are also further exasperated by this further cementing of the process.

5.1 Knowledge Management Effort [7]

In the form of an integrated expert system and database, the Microwave Manufacturing Department built a knowledge management system. At the time of the case study, Texas Instruments was organized into 8 major groups, including Defense Systems & Electronics Group (DSEG). Each group consisted of entities. For example, DSEG had six entities, including the Business Development Entity. Each entity had about four divisions, e.g., the Business Development Entity included the Microwave Technology Products Division. Within divisions there were multiple departments, e.g., the Microwave Manufacturing Department. This basic organization structure is illustrated in figure 2.

Texas Instruments Organization Structure

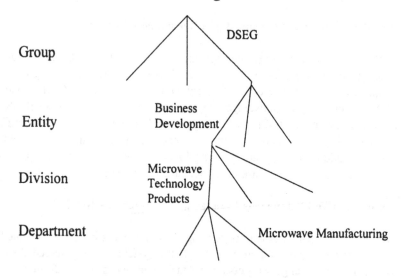

Fig. 2. Texas Instruments has an extensive organization structure. The system developer, the Microwave Manufacturing Department, is at the bottom of the hierarchy.

Unfortunately, the capital budgeting process had a number of limitations at the time. Capital expenditures required substantial documentation and committee review for any expenditure of $1,000 or more. Larger expenditures could require up to four levels of management committees. DSEG prepared over 1,500 requests in a typical year, each of which could require substantial review time.

The knowledge management system, was built to facilitate the construction of proposals to be submitted for funding, as part of the capital budgeting process. The system was based on knowledge gathered at the Microwave Manufacturing department level and was designed to meet the needs of a rapidly growing department, with large capital requirements. Because the department had experience at generating (successful) capital packages, they had accumulated substantial expertise in knowing what the committees wanted to see in a capital proposal.

The system had knowledge about depreciation, income taxes, and division production plans. A system user provided information about a particular capital proposal and then determined what would need to be done to make the proposal acceptable to the committee(s) responsible for evaluating capital proposals. For example, if the proposal included a request for a new welder, then the system would ask the user questions about when the welder would be needed and how many welds would be required. Based on past experience the system would determine if the welder would be approved based on the parameters gathered.

Whereas, the rest of the company averaged an 80% success rate on their capital proposals, the Microwave Manufacturing Department was able to generate a higher acceptance rate. For one set of 50 proposals, the system indicated that three proposals would not be acceptable by the capital proposals group, whereas the other forty-seven would be acceptable. The system was right on all fifty. The system apparently was so successful at generating budget proposals, that other groups, entities, divisions and departments became interested in acquiring the system for their own use.

5.2 Some Limitations in the Knowledge Management Effort

Although the system has been hailed as a success story for expert systems, there is another perspective. The Texas Instrument knowledge management effort was limited in a number of ways. First, the group that built the system was not in a position to make any changes in the existing capital budgeting process. The development group was a "process taker." For example, even though the $1,000 requirement was very low, there was no change in the process. Second, the group took the existing processes and developed a system that would help them best function within the context of the existing processes. The department needed capital, and the system could be used to help them develop proposals that met the requirements of the review committees. The department saw the existing processes as those that needed knowledge management support. They optimized the knowledge management system, subject to the existing processes, that the department saw as constraints. Third, the development of the knowledge management system ultimately further embraced the existing set of processes. As the system was given to other divisions, units, etc. the existing policies would be further cemented in the organization. As a result, there was no re-thinking of budgeting policy and knowledge. The organization as a whole ultimately was driven to using a system that contained the policies and other knowledge of the organization, from the viewpoint a lower level department.

6 Reengineering and Ontologies

Reengineering and ontology development also must be sequenced. Currently, much of the reengineering uses ERP systems to facilitate and enable reengineering of transaction processing systems. Implementation of those systems typically requires that an organization change its organizational design and flows of information and knowledge from a functional approach to process-oriented approach in order to accommodate the ERP software.

Process oriented ontologies are likely to be substantially different than functionally oriented ontologies. Some differences in information flows are summarized in figure 3, which illustrates the basic differences in functional and process flows in SAP's R/3 ERP system.

Order Management Process

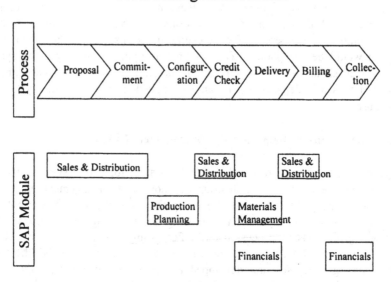

Fig. 3. Sample Mapping of a Reengineered System to a Process, based on SAP's R/3 enterprise resource planning system.

Process-based technologies are not just used in transaction-based systems. Process-based ontologies are also used in knowledge management systems. For example, a number of consulting firms have developed process-oriented ontologies that they use internally to organize best practice databases. A sample model of such an ontology is included as figure 4. A functional based ontology would be substantially different, focusing on stove-piped functional needs rather than cross functional value creation.

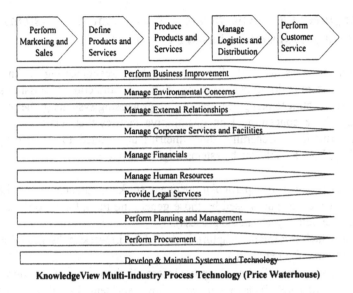

KnowledgeView Multi-Industry Process Technology (Price Waterhouse)

Fig. 4. One firm's model of their ontology for their best practices knowledge base.

7 Reengineering and Knowledge Bases

Reengineering also influences the type and content of knowledge bases developed or required for knowledge management.

7.1 Knowledge Base Types

The types of knowledge bases will differ between reengineered process organizations and functional organizations. For example as seen in figure 3, a process oriented organization's "Order Management Process" requires tight "linkages" between Sales & Distribution, Production Planning, Materials Management and Financials. However, in a classic functional organization, there are only limited linkages between the functional areas.

7.2 Knowledge Base Content Differences

A "lessons learned" knowledge base could have substantially different content in a reengineered process oriented organization, as opposed to a functionally oriented organization. In the process organization, linkages with other functions could force development of different lessons learned.

The same lesson ultimately could appear in either knowledge base, but different people could be interested in it. For example, as seen in figure 3, all of those interested in the efficiency of the Order Management process, would be concerned with the financial aspect of collection. However, in a functionally oriented organization, only the financial department would be interested.

8. Reengineering Knowledge Management Systems vs. Reengineering Transaction-based Systems

This section provides a brief discussion of how reengineering a knowledge management system is different than reengineering a transaction processing system. AI-based systems built to reengineer transaction processing systems (either explicitly or implicitly) have concentrated on quantitative metrics that relate to measuring flows of information. Generally, those metrics are related to the principles of reengineering. For example, such systems might measure the

- number of hand-offs of a particular document (task vs. outcome orientation),
- extent to which output is used by those generating the information (have those who use the output perform the process),
- extent to which information capture is embedded in work (subsume information processing into the real work),
- information capture efficiency (capture information once and at the source),
- the amount of parallelism in a network flow representation of a process (link parallel activities rather than integrating their results),
- extent to which a process is manual or automated,
- extent to which flows are reviewed (e.g., internal audit function of checking documents).

Heuristics easily can be developed to take an existing graph representation of information flow and reengineer it to optimize across these metrics. In some cases authors have used these same metrics to begin to try to reengineer knowledge management systems.

Unfortunately, such a reengineering of knowledge management systems would likely be the wrong path to pursue. Knowledge management is not generally concerned with transaction information flows. Instead, reengineering of a knowledge management system needs to consider the principles on which a knowledge management system is based. One such approach to capture some of the principles of knowledge management was initiated in O'Leary (1998) (others have also pursued these principles). O'Leary (1998) argued that the principle functions of a knowledge management system are to facilitate (the five C's)

- conversion of data and text into knowledge,
- conversion of individual and group's knowledge into accessible knowledge,
- connection of people and knowledge to other people and other knowledge,
- communication of information between users,
- collaboration between different groups, and
- creation new knowledge that would be useful to the organization.

Some quantitative measures that relate to these functions include

- percentage of data analyzed using knowledge discovery approaches,
- percentage of text analyzed using knowledge discovery approaches,
- number of links connecting knowledge
- nature of network connecting knowledge (e.g., single level tree)
- percentage of groups or individuals actually collaborating,
- percentage of time spent collaborating

Unfortunately, these measures don't really capture how useful the system was or the quality of the interactions. Although reengineering of transaction-based systems can pursue quantitative measures, reengineering of knowledge management systems also seems to required more qualitative data, as captured in the following (and other) questions.

- Does the knowledge management system accomplish these functions?
- To what extent does the system make converted or created information available?
- Do all who need the system have access to the system?
- How can the system be modified to accomplish these functions?

9 Simultaneous Reengineering and Knowledge Management

Generally, this paper has portrayed a sequence of reengineering and then knowledge management of a process. However, from an alternative point of view, knowledge management is a technology that needs to be exploited as part of the reengineering process, suggesting simultaneity between reengineering and knowledge management.

To-date there has been limited research and real world implementation designed to address simultaneous development of a reengineered system and its supporting knowledge management system. Much of the technology designed to enable either reengineering or knowledge management is not designed to facilitate generation of the other.

10 Summary

This paper has argued that knowledge management and reengineering are tightly bound together, and generally, reengineering should proceed prior to knowledge management, or simultaneously.

When considered in the context of reengineering, some knowledge management computing artifacts that have been proposed and developed put the knowledge management first. Although some KMCA are based in broad human experience, others replicate out-dated environments that could be reengineered.

In order to provide high quality processes, generally reengineering is pursued prior to knowledge management. If not, there can be a number of problems.

- Knowledge management further cements existing processes. As a result, if processes are not efficient or need to be improved, those inefficiencies will be further entrenched. Accordingly, it is critical to reengineer before the knowledge management systems are built.

- Knowledge management needs to be pursued carefully. Without reengineering, knowledge built into systems may come from the perspective of knowledge and policy takers. The system may be built to "optimize" across the department's view, rather than the overall organization. Ultimately, this can lead to a very different system than that developed with the overall organization in mind.

- Ontologies developed for functional organizations are not generally applicable to process-based organizations. As a result, if firms are planning to move toward a more process-based approach, then it can be important to reengineer and then develop the ontology.

- The knowledge bases that come from first reengineering and then developing a knowledge management system would differ substantially from those that would result without first reengineering.

References

1. Brown, John Seely, "Calm Computing," 32nd Annual Hawaii International Conference on System Sciences, Thursday, January 7, 1999.

2. Davenport, T., Process Innovation: Reengineering Work through Information Technology, Harvard Business School Press, Boston, 1993.

3. Hammer, M., "Reengineering Work," Harvard Business Review, July/August 1990, pp. 104-112

4. Hammer, M. and Champy, Reengineering the Corporation: A Manifesto for Business Revolution, Harper Business Press, New York, NY, 1993.

5. McAfee, A. and Upton, D., "Vandelay Industries," Harvard Business School, 1996.

6. O'Leary, D., Knowledge Management Systems: Converting and Connecting, IEEE Intelligent Systems, May/June 1998, pp. 30-33.

7. Sviokla, John, "Texas Instruments: Using Technology to Streamline the Budgeting Process," Harvard Business School, 1988.

Knowledge Navigation
in Networked Digital Libraries*

Mike P. Papazoglou and Jeroen Hoppenbrouwers

Tilburg University/Infolab
PO Box 90153, NL-5000 LE Tilburg
The Netherlands
{mikep,hoppie}@kub.nl

Abstract. Formulating precise and effective queries in document retrieval systems requires the users to predict which terms appear in documents relevant to their information needs. It is important that users do not retrieve a plethora of irrelevant documents due to underspecified queries or queries containing ambiguous search terms. Due to these reasons, networked digital libraries with rapid growth in their volume of documents, document diversity, and terminological variations are becoming increasingly difficult to manage.

In this paper we consider the concept of knowledge navigation for federated digital libraries and explain how it can provide the kind of intermediary expert prompting required to enable purposeful searching and effective discovery of documents.

Keywords: digital library, meta-data, ontology, clustering, browsing, navigation, semantic indexing, concept searching.

1   Introduction

Digital libraries bring large volumes of information to the user, whether researcher, analyst, student or casual browser. The classical approach by Information Retrieval (IR) is to define scalable techniques such as the vector-space model for matching queries against many thousands of documents efficiently [21]. This technique attempts to maximize the relevance of a document to a query. AI approaches have also been similarly intensioned although focusing on applying domain knowledge and analogical reasoning rather than numeric matching techniques. For example, an analogical reasoning system can be used to construct the possible interpretations of query terms corresponding to alternative paths in the inference network and to negotiate them with the user. In this way the user is able to select his/her intended interpretation of an unstructured query.

The relevance of query terms to documents is only one part of a complex problem. Currently, there is a massive investment world-wide in making digital document repositories accessible over networks. The result of this is that users

---

* This research has been partially funded by the European Union under the Telematics project Decomate LIB-5672/B.

of Digital Libraries (DLs) are overwhelmed by the amount of documents that are required to assimilate but also of the constant influx of new information. At the same time there is also a major investment in providing indexing, categorization, and other forms of meta-data for DL documents and a large number of IR techniques have been developed for automatic categorization of repositories for which human indexing is unavailable. These activities result in quite diverse meta-data vocabularies, e.g., index and thesaurus terms, that characterize documents. Therefore, the number of meta-data vocabularies that are accessible but unfamiliar for any individual searcher is increasing steeply.

1.1 Limitations of Index Terms

Despite user knowledge that several terms within a particular domain may have the same meaning, known IR technology can only match terms provided by the searcher to terms literally occurring in documents or indexing records in the collection. Unfortunately, keyword expansion techniques have shown no significant improvements over other standard IR techniques as it is usually very difficult to choose which keywords to expand [5]. This implies that there are too many potentially matching documents which may not be retrieved due to the variation of the index terms used, and the fluidity of concepts and vocabularies in different domains.

The situation described above is particularly acute in digital libraries with spatial distribution which aim to make widely distributed collections of heterogeneous documents appear to be a single (virtually) integrated collection. Such federated digital libraries (FDLs) typically specialize in a fairly *narrow* and *specific domain area*, e.g., Biomedicine, Computer Science, or Economics. Although the amount of searching in FDLs is expected to rise, diminishing search effectiveness and less reliable answers is the predictable result as a consequence of the explosive increase in meta-data heterogeneity due to terminology fluctuations. The challenge is to provide automatically the kind of expert assistance that a human search intermediary, familiar with the source being searched, would provide. In [3] has been argued that the most effective solution to improving effectiveness in the search of digital repositories would be technology to assist the information searcher in coping with unfamiliar meta-data vocabularies.

1.2 From Terms to Knowledge

A particularly promising methodology for addressing these objectives is *knowledge navigation*. This methodology relies on the use of computer assisted support for acquiring and relating digital information originating from diverse heterogeneous document repositories. Knowledge navigation combines techniques from knowledge representation and natural language processing with classical techniques for indexing words and phrases in text to enable a retrieval system to make connections between the terminology of a user request and related terminology in the information provided in an FDL.

At this juncture it is useful to discriminate between *terms* and *concepts*. Terms may appear in documents or meta-data descriptions and may originate from a controlled vocabulary of terms such as a thesaurus and have a predominantly structural flavor. Concepts, on the other hand, are used to organize index terms into distinct, higher-level, conceptual categories that have a distinct meaning.

The purpose of knowledge navigation is to help users negotiate a pathway through an overwhelming universe of information in order to improve their understanding. This requires locating, identifying, culling, and synthesizing information into knowledge. Knowledge navigation does this by analyzing the conceptual structure of terms extracted from document indices and using semantic relationships between terms and concepts to establish connections between the terminology used in a user's request and other related terminology that may provide the information required.

We consider the development of a methodical, scalable search process critical to the successful delivery of information from networked digital library systems. Hence, in order to provide users with tools for knowledge navigation, a four step process may be introduced: (i) *Determining* the information needs of users by means of different term suggestions; (ii) *Locating* candidate documents that may address these needs; (iii) *Analyzing* the structure, terminology and patterns of use of terms and concepts available within these information sources; and finally, (iv) *Retrieving* the desired documents. The very nature of this process suggests that we should provide facilities to landscape the information available in FDLs and allow the users to deal with a controlled amount of material at a time, while providing more detail as the user looks more closely.

To support the process of knowledge navigation while overcoming the complexity of wide-area information delivery and management, we cannot rely on a collection of meta-data index terms which simply contain terms reflecting the content of documents in an FDL. A more structured and *pro-active* approach to searching is required. In such situations, *concept browsing* can be particularly beneficial [10, 18]. The precursor of such an advanced browsing approach assumes that we are in a position to impose some logical organization of the distributed information space in such a way that potential semantic relationships between related documents in the network can be explored. Accordingly, the objective of knowledge navigation systems is to be able to handle a spontaneous description of the information required while minimizing the need for an information seeker to engage in repeated query reformulation in order to discover the exact terminology that will retrieve the information required.

In this paper we discuss how the use of knowledge knowledge navigation techniques can be used to transform an FDL from a passive warehouse of navigatable information to an environment that supports pro-active distributed document searching and retrieval. The paper is organized as follows. First we introduce the precursors of knowledge navigation such as a common ontology and rich meta-data sets. Following this, we discuss the benefits of knowledge navigation for FDLs and introduce a conceptual FDL architecture. Subsequently, we discuss different dimensions of browsing and querying and report on related research. Finally, we summarize the main points of this paper.

2 Conceptual Network Creation and Maintenance

For knowledge navigation to be effective it should provide an efficient network of pathways that can allow a person to navigate through conceptual space in a DL and can also reveal relationships between concepts. It should support human browsing and navigation in "conceptual space" by providing a structured map of the concepts used in the indexed material and allowing a user to move conveniently back and forth between concepts in a classification scheme and thus locate the text material where these concepts occur. It should also be able to use paths in the conceptual index to find relationships between terms in a request and related terms that may occur in relevant material. In the following we present some relevant terminology and explain why the use of ontologies and conceptual networks can be beneficial to knowledge navigation.

2.1 From Indexing Terms to Conceptual Networks

Indexing terms are used when adding a document to a (digital) library for efficient retrieval of the document. Surrogates of the documents in a digital library, commonly known as meta-data, are created by professional catalogers and indexers. The concept of meta-data is examined further in section 3.

Vocabulary in information retrieval usually refers to the stylized adaptation of natural language to form indexing terms. In such situations we tend to define a vocabulary purely in terms of word structures that can be manipulated, but the meanings of the words are constructed subjectively and situationally and the use of the vocabulary is predominantly social [3].

A thesaurus in the field of information and library science is defined as "a compilation of words and phrases showing synonyms, hierarchical and other relationships and dependencies, the function of which is to provide a standardized vocabulary for information storage and retrieval systems" [20]. Such a list of thesaurus terms, also called an authority list, is useful in showing terms, which may be used in indexing, and which should be not.

Conventional thesauri often represent a general subject area, so that they usually need significant enhancement to be tailored to a specific domain. This has triggered AI research to attempt to represent knowledge of a domain in a declarative formalism, with the goal of permitting knowledge to be expressed with such detail that it can be manipulated automatically.

An ontology may be generally defined as a representation of a conceptualization of some domain of knowledge [8]. It is a formal and declarative representation which includes the vocabulary (or names) for referring to the terms in that subject area and the logical statements that describe what the terms are, how they are related to each other, and how they can or cannot be related to each other. Ontologies therefore provide a formal vocabulary for representing and communicating knowledge about some topic and a set of relationships that hold among the terms in that vocabulary. This consensus knowledge about a specific and narrow domain is meant to be relatively stable over time, and reusable to solve multiple problems.

Formal ontologies define vocabulary with logic. The exact syntax and semantics depends on the representation language, e.g., description logics [27]. Formal ontology concept definitions are usually constructed as frames with definitions including a name, a set of relations to other concepts, and a natural language description that serves strictly as documentation [27].

Informal ontologies, such as WordNet [13], use a dictionary style natural language description, and this description provides the authoritative meaning of the term. Informal ontologies use richer kinds of relationships than subsumption and are directed graphs rather than trees as in the case of formal ontologies.

Compared to description systems in DLs, ontologies are more expressive, precise and powerful. They are powerful because their precision supports reasoning. Ontologies can be used to define sets of of descriptive meta-data, e.g., the Dublin Core elements, see section 3, as well as systems for classifying knowledge [27].

A conceptual network is a collection of semantic nodes with links between them, in such a way that many relationships are captured. Detailed coverage of a domain is an elaborate process involving rich semantic relationships, e.g., semantic roles and part-of relationships [13], usually more than those that a typical thesaurus can sustain. However, newer generation thesauri and ontologies contain richer information that can be used as basis to construct conceptual networks [14].

As the vocabulary of each living language grows continuously, especially in the technical-scientific domains, it will be very hard to claim that *any* thesaurus is ever complete. Regular updates must be applied to every thesaurus to keep it abreast of terminology evolution and changes [1].

2.2 Managing Network Growth

The dynamic nature of thesauri and conceptual networks means that most static, hierarchically organized classifications such as the UDC tree[1] or the classification of the Journal of Economic Literature (JEL)[2] are not adequate to serve as a complete conceptual network. More specifically, classification tools do not aim at covering the complete terminology of a domain, instead they aim to identify specific subfields (subjects) within broader fields. Of course their subject headings can be used as a starting point for thesaurus construction, and they can be included as generic 'see also' (related term) pointers in a conceptual network.

Conceptual networks such as WordNet [13] contain enough terminology and relationship information to be usable. However, these are usually too static and

---

[1] http://main.bib.uia.ac.be/MAN/UDC/udce.html

[2] http://www.econlit.org/elclasbk.htm

cover a broad range of common fields while being sparse on specialized domains – which are far better suited to assist users in knowledge navigation [2, 11]. It is especially important to have the conceptual network organized in terms of concepts instead of plain index terms. WordNet uses the *synset* primitive to group highly synonymous terms together while the EuroWordNet project extends the synonymy relation to include multiple languages [24, 25]. Other work on Lexicons, aimed specifically at conceptual modeling [9], also suggests ways of organizing terminology to properly present a conceptual space to users.

Acquiring a suitable conceptual network therefore is not just a matter of copying existing thesauri or term lists. Considerable effort should be put into the creation and maintenance of a conceptual network for knowledge navigation purposes. Any semantic network which models a piece of reality needs regular updating in order to stay synchronized with the world it represents. It is unreasonable to expect that a network can be constructed once and remain stable for an extended period of time. According to [16]: "The danger is that if the thesaurus is permitted to become monolithic and resistant to change, it can actually hinder both indexing and retrieval."

In the case of a virtual library system – which exhibits spatial distribution and which specializes in one particular scientific field, such as economics, astronomy or chemistry – the network should be maintained by experienced librarians and catalogers. These people can quickly recognize the particular places in the conceptual network where potential new concepts should be placed, and can update and verify the network as part of their regular work. In this way they help develop a 'conceptual map' of their domain, which can be very useful for other purposes besides knowledge navigation support.

3 Meta-data: the Foundations of Document Description and Discovery

Surrogates of the documents in a digital library – called *document index records* (DIRs), or *meta-data* – are usually created by professional catalogers and indexers. The concept of meta-data (index records) when applied in the context of digital libraries typically refers to information that provides a brief characterization of the individual information objects in a DL and is used principally in aiding searchers to access documents or materials of interest [22]. The purpose of meta-data is to describe a certain the type of a resource and provide the means of identifying topics related to the search terms.

In recent years there has been a focus on meta-data in relation to describing and accessing information resources through digital libraries, or the World Wide Web in general.[3] In contrast to traditional descriptive cataloging, which relies on very complex rules requiring extensively trained catalogers for successful application, simpler descriptive rules are employed which are sufficiently simple to be understood and used by the wide range of authors and publishers who

---

[3] http://ifla.inist.fr/II/metadata.htm

contribute information to the Web. Many librarians and organizations create handicraft collections of records (portals) that are more informative than an index entry but is less complete than a formal cataloging record to characterize document resources. Some of these collections of "third-party" meta-data records classify the document resources using organizational methods such as the Library of Congress classifications, UDC codes, or home grown schemes. The collections also include subject or keyword information, as well as title and authority information.

The term meta-data in the context of DLs has been used in conjunction with the "Dublin Core" [26] which is being developed as a generic meta-data standard for use by libraries, archives, government and other publishers of online information. The Dublin Core was intended to be limited to describing "document like objects" such as HTML pages, PDF files and graphic images. It was intended to be descriptive, rather than evaluative. The Dublin Core standard was deliberately limited to a small set of elements which would have applicability over a wide range of types of information resources. However, the descriptive rules suggested by the Core do not offer the retrieval precision, classification and organization that characterizes library cataloging.

To support pro-active searching FDLs need to rely on higher-level (and more structured) meta-data than that of descriptive cataloging to support dealing with the problems of large-scale searches and cross disciplinary semantic drifts. The meta-data *schema*[4] should capture in its fields the contents and topics of documents based on elements of the Dublin Core, e.g., title, creator, subject and textual summaries (description), and also provide fields that allow to associate search terms and concepts to related sets of terms and topics in other documents. It is particularly useful to be able to combine meta-data descriptions with ontologies. If an ontology underlies meta-data descriptions, then it can represent the meta-data terms associated with documents in a precise and explicit manner. It can help alleviate term mismatch problems by grounding meta-data supplied terms to commonly used and understood terms. It can also ontologically define implicit (narrower, broader, part of) relationships between meta-data supplied terms, thus, making them amenable to computational reasoning.

4 Requirements for Effective Knowledge Navigation

It is evident that facilitating access to a large number of distributed document repositories and libraries involves a range of requirements that cut across both user and system needs.

Topic classification schemes In order to be able to search large information spaces an important requirement is to partition them into distinct subject (topic) categories meaningful to users. This makes searches more directed and efficient. It also facilitates the distribution and balancing of resources via appropriate allocation to the various partitions.

---

[4] http://www.imsproject.org/md_overview.html

Abstracting meta-information Support for meta-information concentrates not on the descriptions (meta-data) of network-accessible information items but rather on high-level information whose purpose is to cross-correlate, collate, and summarize the meta-data descriptions themselves. This type of summarization or synoptic topic knowledge is called *meta-information*. Thesaurus-assisted explanations created for each such subject-based abstraction (and its contents) can serve as a means of disambiguating term meanings and addressing terminology and semantic problems.

Incremental discovery of information As users are confronted with a large, flat, disorganized information space it is only natural to support them in negotiating this space. Accordingly a knowledge navigation system should provide facilities to landscape the information available and allow the users to deal with a controlled amount of material at a time, while providing more detail as the user looks more closely.

Domain specific query formulation assistance An important service is user assistance with the formulation of information retrieval queries. For example, users may not know or understand the idiosyncratic vocabularies used by information sources to describe their information artifacts and may not know how to relate their functional objectives to these descriptions. Any system that provides global information access must help the user formulate meaningful queries that will return more useful results and avoid inundating them with unwanted material. This can be achieved by allowing a query-based form of progressive discovery in which the user finds out about subject-areas of interest rather than specific information items, viz. index terms.

Relevance feedback and results explanation The need to provide information users with explanations regarding the rationale for the relevance of information presented in response to queries and of the meanings of the terms occurring in the presented information is apparent.

Scalability support Scalability is an important issue for any large distributed system as it deals with the management of distributed resources, repositories, and document collections. A scalable system is one that can grow piecemeal without hindering functionality or performance if the current system configuration expands beyond the resources available.

5   Federating Digital Libraries

The issues presented in the previous sections illustrate the wide range of problems to be considered when designing and implementing an FDL. This section presents a conceptual architecture for an FDL and illustrates how issues identified in the previous can have implications in several areas of this architecture.

In the following we will describe two different approaches to the problem of federating digital libraries. The first approach is based on the premise that the interconnected DLs agree on using a single standard ontology (or thesaurus) for cooperation. The second approach is based on the premise that although individual DLs agree on cooperating they wish to retain complete control and autonomy of their local thesauri – which can also continue to evolve with the passage of time. This second configuration is typical of cases where there is an element of multi-linguality involved.

In both cases our approach to knowledge navigation in FDLs is based on linguistic techniques and ontology-based categorization. Large-scale searching is guided by a combination of lexical, structural and semantic aspects of document index records in order to reveal more meaning both about the contents of a requested information item and about its placement within a given document context. Prior to describing the two different configurations to federating DLs we will describe a conceptual architecture for FDLs which will be used as a reference to explicate their differences.

5.1 Conceptual Architecture for Federated Digital Libraries

To exemplify the FDL environment we use a comprehensive example from a federated library in Economics embracing various institutional libraries scattered over the European continent. Each library maintains its own collection of documents, using both full text and controlled vocabulary indexing. Users of the FDL in Economics should be able to search and access documents no matter where they originate from and irrespectively of the terms used to index the documents in the individual libraries.

Figure 1 shows a conceptual view of this FDL. The architecture is in a position to provide a conceptually holistic view and cross-correlate information from the multiple libraries (repositories). The in the FDL meta-data schemas contain meta-data terms in addition to other descriptive information such as geographical location of documents, access authorization and usage roles, charge costs, and so on. An aggregation of meta-schema terms for semantically related documents will result in forming a subtopic. For example, meta-data schemas individual libraries may abstract documents about market structure and pricing and may contain such index terms as monopoly, oligopoly, auction, rationing, licensing, etc. The aggregation of these terms generates a more generic subtopic (*concept*) called Market Models, step 2 in Figure 1. Although this concept is semantically clear to many users, it is highly unlikely that the term 'market models' appears as such in the documents. Finally, semantically related concepts such as Industrial Economics, Household Economics, Consumer Economics and Market Models are aggregated in their turn into the higher-level concept Micro-Economics, see step 3 in Figure 1. We refer to this type of construct as *Topic* or *Generic Concept* [19]. In this example, we assume for reasons of simplicity that terms are connected to topics via a single level of concepts. However, in a reality terms may be connected to topics via an elaborate hierarchy of concepts.

Topics thus represent semantically related DIR clusters (via their respective meta-data schemas) and form topically-coherent groups that unfold descriptive textual summaries and an extended vocabulary of terms for their underlying documents. A topic is thus a form of a logical object (a kind of *a contextualized*

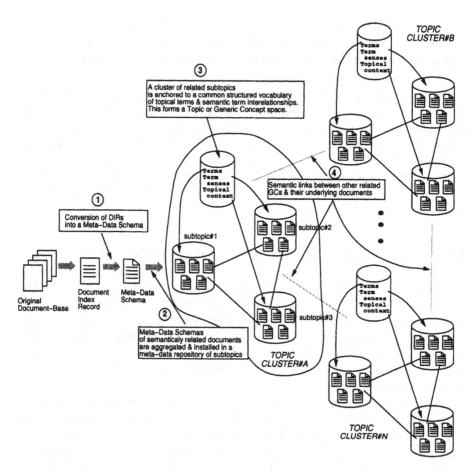

Fig. 1. Connecting meta-data schemas and forming the Topic space.

abstract view over the content of large semantically related document collections) whose purpose is to cross-correlate, collate, and summarize the meta-data descriptions of semantically related network-accessible data.

Overall a networked digital library system (representing a narrow domain, e.g., economics, astronomy or engineering) may be viewed in terms of four logical layers, as depicted in Figures 1 and 2, where

1. the top most layer corresponds to the *topic or generic concept* layer;
2. the second layer from the top represents the *subtopic or concept* layer associated with the meta-data schemas;
3. the third layer represents the *index terms* associated with the documents;
4. the bottom layer corresponds to the *document collection* layer (document base in Figure 1).

This four-tier architecture is the key ingredient to knowledge navigation in federated DLs. It generates a semantic hierarchy for document terms in layers of increasing semantic detail (i.e., from the name of a term contained in a document index, to its structural description in the subtopic layer, and finally to the generic concept space layer where the entire semantic context – as well as patterns of usage – of a term can be found). Searches always target the richest semantic level, viz. the topic layer, and percolate to the schema layer in order to provide access to the contents of a document cluster. This methodology results in a simplification of the way that information pertaining to a large number of interrelated collections of documents can be viewed and more importantly it achieves a form of global visibility.

This type of topic-based clustering of the searchable information space provides convenient abstraction demarcators for both the users and the system to make their searches more targeted, scalable and effective. This type of subject partitioning creates smaller semantically related collections of documents that are more efficient for browsing and searching. Concept searching can be utilized as opposed to keyword searching which is the traditional method employed by most contemporary search engines.

5.2   Tight Coupling: a Common Ontology-based Approach

The tightly coupled architecture describe in this section is based on earlier research activities on the TOPICA federated digital library system [19]. The architecture has as its main objective to impose a logical order to an otherwise flat information space by categorizing the content of document meta-data schemas and clustering them into topically-coherent, disjoint groups which are anchored on standard ontologies. Classical document clustering techniques from IR are used for this purpose [15]. The information space in FDLs is logically partitioned into meaningful subject areas. This results in clusters of documents formed around specific topic categories where different kinds of term suggestions – automatically generated by a thesaurus (ontology) – can be used to enhance retrieval effectiveness. We refer to this setup as the *topic space* for each group of semantically related documents, see Figure 2. After individual contextual spaces of documents are formed, subject-specific browsing or searching can be performed by a variety of tools that concentrate on concept (as opposed to term) browsing. Only in this way we can allow tools and searchers to selectively access individual document aggregations while ignoring others. The inclusion of a complete vocabulary and semantic information in the topic space provides the opportunity for "intelligent" navigation support and retrieval, with the system taking a more active role in the navigation process rather than relying purely on manual browsing.

To resolve terminology mismatches and semantic drifts between disparate index terms, topical synoptic knowledge and a standard vocabulary for term suggestions is supported by each topic. A common ontology is used to disambiguate topic-related terms and concepts and terms originating from different meta-data sets in the networked DLs. The common (canonical) ontology, e.g., an appropriate extension of the in-house Attent thesaurus, is used to represent concepts, terms and their relationships in a conceptual graph structure, akin to an

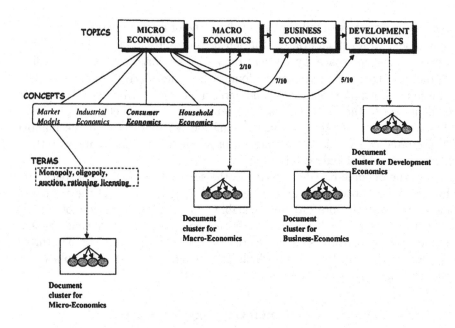

Fig. 2. Forming a conceptual network by linking documents to concepts and topics.

associative thesaurus. Term disambiguation for the diverse meta-data terms and their surrounding concepts is achieved with reference to this conceptual network to make connections between requested items and indexed terms of information.

A topic is materialized by a class hierarchy depicting all concepts and terms sampled by the topic, e.g., Micro-Economics. Each topic is characterized by its name and the context of its concepts and terms. A topic's concept space consists of abstract descriptions of terms in the domain, ontological relationships between these terms, composition of terms, terminology descriptions, hypernym, hyponym, antonyms-of, part-of, member-of (and the inverses), pertains-to relations, selected term usage and definitions (narrative descriptions), domains of applicability, list of keywords, and other domain specific information that apply to the entire collection of members of a topic. For example, if the user chooses to explore the topic Micro-Economics (s)he will view the terms shown by the concept browser on Figure 3. Once the concept Household Economics has been selected then a term bucket containing all possible terms under this topic is revealed. Subsequently, the user is free to choose terms that reflect her/his own preferences to form queries against the entire FDL. Terms in documents are matched to those appearing in the term bucket by word analysis techniques [15]. Hence, the user is pointed to the relevant documents where in the first instance (s)he can see (and possibly query) the document meta-data schema. The topic-areas, described by the topic descriptor classes, are interconnected by weighted links to make the searches more directed, see Figure 2. When dealing with a specific concept such as Market Models we are not only able to source appropriate information from remote document-based on the same topic but also to provide information about semantically related topics, e.g., Business Economics in the case of the Micro-Economics topic. The stronger the weight the closer the relatedness between two topics. Documents within a topic are all connected to this topic by a weight 10/10. Currently, the weights to topics are manually assigned by catalogers. This can be replaced in the future by text analysis techniques and IR ranking algorithms to determine the relatedness of topics.

In summary, the topic structure is akin to an associative ontology (thesaurus) and on-line lexicon (created automatically for each topic category). Ontology-assisted explanations created for each topic-based information space serve as a means of disambiguating term meanings, and addressing terminology and semantic problems. Therefore, the topic structure assists the user to find where a specific term that the user has requested lies in its conceptual space and allows users to pick other term descriptions semantically related to the requested term.

5.3   Loose Coupling: Inter-linking Independent Thesauri

One problem with the approach outlined above is that an agreed upon conceptual network needs to be maintained on the basis of a common ontology (thesaurus). In many cases, the individual libraries contributing to the virtual library will demand complete freedom in maintaining their own, specialized, localized system, including the index vocabulary (thesaurus). However, these libraries would not object against re-using their thesauri, and would favor mutual linking of concepts between thesauri. In such cases we need to provide software solutions that permit users to pose queries using terms from a thesaurus (source thesaurus) that was not used to index the documents being searched. A *cross-thesaurus gateway* will then translate the query into terms from the remote thesaurus (target thesaurus) that was used to index the documents. We will explain this approach based on our experience with working on the European virtual library for Economics.

The Decomate Project[5] is an example of a truly federated, virtual library for Economics. The contributor libraries are geographically distributed over Europe and each partner maintains several databases, indexed using different thesauri, e.g., EconLit/JEL, IBSS, Attent, in different languages (English, Spanish, and Italian).

In Decomate, a Multi-Protocol Server is capable of simultaneously querying all relevant thesauri: a 'horizontal' multi-query can be issued that retrieves all matching terms out of all thesauri. Decomate does not directly support integration of the federated thesauri. However, it provides a cross-thesaurus linkage (bridging) facility which allows generating a virtual concept network involving terms from any two interacting thesauri based on semantic closeness, see Figure 4. A connection can still be made if we follow neighboring, viz. semantically related, concepts in the conceptual network which may lead to matching concepts in the thesauri. When concepts are semantically matched, the terms contributed

---

[5] http://www.bib.uab.es/decomate2

by all thesauri can be collected in a virtual term bucket, originating from the meta-data underlying the matched documents, in order to facilitate the accessing of documents whose terms are missed by the indexers (Figure 4).

Some thesauri (such as JEL) include unique codes for concepts. For example, Household Behavior: General has the JEL code D10, irrespective of the actual term or language used for its description. Related JEL codes are D11 Consumer Economics: Theory, D12 Consumer Economics: Empirical Analysis, and D13 Household Production. Linking up such instances of the JEL thesaurus in different languages is therefore an easy task.

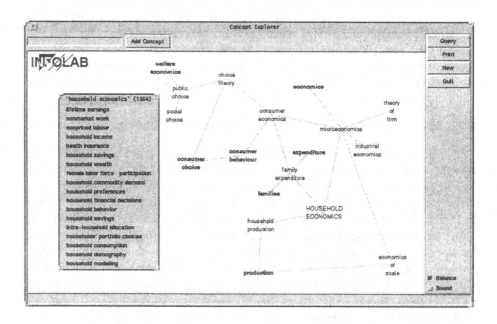

Fig. 3. Browsing the Attent Thesaurus

The virtual conceptual network is, just like a view in the database parlance, created dynamically, and in bottom up fashion, every time a user fires a query containing a term that matches a local thesaurus. This is contrast to the approach taken in section 5.2 where a a fixed ontology is used as a basis for matching concepts from different DLs in a top down fashion. The virtual conceptual network is not only used for concept matching but also for user browsing purposes.

6 Information Discovery Strategies

An interesting dichotomy in the space of document retrieval strategies is the distinction between *searching* and *browsing*.

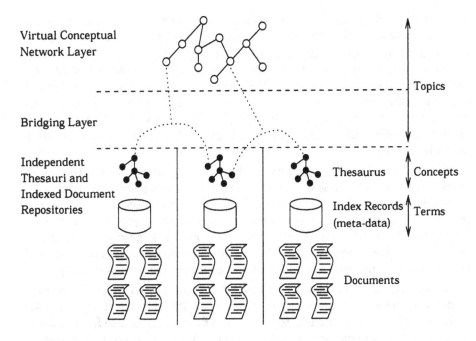

Virtual Conceptual
Network Layer

Topics

Bridging Layer

Independent
Thesauri and
Indexed Document
Repositories

Thesaurus | Concepts

Index Records | Terms
(meta-data)

Documents

Fig. 4. Using a bridging layer to create a virtual conceptual network of concepts and related terms

Searching implies that the searcher knows exactly what s/he is looking for. If the collection to be searched is small *compared to the precision of the query*, the resulting number of 'hits' will be sufficiently small to allow further processing. Searching falls short, however, when the user is required to know (or remember) the valid keywords, how these keywords correlate with concepts that s/he wishes to find, and how the keywords may be combined to formulate queries.

Traditional IR queries are considered as an analytical strategy, requiring planning, cognitive overhead, goal-driven and batch-oriented techniques. However, when faced with ill-defined problems requiring information access, users often wish to explore the resources available to them before exploiting them. This exploration may be partly aimed at refining their understanding of the potential information space or content that is available to, and partly aimed at formulating a concrete course of action for retrieving specific documents. Tools that support the browsing of document meta-data collections, as opposed to searching, are aimed at satisfying this need to learn more about documents in a collection before taking any action.

The purpose of browsing is to provide an open, exploratory information space to the user. Browsing can be accomplished by providing links between terms that can be explored at will as the focus of exploration changes. In many cases as new information is obtained in the process of browsing the goal may change. Strategies can be selected in response to these conditions to pick up new chunks of information. We can view browsing as a semi-structured, heuristic, interactive and data-driven activity of exploratory nature quite distinct from keyword (boolean) searching. Navigation can be seen as a special form of browsing characterized by high interactivity in a structured environment with the destination seldom predetermined. Navigation balances user and system responsibility with the user making choices from directions provided by the system. Navigation provides "pathways to discovery instead of answers to queries" [6]. Therefore, navigation is an ideal guide for *serendipity of information*, where users browse at random seeking information that is unknown, often not knowing what their target is unless it is seen.

Knowledge navigation is an advanced form of navigation where the system plays a more pro-active role by locating, identifying, culling, and synthesizing information into knowledge that it uses to assist the information seeker to discover the exact terminology that will retrieve the information required. It is not surprising that knowledge navigation concentrates on browsing prior to embarking on searching (querying) activities. In this way searches become more directed and effective as unwanted material is discarded during the process of navigation.

In section 5.2 we explained how navigation can be used to guide the user to discover the exact terminology required to retrieve documents dealing with specific issues under the broader topic of Micro-Economics, see also Figures 2 and 3. This is one form of navigation that can be provided with the FDL configurations described in section 5. We refer to this mode of navigation as *index-induced* navigation.

Another form of navigation that can be used with systems that provide weighted relationships among topics, see Figure 2, is that of *topic-driven navigation* which is when the user embarks on explorative searches and is most likely interested to find data closely related to a local document by following topic link-weights. We will use the topic connections shown in Figure 2 to illustrate this form of navigation. The concept-driven search is based on the weights with which a specific document base, e.g., Market Models – which is the subject of interest of some users – is linked to the various other topics in the system. This document base's weight to the Micro-Economics (its own topic) is 10/10, whereas its links to the topics Macro-Economics, Business Economics, and Development Economics are weighted with 2/10, 7/10 and 5/10, respectively. The Micro-Economics topic is in closer proximity to the Market Models document-base, followed by the Business Economics, Development Economics, and Macro-Economics topics. The user may then choose to explore concepts and meta-data information contained in the Micro-Economics topic first. Subsequently, s/he may choose to explore the Business Economics topic, followed by the Development Economics, and so on. The two modes of navigation can be mixed: when exploring these topics the user may embark on index-driven navigation to gain more insight into the concept found.

When the user needs to further explore the search target, *intensional*, or schema queries [17] – which explore meta–data terms – can be posed to further restrict the information space and clarify the meaning of the information items under exploration. Sample intensional queries related to the topics in the previous sections may include the following:

query-1: *Give me all terms similar to "value theory" under JEL AND Attent.*
query-2: *Give me all terms more specific than "value theory" and all their parts under JEL.*

The previous two queries return definitions and connections between concepts and terms under different thesauri.

Finally, when the users are sufficiently familiar with the terminology and understand the uses of the terms employed in an FDL they can issue *extensional queries* which retrieve documents or document meta-data (in case of non-electronic documents). Some representative extensional queries may be:

query-3: *Give me all documents dealing with "Household Behavior: General" under JEL AND "Family Expenditure" under Attent.*
query-4: *Give me all documents similar to author = "S. Hochguertel" AND "A. van Soest" AND title = "The relation between financial and housing wealth of Dutch households".*

Query-3 returns documents which belong to the intersection of two concepts in two different thesauri, wile query-4 tries to match a certain book pattern (through its associated meta-data) to that of other documents.

7 Related Work

Related work can be broken into two broad categories. First, work that spans different IR techniques such as query modifications and query refinement and clustering techniques. Second, activities in the area of digital libraries that concern themselves with subject-based information gateways.

7.1 Query Modification and Refinement

Related work on query modification has focused on automatic query expansion [7, 4] by means of addition of terms to a query to enhance recall. Query expansion has been done using thesauri or based on relevance feedback. Automatic query expansion techniques rely mainly on fully automatic expansion of terms to the query according to a thesaurus with no user intervention. The thesaurus itself can be either manually or automatically generated. With relevance feedback [4] query terms are selected or weighted based on a retrieved result set where terms are added to the query based on evidence of usefulness. Interactive query expansion can be used on basis of relevance feedback, nearest neighbors and terms variant of the original query terms that are suggested to the user.

Query refinement tries to improve precision (and not recall) by perusing the documents and selecting terms for query expansion which are then suggested to the user [23]. Automatically generated thesauri are used for suggesting broader and narrower search terms to the user.

Our approach differs from these activities as we place emphasis on characterizing document sets, logically partitioning them into distinct sets and then interactively querying these sets based on concept rather than term retrieval. As basis of comparison we use a standard ontology. In this way users are assisted to formulate meaningful queries that return a large number of desirable documents.

7.2 Clustering Techniques

In most clustering IR techniques the strategy is to build a static clustering of the entire collection of documents and then match the query to the cluster centroids [28]. Often a hierarchical clustering is used and an incoming query is compared against each cluster in either a top-down or a bottom-up manner. Some variations of this scheme were also suggested in which a document that had a high similarity score with respect to the query would first be retrieved and then would be used for comparison to the cluster centroids. However, if a query does not match any of the pre-defined categories then it would fail to match any of the existing clusters strongly. As a remedy to this problem previously encountered queries are grouped according to similarity and if a new incoming query is not similar to any of the cluster centroids it might be instead similar to one of the query groups, which in turn might be similar to a cluster centroid.

Our clustering techniques, although employing many of the traditional IR clustering algorithms, follow a different approach. First documents are sorted and tied to their high-level centroids (called generic concepts in this paper) and then interactive tools are provided for the user to expand or narrow her/his context and disambiguated her/his terms (via navigation through a lexical network). Once the centroid that contain these terms is determined then queries can be issued against its underlying document sources.

7.3 Subject-based Information Gateways

Of particular interest to our work are *subject gateways*. These are facilities that allow easier access to network-based information resources in a defined subject area [12]. Subject gateways offer a system consisting of a database and various indexes that can be searched through a Web-based interface. Each entry in the database contains information about a network-based resource, such as a Web page, Web site or document. Entries are usually created by a cataloger manually by identifying a resource, describing the resource in appropriate template which is submitted to the database for indexing.

Typical examples of subject gateways are: the Social Science Information Gateway (SOSIG),[6] which incorporates a complete thesaurus containing social science terminology, and the Organization of Medical Networked Information (OMNI)[7] which allows users to access medical and health-related information. The key difference between subject gateways and the popular Web search engines, e.g., Alta Vista, lies in the way that these perform indexing. Alta Vista

---

[6] http://www.sosig.ac.uk/
[7] http://omni.ac.uk/

indexes individual pages and not resources. For example, a large document consisting of many Web pages hyper-linked together via a table of contents would be indexed in a random fashion. In contrast to this, subject gateways such as OMNI index at the resource level, thus, describing a resource composed of many Web pages in a much more coherent fashion. In this way the resource containing numerous pages can be returned as an individual hit even by a search engine that indexes each Web page as a distinct entity.

8 Summary

In this paper we presented the concept of knowledge navigation for federated digital libraries and explained how it can provide the kind of intermediary expert prompting required to enable purposeful searching and effective discovery of documents.

We have argued that knowledge navigation in federated digital libraries should be guided by a combination of lexical, structural and semantic aspects of document index records in order to reveal more meaning both about the contents of a requested information item and about its placement within a given document context. To surmount semantic-drifts and the terminology problem and enhance document retrieval, alternative search concepts and terms and terms senses are suggested to users. Finally, we have briefly outlined two FDL architectures, that are currently under development, which enable users to gather and rearrange information from multiple digital libraries in an intuitive manner.

References

1. J. Aitchison and A. Gilchrist. *Thesaurus Construction*. Aslib, London, 1987. 2nd edition.
2. R. Bodner and F. Song. Knowledge-based approaches to query expansion in information retrieval. In *Lecture Notes in Computer Science*, volume 1081, pages 146–158. 1996.
3. M. Buckland et al. Mapping entry vocabulary to unfamiliar meta-data vocabularies. *Digital Libraries Magazine*, Jan. 1999.
4. C. Buckley et al. Automatic query expansion using SMART. In *3rd Text Retrieval Conference: TREC-3*, Gaithersburg, MD, Nov. 1994.
5. J. W. Cooper and R. J. Byrd. Lexical Navigation: Visually Prompted Query Expansion and Refinement. In R. B. Allen and E. Rasmussen, editors, *Proceedings of the 2nd ACM International Conference on Digital Libraries*, 1997.
6. D. Cunliffe, C. Taylor, and D. Tudhope. Query-based Navigation in Semantically Indexed Hypermedia. In *ACM Hypertext Conference, Southhampton*, June 1997.
7. E. Efthimiadis. A user-centered evaluation of ranking algorithms for interactive query expansion. In *16th Annual Int'l ACM SIGIR Conference on Research and Development in Information Retrieval, Pittsburgh, PA*, June 1993.
8. T. Gruber. Toward principles for the design of ontologies used for knowledge sharing. Technical Report KSL-93-04, Knowledge Language Laboratory, Stanford Univ., 1993.

9. J. Hoppenbrouwers. *Conceptual Modeling and the Lexicon.* PhD thesis, Tilburg University, 1997. http://infolab.kub.nl/people/hoppie.

10. J. Hoppenbrouwers. Browsing Information Spaces. In J. Prinsen, editor, *International Summer School on the Digital Library 1998*, Tilburg, The Netherlands, 1998. Ticer B.V. http://infolab.kub.nl/people/hoppie.

11. H. Howard. Measures that discriminate among online searchers with different training and experience. *Online Review*, 6:315–327, 1992.

12. J. Kirriemuir, D. Brickley, S. Welsh, J. Knight, and M. Hamilton. Cross-Searching Subject Gateways—the Query Routing and Forward Knowledge Approach. *D-Lib Magazine*, Jan. 1998.

13. G. Miller. Wordnet: A lexical database for english. *Communications of the ACM*, 38(11), 1995.

14. U. Miller. Thesaurus Construction: Problems and their Roots. *Information Processing and Management*, 33(4):481–493, 1997.

15. S. Milliner, M. Papazoglou, and H. Weigand. Linguistic tool based information elicitation in large heterogeneous database networks. In R. van de Riet, J. Burg, and A. van der Vos, editors, *Applications of Natural Language to Information Systems*, pages 237–246. IOS Press/Omsha, 1996.

16. J. Milstead. Methodologies for subject analysis in bibliographic databases. *Information Processing and Management*, 28:407–431, 1992.

17. M. Papazoglou. Unraveling the Semantics of Conceptual Schemas. *Communications of the ACM*, 38(9), Sept. 1995.

18. M. Papazoglou. Knowledge Navigation and Information Agents: Problems and Issues. 1997.

19. M. Papazoglou, H. Weigand, and S. Milliner. TopiCA: A Semantic Framework for Landscaping the Information Space in Federated Digital Libraries. In *DS-7: 7th Int'l Conf. on Data Semantics*, pages 301–328. Chapman & Hall, Leysin, Switzerland, Oct. 1997.

20. J. Rowley. A comparison between free language and controlled language language indexing and searching. *Information Services and Use*, 10:147–155, 1990.

21. G. Salton. *Automatic Text Processing.* Addison–Wesley, Reading Mass., 1989.

22. T. Smith. The Meta-Data Information Environment of Digital Libraries. *Digital Libraries Magazine*, July/August 1996.

23. B. Velez et al. Fast and effective query refinement. In *20th 16th Annual Int'l ACM SIGIR Conference on Research and Development in Information Retrieval, Philadelphia*, July 1997.

24. P. Vossen. EuroWordNet: a multilingual database for information retrieval. In *Proceedings of the DELOS workshop on Cross-language Information Retrieval, March 5-7, 1997, Zürich*, 1997.

25. P. Vossen, P. Diez-Orzas, and W. Peters. The Multilingual Design of the EuroWordNet Database. In *Proceedings of the IJCAI-97 workshop Multilingual Ontologies for NLP Applications, August 23, 1997, Nagoya*, 1997.

26. S. Weibel, J. Goldby, and E. Miller. OCLC/NCSA Meta-Data Workshop Report. http://www.oclc.org:5046/oclc/research/conferences/metadata/ dublin_core_report.html, 1996.

27. P. Weinstein. Ontology-based meta-data. In *21th Annual Int'l ACM SIGIR Conference on Research and Development in Information Retrieval, Pittsburgh, PA*, 1988.

28. P. Willett. Recent trends in hierarchical document clustering: A critical review. *Information Processing and Management*, 24(5), 1988.

Towards Brokering Problem-Solving Knowledge on the Internet

V. Richard Benjamins[1], Bob Wielinga[1], Jan Wielemaker[1] and Dieter Fensel[2]

[1] Dept. of Social Science Informatics (SWI), University of Amsterdam, Roetersstraat 15, 1018 WB Amsterdam, The Netherlands, richard@swi.psy.uva.nl, http://www.swi.psy.uva.nl/
[2] University of Karlsruhe, Institute AIFB, 76128 Karlsruhe, Germany, dfe@aifb.uni-karlsruhe.de, http://www.aifb.uni-karlsruhe.de/WBS/dfe/

Abstract. We describe the ingredients of an intelligent agent (a broker) for configuration and execution of knowledge systems for customer requests. The knowledge systems are configured from reusable problem-solving methods that reside in digital libraries on the Internet. The approach followed amounts to solving two subproblems: (*i*) the configuration problem which implies that we have to reason *about* problem-solving components, and (*ii*) execution of heterogeneous components. We use CORBA as the communication infrastructure.

1 Introduction and motivation

We think that software reuse will play a more and more important role in the next century, both general software components, as well as so-called knowledge components. Knowledge components are object of study in the knowledge engineering community and include problem-solving methods and ontologies. In this paper, we are concerned with problem-solving methods (PSMs). Nowadays, many PSM repositories exist at different locations [4, 24, 7, 29, 2, 31, 8, 20], which opens, in principle, the way to large-scale reuse. There are, however, at least two problems that hamper widespread reuse of these problem-solving components: they are neither *accessible* nor *interoperable*. In this paper, we present an approach aimed at remedying these two problems. We will present a software agent –a broker– that is able to configure PSMs into an executable reasoner. The work presented here forms part of an ESPRIT project whose aim is to make knowledge-system technology more widely available at lower costs.

Our approach is based on the integration of different technologies: knowledge modeling, interoperability standards and ontologies. PSMs are made accessible by describing them in the product description language UPML (Unified Problem-solving Method description Language) whose development is based on a unification of current knowledge-modeling approaches [25, 9, 28, 1, 23, 27]. For letting heterogeneous PSMs work together, we use CORBA [22, 15]. Ontologies are used to describe the different worlds of the agents involved, which have to be mapped onto each other.

In a nutshell, the two tasks we aim to solve, are the following (illustrated in Figure 1). A broker program *configures* individual PSMs –that reside in different

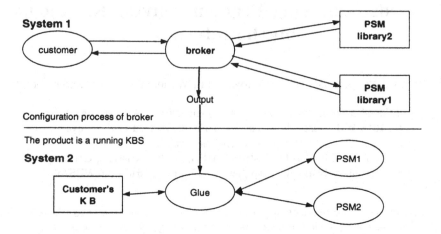

Fig. 1. Distinction between two systems: (1) the broker configures a problem solver by reasoning with UPML, and (2) the output of the broker is a knowledge system, which consists of executable code fragments corresponding to the selected PSMs, along with "glue" for their integration to make them interoperate. The arrows in system1 denote UPML expressions, whereas the arrows in system2 stand for CORBA structures.

libraries on the Internet– into a coherent problem solver. The task is carried out at the UPML-level and involves: interaction with a customer to establish the customer requirements, matching the requirements with PSMs, checking the applicability of the identified PSMs (see also Figure 3), deriving components for glueing the PSMs to the customer's knowledge base, and imposing a control regime on the selected components (System1 in Figure 1). The other task we have to deal with is to actually *execute* the configured problem solver for the customer's problem (using its KB). It does not really matter whether the PSMs are retrieved from the libraries and migrated to the broker or the customer's site, or whether they remain in the respective libraries and are executed distributively. CORBA makes these options transparent. The only requirement is that the site where a PSM is executed should support the language in which the PSM is implemented (System2 in Figure 1).

In Section 2, we briefly review the ingredients needed to explain our approach. Section 3 describes the configuration task of the broker. In Section 4, we outline how the configured problem solver is executed and in Section 5 we sketch the CORBA architecture to implement our approach. Finally, Section 6 concludes the paper.

2 Ingredients

Before we explain our approach in detail, we first briefly explain its ingredients: PSMs, ontologies, UPML and CORBA.

2.1 Problem-solving methods

The components we broker are problem-solving methods, which are domain-independent descriptions of reasoning procedures. PSMs are usually described as having an input/output description, a competence description (what they can deliver), assumptions on domain knowledge (what they require before they can deliver their competence). We distinguish between two kinds of PSMs; primitive and composite ones. Composite PSMs comprise several subtasks that together achieve the competence, along with an operational description specifying the control over the subtasks. Primitive PSMs are directly associated with executable code.

2.2 Ontologies

An ontology is a shared and common understanding of some domain that can be communicated across people and computers [17, 32, 17, 30]. Most existing ontologies are *domain* ontologies, reflecting the fact that they capture (domain) knowledge about the world independently of its use [18]. However, one can also view the world from a "reasoning" (i.e. use) perspective [19, 14, 10]. For instance, if we are concerned with diagnosis, we will talk about "hypotheses", "symptoms" and "observations". We say that those terms belong to the *task ontology* of diagnosis. Similarly, we can view the world from a problem-solving point of view. For example, Propose & Revise sees the world in terms of "states", "state transitions", "preferences" and "fixes" [14, 20]. These terms are part of the *method* or *PSM ontology* [16] of Propose & Revise.

Ontologies can be used to model the worlds of the different agents involved in our scenario (illustrated in Figure 3). So we have task ontologies, PSM ontologies and domain ontologies to characterize respectively the type of task the customer wants to solve, the PSM, and the application domain for which a customer wants a KBS to be built. These different ontologies are related to each other through what we call *bridges*.

2.3 A product description language

In order to reason about the different components involved, we need a component-description language. The idea is that providers of PSMs (library builders) *characterize* their products (i.e. PSMs) using a standard language. Note that providers are free to use any particular *implementation* language. The broker understands this product language and reasons with it. The language we developed is the Unified Problem-solving Method description language (UPML) and integrates notions from various existing knowledge modeling approaches [12]. UPML allows to describe in an integrated way task ontologies, task specifications, domain ontologies, PSM ontologies, and bridges between these components. The syntax of the language is specified in the ProtegeWin[3] tool [21]

---

[3] http://smi-web.stanford.edu/projects/prot-nt/

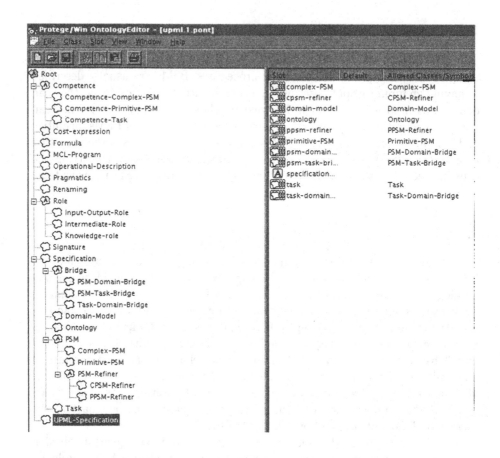

Fig. 2. The class hierarchy of the UPML language (left), and the attributes of a UPML specification (left).

which is a tool that allows one to write down a meta-description of a language. Figure 2 gives the class hierarchy of UPML (left part of figure). A UPML specification consists of, among others, tasks, PSMs, domain models, ontologies and bridges (see right part of Figure 2). Bridges have to fill the gap between different ontologies by renaming and mapping.

Having specified the structure and syntax of UPML, ProtegeWin automatically can generate a knowledge acquisition tool for it, that can be used to write instances in UPML (i.e. actual model components). For describing the competence of PSMs, FOL formulas can be used. Typically, library providers use a subset (the part related to PSM) of UPML to characterize their PSMs, using the generated KA tool.

2.4 Interoperability standard

CORBA stands for the Common Object Request Broker Architecture [22] and allows for network transparent communication and component definition. It enables distributive execution of heterogeneous programs. Each of the participating programs needs to be provided with a so-called IDL description (Interface Definition Language), which defines a set of common data structures. Programs then can exchange data that comply with the IDL definition.

In our approach, we use CORBA both for exchanging data during execution of the problem solver, as well as for exchanging UPML specifications between the broker, the libraries and the customer, during the configuration task (note that for clarity reasons, in Figure 6, the use of CORBA is only depicted for the execution part, and not for configuration part).

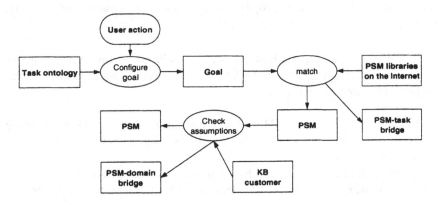

Fig. 3. The steps the broker needs to make for selecting a PSM.

3 Configuration task of the broker

In order to configure a problem solver, the broker reasons with characterizations of components (instances) written in UPML. In Section 5, we will explain how the broker gets access to UPML descriptions of PSMs. Figure 3 illustrates the different steps the broker takes. The current version of the broker is implemented in Prolog[4]. Therefore, we have built a parser that generates Prolog from UPML specifications written with the KA-tool generated by ProtegeWin.

Broker-customer interaction The first task to be carried out is to get the customer's requirement, that is, what kind of task does s/he wants to be solved. We use the notion of task ontology for this. A task ontology describes the terms and relations that always occur in that task, described by a signature. When a

---

[4] SWI-Prolog [33].

task is applied to a specific domain, it imports the corresponding domain ontology. A task ontology additionally describes axioms that define the terms of the signature.

With a particular task ontology, a whole variety of specific instances of the tasks can be defined. In other words, a customer can construct a specific goal s/he wants to have achieved by combining terms of the task ontology. For example, in a classification task, the task ontology would define that solution classes[5] need to satisfy several properties. Additional requirements on the goal are also possible like complete classification and single-solution classification. A specific goal would consist of some combination of a subset of these axioms, along with the input and output specification (i.e. observations and classes, respectively). Goals can be specified in FOL (which the customer does not need to be aware of) such as: $\forall$ x:class in(x,output-set) $\Rightarrow$ in(x, input-set) $\wedge$ test(x, properties), which says that the output class is a valid solution if it was in the original input and if it its properties pass some test (namely, that they are observed).

Broker-library interaction and broker-customer's KB interaction Given the goal of the customer, it is the broker's task to locate relevant and applicable PSMs. Two problems need to be solved here:

- Matching the goal with PSM competences and finding a suitable renaming of terms (the ontology of the task and the ontology of the PSMs may have different signatures).
- Checking the assumptions of the PSM in the customer's knowledge base, and generating the needed PSM-domain bridge (for mapping different signatures).

These tasks are closely related to matching software components in Software Engineering [34, 26], where theorem proving techniques have shown to be interesting candidates. For the current version of our broker, we use the lean$T^A\!P$ [3] theorem prover, which is an iterative deepening theorem prover for Prolog that uses tableau-based deduction.

For matching the customer's goal with the competence of a PSM, we try to prove the task goal given the PSM competence. More precisely, we want to know whether the goal logically follows from the conjunction of the assumptions of the task, the postcondition of the PSM and the assumptions of the PSM. Figure 4 illustrates the result of a successful proof for a classification task (set-pruning) and one specific PSM (prune). In Figure 4, Formula (1) represents the task goal to be proven (explained in the paragraph on "broker-customer interaction"), Formula (2) denotes the assumption of the task, Formula (3) the postcondition of the PSM and Formula (4) represents the assumption of the PSM. The generated substitution represents the PSM-task bridge needed to map the output roles of

---

[5] Note that "class" is used in the context of classification, and not in the sense of the OO-paradigm.

```
---------------------------------------------------------------------
9 ?- match_psm('set-pruning,prune,Substitution,10).
The goal to be proven is :
formula(forall([var(x, class)]),                                  (1)
        implies(in(x, 'output-set'),
                and(in(x, 'input-set'), test(x, properties)))).
The theory is:
and(formula(forall([var(x, class)]),                             (2)
        equivalent(test(x, properties),
                formula(forall([var(p, property)]),
                        implies(in(p, properties),
                                implies(true(x), true(p)))))),
    and(formula(forall([var(x, class)]),                         (3)
            implies(in(x, output),
                and(in(x, input),
                        formula(forall([var(p, property)]),
                            and(in(p, properties),
                                has_property(x, p)))))),
        formula(forall([var(x, element), var(p, property)]),     (4)
            implies(has_property(x, p), implies(true(x), true(p)))))).

Substitution = ['input-set'/input, properties/properties,
                'output-set'/output]

Yes
---------------------------------------------------------------------
```

Fig. 4. Matching the task goal of the "set-pruning task" with the competence description of the "prune" PSM using a theorem prover. The task provides the goal to be proven (1). The theory from which to prove the goal is constituted by the assumptions of the task (2), the postcondition of the PSM (3) and the assumptions of the PSM (4). The "10" in the call of the match denotes that we allow the theorem prover to search 10 levels deep. The resulting substitution constitutes the PSM-task bridge.

the task and PSM onto each other. The output of the whole matching process, if successful, is a set of PSMs whose competences match the goal, along with a renaming of the input and output terms involved. If more than one match is found, the best[6] needs to be selected. If no match is found, then a relaxation of the goal might be considered or additional assumptions could be made [5].

Once a PSM has been selected, its assumptions need to be checked in the customer's knowledge base. Because the signatures of the KB ontology and PSM

---

[6] In the current version, we match only on competence (thus on functionality). However, UPML has a slot for capturing non-functional, pragmatic factors, such as how often has the component be retrieved, was that successful or not, for what application, etc. Such non-functional aspects play an important role in practical component selection.

```
-------------------------------------------------------------------------
10 ?- bridge_pd(prune, apple-classification, B).
The goal to be proven is :
formula(forall([var(x, element), var(p, property)]),              (1)
        implies(has_property(x, p), implies(true(x), true(p)))).
The theory is:
and(formula(forall([var(c, class), var(f, feature)]),             (2)
            implies(has_feature(c, f), implies(true(c), true(f)))),
    forall([var(x, class), var(y, feature)],                      (3)
           equivalent(has_feature(x, y), has_property(x, y)))).

Limit = 1
Limit = 2
Limit = 3
Limit = 4

B = [forall([var(x, class), var(y, feature)],
       equivalent(has_feature(x, y), has_property(x, y)))]

Yes
-------------------------------------------------------------------------
```

Fig. 5. Deriving the PSM-domain bridge: ∀ x:class, y:feature (has_feature(x,y) ⇔ has_property(x,y)) at the fourth level.

ontology are usually different, we may need to find a bridge for making the required proof possible. Figure 5 illustrates the result of a successful proof for deriving a PSM-domain bridge. In the figure, we ask to derive a PSM-domain bridge to link together the prune PSM and a KB for apple classification. Formula (1) represents the PSM assumptions (same as Formula (4) in Figure 4). We want to prove Formula (1) from the assumption of the KB (Formula (2)) and some PSM-domain bridge (if needed). In our prototype, a PSM-domain bridge is automatically constructed, based on an analysis of the respective signatures. This involves pairwise comparison of the predicates used by the PSM and the KB that have the same arity. A match is found if the respective predicate domains can be mapped onto each other. The constructed bridge is added to the theory (Formula (3)) and then the theorem prover tries to prove the PSM assumption from this theory (i.e., from the conjunction of Formula (2) and (3)), which is successful at the fourth level of iteration (Figure 5). Note that, in general, it is not possible to check every assumption automatically in the KB; some of them just have to be believed true [6].

Figure 3 shows the case for primitive PSMs. In case of composite PSMs the following happens. When a composite PSM has been found to match the task goal, its comprising subtasks are considered as new goals for which PSMs need to be found. Thus, the broker consults again the libraries for finding PSMs. This continues recursively until only primitive PSMs are found.

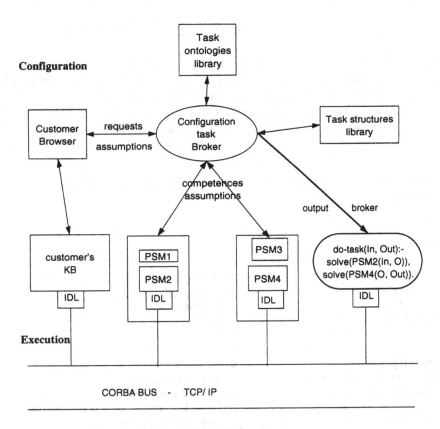

Fig. 6. The whole picture.

Integration of selected PSMs The result of the process described above is a set of PSMs to be used for solving the customer's problem. In order to turn these into a coherent reasoner, they need to be put together. In the current version, we simply chain PSMs based on common inputs and outputs, taking into account the types of the initial data and the final solution. This means that we only deal with sequential control and not with iteration and branching. We plan to extend this by considering the control knowledge specified in the operational descriptions of composite PSMs (controlling the execution of their subtasks). This knowledge needs to be kept track of during PSM selection, and can then be used to glue the primitive PSMs together. The same type of control knowledge can be found explicitly in existing task structures for modeling particular task-specific reasoning strategies [9, 2, 11]. Task structures include task/sub-task relations along with control knowledge, and represent knowledge-level descriptions of domain-independent problem solvers. If the collection of PSMs selected by the broker matches an existing task structure (this can be a more or less strict match), then we can retrieve the corresponding control structure and apply it.

Output of the configuration task of the broker The output of the broker is thus a program in which each statement corresponds to a PSM (with the addition of the derived PSM-domain bridge to relate the PSM predicates to the needed KB predicates), as illustrated –in an oversimplified way– in Figure 6. The next step is to execute this program, which may consist of heterogeneous parts.

```
--------------------------------------------------------------------------
module ibrow
{

typedef string atom;

enum simple_value_type                enum value_type
{ int_type,                           { simple_type,
  float_type,                           compound_type,
  atom_type                             list_type
};                                    };

union simple_value                    union value
switch (simple_value_type)            switch (value_type)
{ case int_type:                      { case simple_type:
    long int_value;                       simple_value simple_value_value;
  case float_type:                      case compound_type:
    float float_value;                    sequence<value> name_and_arguments;
  case atom_type:                       case list_type:
    atom atom_value;                      sequence<value> list_value;
};                                    };

interface psm
{ value solve(in value arg);
};
};
--------------------------------------------------------------------------
```

Fig. 7. The IDL description for list-like data structures. For space reasons we printed it in two columns, but it should be in one column.

4 Execution of the problem solver

Once we have selected the PSMs, checked their assumptions and integrated them into a specification of a problem solver, the next step is to execute the problem solver applied to the customer's knowledge base. Figure 6 situates the execution process in the context of the overall process.

Since we use CORBA, we need to write an IDL in which we specify the data structures through which the PSMs, the KB and the broker communicate [15]. Figure 7 shows the IDL. In principle, this IDL can then be used to make inter-operable PSMs written in any language (as long as a mapping can be made from the language's internal data structures to the IDL-defined data structures). In our current prototype, we experiment with Prolog and Lisp, and our IDL provides definitions for list-like data structures with simple and compound terms. This IDL is good for languages based on lists, but might not be the best choice for including object-oriented languages such as Java. An IDL based on attribute-value pairs might be an alternative. Figure 8 illustrates the role of IDL in the context of heterogeneous programs and CORBA. Given the IDL, compilers generate language specific wrappers that translate statements that comply with the IDL into structures that go into the CORBA bus. The availability of such compilers[7] depends on the particular CORBA version/implementation used (we used ILU and Orbix).

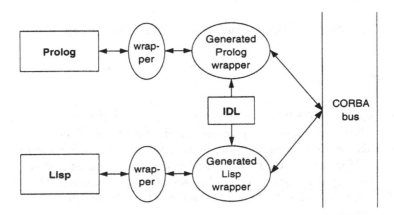

Fig. 8. The role of IDL.

The last conversion to connect a particular language to the CORBA bus is performed by a wrapper (see left wrappers in Figure 8) constructed by a participating partner (e.g. a library provider of Prolog PSMs). This wrapper translates the internal data structures used by the programmer of the PSM or KB (e.g. pure Prolog) into statements accepted by the automatically generated wrapper (e.g. "IDL-ed" Prolog). Figure 9 shows an example of a simple PSM written in Prolog and wrapped to IDL. Wrapping is done by the module convert, which is imported into the PSM and activated by the predicates in_value and out_value).

---

[7] The compiler for Prolog has been developed inhouse.

```
-----------------------------------------------------------------
:-module(prune,[
                    psm_solve/3
                    ]).
:- use_module(server(client)).
:- use_module(convert).

psm_solve(_Self, Arg, Return) :-
        in_value(Arg, prune(Classes,Features)),!,
        prune(Classes,Features,Out),
        out_value(Out, Return).

prune([], _, []):-!.
prune(Classes, Features, Candidates) :-
        setof(Class,
                (   member(Class, Classes)
                ,   forall(member(Feature,Features),
                            has_property(Class, Feature))),
                Candidates).
-----------------------------------------------------------------
```

Fig. 9. A simple "prune" PSM implemented in Prolog.

5 Architecture

In the context of CORBA, our PSMs are *servers* and the statements in the problem solver (the program configured by the broker, see Figure 6) are the *clients*. This means that each PSM is a separate server, the advantage being modularity. If we add a new PSM to the library, and assuming that the PSMs run distributively at the library's site, then we can easily add new PSMs, without side effects. The customer's KB is also a server which the broker and the PSMs can send requests to.

During the execution of the problem solver, the broker remains in charge of the overall control. Execution means that when a statement in the problem solver program is called (a client is activated), a request is sent out to the CORBA bus and picked up by the appropriate PSM –a server (through a unique naming service). Execution of the PSM may mean that the PSM itself becomes a client, which sends requests to the customer's knowledge base (a server). Once the PSM finished running and has generated an output, this is sent back to the broker program, which then continues with the next statement.

Another issue is that typically a library offers several PSMs. Our approach is that each library needs a meta-server that knows which PSMs are available and that starts up their corresponding servers when needed. The same meta-server is also used for making UPML descriptions available to the broker. In our architecture, PSMs are considered objects with two properties: (*i*) its UPML description and (*ii*) its executable code. The meta-servers of the various libraries thus have a dual function: (*i*) provide UPML descriptions of its containing PSMs, and (*ii*) provide a handle to the appropriate PSM implementation.

Interaction with the broker takes place through a Web browser. We use a common gateway interface to Prolog (called PLCGI[8]) to connect the broker with the Web.

6 Conclusions

We presented the ingredients of an approach for brokering problem-solving knowledge on the Internet. We argued that this implied solving two problems: (*i*) configuration of a problem-solver from individual problem-solving methods, and (*ii*) execution of the configured, possibly heterogeneous, problem solver. For the configuration problem, we developed a language to characterize problem-solving methods (UPML), which can be considered as a proposal for a standard product-description language for problem-solving components in the context of electronic commerce. We assume that library providers of PSMs characterize their products in UPML. Moreover, we also assume that the customer's knowledge base is either characterized in UPML, or that a knowledgeable person is capable of answering all questions the broker might ask concerning the fulfillment of PSM assumptions. For matching customers' goal with competences of PSMs, we used a theorem prover, which worked out satisfactory for the experiments we did.

With respect to the execution problem, we use CORBA to make interoperability of distributed programs network-transparent. The use of CORBA for our purpose has turned to be relatively straightforward. Our current IDL describes a list-like data structure, making interoperability between for example Prolog and Lisp easy. For including object-oriented languages such as Java, we may have to adapt the current IDL. We assume that the PSMs and the customer's knowledge base come with wrappers for converting their language-specific data structures into those defined in the IDL.

In this paper, we presented our approach by demonstrating the core concepts for a simple case, but additional work is needed to see whether and how the approach scales up. For example, the lean$T^A P$ theorem prover was convenient for our small example, but might not scale up to more complex proofs. Open issues include (*i*) to make the matching of the customer's goal with the competence of the PSMs less strict (partial match), (*ii*) to include other aspects than functionality in this matching process (non-functional requirements), (*iii*) to include other control regimes than sequencing (branching, iteration), (*iv*) to deal with sets of assumptions (possibly interacting), (*v*) to take more complicated tasks than classification.

The interface through which customers interact with the broker, is an important issue. Currently, the broker takes the initiative in a guided dialogue, asking the customer for information when needed. Our plan is to extend this to include

---

[8] PLCGI is only for internal use.

more flexibility in the sense that the customer can browse through the libraries (using Ontobroker's hyperbolic views [13]), select PSMs, check for consistency of her/his selection, and ask for suggestions which PSMs to add to the current selection.

Acknowledgment

This work is carried out in the context of the IBROW project[9] with support from the European Union under contract number EP: 27169.

References

1. J. Angele, D. Fensel, D. Landes, S. Neubert, and R. Studer. Model-based and incremental knowledge engineering: the MIKE approach. In J. Cuena, editor, *Knowledge Oriented Software Design, IFIP Transactions A-27*, Amsterdam, 1993. Elsevier.
2. Barros, L. Nunes de, J. Hendler, and V. R. Benjamins. Par-KAP: a knowledge acquisition tool for building practical planning systems. In M. E. Pollack, editor, *Proc. of the 15th IJCAI*, pages 1246–1251, Japan, 1997. International Joint Conference on Artificial Intelligence, Morgan Kaufmann Publishers, Inc. Also published in Proceedings of the Ninth Dutch Conference on Artificial Intelligence, NAIC'97, K. van Marcke, W. Daelemans (eds), University of Antwerp, Belgium, pages 137–148.
3. B. Beckert and J. Posegga. leanT^AP: Lean tableau-based deduction. *Journal of Automated Reasoning*, 15(3):339–358, 1995.
4. V. R. Benjamins. Problem-solving methods for diagnosis and their role in knowledge acquisition. *International Journal of Expert Systems: Research and Applications*, 8(2):93–120, 1995.
5. V. R. Benjamins, D. Fensel, and R. Straatman. Assumptions of problem-solving methods and their role in knowledge engineering. In W. Wahlster, editor, *Proc. ECAI-96*, pages 408–412. J. Wiley & Sons, Ltd., 1996.
6. V. R. Benjamins and C. Pierret-Golbreich. Assumptions of problem-solving methods. In N. Shadbolt, K. O'Hara, and G. Schreiber, editors, *Lecture Notes in Artificial Intelligence, 1076, 9th European Knowledge Acquisition Workshop, EKAW-96*, pages 1–16, Berlin, 1996. Springer-Verlag.
7. J. Breuker and W. van de Velde, editors. *CommonKADS Library for Expertise Modeling*. IOS Press, Amsterdam, The Netherlands, 1994.
8. B. Chandrasekaran. Design problem solving: A task analysis. *AI Magazine*, 11:59–71, 1990.
9. B. Chandrasekaran, T. R. Johnson, and J. W. Smith. Task-structure analysis for knowledge modeling. *Communications of the ACM*, 35(9):124–137, 1992.
10. B. Chandrasekaran, J. R. Josephson, and V. R. Benjamins. Ontology of tasks and methods. In B. R. Gaines and M. A. Musen, editors, *Proceedings of the 11th Banff Workshop on Knowledge Acquisition, Modeling and Management (KAW'98)*, pages Share–6–1–Share–6–21, Alberta, Canada, 1998. SRDG Publications, University of Calgary. http://ksi.cpsc.ucalgary.ca/KAW/KAW98/KAW98Proc.html,

---

[9] http://www.swi.psy.uva.nl/projects/IBROW3/home.html

also in proceedings of the Workshop on Applications of Ontologies and Problem-Solving Methods, held inconjunction with ECAI'98, Brighton, UK, pp 31–43.

11. D. Fensel and V. R. Benjamins. Key issues for automated problem-solving methods reuse. In H. Prade, editor, *Proc. of the 13th European Conference on Artificial Intelligence (ECAI-98)*, pages 63–67. J. Wiley & Sons, Ltd., 1998.

12. D. Fensel, V. R. Benjamins, S. Decker, M. Gaspari, R. Groenboom, W. Grosso, M. Musen, E. Motta, E. Plaza, A. Th. Schreiber, R. Studer, and B. J. Wielinga. The component model of UPML in a nutshell. In *Proceedings of the First Working IFIP Conference on Software Architecture (WICSA1)*, San Antonio, Texas, 1999.

13. D. Fensel, S. Decker, M. Erdmann, and R. Studer. Ontobroker: The very high idea. In *Proceedings of the 11th International Flairs Conference (FLAIRS-98)*, Sanibal Island, Florida, 1998.

14. D. Fensel, E. Motta, S. Decker, and Z. Zdrahal. Using ontologies for defining tasks, problem-solving methods and their mappings. In E. Plaza and V. R. Benjamins, editors, *Knowledge Acquisition, Modeling and Management*, pages 113–128. Springer-Verlag, 1997.

15. J. H. Gennari, H. Cheng, R. Altman, and M. A. Musen. Reuse, corba, and knowledge-based systems. *International Journal of Human-Computer Studies*, 49(4):523–546, 1998. Special issue on Problem-Solving Methods.

16. J. H. Gennari, S. W. Tu, T. E. Rotenfluh, and M. A. Musen. Mapping domains to methods in support of reuse. *International Journal of Human-Computer Studies*, 41:399–424, 1994.

17. T. R. Gruber. A translation approach to portable ontology specifications. *Knowledge Acquisition*, 5:199–220, 1993.

18. N. Guarino. Formal ontology, conceptual analysis and knowledge representation. *International Journal of Human-Computer Studies*, 43(5/6):625–640, 1995. Special issue on The Role of Formal Ontology in the Information Technology.

19. M. Ikeda, K. Seta, and R. Mizoguchi. Task ontology makes it easier to use authoring tools. In *Proc. of the 15th IJCAI*, pages 342–347, Japan, 1997. International Joint Conference on Artificial Intelligence, Morgan Kaufmann Publishers, Inc.

20. E. Motta and Z. Zdrahal. A library of problem-solving components based on the integration of the search paradigm with task and method ontologies. *International Journal of Human-Computer Studies*, 49(4):437–470, 1998. Special issue on Problem-Solving Methods.

21. M. A. Musen, J. H. Gennari, H. Eriksson, S. W. Tu, and A. R. Puerta. PROTEGE II: Computer support for development of intelligent systems from libraries of components. In *Proceedings of the Eighth World Congress on Medical Informatics (MEDINFO-95)*, pages 766–770, Vancouver, B. C., 1995.

22. R. Orfali, D. Harkey, and J. Edwards, editors. *The Essential Distributed Objects Survival Guide*. John Wiley & Sons, New York, 1996.

23. A. Puerta, S. W. Tu, and M. A. Musen. Modeling tasks with mechanisms. In *Workshop on Problem-Solving Methods*, Stanford, July 1992. GMD, Germany.

24. F. Puppe. Knowledge reuse among diagnostic problem-solving methods in the shell-kit D3. *International Journal of Human-Computer Studies*, 49(4):627–649, 1998. Special issue on Problem-Solving Methods.

25. A. Th. Schreiber, B. J. Wielinga, and J. A. Breuker, editors. *KADS: A Principled Approach to Knowledge-Based System Development*, volume 11 of *Knowledge-Based Systems Book Series*. Academic Press, London, 1993.

26. J. Schumann and B. Fischer. NORA/HAMMR making deduction-based software component retrieval practical. In *12th IEEE International Conference on Automated Software Engineering*, pages 246–254. IEEE Computer Society, 1997.

27. N. Shadbolt, E. Motta, and A. Rouge. Constructing knowledge-based systems. *IEEE Software*, 10(6):34–39, November 1993.

28. L. Steels. Components of expertise. *AI Magazine*, 11(2):28–49, Summer 1990.

29. A. ten Teije, F. van Harmelen, A. Th. Schreiber, and B. Wielinga. Construction of problem-solving methods as parametric design. *International Journal of Human-Computer Studies*, 49(4):363–389, 1998. Special issue on Problem-Solving Methods.

30. M. Uschold and M. Gruninger. Ontologies: principles, methods, and applications. *Knowledge Engineering Review*, 11(2):93–155, 1996.

31. A. Valente and C. Löckenhoff. Organization as guidance: A library of assessment models. In *Proceedings of the Seventh European Knowledge Acquisition Workshop (EKAW'93), Lecture Notes in Artificial Intelligence, LNCS 723*, pages 243–262, 1993.

32. G. van Heijst, A. T. Schreiber, and B. J. Wielinga. Using explicit ontologies in KBS development. *International Journal of Human-Computer Studies*, 46(2/3):183–292, 1997.

33. J. Wielemaker. *SWI-Prolog 2.9: Reference Manual*. SWI, University of Amsterdam, Roetersstraat 15, 1018 WB Amsterdam, The Netherlands, 1997. E-mail: jan@swi.psy.uva.nl.

34. A. M. Zaremski and J. M. Wing. Specification matching of software components. *ACM Transactions on Software Engineering and Methodology*, 6(4):333–369, 1997.

TERMINAE: A Linguistic-Based Tool for the Building of a Domain Ontology

Brigitte Biébow and Sylvie Szulman

Université de Paris-Nord,
Laboratoire d'Informatique de Paris-Nord(LIPN)
Av. J.B. Clément
93430 VILLETANEUSE (France)
Brigitte.Biebow@lipn.univ-paris13.fr
Sylvie.Szulman@lipn.univ-paris13.fr

Abstract. The purpose of TERMINAE is to help building an ontology, both from scratch and from texts, without control by any task. Requirements have been defined for a methodology on the basis of real experiments. TERMINAE fulfills these requirements, involving theoretical bases from linguistics and knowledge representation. Its strong points are integration of a terminological approach and an ontology management, precise definition of concept types reflecting modeling choices, and traceability facilities. This paper presents briefly the experiments leading to the requirements, and focuses on the tool and its underlying methodology.

1 Practical and theoretical basis of TERMINAE

In what follows, we use the term "domain ontology", with the meaning of "ontology" in [33]:
" An ontology is a hierarchically structured set of terms for describing a domain that can be used as a skeletal foundation for a knowledge base ". This definition seems to be totally compatible with that of [16]:
" An ontology is a logical theory accounted for the intended meaning of a formal vocabulary, i.e. its ontological commitment to a particular conceptualization of the world ".
We use also the same distinction between top-level ontology, domain ontology, task ontology and application ontology as in [16]. We agree too with Guarino's definition of a knowledge base as being obtained by specialization of an ontology to a particular state of the world.

In TERMINAE, the computer-aided tool presented in this paper, we often use the term "knowledge base" for "ontology of a generic knowledge base" because what we speak about is always state-independent, and the term "ontology management" is not yet widely used. TERMINAE is used as an "ontology management" tool, even if its representation language allows the description of facts by individual concepts.

1.1 Some practical considerations

TERMINAE is a tool based on a methodology elaborated from practical experiments of ontology building in the domain of telecommunications. The aim of one of these projects was to help the supervision of a telecommunications network [6]. The supervision operators receive alarms from supervised equipment as the result of different kinds of incidents, some of which are minor, others really serious. The operator must rapidly choose the right action, even if the exact cause is not known. The work consisted in building a knowledge base of incidents to help the supervision; the task was well defined, not exactly diagnostic but a clustering of alarms under incident headings in order to classify the incident from the alarm and to know what action to perform.

The difficulty in this modeling was to clarify the domain and to extract relevant information from a large amount of documents, but the choices of the entities to be defined for the application have been considerably facilitated by the final task. The domain modeling led to identify some concepts of the underlying domain which did not correspond to terms in the expert language, but which were immediately recognized as being relevant for structuring the domain. For instance, a concept WorkProblem (PbTravaux in French) was defined during the modeling to cluster all the causes of incidents due to maintenance on the network. But the domain ontology was just a taxonomy of concepts, without formal definition, the concept names being self-explanatory. The formal application ontology was designed for the task and made operational in the BACK description logic [24].

Another project was the building of a knowledge base on software engineering requirements in the domain of telecommunications [5]. These requirements describe ISDN (Integrated Services Digital Network) supplementary services, which means new specific functionalities; the language used is very specialized, specific to the domain of telecommunications and more particularly to the domain of ISDN supplementary services.

Requirements are prescriptive rather than descriptive, with a lot of modal expressions such as " it shall be... ", " ...may.. ", " ...has to... " and there are few precise definitions. For instance, " the SUB (subaddressing) supplementary service allows the called user to expand his addressing capacity beyond that given by the ISDN number ". The objects of the new domain are being defined using objects that are already known. For instance, ISDN exists with its basic services, its calls involve called and calling users, etc.

These new supplementary services define a new domain, with new objects and new terms, for which no terminology, or ontology, exists yet. Building the knowledge base was intended to give a better view of the result of the specification process, and since it was not built for a final application, there was no application bias. The ontology reflects the specification and ISDN domains, neither of which are made up of concrete objects.

1.2 Conclusion about the experiments

The lesson we learnt through our modeling experiments reinforces the literature on ontology: when modeling is controlled by the final task and when the domain is well established or concrete, modeling is easier than without any application bias or when the domain is new, informal, and hardly investigated.

When there is no task to drive the domain building, the modeling looks like the work of a linguist, lexicologist or terminologist. The major difference is that the final modeling has to be used not only for human understanding or translation, but also for automatic inferences, which need more formal modeling. Researchers from computational lexical semantics ([25],[19]) have begun to investigate the close relations between these two approaches, domain ontology modeling and computational lexical semantics. The description of all the possible semantic uses of a word may be possible if it is restricted to a specialized domain relatively to a corpus, while it seems an inaccessible goal in general language. What is needed in both domains is understanding, i.e making " reasonable " inferences. Linguistic methods to define lexical items or terms (lexical items in a specialized domain) are usually introspection (traditional in classical lexicography) and, more recently, corpus analysis (traditional in classical terminology). Even if they are not formal, linguistic methods are rigorous, and there are now usable linguistic tools to help the work.

We think, as others ([30], [2], [22]), that domain modeling would benefit from a close interaction between linguistic methods or tools and computer-aided knowledge engineering methods or tools. Ontology, terminology, and lexical semantics aim to describe the world through the words of the language, in all language's generality for lexical semantics, restricted to a technical domain for terminology and for ontology as we have defined it. Our idea is to push the integration of these disciplines as far as possible into a tool, TERMINAE.

1.3 Some requirements for methods and tools to build a domain ontology

Since the beginning of the 90's, a lot of principles have been elicited for the design of ontologies; the best known may be those of [14], [15]. A lot of ontologies have been designed in big or small projects (see [13] for a review of worldwide known projects and the general literature from the recent conferences or workshops on ontologies or modeling [36], [37] ,[38] ,[39]. But researchers are still asking for guidelines and methodologies, and building usable or reusable ontologies faces the same difficulties.

To these existing principles, we propose to add some requirements that fit the need we met during our work on modeling. All the experiments faced the problem of building an ontology of a domain from texts and we needed a tool to help us. Some exist, but none fitting our needs. We wanted to have a linguistic approach, to take advantage of the method and techniques existing in the terminology domain. We wanted a CAKE tool to help the human task as much as possible. We wanted a formal ontology to help validate the ontology, while avoiding most of the common mistakes such as redundancy and inconsistency, and we also wanted to be able to query the ontology and make inferences. This led to the following requirements for building a domain ontology from scratch and from texts without being task-driven.

* Linguistic-based methods:
  Linguistic methods such as the study of terminology are required. Terminology is studied from domain texts, that is to say a description of a term is elaborated from its occurrences in the texts.
* A typology of concepts to highlight the modeling choices:
  When modeling an ontology, different types of concepts are elaborated. Some come from the text, others from the type of text, from the domain, from meta-knowledge, from common-sense knowledge. Some are introduced to structure the ontology bottom-up or top-down. It is important to be able to distinguish the modeling choices in order to understand and maintain the ontology.
* Formality to avoid as far as possible incoherence and inconsistencies:
  The support of an ontology has to be formal to avoid incoherence and to allow further inferences. The drawback of this option is a loss of meaningful substance but this is the price of correctness and automation.
* Traceability, maintainability, back linking to texts:
  A condition of usability is the ability to understand the ontology, i.e. to be able to decide if the underlying conceptualization fits the addressed problem or domain or not. This implies a documented ontology, with links to its sources and comments on the modeling process.

TERMINAE has been built to meet these requirements.

2 TERMINAE

2.1 Overview of the tool

TERMINAE is a computer-aided knowledge engineering tool written in Java. Its originality is to integrate linguistic and knowledge engineering tools. The linguistic engineering part allows the definition of terminological forms from the study of term occurrences in a corpus. A terminological form defines each meaning of a term, called a notion, using some linguistic relations between notions, such as synonymy. The knowledge engineering part involves knowledge-base management with an editor and browser for the ontology. The tool helps to represent a notion as a concept, which is called a terminological concept.

2.2 Knowledge engineering part

Knowledge-base formalism Knowledge representation formalisms, like conceptual graphs or description logics, describe an epistemological level, in the sense of [10]. They provide logical primitives, the meaning of which is domain-independent, and syntactic rules to build language formulae. They also provide rules for semantic composition, which allows the sense of a formula to be computed from the sense of the primitives which compose it. But the definition of the non-logical primitives of the domain, the interpretation of which is given by the domain, is left to the knowledge engineer. So the task of building a formal ontology of a domain comes down to defining the non-logical primitives of the formalism[4].

The formalism used in TERMINAE belongs to the family of description logics. These formalisms are now well known [34]. They describe concepts by their necessary and sufficient conditions, in order to organize concepts into a taxonomy of subsumption along which the properties are inherited, and to classify concepts in this hierarchy according to their properties. TERMINAE formalism is only a terminological language, close to the T-box language of Back [18], with the following syntax:

Table 1. Syntax of TERMINAE terminological language

Concept Terms	Role Terms
[concept]::[concept-name]	[role]::[role-name]
| anything	| [role] and [role]
| nothing	| domain([concept])
| [concept] and [concept]	| range ([concept])
| all ([role],[concept])	| [role]comp [role]
| atleast([INTEGER],[role])	| trans([role])
| atmost([INTEGER],[role])	| inv([role])

This language has been chosen to facilitate the design, although the classification becomes NP-complex . The operators involved are not used sufficiently often to lead to an unacceptable lack of efficiency in the terminological part.

Typology of concepts for the modeling Moreover, to help the understanding and maintenance of the modeling, concepts have specific labels to express their structuring-type and their linguistic-type. This typology does affect neither the classification nor another inferential process, and the labels are transparent for the formal semantic interpretation. These labels are used as comments by the knowledge engineer when building or maintaining the base, and they reflect everyday experience in knowledge engineering. They emphasize a modeling point of view on the concept, following two methodological dimensions: the usual structuring dimension, and the linguistic one that we have introduced.

Structuring dimension The structuring-type of concept is either top-down or bottom-up, and it expresses the way the concept has been introduced into the ontology.

Top-down structuring (TDS) type concepts partition off the domain early on into large subdomains which are easier to manage. This allows the knowledge engineer to structure his/her conceptualization process. Often the domain differentiates between fundamental objects such as physical object or abstract object in the domain of telecommunications, and data and function in the domain of software specifications.

Bottom-up structuring (BUS) type concepts come from a deeper study of the specialized domain. For instance, in telecommunications, BUS concepts may be exchange, call, or subscriber. Sometimes the limit is not so clear, and a concept may remain unlabeled. A BUS concept may be designed as regrouping BUS concept (RBUS), which means that it has been created to put together a family of concepts with some common properties. These properties may be formally defined at the level of the RBUS concept and then restricted, or just given as a comment on the RBUS concept. This is the case in the telecommunications network supervision application for the concept "work problem", under which all the concepts "incident cause bound to maintenance work" have been clustered. Experts have spontaneously agreed with this conceptualization, which allows them to better structure the huge number of causes they have to keep in mind.

Linguistic dimension The other dimension of a concept is its linguistic accuracy, with respect to the corpus. Terminological (T) concepts are built from the study of the corpus, and they correspond to one or more terms of the specialized domain. One term (the "vedette") is chosen as a name for the concepts. For instance, "ISDN number" is a terminological concept, as is "to-allocate" (affecter in French) that will be modeled further. Pre-terminological (PT) concepts correspond to several expressions, sometimes real sentences (such as "this type of problem occurs when work is programmed on the network, the supervision center has been notified, but all the consequences have not been indicated", or "incident cause bound to maintenance work"), none of them being more used than the others. Ultimately, a specific term will be adopted, but it is not the case for the moment. One expression is chosen as the name for the concept (in the example above, WorkProblem).

The name of a concept may not correspond to a term in the domain studied, for instance the top-level concepts are usually not terminological. It may appear that a not-terminological (NT) concept has the same name as a terminological one, i.e. they are homonyms in the ontology. For instance "domain" may be terminological in a telecommunications text, meaning the set of equipment supervised by a specific exchange (the supervision domain of the exchange); it may also exist to design parts of the general ontology, for instance supervision domain, exploitation domain, taxation domain. In such a case, as in case of polysemic terms, the concepts are distinguished by suffixing their name, domain-1 and domain-2.

It also happens that a concept is needed to structure the ontology and that a known term corresponds to the concept, but this term is not attested in the corpus. For instance, the term "telecommunication" does not occur in the ISDN corpus, it belongs to a domain including that of ISDN, but the concept is needed to structure the ontology. The concept will be defined with the terminological not attested (TNA) type.

Table 2 recapitulates the different types of concept. The two dimensions are

Table 2. Concept types

Dimension	Type of concept
structuring	top-down (TDS)
	bottom-up (BUS)
	regrouping bottom-up (RBUS)
linguistic	terminological (T)
	pre-terminological (PT)
	terminological not attested (TNA)
	not terminological (NT)

independent. A priori, most of the primitive concepts are TDS and NT/TNA, most of the defined concepts are BUS/RBUS and T/PT, but no exact correspondence is possible. For instance, WorkProblem (PbTravaux in French) is a RBUS concept which has been defined to regroup all the causes of incidents due to work programmed on the network. Although this concept is neither linguistically attested in the corpus nor by the expert, the expert is so much in favor of the definition of this new concept that it will certainly become a PT concept very soon. For the moment, it is an NT concept, i.e. not terminological.

The bootstrap top-level ontology TERMINAE has been designed to build an ontology from scratch and the engineers must face the bootstrap problem, that is to say:

* How to describe concepts without first having defined the roles?
* How to describe roles without first having defined the concepts?

In practice, concepts and roles are described at the same time and the structuring process is questioned at each step. But where do we start? TERMINAE proposes around thirty concepts established from the state of the art and a kernel of relations close to linguistic cases, that may be modified depending on the needs [17],[20],[32],[28]. Figure 6 will show some of them in the next section.

2.3 Linguistic engineering part

Theoretical terminological approach The proposed approach follows recent work in terminology [31]. The original postulate of terminology stipulated that scientific knowledge is based on logical reasoning and gave the term as the minimal unit of this knowledge [35]. The term had to be pure, without any emotional or non-cognitive connotation, with a single meaning, precise, mono-referential, which means that to a term corresponds one and only one concept and vice versa. This idea of a purely logical scientific language no longer corresponds to recent knowledge, which considers language and even texts as the basis of scientific work. Moreover, even in restricted domains, term univocity is not respected, and a term may correspond to several notions because of the existence of linguistic phenomena such as metonymy or polysemy. For example, in the domain of the specification of ISDN supplementary services, which is a very restricted domain in telecommunications, the term call forwarding (renvoi d'appel in French) may designate three different notions: a supplementary service, or the action performed when this service is invoked, or the result of this action when the service is invoked.

Practical terminological approach TERMINAE supports a methodology to build terminological concepts from the study of the corresponding term in a corpus. The first step is to establish the list of terms. This requires the constitution of a relevant corpus of texts on the domain. Then LEXTER [8], a term extractor, proposes to the knowledge engineer a set of candidate terms from which the effective terms have to be selected with the help of an expert. The next step is to conceptualize each term. The knowledge engineer analyzes the uses of the term in the corpus to define all the notions (meanings) of the term. He/she gives a definition in natural language for each notion and then translates the definition into a formalism. The new terminological concept finally may or may not be inserted into the ontology, depending on the validity of the insertion. Figure 1 shows the path from text to terminological concepts.

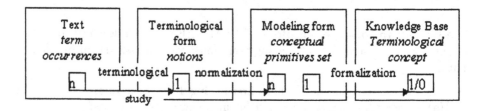

Fig. 1. From text to Knowledge base

Terminological study TERMINAE integrates the results of LEXTER, a tool which extracts candidate terms by means of local syntactic parsing techniques based on surface patterns. Figure 2 presents the graphical user interface to study the occurrences of a term candidate. The right part of the window shows the occurrences of the term selected in the left part. The term "affecter" and its 19 occurrences are extracted from the corpus on the ISDN supplementary services specification. For each occurrence, the user may display its context (the whole paragraph or only the preceding or following sentences).

 A terminological form is created from the study of the term. Figure 3 presents the terminological form of the verb "affecter", which is polysemic. Occurrences 1, 2, 3, ... lead to the notion "to allocate". The others lead to the notion "to modify", with the result that the knowledge engineer fills out two modeling forms. The knowledge engineer binds a distinct notion to each meaning which is defined by a set of occurrences and a text. For instance the notion "affecter-1" is defined by the given occurrences and the text "an exchange allocates something to something".

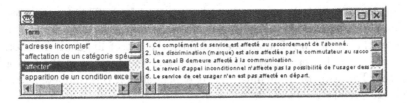

Fig. 2. Terminological study interface

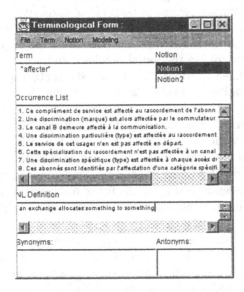

Fig. 3. A terminological form

Normalization and formalization The methodology followed leads us from the study of the text to modeling forms for one term. Each notion underlying a term is described by its uses with the other notions in the corpus. We call this process term normalization, in line with [26]. This means that the choice of corpus is fundamental for the building of the ontology, because the normalization is relative to the corpus. From the analysis of these uses of the term, the engineer fills out a modeling form for each notion, which includes the following fields (see figures[1] 4 and 5):

* a normalized definition of the notion, which is the list of its linguistic relations with other lexical items
* a more formal definition, where each relation is translated into a primitive relation chosen from a list of predefined relations
* a formal definition, where each relation corresponds to a role in the ontology and where the related lexical items are bound to a concept in the ontology

---

[1] Text and term are French. We have tried to translate some elements for a better understanding, that explains the French/English mix presented in some windows.

Each modeling form is bound to the terminological form. This form represents the choice of modeling of the knowledge engineer. It will be saved for the traceability of the modeling. The engineer defines the list of linguistic relations of the notion from the terminological definition and the analysis of the list of occurrences. This is entirely manual and is dependent on the competence of the knowledge engineer.

Then, the linguistic relations are translated into primitive relations with the aid of a list of predefined relations given with their definition and some examples. Most of these relations are defined as roles of the ontology.

Then under the control of the engineer, TERMINAE translates each primitive relation into a role. If the matching is not successful, the engineer has the possibility to add a new role to the initial ontology, and a corresponding relation to the list of predefined relations. An unsuccessful matching means either that the name of the relation is unknown as a role or that the role cannot link the concepts together.

Indeed, a value concept must be defined for each role of the notion which is being defined. The value concept of the role R is the least common subsumer of the concepts bound to the terms which have an R relation with the notion. The classifier of TERMINAE helps to find this least common subsumer, through the analysis and conceptualization of the list of occurrences of the notion. This implies that the notions in relation with the notion which is being defined must themselves be defined, as the modeling process is iterative. Other choices may be to give up a particular notion related to the one being defined or to consider a more generic one. The form keeps trace of the modeling process for traceability and further modeling. The result is a concept with a name and a list of relations with other concepts, and this concept may be inserted into the formal ontology. Let us examine the formalization of the notion "affecter-1" (to allocate). The normalization phase gives the description :

"affecter-1" is an action which has three linguistic relations "agent", "object", "second object". The translation of these relations into primitive ones gives :
"affecter-1" isKindOf action with relations "AGNT", "OBJ", "RCPT".

Each property has to be translated into a role of the knowledge base. These properties will be described by the roles AGNT, OBJ and RCPT which are defined on the concept "action". To define the value concept for each role, the knowledge base is searched for a concept which subsumes the value concepts corresponding to the value terms. So the concepts (subscriber's line, channel, access) are subsumed by the concept "equipment"; the concepts "communication" and "equipment" are subsumed by the concept "entity". Thus the notion studied is formalized into the terminological concept "affecter-1"(to allocate):

to-allocate::= action and (all AGNT exchange) and (all OBJ equipment)
          and (all RCPT entity)

Insertion into the ontology The last step is the insertion of the concept into the knowledge base. The knowledge-base system may give information to the knowledge-base designer. Let us suppose that the knowledge base already

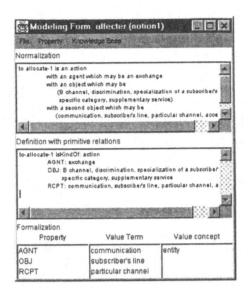

Fig. 4. Modeling form of "affecter-1" (to allocate)

includes some concepts as shown in the figure 6. It informs that the concept "to-allocate" has the same roles as the concept "to-assign". The concept "to-assign" is described by:

to-assign::= descriptive-action and (all AGNT exchange)
and (all OBJ equipment) and (all RCPT spatial-entity)

The knowledge base designer takes either one of the four following decisions:

1. that "to-allocate" is a specialization of "to-assign". The designer defines the concept "to-allocate " as isKindOf the concept "to-assign".
2. that "to-assign" is a specialization of "to-allocate". The designer defines the concept "to-assign" as isKindOf of the concept "to-allocate".
3. that the two concepts are brothers, with the same father "descriptive-action". The designer defines the concept "to-allocate" as isKindOf the concept "descriptive- action".
4. that the underlying notions are synonymous. The designer specifies that the concept "to-assign" also represents a notion of the term "to allocate"; TERMINAE adds a comment to the concept "to-assign", a link between the concept and the modeling form of "to-allocate", and returns to the two terminological forms to specify that "to allocate" and "to assign" terms are synonymous.

In each case, the knowledge-base system will check the validity of the insertion. For example, in case (1), the knowledge-base system will inform the designer that it has detected incoherence on the value role RCPT. Indeed, the "entity" concept is not subsumed by the "spatial-entity" concept. The designer choice

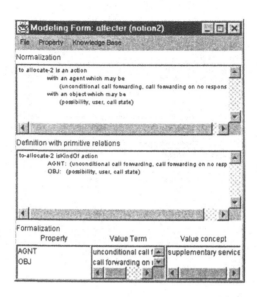

Fig. 5. Modeling form of "affecter-2" (to modify)

has to be changed, or the concept description has to be modified. The designer must explain the choice in a comment linked to the concept. These comments are necessary to understand the modeling and to modify it, they facilitate maintenance and readability. The knowledge-base system allows ontology description and avoids incoherence. The classifier helps to search for similarity and to group concepts together, while the comments facilitate maintenance and readability. The traceability requirement is achieved through the links between the text, the different forms and the terminological concepts in the ontology. The resulting ontology is strongly linked with terminology, and so benefits from the solid experience in semantic modeling of the specialized domain. It is relatively independant from any application, which means that it is necessary to make a new model that is well adapted to the application in question. In particular, the relations may need to be extended by other relations that are closer to the inferences of the application, but its linguistic base makes it directly usable for applications on text retrieval, corporate memory, texts-on-line filtering, etc.

3 State of art

3.1 The terminological knowledge bases

Interactions between knowledge engineering and terminology are studied since 1990, that gave birth to the notion of terminological knowledge base ([30],[2]). In France, the TIA ([9]) group works since 1993 on this theme. A terminological knowledge base (called TKB in what follows) is a terminology, more specifically a term bank, which is electronically accessible. The main difference is that a

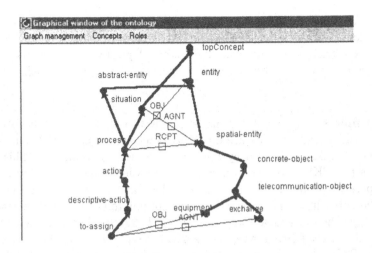

Fig. 6. The part of the ontology involved in an insertion, before the insertion

TKB includes conceptual knowledge "a large and highly structured amount of conceptual information for each term" [21], and its admitted objective is to be used as the knowledge base of some system. The study of the terms in the texts of a domain (any text, interview reports, technical reports, teaching manuals) allows the definition of the domain objects by giving a definition of the terms verified by an expert. A TKB includes the terms of one or more specialized domains, lexical information on these terms, and indications about their use (domain, sub-domain, kind of specific document, kind of specific speaker) and relations with concepts. Several concepts may correspond to one term. A TKB is independent of any application; it is built from texts describing a domain, which may involve several applications. It defines the terms depending on their context, i.e. their uses in texts, linking a concept with the corresponding term occurrences. It may be created by terminologists and used by knowledge engineers as the starting point for building a domain ontology. TERMINAE proposes knowledge engineer to start with a terminological study for defining the concepts of the ontology which corresponds to a term. Its aim is not terminology building but ontology building, the resulting terminology being a side-effect.

CODE, a TKB management tool. The best known TKB management tool is CODE, Conceptually Oriented Design/Description Environment, developed by D. Skuce and his group at Ottawa from 1990 to 1995 ([30], [21], [29]). This tool is a general-purpose knowledge management system. It assists in the various operations necessary to create a knowledge base: inputting, structuring, debugging, retrieving, explaining. CODE uses a frame representation language, allowing consistency-checking based on inheritance mechanism. It provides a highly developed graphic user interface and aims at the production of documents into a pseudo natural language, for linguistic exploitation. The main difference with

TERMINAE, apart from its being wide-spread, is that it was rather designed for a terminologists workstation than as a formal ontology building tool. Technically, the term extraction is very different, and methodologically it does not distinguish between concepts coming from a terminological study and from modeling needs.

A TKB model. [3] proposed a model of TKB in which textual occurrences of terms, terms and concepts are linked together as in usual TKB, but where term-concept links are labeled by the context of use, following [11]. This label structures the TKB into several points of view, which reflect a distinction between specialized domains, such as meteorology and telecommunication. This allows the univocity of the labeled term-concept link to be kept, akin to classical terminology. The concepts are structured into a hierarchical network, where they are defined in a semi-formal way, normalized but still informal. This informality allows the TKB to be adapted to a specific application and its required formalization.
TERMINAE allows for non-univocity of the term-concept link, and focuses on knowledge engineering part and formalization, rather than on manageability of a terminology with multiple views.

3.2 A computational linguistics based knowledge engineering tool

KAWB (Knowledge Acquisition WorkBench)[22] is an example of advanced integration of linguistic tools. It is a semi-implemented tool to acquire semantic features of a domain from large text corpora. It uses methods from computational linguistics, information retrieval and knowledge engineering. A data extraction module includes first a word class identification based on linguistic annotation of texts, statistical word clustering, with access to external linguistic and semantic sources; then a pattern finder collects collocations for words, searches for regularities and proposes lexico-semantic patterns for a conceptual characterization to the knowledge engineer. An analysis and refinement module helps the engineer to test patterns which represent his/her hypotheses, groups together the cases found by the search and generalizes them to ask the engineer for a final decision.
This tool is applied in Medicine,where extensive work has been done, and where a thesaurus exists (UMLS, Unified Medical Language System); it is real NLP technology application independent, even if it requires knowledge engineer intervention, as all knowledge engineering tools. This is a perfect example of how NLP may help acquisition of domain knowledge from texts. Today, TERMINAE tries to use simple NLP tools. For instance, LEXTER uses local syntactic parsing techniques based on surface patterns to extract candidate terms from a tagged text, where KAWB uses a word tagger, a specialized partial robust parser and a case attachment module which requires more lexical information from a knowledge base and external lexical data bases.

3.3 A formal ontology building tool

ONTOSAURUS [33] is an example of browser and editor of ontology based on a formal representation language. It is a user-friendly and Web-based tool for browsing and editing ontologies or knowledge bases, with the Loom knowledge representation formalism. Each concept is described on one HTML page, with all the relevant information; this page contains two types of information, informal or formal. The informal part includes image and textual documentation with reference links to other source documents and references used in formalizing the concept; the formal part includes the concept definition, the related concepts of the hierarchy (super, sub and sibling concepts), its roles, its instances in the knowledge base. Asserted and inferred informations are distinguished, that is useful with description logics tools because the classifier makes sometimes some obscure inferences [24]. Hyper-links abilities facilitate the browsing. The LOOM integration provides ontology maintenance services such as the automatic detection of incoherence, inconsistency and missing definitions.

This tool fulfills our requirements on traceability and formality; but it lacks of methodology guidelines and, as often in knowledge engineering tools, there is no distinction between term and concept. The linguistics used for identifying the concepts to put into the ontology is not made explicit.

3.4 An example of strong principle based methodology

METHOTONLOGY [12] is a very interesting work on the ontology development process. A list of activities to be done is elicited, from planification of task and resources needed to build an ontology to its maintenance. Reuse is strongly recommended, and the conceptualization, formalization, implementation steps are distinguished, even if formalization and implementation come to the same when the formal language is implemented as description logics usually are. It highlights the similarity between ontology and classical software life cycles, such as the needs of an ontology requirements specification. TERMINAE takes place from conceptualization step, and its proposed top-level ontology from state-of-the-art ontologies meets the METHOTONLOGY integration purpose. But in the domains we study, it would have been very difficult to follow more than the first step of conceptualization part, to define data dictionary and concepts classification trees. Indeed, there is no constant, no formula, no constraint, no axiom in the studied domains, which are hardly formalizable. The other steps of conceptualization are not applicable.

4 Conclusion

This paper presents a linguistics-based methodology and tool to help knowledge engineering. We think that domain ontology modeling would benefit from a closer interaction between linguistic methods or tools and computer-aided knowledge engineering methods or tools. Our aim is to push the integration of these disciplines as far as possible into a tool, TERMINAE. The tool, like the methodology it supports, has been developed from the requirements of real applications, to facilitate ontology building from texts.

The requirements were as follows:

* To use the methods and tools from terminology in linguistics to find and define concepts. At present, a term extractor, LEXTER, provides term candidates that may then be modeled through the normalization process.
* To provide traceability for maintenance and back linking from the ontology to texts. This is achieved through the links between the text, the different forms and the terminological concepts in the ontology.
* To highlight the modeling choices. A modeling typology of concepts leads the designer through the ontology.
* To avoid as far as possible incoherences and inconsistencies. A terminological formalism provides a classification mechanism to help the designer to detect redundancies and incompatible definitions.

Today, TERMINAE has been developed in Java. There is still a lot of work to be done to integrate the state-of-the-art in lexical semantics and computational linguistics. Some tools could easily be inserted, such as morphological matchers to align term occurrences one under the other and to facilitate the manual comparison of the uses. As far as we know, very few proposals have been made to help in the elaboration of semantic classes (Zellig [7]), but less sophisticated tools may help, such as LEXICLASS ([1]) that eases to cluster terms according to their "terminological context" given by LEXTER. TERMINAE has been designed through real applications, but it has not yet been extensively used and the methodology needs to be developed further. So far, TERMINAE has been designed as a knowledge engineering tool with an ontology modeling objective, but it could also be used as a terminological knowledge base, since it handles the definition of terminological forms, the links to the text, and the links between notions.

Acknowledgement: We warmly thank Daniel Kayser for his fruitful remarks.

References

1. ASSADI H.: Construction of a regional ontology from text and its use within a documentary system. In Proc. of the 1st International Conference, FOIS'98, Trento, Italy, (1998)
2. AUSSENAC-GILLES N., BOURIGAULT D., CONDAMINES A., GROS C.: How can knowledge acquisition benefit from terminology ? In Proc. of the 9th Banff Knowledge Acquisition for Knowledge-Based Systems Workshop, Banff, (1995)
3. AUSSENAC-GILLES N., SÉGUÉLA P.: Un modèle de base de connaissances terminologiques. In Proc. of the 2nd Conference Terminology and Artificial Intelligence (TIA'97), Toulouse, France,(1997)
4. BACHIMONT B.: Herméneutique matérielle et Artéfacture: des machines qui pensent aux machines qui donnent à penser. Thèse, Ecole Polytechnique, Paris, (1996)

5. BIÉBOW, B., CHARNOIS, T., SZULMAN, S.: ISDN supplementary services: from informality to knowledge representation. In Annals of Telecommunications, 51, n9-10,(1996)440-451

6. BIÉBOW B., NOBÉCOURT J., SZULMAN S.: Elaboration d'une méthodologie pour la création d'un noyau de base de connaissances sur la supervision. Final report, CNRS-Cognisciences-CNET Contract, étude numéro 4, Assistance à la construction et à la réutilisation de connaissances dans le cadre des activités de supervision (1996)

7. BOUAUD J., HABERT B., NAZARENKO A., ZWEIGENBAUM P.: Regroupements issus de dépendances syntaxiques en corpus : catégorisation et confrontation à deux modélisations conceptuelles. In Proc. of the Conference "Journées Ingénierie des Connaissances et Apprentissage Automatique", Roscoff, France,(1997) 207-223

8. BOURIGAULT D.: LEXTER, un Logiciel d'EXtraction de TERminologie. Application à l'acquisition des connaissances à partir de textes. Thèse, EHESS Paris, (1994)

9. BOURIGAULT D., CONDAMINES A.: Réflexions sur le concept de base de connaissances terminologiques. In Proc. of Journées du PRC-GDR-IA, Nancy, France, Teknea ed., (1995)

10. BRACHMAN R. J.: On the epistemological status of semantic networks. In N. V. Findler (ed.), Associative Networks: Representation and Use of Knowledge by Computers, Academic Press,(1979) 3-50

11. CONDAMINES A., AMSILI P.: Terminologie entre langage et connaissances: un exemple de base de connaissances terminologiques. In Proc. of the conference Terminology and Knowledge Engineering, Frankfurt, (1993)

12. FERNANDEZ M., GÓMEZ-PÉREZ A, JURISTO N.: METHOTONLOGY : from ontological art towards ontological engineering. In Proc. of the 1997 AAAI Spring Symposium on Ontological Engineering, (1997) 33-40

13. FRIDMAN NOY N., HAFNER C. D.: The state of the art in ontology design: a comparative review. In Proc. of the 1997 AAAI Spring Symposium on Ontological Engineering, (1997)

14. GRUBER T. R.: Toward principles for the design of ontologies used for knowledge sharing. In International Journal of Human-Computer Studies,43, (1995) 907-928

15. GUARINO N.: Concepts, Attributes, and Arbitrary Relations: Some Linguistic and Ontology Criteria for Structuring Knowledge Bases. In Data and Knowledge Engineering, (1992)

16. GUARINO N.: Formal ontology and information systems. In Proc. of the 1st international conference on Formal Ontologies in Information Systems (FOIS'98), Trento, Italy,(1998)

17. GUARINO N.: Some organizing principles for a unified top-level ontology. In Proc. of the 1997 AAAI Spring Symposium on Ontological Engineering, (1997) 57-63

18. HOPPE T., KINDERMANN C., QUANTZ J., SCHMIEDEL A., FISCHER M.: BACK V5 Tutorial and Manual. KIT-report 100, Technische Universität Berlin, Projekt KIT-BACK, March (1993)

19. KAYSER D.: Ontologically, yours. In Proc. of the 6th International Conference on Conceptual structures, ICCS'98, Montpellier, France,(1998)

20. MARTIN P.: Exploitation de graphes conceptuels et de documents structurés et hypertextes pour l'acquisition de connaissances et la recherche d'informations. Thése, Université de Nice Sophia-Antipolis, (1996)

21. MEYER I., SKUCE D., BOWKER L., ECK K.: Towards a new generation of terminological resources: an experiment in building a terminological knowledge base. In Proc. of the international conference COLING-92, Nantes, (1992) 956-960

22. MIKHEEV A., FINCH S.: A workbench for acquisition of ontological knowledge from natural language. In Proc. of the 9th Banff Knowledge Acquisition for Knowledge-Based Systems Workshop, Banff, (1995)

23. NOBÉCOURT J. Représenter la notion de propriété dans les graphes conceptuels et les logiques de description. In Proc. of the conference Ingénierie des connaissances (IC'98), Nancy, (1998)

24. NOBÉCOURT J.: Une Expérience de Création d'une Base de Connaissances en Logique de Description. In Proc. of the 6th Journées d'Acquisition des Connaissances (JAC'95), Grenoble,(1995)

25. PUSTEJOVSKY J.: Lexical semantics and formal ontologies. In Proc. of the 1st International Conference on Formal Ontologies in Information Systems (FOIS'98), Trento, Italy,(1998)

26. RASTIER F.: Le terme: entre ontologie et linguistique. In La banque des mots, Paris, CLIF, n spécial 7/95, (1995)35-65

27. SCHREIBER A. T., WIELINGA B. J., BREUKER J.A.. KADS: a Principled Approach to Knowledge Engineering. In Knowledge-Based Systems Book Series, Academic Press, London, (1993)

28. SKUCE D.: How we might reach agreement on shared ontologies: a fundamental approach. In Proc. of the 1997 AAAI Spring Symposium on Ontological Engineering, (1997)

29. SKUCE D., LETHBRIDGE T.: CODE4: a unified system for managing conceptual knowledge. International Journal of Human-Computer Studies 42, (1995) 413-451

30. SKUCE D., MEYER I.: Terminology and knowledge acquisition: exploring a symbiotic relation ship. In Proc. of the 6th Banff on Knowledge Acquisition for Knowledge-Based Systems Workshop, (1991)

31. SLODZIAN M.: Comment revisiter la doctrine terminologique aujourd'hui? In La banque des mots, Paris, CLIF, n spécial 7/95, (1995) 11-18

32. SOWA J.: Processes and participants. In Proc. of the 4th International Conference on Conceptual structures, ICCS'96, Sydney, Australia, (1996)

33. SWARTOUT B., PATIL R., KNIGHT K., RUSS T.: Towards distributed use of large-scale ontologies. In Proc. of the 10th Banff on Knowledge Acquisition for Knowledge-Based Systems Workshop, (1996)

34. WOODS W. A., SCHMOLZE, J. G.: The KL-ONE family. Computers Mathematical Applications, 23, (1992) 133-177

35. WÜSTER E.: L'étude scientifique de la terminologie, zone frontalière entre la linguistique, la logique, l'ontologie, et les sciences des choses. In Rondeau, G. et Felber, H., (1981) 56-114

36. Proc. of the 1997 AAAI Spring Symposium on Ontological Engineering, (1997)

37. Proc. of ECAI Workshop on Applications of ontologies and problem-solving methods, 13th Biennal European Conference on Artificial Intelligence, Brighton, UK, (1998)

38. Information modelling and knowledge bases IX, IOS Press, (1998)

39. Proc. of the 1st international conference on Formal Ontologies in Information Systems (FOIS'98), Trento, Italy, (1998)

Applications of Knowledge Acquisition in Experimental Software Engineering

Andreas Birk, Dagmar Surmann, and Klaus-Dieter Althoff

Fraunhofer Institute for Experimental Software Engineering (Fraunhofer IESE),
Sauerwiesen 6, D-67661 Kaiserslautern, Germany
{birk,surmann,althoff}@iese.fhg.de

Abstract. Many tasks in experimental software engineering (ESE) involve the acquisition of knowledge. Only for very few of them systematic knowledge acquisition (KA) practices have been established. It is expected that these ESE tasks can be accomplished more effectively if the application of appropriate systematic KA methods is fostered.

Most reports on KA applications in software engineering address only some selected aspects. A broader ESE perspective with its additional facets (e.g., quality and knowledge management issues) has not yet been presented so far.

This paper surveys applications of knowledge acquisition in experimental software engineering, introduces a repository of knowledge elicitation (KEL) techniques, and suggests a methodology for the development of customised KA methods in experimental software engineering. Repository and methodology aim at fostering the dissemination of systematic KA practices in ESE. They are applied at Fraunhofer IESE to develop methods for the acquisition of experiential software engineering knowledge.

Keywords: knowledge acquisition, knowledge management, experimental software engineering

1 Introduction

Software engineering (SE) involves a multitude of knowledge-intensive tasks: Elicitation of user requirements for new software systems, identification of best software development practice, experience collection about project planning and risk management, and many others.

In addition, the discipline of experimental software engineering (ESE)[1] places particular emphasis on knowledge management and knowledge-based support. It builds on the assumption that continuous learning and systematic reuse of learnt

---

[1] Experimental Software Engineering [1] covers all traditional fields of Software Engineering. It places particular focus on the empirical investigation of Software Engineering concepts such as techniques, methods, or tools. Approaches for managing the gained empirical knowledge play an important role in ESE.

knowledge and experience are crucial for the further development of today's software development and management practices.

Despite the importance of knowledge management in ESE, organised and mature approaches to knowledge acquisition (KA) are rare. Compared to other areas of engineering, SE is still quite young. Technological developments are progressing fast. For these reasons, the often needed KA and knowledge management components of methods and techniques have not yet been developed very far. However, for the same reasons, effective knowledge acquisition and knowledge management (KM) become more and more important for sustained business success.

The objective of our work is to foster the further dissemination and use of advanced KA methods in ESE. This paper presents the approach through which we want to achieve this objective. The approach consists of three elements:

- Survey and characterisation of KA applications in ESE
- A repository of reusable knowledge elicitation (KEL) techniques and experience
- A methodology for developing customised KA methods for specific ESE tasks

The survey of KA applications provides an overview of the various tasks in experimental software engineering that can benefit from advanced and systematic knowledge acquisition practices. The characterisation of these applications illustrates the need for customised KA methods. It also is the first step to identify requirements for the development of such customised methods.

A repository of knowledge elicitation techniques is important for disseminating good KA practice throughout experimental software engineering. Many KEL techniques that could be beneficial to ESE are just not known to software engineers. Operational definitions of these techniques need to be collected and made accessible to software engineers. They must be supplied with experience about when and how to use which technique. This information facilitates the selection of KEL techniques for a specific knowledge acquisition task and supports the application of the KEL techniques.

Such a repository does not only support knowledge acquisition and knowledge management in ESE. It also is a knowledge management application itself, because the repository needs to be kept alive. It must be extended continuously, and experience from the application of KEL techniques should be fed back into it.

A methodology is needed to guide software engineers in the development of customised KA methods. Such a methodology starts with the characterisation of a knowledge acquisition task and selects appropriate KEL techniques from the repository. The KEL techniques must then be integrated with each other and supported by appropriate tools. The result is an operational, customised KA method for the specific application task.

This paper is structured according to the three elements of our approach: Section 2 surveys applications of knowledge acquisition in experimental software engineering, Section 3 presents the repository of KEL techniques, and Section 4 describes the knowledge acquisition methodology. A discussion and an outlook on future work are addressed in Section 5. The remainder of this first section briefly introduces the fields of experimental software engineering and knowledge acquisition. It also lists requirements on KA applications in ESE, which were used to guide the development of the approach presented.

1.1 Experimental Software Engineering

Software engineering aims at providing technologies that can be used for developing software and for managing software development. This involves the definition, selection, tailoring, and integration of principles, methods, techniques, and tools in order to achieve a software product that meets the desired quality, time, and cost requirements. For managing these requirements and for demonstrating that they actually have been achieved, analytical and empirical measures must be applied [2] [1].

Experimental software engineering is a branch of software engineering that addresses problems and research questions of software development and improvement through an experimental approach. It utilises systematically designed experiments and other kinds of empirical studies in order to enhance available knowledge about the software domain. ESE is built on the principle of continuous learning and reuse of experience, which is defined through the Quality Improvement Paradigm / Experience Factory (QIP/EF).

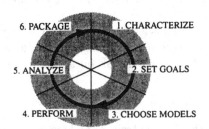

Fig. 1. The Quality Improvement Paradigm

The QIP is a six-step proceeding for structuring software development and improvement activities (see Figure 1). It involves three overall phases: planning, execution, and evaluation of the task. The planning phase is based on the explicit characterisation (QIP1) of the initial situation, the identification of the goals to be achieved (QIP2), and the actual development of the plan (QIP3). The plan then guides the systematic execution of the task (QIP4). The subsequent evaluation phase involves the analysis of the performed actions (QIP5) and the packaging of the lessons learnt into reusable artifacts (QIP6). The evaluation allows to learn for similar tasks in the future.

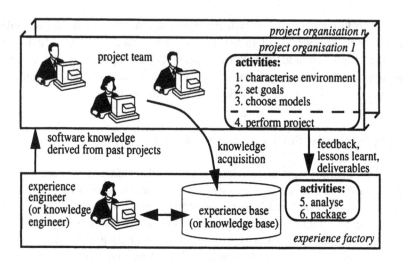

Fig. 2. The Experience Factory

The experience factory is a logical and/or physical organisation that supports project developments by analysing and synthesising all kinds of experience, acting as a repository for such experience, and supplying that experience to various projects on demand. The experience factory complements the project organisation [2]. The experience factory is mainly responsible for conducting steps 5 and 6 of the QIP while steps 1 to 4 mainly concern the project organisation (see Figure 2).

ESE has many relations to knowledge engineering and knowledge management. KA from experienced software professionals is an important means for gaining the knowledge and insight to answer ESE questions.

1.2 Knowledge Acquisition

Knowledge acquisition (KA) is the transfer and transformation of expertise from some knowledge source to some explicit knowledge representation-usually denoted as knowledge base-that enables the effective use of the knowledge. This definition is based on the one by Hayes-Roth et al. from 1983 [3]. It has been generalised slightly to meet the application of knowledge acquisition in experimental software engineering as addressed in the remainder of this paper.

A KA method is an organised approach to knowledge acquisition. It involves a defined process and guidelines for process execution. A knowledge acquisition methodology defines and guides the design of KA methods for particular application purposes. Section 4 suggests a KA methodology for experimental software engineering. Knowledge elicitation (KEL) denotes the initial steps of knowledge acquisition that identify or isolate and record the relevant expertise using one or multiple KEL techniques. A KA method can involve a combination of KEL techniques which is then called KEL strategy. These terms are used differently by different authors. We have chosen our definitions to meet the specific terminology needs of this paper.

Musen [4] lists several characteristics of knowledge acquisition that need to be considered when applying KA methods:

- Knowledge acquisition is a process of joint model building. A model of expertise is built in co-operation between a domain expert (i.e., the knowledge source) and a knowledge engineer.
- Much knowledge is tacit (i.e., it is not directly accessible). Appropriate KEL techniques are needed to make it explicit.
- The results of knowledge acquisition depend on the degree to which the knowledge engineer is familiar with (a) the domain of the knowledge to be acquired, and (b) its later application.
- The results of knowledge acquisition depend on the formalism that is used to represent the knowledge. Knowledge acquisition is most effective if knowledge representation is epistemologically adequate (i.e., all relevant aspects of expertise can be expressed) and usable (i.e., suits all later usage needs).

These characteristics of knowledge acquisition provide guidance for the design of KA methods. For example, they imply that KA methods must assure that the knowledge engineer becomes familiar with the application domain. In Section 4 a knowledge acquisition method is presented that reflects these characteristics.

1.3 Requirements on KA in ESE

Experimental software engineering puts specific requirements on knowledge acquisition that are quite different from KA applications in other engineering sciences or from the development of knowledge-based systems (KBS):

- For most KA applications in ESE, the required knowledge exists only implicitly, codified, and informally. Hence, it can be quite difficult to access the knowledge. This imposes high requirements on the validity of the KEL techniques and strategies used.
- The results of KA in ESE are often the basis for further technical or managerial activities. These activities depend very much on the reliability of KA results. For this reason, the validity of KA methods and their results is an important concern in ESE.
- ESE involves a wide variety of target knowledge representation formats for KA, which can be highly specific to ESE. Many of these knowledge representation (KR) formats are different from the traditional rule-, frame-, or case-based formalisms involved in KBS. For this reason, the target KR format becomes an important criterion to assess the appropriateness of a candidate KEL technique.
- In addition, an ESE artefact (e.g., a design document) often involves multiple different knowledge types (e.g., facts as well as rules and policies). Hence, an appropriate KA method might require a combination of multiple KEL techniques.

- In ESE, KA is not only useful for providing problem-solving support in the form of knowledge-based systems. It can also provide the knowledge to effectively perform technical and managerial tasks, and it can provide input to corporate knowledge management systems and improvement programmes.
- Knowledge-based systems have not yet found their way to wide-spread use in the software industry (cf. [5] [6]). To foster their further dissemination, a gradual transition from current ESE practices via knowledge management implementation to KBS is recommended. This is an additional challenge for KA in ESE, asking for KA methods that adapt to specific needs of KM applications.
- Systematic knowledge acquisition should be integrated into many ESE tasks. As a consequence, KA methods should be applied also by non-knowledge engineers. This requires a strong need for operational definitions of KA methods and guidance for their application.

A KA methodology for ESE must take these requirements into consideration and provide a well-organised approach to the selection of appropriate KEL techniques. The KA methodology suggested in Section 4 reflects these requirements.

2 A Survey of KA Applications in ESE

Experimental software engineering involves a multitude of knowledge acquisition tasks. They can differ in quite a variety of aspects such as involved knowledge types, knowledge sources, knowledge users, modes of knowledge use, and target knowledge representation. A good starting point to provide tailored and effective methodological support to these knowledge acquisition tasks in ESE is to survey these tasks systematically, and to characterise them appropriately.

This section presents such a survey and characterisation of KA applications in experimental software engineering. It thus demonstrates the wide variety of KA-related tasks, which has often not been recognised sufficiently by ESE. For the field of knowledge acquisition, the survey provides a map of possible applications for established KA approaches. The survey is not meant to be comprehensive and complete. It was our intention to build on previous work in SE and to complement it with a specific ESE perspective.

2.1 Literature Review

Applications of knowledge acquisition in software engineering have been described-among others-by [6] [7] [8] [9]. A particular tradition in systematic KA can be found in the field of requirements engineering (RE) (cf. [10] [11] [12] [13]).

Eriksson [7] lists three major application areas of knowledge acquisition in software engineering: Initial feasibility studies, requirements specification, and the identification of solution approaches for design and implementation problems. He summarises that KA is a broad activity which may be useful at many stages in the software development process. Some KA methods were already used in SE, albeit often in a less explicit and systematic manner than in KBS development.

Grogono [6] addresses the mutual interrelations between expert systems and software engineering. Thus, indirectly, he also covers the need for knowledge acquisition in SE. The expert systems that he lists require the following kinds of knowledge: Requirements specifications, expertise on design structures (i.e., products or artifacts), expertise on the design and implementation processes (mainly in the form of rules or heuristics), as well as software process models (i.e., procedure-like representations).

Briand et al. [8] describe a method for estimating software development effort. It is a hybrid approach that combines acquisition of experiential knowledge with empirical data from past projects. The acquired causal models allow for effort predictions that are based on significantly less empirical data than would be needed otherwise. Wilson and Hall [9] use construct elicitation to investigate the perceptions of software quality that they found in a number of IT organisations. The various analogies between knowledge engineering and requirements engineering are surveyed and investigated by Angele and Studer [10] and by Shaw and Gaines [11]. A recent publication by Weidenhaupt et al. [12] surveys and investigates the application of various scenario techniques for the acquisition of system requirements. Maiden and Ncube [13] describe an approach to the acquisition of requirements for the selection of commercial off-the-shelf software that involves multiple semi-structured interview techniques.

2.2 Survey Results

Most reports on KA applications related to software engineering either address only some particular aspects (e.g., requirements elicitation or cost estimation) or focus on software development tasks only. A broader ESE perspective with its additional facets (e.g., quality, improvement, and knowledge management issues) has not yet been presented so far. To gain such a broader perspective on KA applications in experimental software engineering as a basis for our further work, we have investigated multiple literature sources and interviewed SE experts. The results are shown in Table 1. The table demonstrates the wide area of applications of KA in ESE. Each application is characterised briefly.

Starting point of our investigation was a taxonomy of ESE tasks. It is listed in the leftmost column of Table 1. The tasks are grouped into three categories: Product engineering (i.e., the typical software development tasks), management (e.g., project or quality management), and support (i.e., all activities that are not directly related to the product development but that ease, facilitate, and improve it). For each task, a set of knowledge items (i.e., artefacts or concepts) was identified, which are usually gained within the related task by some kind of knowledge acquisition activity. Each knowledge item is characterised using its subject topic and the typical kinds of knowledge encoding (i.e., whether it is contained in documents, available in the minds of humans, or present in the form of processes and procedures).

Each set of knowledge items is supplied with information about the typical knowledge sources (e.g., a SE role or a document), its knowledge users, and the target knowledge representations in which it is documented and used once

ESE Task	Knowledge Items		Knowledge Sources	Knowledge Users	Target Knowledge Representations
	Subject Topics	Encoding			
Product Engineering					
Requirements Analysis	Requirements, Business Processes, Use Cases	H, P, D	U, C, M, SE, PD, S	SE	S, G, U, F
Architecture Design	Reusable Artefacts, Templates, Patterns[1]	D, H	PD, L, SE, S	SE	G, S, F, U
Detailed Design					G, S, F, U
Implementation					F, G
Integration and Testing	Test Plans, Test Cases	D, H, P	U, C, SE, QM, SP	SE	F, G, U, S
Maintenance	Programme Understanding	D, H, P	SE, S, PD	SE	F, G
Software Acquisition	Requirements, Third-Party Products	D, H	PD, L, SE	SE	S, U, G
Management					
Project Management	Time and Effort Estimates, Schedules, Staffing Plans	H, P, D	PM, PD, L, SP	PM	F, S, G
Quality Management	Quality Plans	D, H, P	PD, PM, QM, SP, L	QM	S, G
Risk Management	Risk Mitigation Plans	H, P, D	PM, PD, SP, L	PM	S
Support					
Configuration Management	Configuration Management Plans	D, H, P	PD, SE, QM, SP	SE, QM, PM	F, G, S
Documentation	User Documentation	D, H, P	PD, SE, U, S	TW	S, G
Process Modelling	Process Models	H, D, P	SE, PM, QM, PD, SP	SE, QM, PM	F, G, S, U
Process Enactment	Processes, Guidelines	H, P, D	SE, PM, QM, SP, PD	SE, QM, PM	S, G
Process Automation[2]	Process Models, Configuration Management Plans, System Architecture, Code[3]	D, P, H	PD, SP, SE, PM, QM	SE, QM	F, G, S
Process Assessment	Various aspects of the software engineering practices	P, D, H	SP, PD, SE, PM, QM	PM, QM	S, G, U
Measurement	Quality Goals, Understanding and Definition of Qualities, Products, and Processes, Expected Phenomena, Measurement Plans, Interpretations of Observed Phenomena	D, P, H	PD, SP, SE, PM, QM	PM, QM, SE	F, G, S
Improvement	Improvement Plans	D, H, P	PD, SE, PM, QM, SP	QM, PM	S, G

[1] Typical subjects of these knowledge types are architectures, data models, algorithms, and code.

[2] Note: This involves process automation using CASE tools, and process support using SE environments.

[3] These items are structure- and process-related knowledge about different software engineering artefacts or concepts relevant for setting-up process automation.

Legend: These lists are sorted by relevance. Most relevant items appear first.
Knowledge Types (Encoding): D=Documents, H=Humans, P=Processes.
Knowledge Sources and Knowledge Users: U=User, C=Customer, M=Marketing, PM=Project Management, QM=Quality Management, SE=Software Engineer, TW=Technical Writer, S=Existing System, PD=Existing Project Documentation, L=Literature, SP=Software Process.
Target Knowledge Representation: G=Graphics, U=Unstructured and S=Structured or Semi-Formal Natural Language, F=Formal Language.

Table 1. Overview of KA applications in ESE

it has been acquired. For each set of characteristics, the order in which they are listed indicates an order of relevance.

2.3 Observations from the Survey

The survey and the characterisation of knowledge acquisition applications in experimental software engineering provide an interesting perspective on the detailed, specific KA requirements of ESE. Observations can be made that are useful for selecting KEL techniques and for developing KA methods for application in experimental software engineering. In the following, the most relevant observations are summarised.

Product Knowledge vs. Process Knowledge. Two kinds of knowledge are most important for the gross number of ESE tasks: Product knowledge and process knowledge. Product knowledge addresses structure and other characteristics of artefacts (e.g., system architecture or functionality). Process knowledge deals with how ESE tasks should be performed (e.g., the development process, policies, and guidelines), and how the tasks interact.

Dependency Chains between ESE Tasks. For product engineering and support tasks, especially, it is typical that there are chains of dependent tasks: Design tasks depend on requirements analysis, and implementation depends on design. Likewise, process assessment and measurement depend on process modelling, and improvement depends on process assessment and measurement.

These dependency chains have implications on knowledge encoding: Knowledge that is needed to accomplish the tasks in the chain can mainly be acquired from human experts, especially the first tasks. During KA such knowledge is represented explicitly, so that the subsequent tasks can widely rely on documented knowledge.

High Variety of Knowledge Sources. The lists of knowledge sources for the different ESE tasks can be quite long. The knowledge sources of a certain task can be quite different. This implies that the KEL techniques used to gain the required knowledge must also be quite different, because different groups of persons (e.g., software engineers vs. customers) can show very different communication styles and terminologies.

Support Tasks Have Many Different Knowledge Users. By definition of the taxonomy that is used to structure the ESE tasks, the knowledge users of product engineering tasks are software engineers, and those of management tasks are project or quality managers. In contrast, each support task can have multiple knowledge users, and the sets of users for two support tasks can be different.

The survey of KA applications in experimental software engineering and their characterisations provide a starting point for the development of customised KA methods that can be used to accomplish these tasks. The two following sections suggest an approach by which the development of such methods can be supported.

3 An Experience Base of Knowledge Elicitation Techniques

Software engineering can benefit from the adoption of advanced KA practices. Therefore, a body of knowledge about KA needs to be collected, made accessible, and disseminated to software engineering professionals. Experience about KEL techniques is of particular interest to experimental software engineering, because these are the basic elements needed to develop customised KA methods for the various ESE tasks.

This section presents the repository (or experience base) of KEL techniques that has been built at Fraunhofer IESE. We describe the structure of the chosen knowledge representation and outline how the knowledge was collected and how it is used.

To support systematic KEL practices in ESE, the following information needs to be provided to software engineering personnel:

- Concise and operational definitions of the KEL techniques.
- Information about the application context of the KEL techniques (i.e., in which situations it can be applied, and in which situations it is inappropriate).
- Traceability information and literature references that allow to access further information about the KEL techniques.

The representation structure we have chosen to describe experiences about KEL techniques (in the following denoted as experience packages) meets these requirements. Table 2 shows an example experience package. It has the form of a table with pre-defined information blocks. The upper part of the table contains the definition and classification of the technique as well as references and traceability information (i.e., its name, and slots for sources, classification, relationships, description, and characteristics). The lower part contains information relevant to selecting and using the technique (i.e., its application context). Its slots are: Prerequisites, advantages, disadvantages, risks, and notes.

Each entry that has been acquired from some literature source is supplied with a reference to this source. Information about application context is classified using keywords at the beginning of the statement. The classes indicate aspects of knowledge elicitation to which the statements refer. For instance, KTYP stands for knowledge types and marks statements like "Is appropriate for eliciting facts, conceptual structure, causal knowledge, and justification" in the advantages slot of Table 2. ELIC and EXPT mark statements that refer to the roles of elicitor and expert, respectively.

The experience base currently contains about 30 experience packages. Focus is put on KEL techniques for elicitation from individual human experts in interview-like sessions. Examples are semi-structured interview, retrospective case description, list-related tasks, teachback, construct elicitation using repertory grids, and laddering.

The information contained in the experience packages has been gained from multiple literature sources that survey KEL techniques or report on experiences from using some of them (cf. [14] [15] [16] [17]). The raw information that has been found in these texts has been categorised and structured gradually to gain the experience packages. However, once the experience package structure had been established, it was quite straight-forward to add new KEL techniques or to extend the information about already catalogued ones.

Semi-Structured Interview	
Sources	Cordingly [14], Cooke [15], Welbank [16]
Classification	Interview/Semi-structured Interviews [14]
	Interviews/Structured Interviews [15]
Relationships	Kind of Interview
Description	The interviewer has a list of prepared questions. But the order in which they are covered and the words used to express them may vary from interview to interview.
	Many of the questions are open questions.
	[14], [15]
Characteristics	• Puts more demands on the interviewer than do fully structured and pre-determined interviews. [14]
Prerequisites	• Preparation of generic questions and coarse outline of interview structure.
	• Some basic familiarity of the elicitor with the domain and the tasks for which knowledge needs to be acquired.
Advantages	CNTS Structure provides more systematic and complete coverage of the domain than unstructured interviews. [15]
	STYL EXPT ELIC Structure tends to be more comfortable for both expert and elicitor. [15]
	PERF STYL The interview can flow smoothly. [14]
	CNTS The interviewee's associations between topics can be identified, because he/she has the freedom to follow spontaneous associations during the interview. [14]
	KTYP Is appropriate for eliciting facts, conceptual structure, causal knowledge, and justification. [16]
Disadvantages	PROC ELIC Requires more preparation time and domain knowledge than unstructured interview. [15]
	KTYP Is inappropriate for eliciting expert's strategy. [16]
Risks	KTYP Can be inappropriate when used to elicit rules, weight of evidence, and context of rules. [16]
Notes	• Answers to one question may arise as part of answers in another question. [14]
	• The wording of questions can be adopted to the vocabulary of the interviewee. [14]

Table 2. Example experience package for a KEL technique.

The experience packages can be used by software engineering professionals in multiple ways to gain an overview over KEL techniques, and to select some that meet the requirements of the tasks they have to accomplish. The structure of the experience packages and the keywords that classify each statement allow to search or browse the information for various aspects or subject topics. A KA method that illustrates very well how individual KEL techniques can be integrated in a systematic manner has been presented by Briand et al. [8].

The experience base is extended and updated gradually. Currently, it is provided as versioned electronic documents with some basic hypertext functionality to access structure elements or indexed parts of experience packages. Our future plans are to transfer them into HTML format and offer them as an on-line experience base through the intranet. In addition, we are about to implement the experience base in a prototype knowledge management system that is specialised toward decision support for the selection of SE technologies during project planning. This knowledge management system called *KONTEXT* [2] [18] [19] supports the entire life-cycle of *Technology Experience Packages (TEPs)*, involving (1) knowledge acquisition and modelling of TEPs, (2) decision support for the selection of software engineering technologies, and (3) empirical evaluation of technology application and update of TEPs. *KONTEXT* is a research prototype that is being applied for internal uses at Fraunhofer IESE.

Currently, works are under way to build two variants of *KONTEXT*: One is for offering *Technology Experience Bases* and the TEPs they contain over the internet. The other implements the core functions and data model of *KONTEXT* into Fraunhofer IESE's corporate information network infrastructure. As soon as these works will be completed, the experience base on KEL techniques can be offered as part of a comprehensive knowledge management system that–among other features– allows for knowledge annotation and continuous knowledge evolution of KEL experience.

The knowledge representation of *KONTEXT* in the Fraunhofer IESE corporate information network deploys an object-oriented formalism and associated case-based knowledge representation. Based on a collaboration with a commercial case-based reasoning (CBR) tool provider, a CBR tool has been developed for supporting the retrieval of experience packages [20] [21] [22]. For a public case base a first implementation of the CBR tool has already been validated empirically [23][3]. Further experimental validation of *KONTEXT* is currently being prepared.

4 A KA methodology for ESE

The further dissemination and implementation of systematic knowledge acquisition practices in experimental software engineering requires an appropriate methodological framework. This section suggests a methodology for guiding the development and application of customised KA methods in ESE. The methodology starts with a characterisation of KA tasks (cf. Table 1) as starting point and selects appropriate KEL techniques from the experience base (cf. Section

---

[2] *KnOwledge maNagement base on the application conTEXt of software engineering Technologies.*

[3] http://demolab.iese.fhg.de:8080/

3). It thus integrates the two other elements of our approach that have been introduced in the previous sections.

Table 3 depicts the structure of the methodology. It involves four phases and twelve steps. The initial phase is a pre-study for gaining background information and requirements on design and application of the KA method. The second phase, KEL strategy development, is the core part of the methodology. It defines the KEL strategy. The two subsequent phases are knowledge elicitation and modelling. Hence they address the application of the KA method.

The KA methodology is described in detail in [24]. The following sub-sections outline its overall structure.

Phase	Step / Sub-Step
Pre-Study	Conduct pre-study on subject topic
	Conduct pre-study on usage processes
	Identify knowledge representation
KEL Strategy Development	Identify requirements and candidate KEL techniques • Characterise application situation • Identify applicable KEL technique • Identify further pre-study needs
	Define KEL strategy • Select KEL techniques • Integrate KEL techniques • Document KEL strategy
	Develop support tools and validate KEL strategy • Identify requirements on KEL execution • Develop support tools • Validate KEL strategy and support tools
Knowledge-Elicitation	Plan knowledge elicitation
	Prepare knowledge elicitation
	Conduct knowledge elicitation
Knowledge-Modelling	Construct knowledge model
	Validate knowledge model
	Release knowledge model

Table 3. Overview of the KA methodology.

4.1 Pre-Study

The first phase of the methodology aim at making the knowledge engineer familiar with the subject topic and the usage processes of the knowledge models to be acquired. Pre-study of the subject topic involves an investigation of relevant and available knowledge sources. Based on this information, a suitable knowledge representation formalism is determined or designed from scratch.

4.2 KEL Strategy Development

The core phase of the methodology is the actual design of the KEL strategy. It starts with identification of requirements and candidate KEL techniques. If further pre-study is needed, exploratory knowledge elicitation activities should be planned explicitly. The identification of appropriate techniques can be supported by an experience base of KEL techniques (cf. Section 3). The individual techniques identified must then be integrated, and the method must be defined. Finally, support tools for knowledge elicitation must be provided, and the KEL strategy and its support tools must be validated.

Explicit and operational definition of KA methods is recommended, because it eases the dissemination and re-use of the methods. It also facilitates the planning of KA activities in the context of software projects, which have often tight schedules. Furthermore, in experimental software engineering the KA methods might be applied by persons with little experience in knowledge acquisition. So operational methods can provide beneficial guidance and support.

4.3 Knowledge Elicitation

The actual execution of a customised KA method starts with knowledge elicitation. Knowledge elicitation activities must be planned in accordance with the schedule of the software projects in which the experts are working, and by which the knowledge will be used later. Preparation activities involve customisation of questionnaires and providing the technical infrastructure for knowledge elicitation. During knowledge elicitation sessions, notes or records need to be taken. Possibly some intermediate or mediating knowledge model is being developed.

4.4 Knowledge Modelling

The knowledge modelling phase translates the KEL results into an appropriate knowledge model. The model needs to be validated thoroughly, because many ESE tasks may build on it. Finally, the validated knowledge model is released and disseminated. In some cases release and dissemination of KA results can become a major task. For instance, the dissemination of acquired good design practices may require an entire training programme.

4.5 Example KA Method

The methodology can be illustrated by a method for software development effort estimation called COBRA (COst estimation, Benchmarking, and Risk Assessment) [8]. COBRA applies several KEL techniques in an integrated and very systematic way. It has an operational definition and is based on explicit rationales. COBRA has been applied successfully in industrial environments. Thus it supports the appropriateness and validity of the KA methodology. Details about COBRA and its relation to the presented KA methodology are addressed in [24].

4.6   Validation of the KA Methodology

The KA methodology for ESE needs to be validated further by developing customised KA methods for various ESE applications. Besides COBRA (see above) Fraunhofer IESE has multiple projects ongoing in which KA methods for specialised ESE tasks are being developed. One is the elicitation of descriptive software process models [25]. Others are the acquisition of application prerequisites for SE technologies [26] [18] and the validation of software process improvement methodologies [27] [28]. Past experience supports the appropriateness of the methodology. A detailed validation study is currently ongoing (cf. [27]). Future validation results will be reported in the web [29].

4.7   Tool Support for KA in ESE

The application of a KA methodology for ESE raises the question for possible tool support. In general, whether appropriate tooling is readily available depends very much on the specific kind of KA task to be supported (cf. Table 1). For some tasks SE-specific tools are available (e.g., for requirements engineering and process assessment). For other tasks tools from knowledge engineering can be adapted to ESE (cf. [30]). However, for the majority of KA applications in ESE, effective tool support is still rare. This is probably due to the widely lacking formalisation of knowledge management and problem solving processes in ESE. We expect that the KA methodology for ESE presented above will allow for further formalisation and tool support of knowledge acquisition in ESE (cf. *KONTEXT* [18]).

5   Conclusions and Future Work

Many ESE tasks involve some kind of KA activity. These activities can be expected to become more effective, if advanced KA methods will be used in a systematic manner. Therefore KA methods need to be developed that are customised to the specific requirements of the respective ESE tasks. In general, the dissemination of KA methods in ESE should be fostered.

We have provided a survey of KA applications in ESE. It shows that these applications can have very different characteristics and that they impose quite different requirements on the KA method to be used. For this reason, a methodology has been presented for the development of customised KA methods. The design of such methods is facilitated by an experience base of KEL techniques. The experience base represents an ESE-specific knowledge management application. It is accessible for consultants and researchers within Fraunhofer IESE. It supports the dissemination of KEL techniques in experimental software engineering and the accumulation of experiences about their use.

The approach presented in this paper has been and is being applied at Fraunhofer IESE. Main focus of our work is the acquisition of experiential knowledge in experimental software engineering. Example applications are the acquisition of product/process dependency models [28], lessons learnt about software engineering processes [31], and application prerequisites for SE technologies [26]. Related work addresses the elicitation of software process models [25] as well as cost estimation, benchmarking, and risk assessment of software projects [8].

Future work will address the extension of the experience base of KEL techniques. Additional KEL technologies and experience statements will be added. We have also started to implement the experience base using a knowledge management tool infrastructure. This will allow for case-based knowledge retrieval and interactive decision support for selecting KEL techniques. We are also continuing to develop further our suit of customised KA methods (cf. [24]). Additional information about these activities is provided in [29].

Acknowledgements

We would like to thank Ulrike Becker-Kornstaedt, Frank Bomarius, Lionel Briand, Khaled El Emam, Wolfgang Müller, and Barbara Paech for their valuable feedback on earlier versions of this paper. Sonnhild Namingha has helped us very much to improve our use of the English language.

References

1. H. Dieter Rombach, Victor R. Basili, and Richard W. Selby, editors. *Experimental Software Engineering Issues: A critical assessment and future directions.* Lecture Notes in Computer Science Nr. 706, Springer–Verlag, 1992.
2. Victor R. Basili, Gianluigi Caldiera, and H. Dieter Rombach. Experience Factory. In John J. Marciniak, editor, *Encyclopedia of Software Engineering*, volume 1, pages 469–476. John Wiley & Sons, 1994.
3. Frederick Hayes-Roth, Donald A. Waterman, and Douglas B. Lenat, editors. *Building Expert Systems.* Addison-Wesley, 1983.
4. Mark A. Musen. An overview of knowledge acquisition. In David et al. [32], pages 405–427.
5. Robert L. Glass. Expert systems: Failure or success? *Journal of Systems and Software*, 43(1):1–2, October 1998.
6. Peter Grogono. Software engineering for expert systems. In Jay Liebowitz, editor, *The Handbook of Applied Expert Systems*, pages 25-1-25-15. CRC Press, 1998.
7. Henrik Eriksson. A survey of knowledge acquisition techniques and tools and their relationship to software engineering. *Journal of Systems and Software*, (19):97–107, 1992.
8. Lionel C. Briand, Khaled El Emam, and Frank Bomarius. COBRA: A hybrid method for software cost estimation, benchmarking, and risk assessment. In *Proceedings of the Twentieth International Conference on Software Engineering*, pages 390–399, Kyoto, Japan, April 1998. IEEE Computer Society Press.
9. David N. Wilson and Tracy Hall. Perceptions of software quality: A pilot study. *Software Quality Journal*, 7(1):67–75, 1998.
10. J. Angele and R. Studer. Requirements specification and model-based knowledge-engineering. *Softwaretechnik-Trends: Mitteilungen der GI-Fachgruppen 'Software-Engineering' und 'Requirements-Engineering'*, 15(3):4–16, October 1995.

11. Midred L. G. Shaw and Brian R. Gaines. Requirements acquisition. *IEEE Software Engineering Journal*, pages 149–165, May 1996.

12. Klaus Weidenhaupt, Klaus Pohl, Matthias Jarke, and Peter Haumer. Scenarios in system development: Current practice. *IEEE Software*, March/April 1998.

13. Neil A. Maiden and Cornelius Ncube. Acquiring COTS Software Selection Requirements. *IEEE Software*, 15(2):46–56, March 1998.

14. Elizabeth S. Cordingly. Knowledge elicitation techniques for knowledge-based systems. In Dan Diaper, editor, *Knowledge Elicitation: Principles, Techniques and Applications*, chapter 3, pages 89–176. Ellis Horwood, 1989.

15. Nancy J. Cooke. Varieties of knowledge elicitation techniques. *International Journal of Human-Computer Studies*, 41(6):801–849, 1994.

16. M. Welbank. Knowledge acquisition: a survey and british telecom experience. In T. Addis, J. Boose, and B. Gaines, editors, *Proceedings of the First European Workshop on Knowledge Acquisition for Knowledge Based Systems*. Reading University, 1987.

17. R.R. Hoffman, N.R. Shadbolt, M.A. Burton, and G. Klein. Eliciting knowledge from experts: A methodological analysis. *Organizational Behaviour and Human Decision Processes*, 62(2):129–158, 1995.

18. Andreas Birk and Felix Kröschel. A knowledge management lifecycle for experience packages on software engineering technologies. Technical Report IESE-Report No. 007.99/E, Fraunhofer Institute for Experimental Software Engineering, Kaiserslautern, Germany, 1999.

19. Felix Kröschel. A system for knowledge management of best software engineering practice. Master's thesis, University of Kaiserslautern, Kaiserslautern, Germany, November 1998.

20. Klaus-Dieter Althoff, Frank Bomarius, and Carsten Tautz. Using case-based reasoning technology to build learning organizations. In *Proceedings of the the Workshop on Organizational Memories at the European Conference on Artificial Intelligence '98*, Brighton, England, August 1998.

21. Klaus-Dieter Althoff, Andreas Birk, Christiane Gresse von Wangenheim, and Carsten Tautz. Case-based reasoning for experimental software engineering. In Mario Lenz, Brigitte Bartsch-Spörl, Hans-Dieter Burkhard, and Stefan Wess, editors, *Case-Based Reasoning Technology - From Foundations to Applications*, number 1400, chapter 9, pages 235–254. Springer-Verlag, Berlin, Germany, 1998.

22. Christiane Gresse von Wangenheim, Alexandre Moraes Ramos, Klaus-Dieter Althoff, Ricardo M. Barcia, Rosina Weber, and Alejandro Martins. Case-based reasoning approach to reuse of experiential knowledge in software measurement programs. In Lothar Gierl, editor, *Proceedings of the Sixth German Workshop on Case-Based Reasoning*, Berlin, Germany, 1998.

23. Markus Nick and Carsten Tautz. Practical evaluation of an organizational memory using the goal-question-metric technique. In *Proceedings of the Workshop on Knowledge Management, Organizational Memory and Knowledge Reuse during Expert Systems '99 (XPS-99)*, Würzburg, Germany, March 1999.

24. Andreas Birk. A knowledge acquisition methodology for use in experimental software engineering. Technical Report IESE-Report No. 062.98/E, Fraunhofer Institute for Experimental Software Engineering, Kaiserslautern (Germany), 1998.

25. Ulrike Becker, Dirk Hamann, and Martin Verlage. Descriptive Modeling of Software Processes. In *Proceedings of the Third Conference on Software Process Improvement (SPI '97)*, Barçelona, Spain, December 1997.

26. Andreas Birk. Modelling the application domains of software engineering technologies. In *Proceedings of the Twelfth IEEE International Automated Software Engineering Conference.* IEEE Computer Society Press, 1997.

27. Andreas Birk, Janne Järvinen, and Rini van Solingen. A validation approach for product-focused process improvement. Technical Report IESE-Report No. 005.99/E, Fraunhofer Institute for Experimental Software Engineering, Kaiserslautern, Germany, 1999.

28. PROFES. ESPRIT project 23239 (Product-FOcused improvement of Embedded Software processes). http://www.ele.vtt.fi/profes/.

29. AXIS. Acquisition of Experiential Knowledge in Software Engineering. http://www.iese.fhg.de/axis.html.

30. Barbara Dellen, Frank Maurer, Jürgen Münch, and Martin Verlage. Enriching software process support by knowledge-based techniques. *International Journal of Software Engineering & Knowledge Engineering,* 7(2):185–215, 1997.

31. Andreas Birk and Carsten Tautz. Knowledge management of software engineering lessons learned. In *Proceedings of the Tenth Conference on Software Engineering and Knowledge Engineering,* San Francisco Bay, CA, USA, June 1998. Knowledge Systems Institute, Skokie, Illinois, USA.

32. Jean-Marc David, Jean-Paul Krivine, and Reid Simmons, editors. *Second Generation Expert Systems.* Springer, 1993.

Acquiring and Structuring Web Content with Knowledge Level Models

Louise Crow & Nigel Shadbolt

Artificial Intelligence Group,
Department of Psychology,
University of Nottingham,
University Park, Nottingham
NG7 2RD
U.K.
+44 (0) 115 9515280
{lrc, nrs} @psychology.nottingham.ac.uk

Abstract. Increasingly diverse and useful information repositories are being made available over the World Wide Web (WWW). However, information retrieved from the Web is often of limited use for problem solving because it lacks task-relevance, structure and context. This research draws on software agency as a medium through which model-driven knowledge engineering techniques can be applied to the WWW. The IMPS (Internet-based Multi-agent Problem Solving) architecture described here involves software agents that can conduct structured on-line knowledge acquisition using distributed knowledge sources. Agent-generated domain ontologies are used to guide a flexible system of autonomous agents arranged in a server architecture.

1 Introduction

Much useful information is available over global electronic networks, particularly the World Wide Web (Web). The Web could be a valuable resource for knowledge engineers, supplying knowledge covering many subject areas. However, there is often simply *too much* information available to each Web user. The lower bound of the size of the "indexable Web" was estimated at 320 million pages in December 1997 [1]. This may be a serious underestimate as (among other things) it excludes dynamic on-the-fly information serving over the Web. This exclusion is significant because increasingly, the Web is being used as a gateway for dynamic information transfer rather than simple delivery of static HTML pages.

There are other factors to be considered when using information from the Web. The use of multiple formats and the distributed nature of the Web makes the integration of this information a non-trivial task. Firstly each piece of information must be retrieved from its location using network protocols, and re-represented in a common format. Secondly, the pieces of information must be integrated with respect to their meaning. This poses problems as information from different sources may have been created from different, possibly contradictory, perspectives on the subject concerned.

Knowledge can be thought of as information applied to a problem in order to reach a goal. The Web holds information on a vast number of domains. However, it does not present convenient packages of knowledge indexed by the kind of problems they could be applied to. Within each domain represented on the Web, information is available which could be used for solving many possible problems.

This paper presents the IMPS (Internet-based Multi-agent Problem Solving) architecture. IMPS is an agent-based architecture driven by knowledge level models. It is designed to facilitate the retrieval and restructuring of information from the Web. Our purpose is to use the resulting knowledge as problem solving knowledge suitable for use in an knowledge based system. IMPS uses an approach which extracts and transforms information based on two criteria. The approach considers firstly the domain (e.g. geology, respiratory medicine, electronic engineering), and secondly the kind of task in which the information is to be used (e.g. classification, diagnosis, scheduling). In effect, this approach describes on-line knowledge acquisition using knowledge level models.

The structure of the rest of this paper will be as follows: We will describe how knowledge level models such as problem solving methods and ontologies may be useful in extracting information from the Web. Next we will present IMPS as an architecture and a prototype. We will discuss the scalability of the architecture and evaluation of the prototype. We will end with some conclusions.

2 Knowledge Level Models

Different kinds of knowledge model generally represent a particular perspective on the knowledge level. Van de Velde [2] points out that in practical terms, knowledge can be divided into relatively stable structures.

"A KL-model is a structure that is imposed on knowledge when it is being put to use in a class of problem situations."

The common feature of this class of problem situations may be that they are all in the same domain. In this case, the model imposed may be described as a domain model. This model would describe features of the domain and could be useful in various tasks within the domain.

Alternatively, the common feature of the class of problem situations might be that they share a common task structure, although they appear in different domains. In this case, the knowledge level model is a task model. There may be more than one way to solve problems which share a task model. For instance, there are many problem solving methods for carrying out classification tasks.

A full knowledge level model for a task would bring together the task model, domain model and problem solving method into a coherent model which is sufficient to solve the task. If this is the case, one may ask "Why use the separate models in the first place?". One of the reasons that these different knowledge models are used is to guide knowledge acquisition. If a new domain is being tackled, a task model may impose a structure on knowledge that can guide acquisition, even though a full domain model has not yet been formed.

Another reason for using the separate models is the potential for knowledge reuse. Full knowledge level models will rarely be reused as it is unlikely that knowledge engineers will encounter exactly the same problem again. However, domain models, task models and problem solving methods all have the potential to be reused in problems which are similar in domain (in the case of domain models), or task (in the case of task models and problem solving methods).

2.1 Problem Solving Methods

Reusable problem-solving methods (PSMs) focus on the idea that certain kinds of common task can be tackled by using the same problem-solving behaviour (e.g. generate and test a set of hypotheses), regardless of the domain in which they appear. An abstract model of this behaviour is a problem solving method. This method relates the task and domain models together so that goals can be accomplished.

The separation of a problem solving method from domain knowledge is a feature of various well known knowledge acquisition methodologies [3] [4] [5] [6]. What these approaches have in common is the use of a finite library of domain independent problem solving methods, which may need some tuning to suit the domain of application.

Some methods, such as 'generate and test' or 'heuristic search' are so weak in their assumptions of domain knowledge that they can be applied to a wide range of tasks with little fine-tuning. However, these weak methods tend not to be very efficient. Stronger, more efficient methods have more requirements in terms of the type and structure of domain knowledge and are therefore less widely applicable [7]. Figure 1 shows a typical domain knowledge schema for classification.

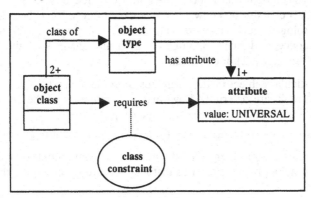

Fig. 1. Typical domain-knowledge schema for classification
tasks [8]

Additionally, problem solving methods are usually specified not as a homogenous whole, but as a series of components or inference steps. Each of these components describes a relatively independent step taken in the problem solving method. Each oval in Figure 2 represents an inference step taken in the pruning classification method. There is often some flexibility regarding the order these steps are taken in.

Methods with larger grainsize – fewer and larger components – are less reusable and require more tuning for new uses. Therefore the approach is moving towards a smaller grainsize, with finer-grained problem-solving strategies which can be configured together to form a knowledge based system [9] [10].

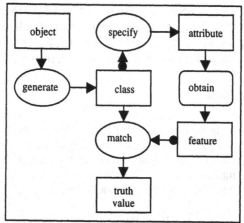

Fig. 2. Inference structure for the pruning classification
method [8]

2.2 Ontologies

As we have discussed, it is the conjunction of the domain and task models with
the problem solving method that allows a knowledge based system to achieve goals.
The idea of a library of domain independent problem solving components, such as
task models and problem solving methods implies the availability of domain models
to instantiate these components and turn them into knowledge based systems.

Domain models can also be known as domain ontologies. It has been argued [11]
that explicit ontologies can be used to underpin the knowledge engineering process.
However, the concept 'domain ontology' is used ambiguously in the knowledge
engineering community [12]. It can mean:

"...the particular subject matter of interest in some context...The nature and
scope of a domain are determined by what is of interest and the context. The
context includes the purpose for delimiting a subject area."

An alternative perspective (also taken from [12]) sees the ontology covering

"the particular subject matter of interest in some context *considered
separately* from the problems or tasks that may arise relevant to the subject."

According to the first definition, an ontology can be task dependent – so a
domain ontology might only contain concepts and relationships relevant to the
particular problem solving method it was used with. An example of this might be an
ontology of rocks to be used in a simple classification task. This could contain the
mineral properties of different types of rock necessary for identifying them, but
would not necessarily contain information about the causal processes that
contributed to rock formation. These causal concepts would be relevant to a
different problem solving method in which some causal model of process was used.

The second conceptualization proposes that a domain ontology should be
constructed with no reference to the kind of tasks that the knowledge engineer
would be hoping to tackle with it. This kind of domain ontology in the field of
geology would contain all the information available about rocks. It has been

suggested that a library of such task-independent domain ontologies would complement the existing libraries of task models and problem solving methods.

We have discussed how problem solving methods can make assumptions about the nature and structure of the domain knowledge which can be used with them. Therefore, if a domain ontology is not oriented towards the specific task to be carried out in the domain, there may have to be extensive modification of the information in the domain ontology, or 'mapping', to allow it (and subsequent knowledge acquisition based on the ontology) to be fitted into the constraints of the problem solving model.

2.3 Mapping

Significant obstacles would need to be overcome in the creation of a comprehensive library [11] of domain ontologies. In order to provide usable ontologies for a significant range of domain areas, the library itself would have to be huge. In order to make a system useful in areas not covered by the library, some method for supplying ontologies to 'cover the gaps' would be required.

Nevertheless, knowledge based system metatools have appeared [13] [14] which store reusable components in libraries and configure them according to the requirements of each application. The advantages of an explicit mapping step between knowledge level models are expressed in terms of reuse [15]. The idea is that in order to allow reuse of methods and knowledge bases, knowledge engineers must isolate, as much as possible, method knowledge from domain knowledge. When an application is being constructed, the methods and domains must be connected by defining declarative mapping relations between them. Ideally, the end result is a high payoff in terms of saved effort.

However, the instantiation of mapping methods is part of the overhead cost for reuse. This cost must include all the work needed to find, understand, and adapt pre-existing knowledge for reuse. Therefore, unless the mapping relations defined are simple these overheads could outweigh the benefits completely.

One problem we have already mentioned for knowledge reuse with this method is that representational choices in encoding domain knowledge depend on the particular problem solving method being used. So the mapping step could involve re-representing a domain ontology entirely. This would involve a significant effort.

Uschold et. al [16] point out that there are still few examples of existing ontology reuse in the literature. From their own experiences of reusing an ontology in the engineering domain, they found translation from one representation to another a significant problem, stating that fully automatic translators are "unlikely to be forthcoming in the foreseeable future". Although they were ultimately successful and cautiously optimistic about reuse of ontologies, it must be recognised that they started with a high quality ontology. We are still far from the situation where such high quality ontologies describe a significant proportion of human knowledge.

There are other problems with the reuse of existing ontologies. Unlike PSMs and task models, domain ontologies are not abstract. Usually they represent the 'state of the art' in some specialist branch of human expertise. Although obsolescence is more of a problem with instantiated knowledge bases, domain conceptualisations also change as disciplines advance, and ontologies will need updating. Stable ontologies do occur in some fields through standardisation efforts and/or years of conceptual development (e.g. the Periodic Table in the physical sciences). It may be the case that such an ontology is sufficient for new applications. Alternatively, the problems being tackled may require some modifications or additions to existing representations. The specialist nature of the domain ontologies used in knowledge-based systems makes it less likely that an existing ontology will capture all the knowledge needed for a new application.

These problems may indicate that an alternative to the idea of ontology libraries might be appropriate. We argue that mapping will always be a significant hidden cost in ontology reuse and is very far from being automated. Our hypothesis is that more effective use and reuse will be obtained from a system that constructs ontologies at runtime from some set of source material, fitting the ontologies to the requirements of the problem solving method being used. Such an approach is more adequate in dealing with a changing information environment, and reflects a move towards "living ontologies" [17] whose development is integrated with that of the system they are to be used in. A system which can integrate and use knowledge from different sources to construct a domain-specific, task-specific ontology could be used both to create new ontologies for domains, and also to update existing ontologies, or adapt ontologies created for different tasks.

Although high quality specialist ontologies may not be available, the availability of high level ontologies on the Internet is increasing. The idea of generating domain ontologies automatically from high-level ontologies was explored in the SENSUS project [18]. This involved the use of a broad coverage general ontology to develop a specialized, domain specific ontology semi-automatically. Systems such as the Generalized Upper Model [19], the 'upper CYC® ontology' [20], Ontolingua [21] and WordNet [22] are knowledge structures which provide a framework which could organize all of the concepts we use to describe the world, aiming to cover every possible subject area with at least a low level of detail. These ontologies may be used to as a 'bootstrapping' method to bridge the gap between "common sense" knowledge and domain specific knowledge which can be obtained from specialist sources by providing a general high-level structure in which to situate domain specific knowledge. Existing high-quality high-level ontologies within a domain could also play this role.

The general ontology we use is the WordNet semantically organized lexical database [23] which contains approx. 57,000 noun word forms organized into around 48,800 word meanings (synsets). Several studies have used WordNet in the role of domain independent ontology. Burg and van de Riet [24] regard WordNet as a rich source of conceptual models.

> "We see the lexicon as the central repository of all terminology and related linguistic elements that we need to describe communication in and about the world we live in. As such, it is much more than a list of terms. The lexicon contains the concepts that make up our communications, and it defines the relationships between these concepts."

Additionally, a domain specific ontology of 5200 terms has been constructed and linked to WordNet [25]. The resulting composite ontology was used to generate semantic lexical representations of domain specific and domain independent concepts [26]. These representations were used in a concept-based full text retrieval system. O'Sullivan, McElligott and Sutcliffe [25] also report a psychometric study in which the results produced by this method on a lexicon of computer terms were comparable with judgements regarding the same terms which were made by people.

3 The IMPS Architecture

Having outlined the theoretical roots of the IMPS architecture in the knowledge engineering field, this section will describe the architecture in specific terms. We will trace the ideas introduced earlier to their software implementations. IMPS is made up of agent programs. A popular Internet agent architecture is one in which the agent's behaviour is informed by some kind of user model (e.g. [27]).

In IMPS, the model used to guide information retrieval is a task model rather than a user model. The profile maintained describes the requirements of a particular task type (selected by the user) in terms of domain information. Thus an agent primed with a model of classification will be highly 'interested' in information about object classes and properties. For a fuller discussion of the use of agency in IMPS, see [28]. While the IMPS agents are independent, they cooperate at a high level to extract information from Internet sources. They reformulate this information so that it can be used in the kind of problem solving that is typically seen in knowledge based systems. To do this, the agents act together in a server architecture. The architecture will be described in two sections, the first detailing the internal structure and function common to all the IMPS agents and the second relating the agents together as a multi-agent system.

3.1 The Agent Level Architecture

Although each agent specializes in performing a certain task and may therefore have abilities that the other agents lack, all the agents are based on the same fundamental structure. This allows them to communicate with other IMPS agents via messages, retrieve information from the Web and manipulate it internally. For a more complete discussion of the IMPS agent-level architecture, see [28].

The basic structure on which all the IMPS agents are based is supplied by the Java Agent Template (JAT) 0.3 [29]. The template provides Java classes to support a multi-agent architecture composed of agents with individual knowledge bases. In IMPS, the JAT is supplemented with Jess. Jess is a version of the popular expert system shell CLIPS, rewritten entirely in Java [30]. It provides the agents with internal representation and inference mechanisms. In effect, the addition of Jess means that whilst the agents share a common architecture, each agent reasons and acts like a small knowledge-based system following its own set of rules. Jess can be used to manipulate external Java objects in a rule-based manner. This means the agent's low level behaviours can be directly controlled by the inference engine.

IMPS uses the Knowledge Query and Manipulation Language (KQML) for inter-agent communication, as specified and supported by the JAT. KQML has been proposed as a standard communication language for distributed applications in which agents communicate via "performatives"[31]. KQML is indifferent to the format of the information itself, so expressions can contain sub-expressions in other languages. In IMPS, KIF statements are embedded in KQML. Each IMPS agent has a KIF (Knowledge Interchange Format)[32] parser which allows it to read KIF text messages. KIF is maintained as a possible means of more sophisticated knowledge representation and sharing with other systems.

3.2 The Multi-Agent Architecture

As a model-driven architecture, IMPS aims to take the task-oriented nature of agent software much further. It uses PSM-oriented knowledge acquisition to create an explicit domain ontology for a task. The PSM used provides templates that describe the kind of knowledge required, the types of role that this knowledge might play and the inferences in which this knowledge might figure. The ontology provides a conceptual framework for the organization of knowledge. As it becomes instantiated with further structured acquisition, it produces a domain knowledge base which could in turn underpin agent-based problem solving guided by the same PSM structure.

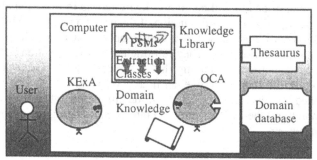

Fig. 3. The IMPS server agents

In order to apply these knowledge level models, IMPS uses a server architecture (see Figure 3), in which two specialist server agents, the Knowledge Extraction Agent (KExA) and the Ontology Construction Agent (OCA) provide knowledge to Inference Agents (IAs) on demand. IAs represent KADS primitive inference types [8] embodied in agent shells to produce agents that specialize in performing a particular kind of inference (see Figure 2). For a classification task, agents might specialize in generation of classes, specification of attributes, or matching features. The knowledge based system arises from the dynamic configuration of problem solving agents reasoning over the external domain knowledge representation as served to them by the OCA. The discussion of the prototype will focus on the server agents (see Section 4).

When IMPS is used on the Internet, the PSM drives agent knowledge acquisition over highly implicit, heterogeneous and distributed knowledge sources. Therefore, standardization must occur at some point to allow the system to use uniform modular components. This happens in the knowledge library where the knowledge extraction modules and PSM modules are stored. These modules can be viewed as mediators as described by [33] in the database community.

The knowledge library component of IMPS is as essential to its operation as the agent component. The extraction classes used to obtain particular kinds of knowledge from knowledge sources are all based around a common Java interface, with standard inputs and outputs. The actual mechanisms by which the class extracts information from a source and parses it into a form comprehensible to Jess are completely hidden from the agent loading the class. New classes can be added to the library as appropriate, in a 'plug-and-play' manner, without any change to the rest of the architecture. This is also true of the PSM components, which are based around a (different) common interface. Within the library, the knowledge sources are indexed by type - e.g. database, plain text file, etc., so new instances of a particular type of source just need to be identified as such to be used by the system.

Knowledge sources available to the IMPS architecture do not have to be static. In recognition of a global network in which an increasing amount of the information available is dynamically created, the classes can be written in such a way that they allow agents to interact with programs available over the network, such as search engines.

4 The Prototype

Currently, the prototype IMPS system (P-IMPS) focuses on the ontology construction stages of IMPS, rather than the later problem solving phase. It constructs a domain ontology from online sources using two agents. The sources are accessed dynamically at runtime through the Internet, using HTTP. The agents can be accessed at http://www.psychology.nottingham.ac.uk/staff/lrc/agent.html. In the immediate future, we plan to extend the system beyond ontology construction. We intend to add the Inference Agents which will use the ontologically organized knowledge to make problem solving inferences. At the moment, the system has two PSMs – pruning classification and diagnosis, and two agents, which are:

- The Knowledge Extraction Agent (KExA), acting as an Agent Name Server (ANS) and the interface through which the user interacts with IMPS during initialization.
- The Ontology Construction Agent (OCA), which is able to use modules from the knowledge library to extract information from networked knowledge sources (in this example, WordNet, the online thesaurus/lexical database and a plain text domain database in the field of geology – the IGBA dataset).

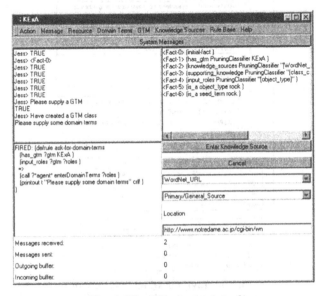

Fig. 4. The KExA user interface

Suppose a user is interested in performing a task in a domain but has little or no information to work with. Using a simple knowledge acquisition interface (Figure 4), the user provides the KExA with domain keywords, and chooses a PSM from a list.

The KExA selects and loads from the knowledge library a Java code module giving details of the PSM to be used. Then the user suggests knowledge sources. The KExA passes on the information it has gathered to the OCA and extracts classes for handling the knowledge sources (whatever format they are in) from the knowledge library. Currently, the prototype has classes for handling WordNet HTML documents and plaintext database files. A module for handling XML is under construction.

Control rules organize the behaviour of the OCA into consecutive phases. The first phase is initialization – the OCA gets information from the PSM module about what kind of relationships between concepts and entities the PSM requires.

Next, the agent uses the general knowledge sources to get information on the domain keyword(s) given by the user – this involves matching between the kinds of

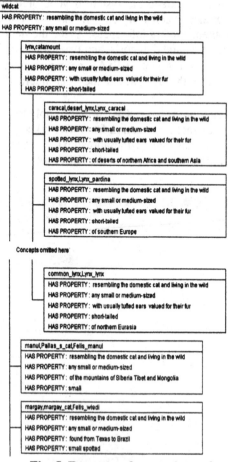

Fig. 5. Fragment of an ontology of
cats developed for a classification PSM

information required by the PSM and the information available about the keyword(s) from the source. The latter is obtained through the knowledge source interface class which has a method for scanning the knowledge source and producing a list of the kinds of information that are likely to be available from it. This interface is implemented by all the knowledge extraction classes (in different ways). At this point, an interaction with the user occurs in which the OCA offers definitions of the keyword which have been extracted from the general source to the user for them to pick the one which most closely matches the concept they had in mind. A structured node in ontology representation is made for the concept represented by the keyword, containing all the information that has been found for it – synonyms, definitions etc. New nodes are also added for entities which are linked to the seed term in ways that are 'interesting' to the PSM. If the task structure is classification, the significant parts of the ontology will be hierarchical, and significant relations will be 'is-a' (to elicit object classes) and 'has-a' (to elicit attributes which will distinguish between the classes).

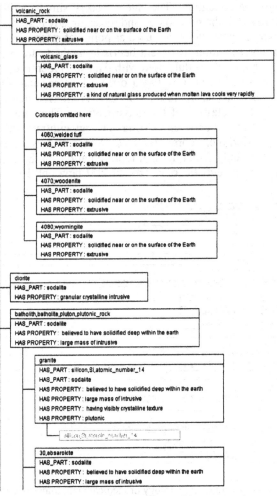

Fig. 6. Fragment of an ontology of igneous rocks developed for a classificatory PSM

Next the agent uses the generalized source to develop a simple ontology around the keyword concept. Each of the 'leaf' nodes that have been added is focused on in turn, and the generalized knowledge source is queried for new concepts related to these nodes in ways that are significant to the PSM. When each node has been added to the external ontology representation, the OCA removes information relating to the nodes that have been created from its working memory, keeping the agent itself 'light' and fast. The objects and relations extracted from the lexical database are presented back to the user graphically (Figure 5). This 'first pass' creates a skeletal ontology for the domain. The "HAS_PROPERTY" attributes of the nodes in Figure 5 have been generated by using very simple parsing on the textual definitions of concepts returned by WordNet.

Finally the agent uses the secondary specialised source to supplement this ontology with information obtained from data representations which contain explicit or implicit ontological statements. To the agent, this phase is similar to the last one, but the sources used here are more specialised to the domain and are providing more detailed information. The information also needs to be integrated seamlessly into the existing ontology representation. The agent makes simple string-based matches between entities found in the new source and those already represented and confirms these with the user. These matches are used as points of reference in integrating new entities into the representation. Different heuristic methods are used for extraction. For example, the extraction module used with databases identifies 'unique' columns in the database in which each row has a different value, and 'classifications', in which each value may appear more than once. It is inferred that the unique values may be hyponyms (sub-classes) of the classifications. They are then added to the ontology using the matches between existing ontology entities and concepts found in the database to position them correctly. This process creates an enriched ontology both in terms of size and correct domain representation. In the domain of geology, using only this simple heuristic rule, around 200 new entities were added to an

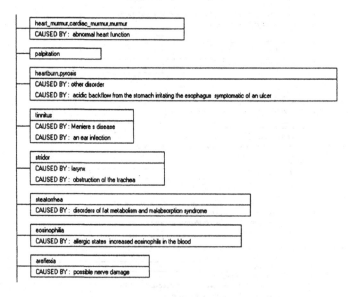

Fig. 7. Fragment of an ontology of medical symptoms created for a diagnosis PSM

ontology of igneous rocks at this stage. The categorical concepts 'volcanic' and 'plutonic' were matched with existing concepts in the ontology and the new subclass entities were added in hyponymical relationships to the concepts (Figure 6). The concepts marked with numbers have been added from the second source.

It should be noted that there is a wide variety of PSMs in standard libraries. If a different PSM is used, the concepts and relationships featured in the ontology are qualitatively different. For example, if the prototype is initialized with a diagnosis PSM and a domain term from the field of medicine, the kind of initial ontology produced is structurally very different, as the focus is on causal relationships (see Figure 7). Again, the causal attributes are extracted by simple textual parsing.

5 Scalability

The success of the prototype begs the question "Could such a system be driven by a larger range of PSMs over more diverse knowledge sources and produce useful results?". The prototype can extract much more information for pruning classification than for diagnosis. This is because the general source we are using is basically classificatory in structure – less transformation needs to be performed in order to get the correct domain knowledge schema for classification.

If the bias towards representing classificatory information is widespread, this could be a serious problem for the scalability of the architecture. However, there are several factors to consider. Firstly, our exploitation of WordNet is not exhaustive at this time. IMPS uses only the noun portion of the database – WordNet also contains some 19,500 adjectives [34], and 21,000 verbs [35]. It also has some unused semantic structure based in causality – "cause" has the status of a semantic relation in WordNet linking verb pairs such as 'teach' and 'learn'. In addition, P-IMPS uses the source in a very straightforward way by 'mining' only the domain concepts provided by the user. A more sophisticated approach can be envisioned in which more information about the nature of the PSM is stored in IMPS so that a more complex query is made to the general source. The selection of a prediction PSM for tides would instigate a search around the term. It would also start a search around the abstract concepts 'time' and 'event', which are implicit in the task. This kind of approach would require another step of semantic integration of the two concept clusters and might be more compatible with a different higher level ontology.

In general terms, we believe that higher level ontologies have much to offer knowledge structuring at the border between 'common sense' and specialist knowledge with relation to a complete range of PSMs. The existence of a relatively stable set of problem solving inferences [8] which include but are not limited to classificatory inferences indicates that human problem solving knowledge has a wider scope. Attempts to use high level ontologies for automated problem solving may prompt more explicit representation of the relationships that support this broader range of inferencing. Concepts like causality are central to our understanding of the world but seem to be under-represented in these general knowledge structures.

The second dimension of scalability is the use of other information sources. Like Ontobroker [36], the IMPS approach views the Web as a very large knowledge base, and attempts to increase the inferential capability that can be applied to it. However, whilst recognising that there are only two main types of standardisation for knowledge representation in the Web – HTML and natural language, we believe that the semi-structured sources that exist within these representations can be exploited with PSM driven extraction. Our approach does not rely on ontological annotation by information providers, but exploits the implicit ontologies contained in the structure of sources. The semi-automatic generation of wrappers for semi-structured Web sources is becoming a trivial task [37].

Although not reliant on content tagging, the open ended nature of the architecture anticipates the evolution of one or more meta-content languages on the Web (the frontrunner for this role at the moment seems to be extensible Markup Language (XML)). The widespread use of content-based tagging on the Web would increase the power of IMPS considerably by making the semantic structure of information presented on the Web more explicit. This could in turn increase the set of PSMs that are viable.

6 Evaluation

It is difficult to thoroughly evaluate a system such as the IMPS prototype, which draws on several areas of research and integrates various technological components. However, some aspects of the system can be earmarked as suitable for formal evaluation. The ontologies created by IMPS are the most obvious example.

We plan to perform some empirical evaluations on the ontologies produced by the prototype to test several hypotheses. These include the proposition that IMPS produces initial domain ontologies for tasks that are comparable in quality to those produced by hand, within the representation system used. We would also like to find out whether IMPS produces initial domain ontologies for tasks using PSM oriented domain schema that are adequate for a problem solving task. Additionally we would like to know whether these PSM-oriented ontologies are superior in terms of that task to those produced by IMPS using another PSM domain schema or those produced without using a PSM domain schema.

At the moment, the proposed general experimental design is one in which the IMPS ontologies will be compared to handcrafted ontologies created by subjects who are experienced both in knowledge engineering (i.e. in the process of eliciting and representing knowledge) and in using the Web. These subjects will not, however, be expert in the domains in which they will be constructing ontologies.

The IMPS and handcrafted ontologies will be presented to domain experts who will evaluate them. This evaluation will be conducted on the basis of qualitative measures of ontology 'goodness' as used in Tennison's [38] evaluation of a collaborative ontology construction tool. The criteria used in that evaluation were precision, breadth, consistency, completeness, readability and utility.

The reasoning behind the choice of subjects in these proposed experiments is that these subjects are the kinds of people who might be expected to use a system such as the IMPS prototype to assist them. Therefore if it can show significant improvements over what the subjects can do by hand, this will be an indication that it could be an asset in the knowledge acquisition process.

Some aspects of the system are not yet mature enough for formal evaluation. This is the case with the Inference Agents that embody inference steps from PSMs and act over the domain ontologies. Long term evaluation aims would be to assess whether the complete IMPS architecture could perform PSM construction and opportunistic collaboration, together with ontology construction and knowledge, to create an on-line expert system on-the-fly.

7 Conclusions

In this paper, we have described a model-driven approach to the problem of getting useful knowledge from distributed and implicit information sources. In [28] we describe the position of IMPS with respect to other related work. The IMPS architecture features clean syntactic integration of information presented originally in different formats, and rule-based semantic information integration. It does this through the use of standardised modular components to filter information while maintaining a lightweight agent architecture. The modular design means that IMPS is open to the use of new technologies and standards.

IMPS applies knowledge level models to Web information sources through a server architecture. In this way, it accomplishes preliminary ontology construction, KA and problem solving. We believe that the partitioning of semi-structured Web information according to the domain schema of problem solving methods can be exploited in order to drive Web-based KA and will be rich in potential reuse.

Acknowledgements

Louise Crow is supported by a University of Nottingham Research Scholarship.

References

1. Lawrence, S., and Giles, C. L. 1998. Searching the World Wide Web. *Science* 280: 98-100.
2. Van de Velde, W. 1993. Issues in Knowledge Level Modelling. In David, J. M., and Krivine, J. P, and Simmons, R. eds. *Second Generation Expert Systems.* Berlin.: Springer Verlag.
3. Weilinga, B.; Van de Velde, W.; Schreiber, G.; and Akkermans, H. 1991. Towards a unification of knowledge modelling approaches, Technical Report KADS-II/T1.1/UvA/004/2.0, Dept. of Social Science Informatics, University of Amsterdam.
4. Klinker, G.; Bhola, C.; Dallemagne, G.; Marques, D.; and McDermott, J. 1991. Usable and reusable programming constructs. *Knowledge Acquisition* 3 (2):117-136.
5. Steels, L. 1990. Components of Expertise. *AI Magazine* 11 (2):29-49.
6. Chandrasekaran, B. 1986. Generic tasks in knowledge-based reasoning: High-level building blocks for expert system design. *IEEE Expert* 1 (3):23-30.
7. Bylander, T., and Chandrasekaran, B. 1988. Generic tasks in knowledge-based reasoning: the right level of abstraction for knowledge acquisition. In Gaines, B and Boose, J. eds. *Knowledge Acquisition for Knowledge-based Systems* 1:65-77. London: Academic Press.
8. Schreiber, A Th.; Akkermans, J. M.; Anjewierden A. A.; de Hoog H., Shadbolt, N. R.; Van de Velde, W.; and Weilinga, B. J. 1998. Engineering and Managing Knowledge.

The CommonKADS Methodology [version 1.0]. Amsterdam, The Netherlands.: Department of Social Science Informatics, University of Amsterdam.

9. Puerta, A. R.; Eriksson, H.; Egar, J. W.; and Musen, M. A. 1992. Generation of Knowledge-Acquisition Tools from Reusable Domain Ontologies, Technical Report KSL 92-81 Knowledge Systems Laboratory, Stanford University.

10. Gil, Y., and Melz, E. 1996. Explicit representations of problem-solving strategies to support knowledge acquisition. *Proceedings of the Thirteenth National Conference on Artificial Intelligence*, 469-476. Menlo Park, CA.: AAAI Press/MIT Press.

11. van Heijst, G.; Schreiber, A. Th.; and Wielinga, B. J. 1997. Using Explicit Ontologies for KBS Development. *International Journal of Human-Computer Studies/Knowledge Acquisition*, 2(3):183-292.

12. Uschold, M. 1998. Knowledge Level Modelling: Concepts and terminology. *The Knowledge Engineering Review* 13 (1):5-30.

13. Walther, E.; Eriksson, H.; and Musen, M. 1992. Plug-and-Play: Construction of task-specific expert-system shells using sharable context ontologies. Technical Report KSI-92-40, Knowledge Systems Laboratory, Stanford University.

14. Studer, R.; Eriksson, H.; Gennari, J.; Tu, S.; Fensel, D.; and Musen, M. 1996. Ontologies and the Configuration of Problem-solving Methods. In Proceedings of the Tenth Banff Knowledge Acquisition for Knowledge-Based Systems Workshop. Banff, Canada.: SRDG Publications.

15. Gennari, J., Tu, S., Rothenfluh, T.; and Musen, M. 1994. Mapping domains to methods in support of reuse. In Proceedings of the Eighth Knowledge Acquisition for Knowledge-Based Systems Workshop. Banff, Canada.: SRDG Publications.

16. Uschold, M., Clark, P., Healy, M.Williamson, K.; and Woods, S. 1998. An Experiment in Ontology Reuse. In Proceedings of the Eleventh Banff Knowledge Acquisition for Knowledge-Based Systems Workshop. Banff, Canada.: SRDG Publications.

17. Tennison, J., and Shadbolt, N. R. 1998. APECKS: A Tool to Support Living Ontologies. In Proceedings of the Eleventh Banff Knowledge Acquisition for Knowledge-Based Systems Workshop. Banff, Canada.: SRDG Publications.

18. Swartout, B.; Patil, R.; Knight, K.; and Russ, T. 1996. Toward Distributed Use of Large-Scale Ontologies. In Proceedings of the Tenth Banff Knowledge Acquisition for Knowledge-Based Systems Workshop. Banff, Canada.: SRDG Publications.

19. Bateman, J.; Magnini, B.; and Fabris, G. 1995. The generalized upper model knowledge base: Organization and use. In Mars, N. ed., *Towards very large knowledge bases: knowledge building and knowledge sharing* 60-72. Amsterdam.:IOS Press.

20. Cycorp, Inc. 1997. The Cycorp homepage. WWW: http://www.cyc.com

21. Gruber, T. R. 1993. A Translation Approach to Portable Ontology Specifications. *Knowledge Acquisition* 5(2): 199-220.

22. Miller, G. 1990. WordNet: An on-line lexical database. *International Journal of Lexicography* 3 (4): 235-302.

23. Beckwith, R., and Miller, G. A. 1990. Implementing a lexical network. *International Journal of Lexicography* 3 (4): 302 - 312.

24. Burg, J. F. M., and van de Riet. R. P. 1995. The impact of linguistics on conceptual models: consistency and understandability. In: Bouzeghoub, M. and E. Métais, eds., Proceedings of the 1st International Workshop on Applications of Natural Language to Databases. Versailles.

25. O'Sullivan, D., McElligott, A.; and Sutcliffe, R. F. E. 1995. Augmenting the Princeton WordNet with a Domain Specific Ontology. In Proceedings of the IJCAI'95 Workshop on Basic Ontological Issues in Knowledge Sharing. Montreal, Canada.

26. Sutcliffe, R. F. E., O'Sullivan, D.; and McElligott, A. 1995. The Creation of a Semantic Lexicon by Traversal of a Machine Tractable Concept Taxonomy. *Journal of Quantitative Linguistics* 2(1): 33-42.

27. Lieberman, H. 1995. Letizia: An Agent that Assists Web Browsing. In Working Notes of AAAI-95 Fall Symposium Series on AI Applications in Knowledge Navigation and Retrieval 97-102. Cambridge, MA.: The AAAI Press.

28. Crow, L. R., and Shadbolt, N. R. 1998. Internet Agents for Knowledge Engineering. In Proceedings of the Eleventh Banff Knowledge Acquisition for Knowledge-Based Systems Workshop. Banff, Canada.: SRDG Publications.

29. Frost, H. R. 1996. Documentation for the Java(tm) Agent Template, Version 0.3. Center for Design Research, Stanford University. WWW: http://cdr.stanford.edu/ABE/documentation/index.html

30. Friedman-Hill, E. J. 1998. Jess, The Java Expert System Shell, Technical Report, SAND98-8206 (revised), Sandia National Laboratories, Livermore. WWW: http://herzberg.ca.sandia.gov/jess

31. Finin, T.; Labrou, Y.; and Mayfield, J. 1997. KQML as an agent communication language. In Bradshaw J. M. ed. *Software Agents*. Cambridge, MA.: AAAI/MIT Press.

32. Genesereth, M. R., and Fikes, R. E. 1992. Knowledge Interchange Format Version 3.0 Reference Manual, Technical Report, Logic-92-1, Computer Science Department, Stanford University.

33. Wiederhold, G.1992. Mediators in the Architecture of Future Information Systems. *Computer* 25(3):38 - 49.

34. Fellbaum, C., Gross, D.; and Miller, K. 1993. Adjectives in WordNet. Unpublished report.

35. Fellbaum, C. 1990. English verbs as a semantic net. *International Journal of Lexicography* 3 (4):278 - 301.

36. Fensel, D., Decker, S., Erdmann, M.; and Studer, R. 1998. Ontobroker: Or How to Enable Intelligent Access to the WWW. In Proceedings of the Eleventh Banff Knowledge Acquisition for Knowledge-Based Systems Workshop. Banff, Canada.: SRDG Publications.

37. Ashish, N., and Knoblock, C. 1997. Semi-automatic Wrapper Generation for Internet Information Sources. In Proceedings of the Second IFCIS Conference on Cooperative Information Systems. Charleston: South Carolina.

38. Tennison, J. 1998. Collaborative Knowledge Environments on the Internet. Forthcoming Ph.D. Thesis, Dept of Psychology, University of Nottingham.

A Knowledge-Based News Server Supporting Ontology-Driven Story Enrichment and Knowledge Retrieval

John Domingue and Enrico Motta

Knowledge Media Institute
The Open University
Walton Hall,
Milton Keynes, UK

{j.b.domingue, e.motta} @open.ac.uk
http://kmi.open.ac.uk/people/{domingue, motta}

Abstract. We consider a knowledge management scenario in which members of an academic community collaboratively construct and share a common archive of news items. Given this scenario, a number of knowledge management challenges arise: how to organize a speedy, low overhead publication process which can nevertheless yield high quality results; how to provide semantic search and knowledge retrieval facilities in an effective and sustainable way; how best to provide individualized presentations and news alerts. To address these questions we have drawn on a number of technologies, including knowledge modelling, autonomous agents, software visualization, knowledge acquisition and distributed computing. In the paper we describe the resulting *Planet-Onto* architecture, which provides an integrated set of tools to support news publishing, ontology-driven document formalization, story identification and personalized news feeds and alerts.

1 Introduction

Loosely speaking, *knowledge management* is about facilitating the generation, sharing and use of knowledge. Thus, any activity or tool which fosters communication and sharing in a community can be seen in principle as an exercise in knowledge management – for instance, bandwidth improvements to an Intranet. Having said so, when discussing knowledge management it is useful to try and refine the all-encompassing span of this research area, by circumscribing the range of issues and technologies under examination. In the context of this paper, rephrasing and refining the definition given by O'Leary [29], we say that we are interested in the *computer-*

mediated management of explicitly represented knowledge. That is, we focus on issues of organisation, formalisation and distribution of knowledge stored in a network of computers. It is important to emphasise that we do not impose any constraint on the form of the representation – e.g. whether the knowledge in question is represented as text, in a conventional database, or in some knowledge representation formalism.

In particular, in this paper we consider a scenario in which members of an academic community collaboratively construct and share a common archive of news items. Given this context, our main research goal is to develop a suitable computational infrastructure, which can effectively support the publishing process, as well as facilitating access to the archive of news items.

To characterise the activities implied by our scenario we can use the framework proposed by O'Leary [29], which proposes an elegant typology of knowledge management activities as specialised *connecting* and *converting processes*. Specifically, using O'Leary's terminology, our goal is to provide solutions for the following classes of knowledge management processes:

- *Converting individual to group knowledge.* In our context this means the provision of tools for supporting 'journalists' submitting stories to a news archive.
- *Converting text to knowledge.* That is, formalising the knowledge expressed by the news item and integrating it into a knowledge base associated with the archive.
- *Connecting people to knowledge.* That is, providing integrated visualisation, search and query answering facilities, to allow users of the archive to quickly home in on information at different levels of granularity, from (sub-)collections of stories to specific data (whether they are explicitly included in a document or implied by the collection of documents).
- *Connecting knowledge to people.* That is, pro-actively contacting journalists and readers. The former should be contacted to solicit stories useful to plug 'holes' in the archive; the latter should be contacted when items of interest are published.

Actually, while O'Leary's framework provides a useful typology for characterising knowledge management activities, we ought to point out that his use of the term "converting" is not necessarily the correct way to talk about knowledge transformation activities in our (and maybe any other) scenario. The problem is that the term "converting" has a translation-centred connotation, which is misleading. In particular, in our scenario the formalisation process is driven by an *ontology* [18], which defines the concepts needed to describe events related to academic life, e.g. projects, products, seminars, publications, etc. This means that the parts of a news story not relevant to the ontology are ignored, much as in template-driven *information extraction* approaches [9] [33]. That is, not all knowledge expressed in textual form in a news item is expected to be formalised. On the other hand, because i) the formalisation is ontology-driven and ii) instantiating an ontology might require the specification of knowledge not given in the story, the knowledge base associated with the news archive would normally contain knowledge that is not present in the archive. In sum, the knowledge base associated with the news archive provides neither a subset nor a superset of the knowledge expressed in the stories. This is of course not very surprising. We know that any translation or encoding process has more to do with reconstructing meaning than with replacing representations. This is true not only for translations between different natural languages, but also for translations from text to code [6] and from code to code [8]. Hence, the metaphor of converting is not the right one when talking about formalising knowledge in a document, both for fundamental reasons and, in our case, because of the different roles played by the news stories and the associated representations. For these reasons we prefer to use the metaphor of *enriching a representation* [40].

The paper is organised as follows. In the next section we provide an overview of the overall architecture, which is called *Planet-Onto*. In section 3 we describe the *Planet* news server [11]. In section 4 we describe the ontology which we use to drive the representational enrichment of news items. In section 5 we illustrate the ontology-driven formalisation process. In section 6 we discuss the aspects related to "connecting people to knowledge" and "connecting knowledge to people". Specifically, we illustrate i) the interface which allows users to access the archive and the associated knowledge base and ii) the *push technology* [32], which alerts journalists to gaps in the archive and readers to new, relevant stories. Finally, in sections 7 and 8 we discuss related work in knowledge management and ontological engineering, we assess the current state of the architecture and we outline outstanding research issues.

2   The Architecture of Planet-Onto

The overall scenario introduced in the previous section is graphically shown in figure 1, which summarises both the architecture of Planet-Onto and the associated process model. The architecture of Planet-Onto extends that of the original Planet news server [11]. In the 'basic' scenario supported by the Planet news server a 'journalist', who is normally a KMI member, writes a story about some KMI-related event and emails it to the Planet server. The Planet agent formats the story and adds it to the news archive. Periodically an agent informs the Planet readership about new stories that have been added to the archive. Readers can browse the archive and access stories through a standard web browser, such as Netscape Navigator™ or Microsoft Explorer™.

This basic publish/find out/read scenario supported by KMI Planet has now been augmented in Planet-Onto, as we have developed i) tools which allow the specification and association of knowledge structures to stories, ii) an end user interface, *Lois*, which integrates web browsing with search and knowledge retrieval, and iii) specialised agents which, alert journalists to gaps in the archive and readers to relevant new stories.

Specifically, as shown in figure 1, Planet Onto supports seven main activities with respect to three types of users. These are:

Journalists. Those who send stories to KMI Planet.

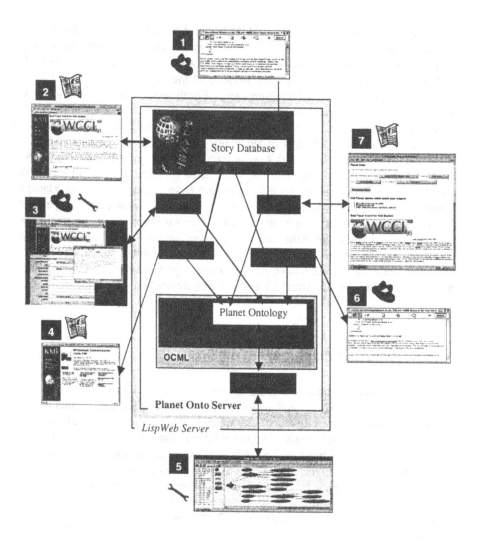

Fig. 1. The Architecture of Planet Onto

Knowledge Editors. Those who are responsible for maintaining the Planet Ontology and the Planet knowledge base. In some cases they may annotate the stories in place of journalists.

Readers. Those who read the Planet stories.

The seven main activities supported by Planet-Onto are:

1. *Story submission.* A journalist submits a story to KMI Planet by plain email. The story is formatted and stored within KMI Planet's story database.

2. *Story reading.* A Planet reader browses through the latest stories using a standard browser.

3. *Story annotation.* Either the journalist submitting the story or one of the Planet knowledge editors uses *Knote* to perform ontology-driven association of knowledge structures to a story.

4. *Provision of customised alerts.* An intelligent agent, *NewsBoy*, which is able to build user profiles from patterns of access to Planet-Onto, uses these profiles to alert readers about relevant new stories.

5. *Ontology editing.* The Planet-Onto architecture also includes sophisticated support for knowledge modelling to be used by skilled knowledge editors. In particular, the *Web-Onto* tool [10] provides web-based visualisation, browsing and editing support for developing and maintaining knowledge models specified in *OCML* [27]. The latter is an operational knowledge modelling language, which supports the specification and instantiation of ontologies and the specification and execution of *reusable problem solving methods* [1].

6. *Story soliciting.* An intelligent agent, *NewsHound*, periodically gathers data about 'popular' news items and uses these data to solicit potentially popular stories from the appropriate journalists. This is accomplished by identifying 'gaps' in the knowledge base, e.g. projects about which there is no information, which can be filled by potentially interesting stories.

7. *Story retrieval and query answering.* An end-user interface, *Lois*, integrates traditional web browsing and search with knowledge-based query retrieval, to support integrated access to the archive of Planet stories and to the associated knowledge base.

All the tools included in the Planet-Onto architecture are web-based and can be accessed through ordinary web browsers. As a result, both the development and use of the archive and associated knowledge base are carried out in a distributed fashion, by a community of users playing specialised roles. The underlying technology is provided by an *HTTP server* written in Common Lisp, *LispWeb* [34].

In the rest of the paper we will discuss the Planet-Onto architecture and process model in detail, focusing in particular on the 'external' knowledge management activities and tools rather than on the 'internal' knowledge modelling support and web-based infrastructure.

3 KMI Planet: A Newsroom Agent on the Web

KMI Planet was designed to support the creation of high quality web based newsletters whilst minimising the load for journalists submitting stories. Our approach to attaining this objective was to develop a news server which accepts stories submitted in the lowest common-denominator medium - an email message - yet is able to create a high quality web page. Thus, the system minimises overheads for journalists and editors by making their contributions entirely lightweight: the web based news server takes on most of the work.

In our model a journalist sends an email message to the KMI Planet story account. The subject line of the message becomes the headline of the story, the body of the message becomes the text of the story. If an image has been attached to the message, it is added into the story in an appropriate place. If no image has been attached, then Planet searches its database of images for a suitable one – e.g. a photo of the journalist in question, the logo of the project described in the story, a screen snapshot of a relevant system, etc.

Fig. 2. A story presented in KMI Planet

In figure 2 we see a single story web page rendered from an email message. The message header is shown at the top and the attached image follows beneath. Next to the image are the name of the journalist who sent the message (linked to his home page) and the date of the submission. The message body is below the image, with web links appropriately anchored to their destinations. Although the journalist is responsible for sending in a good story, the rest of the process is handled by the software.

This low-overhead approach to news publishing has proven very successful. Our archive is growing steadily and now contains 73 stories, submitted by 13 journalists. We now have 480 registered readers – i.e. not just readers who have accessed the Planet server but users who subscribe to the Planet alert services. Moreover, the Planet technology has attracted interest from other organisations, both within and outside the Open University. However, it is apparent that, as the Planet archive and readership grow, more sophisticated mechanisms supporting semantic searches and individualised presentations and alerts are needed. In the rest of this paper we will discuss the tools that we are developing to fulfil these needs.

4   An Ontology for Characterizing Academia-Related Events

An ontology provides a partial specification of a shared conceptualisation, to be used for formulating knowledge-level theories about a domain [18] [20] [27]. Our domain comprises the range of events associated with a university department, the persons who take part in these events and the entities required to characterise these events and these persons in the context of academic life.

Several approaches to ontology development have been proposed in the literature, which introduce distinctions along different dimensions. For instance van der Vet and Mars [42] propose a *bottom-up* approach to concept identification, which contrasts with the *top-down* approach normally used by researchers and practitioners – e.g., see [39]. Uschold and Gruninger [41] argue that a *middle-out* approach is most effective, in which the basic concepts in a domain are identified first (e.g., dog), and later generalised (mammal) and/or specialised (cocker spaniel)[1]. Another distinction is whether an ontology is developed in a *task-oriented* [27] or a *task-independent* style [5] [15]. However, hardly any approach affords detailed, prescriptive guidelines. A notable exception is provided by Uschold and Gruninger [41], who propose a *purpose-driven* skeletal lifecycle for developing ontologies.

In developing the Planet ontology we have followed a task-independent, purpose-driven approach. In particular, the main role of the Planet ontology is to drive the annotation of news items relating events in KMI. Thus, we have taken the concept of *news item* as our starting point. The essence of a news item is that of relating one or more *events*.

4.1   Modelling Events

The notion of event is central to problem solving and several ontological characterisations are available in the literature – e.g., see [25] [37]. Thus, rather than trying to reinvent a pretty complex wheel we looked at existing definitions with the aim of reusing them. In particular, the public version of the CYC upper level ontology [25], which is called *HPKB upper level*[2], is now available on the Stanford ontology server [13]. Thus, we decided it would be a useful exercise to try and reuse this one. Unfortunately this turned out to be a problem. The definition of class event in the UPKB upper level ontology contains 94 slots. Obviously this definition has been designed with the aim to maximise *reusability*, by trying to account for all features which can possibly be associated with an event. On the contrary, given the purpose of our ontology (to allow story annotation by users who are not necessarily knowledge engineers), we are mainly interested in *usability*: that is, our ontology ought to minimise the knowledge engineering overhead associated with story annotation. Otherwise, this task would have to be carried out by specialist knowledge

---

[1] Incidentally, this claim is consistent with much psychological literature, which shows that human subjects are much better are recalling information about basic categories, than they are at recalling information about superordinates or subordinates – see e.g., [35].

[2] HPKB stands for "High Performance Knowledge Bases" and is the name of an ongoing research project in the United States [23].

editors, resulting in an unsustainable approach. In practice, imposing a low overhead on the annotation process means adhering to two modelling guidelines:

- *Minimal ontological commitments.* The definition of class event in the HPKB upper layer provides an extreme case of a *coverage-centred* approach to reuse. That is, the definition aims to cover all potential attributes which *can* be relevant to a *generic instance* of the class. However, typically only few slots will *actually* be relevant for any *specific instance* of the class. An alternative approach consists of *minimising ontological commitments* [19]. That is, to try and provide only the minimal set of attributes needed to define the class. This approach has the advantage that, when populating the ontology, users don't have to face lots of irrelevant attributes.
- *User-centred definitions.* This guideline requires that the terminology used by the ontology needs to be easy to understand for a user who is not necessarily a knowledge engineer. There are two aspects here: heavily technical modelling concepts – e.g. sophisticated modelling solutions for representing time – ought to be avoided. Moreover, the terminology should be as context-specific as possible. For instance, while we can talk about "agents performing events" when describing events in general, we should use the class-specific terminology "awarding body assigns awards", when talking about an award-giving type of event. This latter guideline implies that the underlying modelling language should support slot renaming along *isa hierarchies* – i.e. inherited slots should get subclass-specific names. The importance of domain-specific, user-oriented terminology has been recognised in knowledge acquisition for a long time [28] and arguably it provides an important difference between the criteria associated with modelling for knowledge acquisition and those associated with modelling for system development.

For these reasons we decided we could not just 'cut & paste' the definition in HPKB, but we needed to build our definitions by means of a more use-oriented approach – i.e. starting with minimalist concepts and then enriching them when defining specialised subclasses. The definition of class event used in our ontology is shown below.

The definition shown in the box defines the essential aspects of an event. For the sake of compatibility the terminology reflects the one used in the HPKB ontology. However, as already pointed out, this generically reusable terminology scores lowly on usability and therefore different refinements of this class provide specialised terminology. For example class award-to-kmi-member renames slot main-agent to awarding-body and slot object-acted-upon to awarded-prize.

In total, KMI-Planet-Ontology comprises 452 definitions, based around 6 epistemological building blocks: story, event, person, organisation, project and technology. We shall describe how the ontology has been deployed within Planet-Onto in the following sections.

```
(def-class event (temporal-thing)
 ((main-agent
   :min-cardinality 1
   :documentation
   "The agents causing the event to happen.
    At least one main agent is assumed but
    there can be others")
  (other-agents-involved
   :documentation
   "Other agents involved in the event")
  (instrument-used :documentation
                   "The instrument used by the main
                    agent to carry out the action")
  (Object-Acted-On
   :documentation "The things which are affected by
                   the event. e.g. in 'john broke the
                   stone with a hammer', the stone is
                   the object acted on")
  (recipient-agents
   :documentation
   "The agents which are affected by the event")
  (location-at-start
   :type location
   :documentation "The location at which an event
                   takes place - or starts in the case
                   of events which change the position
                   of something)")))
```

5   Ontology-driven Story Annotation using Knote

Our goal is to enable as wide an audience as possible to annotate stories. Encoding representations of even a moderately growing repository such as KMI Planet can only succeed if the process is 'farmed out' as much as possible. We thus envisage that users of Knote will not form a homogeneous group, but will range from regular Planet journalists to experienced ontology engineers. Knote was therefore designed to be 'low entry', so that users would not necessarily require a background in knowledge modelling. At the same time Knote should allow experienced ontology engineers the freedom to create arbitrarily complex OCML expressions.

As we discussed in the previous section, the Planet ontology is based around the epistemological tenet that a KMI Planet story describes a number of KMI related events. Story annotation is therefore the description of one or more events occurring within the story to be described. The four main steps in annotating a story are:

1. Choosing a story to annotate,
2. Selecting a particular event in the story to describe,

3. Classifying the event in terms of the hierarchy of event types provided by the KMI-Planet-Ontology.

4. Filling in an automatically created *instance definition form* to characterise the new instance of class event.

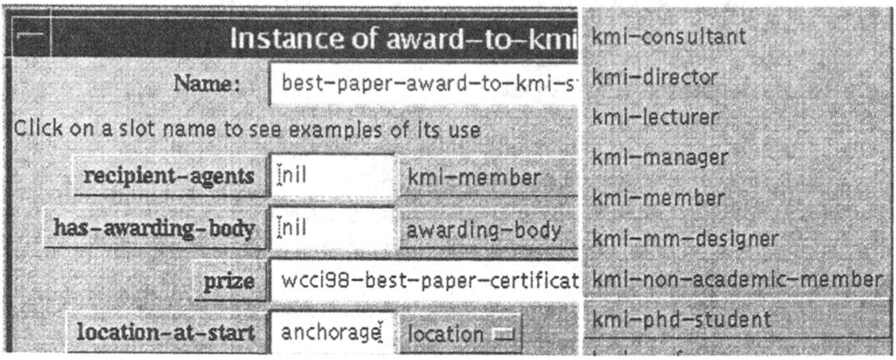

Fig. 3. A partially filled in form for an instance of class award-to-kmi-member

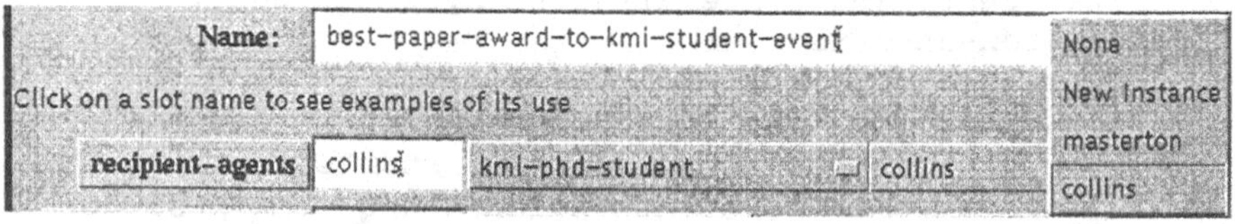

Fig. 4. The appearance of figure 3 as the journalist fills in the value of the recipient-agents slot with the instance collins

We shall describe how Knote supports the annotation process through a small scenario. A Planet journalist decides to annotate the 'Best Paper Award for KMI Student' story shown in figure 2. The journalist elects to describe the main event in the story, that is Trevor Collins receiving a best paper award from IEEE. After a little consideration the journalist classifies the event in question as an instance of class award-to-kmi-member and hits the "Describe Event" button. An event instance definition form, partly shown in figures 3 and 4, is created which the journalist begins to fill in. We will illustrate the annotation support provided by Knote by showing how the tool helps the user fill in the slot recipient-agents.

The journalist can see from figure 3 that the value for the recipient-agents slot must be of type kmi-member. She decides to see which more specific types are currently available by clicking on the kmi-member menu. After choosing class kmi-phd-student, the journalist checks whether there are any instances of kmi-phd-student currently defined. She does this by clicking on the rightmost menu of the recipient-agents row – see figure 4. She chooses collins from the menu and the text "collins" is inserted into the recipient-agents value window. Alternatively, the journalist could have chosen to create a new instance of class kmi-phd-student, by clicking on the menu item "New Instance". In this case a new instance form would be created and the name of the new instance inserted as the value of slot recipient-agents.

The instance forms described here are modelled on the *Dynamic Forms* of Girgensohn et al. [17] and provide a subset of the functionalities found in the Dynamic Forms system. The key difference between dynamic forms and instance forms in Knote, however, is that forms in Knote are generated directly from the ontology and not from a user description. The forms in Knote are similar to the forms found in the Mecano environment [31].

6   Connecting People to Knowledge

6.1   Lois: A Flexible Form-Based Interface for Knowledge Retrieval

As the number of stories in KMI Planet grows, it becomes harder for users to find relevant stories quickly. In addition, browsing and reading stories is but one way to find information about events in KMI. Readers may wish to know about specific technologies, specific projects or specific members of staff. For instance, after reading the story about the award to Trevor Collins, a reader might want to find out who else in KMI works on software visualisation, what papers have recently been produced, what projects tackle software visualisation issues, etc. An important feature of the Planet-Onto architecture is the integration of traditional web browsing, including lexical search, with deductive knowledge retrieval. In particular, various levels of knowledge retrieval support are provided. Experienced ontology engineers can directly access the Planet knowledge base and pose arbitrary queries expressed in OCML, using the Web-Onto tool [10]. However, our assumption is that most readers either are not experienced knowledge engineers, or, even if they are, might not want to interact with Planet-Onto at the OCML level.

To support semantic access to Planet by 'ordinary' readers we have developed a form-based interface, called Lois. The aim of this interface is to allow users to express a wide range of queries, ideally any query that can be expressed directly in OCML, while at the same time shielding them from formalism-related aspects.

The solution we have taken is to use the basic epistemological building blocks (people, organisations, stories, events, projects and technologies) of the Planet knowledge base to organise a form-based query interface. The rationale for this approach is that, almost without exception, any useful query to Planet-Onto must include one or more subclasses or instances of these six building blocks. For instance, figure 5 shows a query which asks for KMI researchers involved in software visualisation. This query was constructed by selecting the class kmi-member (pressing the button "Member of KMi"), specialising it to kmi-researcher (using the "Index Aspect" and "Aspect Type" windows), selecting the relation develops-technology and then circumscribing the range of this relation to kmi-software-visualisation-technology. To ensure that 'naïve' users can indeed construct queries out of these six building blocks, when designing the ontology we have ensured that all the 'obvious' binary relations between these six classes are *explicitly* included in the ontology (as opposed to be derivable through chains of inferences). Because stories are only interesting with respect to the associated events, they are not linked to the other main classes (and correspondingly no button is provided for the story class). Hence, only 24 relations had to be specified.

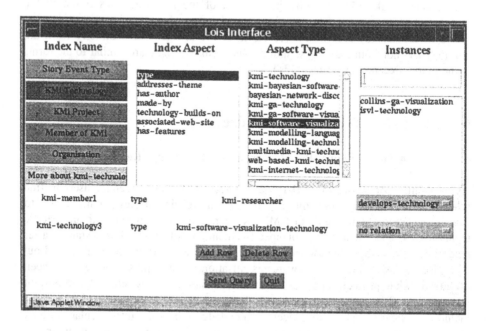

Fig. 5. Finding a KMI researcher who works on software visualisation

6.2 Story Chasing with NewsHound

An important goal in the design of KMI Planet was that the system should try and emulate a news room team. One of the tasks that a news editor carries out is to identify potentially popular stories and assign them to one of the journalists in the staff. In order to emulate this behaviour we are developing an intelligent agent, NewsHound, whose job is to identify potentially popular stories and to assign them to the appropriate journalists. These requests for new stories are carried out simply by sending the relevant journalist an email.

In order to identify potentially interesting stories, NewsHound uses two main types of data: statistics on access to individual stories in KMI Planet and records of the queries posed through Lois. Each story within Planet keeps a record of its own popularity by counting the number of times the full text is requested from the KMI Planet server. Once NewsHound identifies a story as 'popular', then it tries to identify related stories which have the potential to be popular. To perform this task NewsHound analyses the knowledge base trying to find items of interest that have not yet been covered by Planet stories. Typically, these would be projects and technologies which i) are known to NewsHound, ii) are 'related' to 'popular' projects and technologies, but iii) have not yet been covered by a story. The term 'related' is the key here. NewsHound uses various heuristics to define 'relatedness': for instance direct subclasses of the same class are considered related; technologies are related if they build on the same underlying technology; projects are related if they tackle the same areas. These heuristics are of course completely 'soft' and modular and therefore any new one can be added without affecting the existing ones. However, in our view the most interesting feature of NewsHound has not so much to do with the specific adopted heuristics but rather with the unique scenario in which it examines a knowledge base for gaps. Typically, completeness in a knowledge base is defined with respect to logical or task-related properties [22]. In our scenario incompleteness is defined in pragmatics terms: publications need popular stories.

6.3   Providing Personalised Alerts with NewsBoy

Lois is designed (among other things) to help users to track down Planet stories with very specific characteristics. However, a significant number of users prefer to work with push technology, that is they prefer to be automatically notified about potentially interesting stories, rather than having to query Lois about them. We therefore designed an agent, NewsBoy, to provide a mode of use that was complementary to the one supported by Lois. NewsBoy enables users to create a personalised front-page to which interesting stories are pushed.

When a new story is annotated using Knote, NewsBoy matches the story knowledge base against the specified interests of registered readers. Readers whose interests match that of the newly annotated story are notified that a new story has been added to their personal Planet page. For example, if a reader has specified that they would like to read stories about visitors to KMI, she would receive an email stating that her personal Planet page has been updated to look like figure 6.

The primary interface to NewsBoy is via a settings page where registered users can:

1. Set their name and password.
2. Set the criteria for a notification to be sent.
3. Declare what sort of stories their interests cover.

Passwords enable groups of users to create a secure communal newsletter where confidential information can be communicated. Readers can elect to be sent an automatic notification by NewsBoy every time a relevant story is found, or to be sent an update every week or month. Moreover, readers can either explicitly declare the types of stories which interest them or allow NewsBoy to infer them. One of the prime goals when designing Planet-Onto was to make the system as easy to use as possible. For this reason we decided to reuse the Lois interface as far as possible, rather than creating a whole new interface for readers to communicate their interests to NewsBoy.

To make an explicit declaration a reader simply specifies a number of queries using the Lois interface. The reader is then informed when a new story matches at least one of the logged queries. Alternatively, a reader can state that she would like NewsBoy i) to log all the queries she makes using Lois and ii) to create a user profile from the log. The resulting user profile is simply the logical disjunction of the queries contained within the log.

It is interesting to compare NewsBoy to other approaches which attempt to infer user profiles from analysing patterns of access to documents – see e.g., [26] [24]. These approaches try to induce user interests using empirical methods. Our approach is semantic-centred: the user herself specifies the range of documents of potential interest through unambiguous declarative specifications.

Fig. 6. A personalised Planet Web page showing stories concerning visits to KMI

7   Related work

The work described in this paper is related to research in a number of areas, including *information retrieval* [38] and *extraction* [33] [9], *knowledge management* [29], *ontological engineering* [18], *agent technology* [7] *knowledge engineering* [14] and *model-based knowledge acquisition* [22] [36] [12]. Because we have already compared individual tools in Planet-Onto to related technology and (more importantly) because this paper should not exceed the 18 page limit, we will confine ourselves to discuss related approaches to ontology-driven knowledge management.

The SHOE project [21] has proposed an extension to HTML to allow the specification of ontological information in web pages. The project team has also developed an editor to support the page annotation process. This work is mainly at the infrastructure level. That is, they suggest a mechanism to allow the representation of information and provide tools to edit and retrieve it. In Planet-Onto we take a holistic approach to the publish-annotate-retrieve process and we look at the wider issues concerning usability and sustainability. Thus, we are not just concerned with providing a mechanism for associating knowledge structures to text but we wish to develop a comprehensive architecture addressing all the relevant issues, from the 'right' approach to ontology development to the required visualisation and interface tools needed to facilitate the publish-annotate-access process. Having said so, the technical solutions provided by SHOE could be easily integrated within the Planet-Onto framework. For instance OCML structures could be represented in terms of the relevant SHOE tags.

The (KA)2 initiative also shares a number of commonalities with our work. As in the case of Planet-Onto the aim of (KA)2 is to allow a community to build a knowledge base collectively, by populating a shared ontology. In the case of (KA)2 the knowledge base is meant to document the activities of the knowledge acquisition community. Similarly to the approach used in SHOE the knowledge base is constructed by annotating web pages with special tags, which can be read by a specialised search engine cum interpreter, Ontobroker [16]. In this paper we have emphasised that the feasibility of the idea of a collective construction of a knowledge base crucially depends on the availability of i) a carefully defined ontology; ii) an underlying modelling language providing user-oriented facilities, such as context-dependent renaming; iii) a user-friendly annotation environment; and iv) the right motivational stimuli for the participants. In their paper on the (KA)2 initiative, [2], the authors mainly focus on the latter issue. However it seems to us that a careful analysis of all the issues associated with collaborative ontology development and instantiation is required, in order to manage the risks associated with such enterprises. In particular we believe that a careful design of the underlying ontology is particularly important. For this reason, in contrast with the case of (KA)2, the design of the ontology is centralised in our approach. Members of the community are not expected to develop ontologies, only to populate existing ones.

Related work in knowledge management here in KMI has (naturally) many points of contact with Planet-Onto. The work in the *Enrich* project [40] aims to support organisational learning through the enrichment of web-based documents. This enrichment is carried out both through ontologies, as in our scenario, and through hypertext-based argumentation [4]. Although the Enrich scenario is very different from the one addressed by Planet-Onto, the underlying assumptions are the same for both projects: ontology-driven enrichment of documents play an important role in knowledge management. However, effective support for knowledge management requires a holistic approach, which carefully analyses both technological and organisational issues and emphasises the usability of the deployed technology and the sustainability of the overall process model.

Buckingham-Shum and Sumner [3] have produced an ontology to support the tracking of research within the Journal of Interactive Media in Education (http://www-jime.open.ac.uk/). Their emphasis is to support the development of shared viewpoints in a community and the discovery of relationships between documents. As for Planet-Onto populating the ontology is a collaborative process. In contrast with Planet-Onto only an informal ontology is provided.

8   Conclusions

The Planet-Onto architecture provides an example of an ontology-centred approach to knowledge management. With the exception of NewsBoy and NewsHound, which are still at a preliminary implementation stage, all components of the architecture are now in place and are undergoing preliminary user testing. Once this preliminary evaluation and testing phase has been completed, Planet-Onto will become fully operational. We also plan to apply the Planet-Onto technology to support semantic access to medical guidelines. This work will be done in the context of the *PatMan* project [30].

Obviously, several research issues are still open. In particular, the main obstacle to this kind of enterprises is provided by the collaborative construction of the knowledge base. While usability has been our main criterion when designing the ontology and the knowledge annotation tool, we realise that this approach is only sustainable in restricted scenarios, where users are reasonably motivated and skilled and the annotation process relatively lightweight. Thus, the major challenge for this and other similar enterprises remains to develop tools that take the burden of ontology annotation off the writers of the documents to be annotated. Investigating the feasibility of such tools will be one of our main research goals for the near future.

Acknowledgements

Many thanks to Simon Buckingham-Shum and Paul Mulholland for the insightful discussions on topics related to Planet-Onto and especially to Simon for the important feedback on the usability of Planet-Onto.

References

1. Benjamins, V. R. and Fensel, D.: Special Issue on Problem Solving Methods. International Journal of Human-Computer Studies, **49**(4), (1998) 305-650
2. Benjamins, R., Fensel, D. and Gomez Perez, A.: Knowledge Management through Ontologies. In U. Reimer (editor), Proceedings of the Second International Conference on Practical Aspects of Knowledge Management. Basel, Switzerland (1998)
3. Buckingham-Shum, S. and Sumner, T.: Publishing, Interpreting and Negotiating Scholarly Hypertexts: Evolution of an Approach and Toolkit. Technical Report KMI-TR-57, Knowledge Media Institute, The Open University, Milton Keynes, UK (1997. Available from http://kmi.open.ac.uk/kmi-abstracts/kmi-tr-57-abstract.html.
4. Buckingham-Shum, S. and Sumner, T.: New Scenarios in Scholarly Publishing and Debate. In M. Eisenstadt, and T. Vincent, (editors) The Knowledge Web: Learning and Collaborating on the Net, Kogan Press, (1998) 135-152
5. Beys, P., Benjamins, R., and Van Heijst, G.: Remedying the Reusability-Usability Trade-off for Problem-Solving Methods. In B. R. Gaines and M. Musen (editors), Proceedings of the 10th Banff Knowledge Acquisition for Knowledge-Based System Workshop (KAW´96), Banff, Canada, (1996)

6. Bowker, G. C.: Lest We Remember: Organizational Forgetting and the Production of Knowledge. Accounting, Mangement and Information Technologies, 7(3) (1997) 113-118. Available from http://www.lis.uiuc.edu/~bowker/forget.html

7. Bradshaw, J.: An Introduction to Software Agents. In J. Bradshaw (editor), Software Agents. AAAI Press/MIT Press, Menlo Park, California (1996)

8. Clark, P., Healy, M., Uschold, M., Williamson, K. and Woods, S.: An Experiment in Ontology Reuse. In B. Gaines and M. Musen (editors), Proceedings of the 11th Knowledge Acquisition for Knowledge-Based Systems Workshop, Banff, Canada (1998)

9. Craven, M., Di Pasquo, D., Freitag, D., McCallum, A., Mitchell, T., Nigam, K. and Slattery, S.: Learning to Extract Symbolic Knowledge from the World Wide Web. Proceedings of the 15th National Conference on Artificial Intelligence (AAAI-98) (1998)

10. Domingue, J.: Tadzebao and WebOnto: Discussing, Browsing, and Editing Ontologies on the Web. In B. Gaines and M. Musen (editors), Proceedings of the 11th Knowledge Acquisition for Knowledge-Based Systems Workshop, April 18th-23th, Banff, Canada (1998).
Available from http://kmi.open.ac.uk/people/domingue/banff98-paper/domingue.html

11. Domingue, J. and Scott, P.: KMI Planet: Putting the Knowledge Back into Media. In M. Eisenstadt, and T. Vincent, (editors), The Knowledge Web: Learning and Collaborating on the Net, Kogan Press, (1998) 173-184

12. Eriksson, H., Puerta, A. R. and Musen, M. A.: Generation of Knowledge Acquisition Tools from Domain Ontologies. In B. Gaines and M. Musen (editors), Proceedings of the 8th Knowledge Acquisition for Knowledge-Based Systems Workshop (1994)

13. Farquhar, A., Fikes, R. and Rice, J.: The Ontolingua Server: A Tool for Collaborative Ontology Construction. In B. Gaines and M. Musen (editors), Proceedings of the 10th Banff Knowledge Acquisition for Knowledge-Based Systems Workshop. Banff, Alberta, Canada (1996)

14. Feigenbaum, E. A.: The Art of Artificial Intelligence: Themes and Case Studies of Knowledge Engineering. Proceedings of the Fifth International Joint Conference on Artificial Intelligence, Cambridge, MA (1977)

15. Fensel, D., Motta, E., Decker, S. and Zdrahal, Z.: The Use of Ontologies for Specifying Tasks and Problem Solving Methods: A Case Study. In R. Benjamins and E. Plaza (editors), Knowledge Acquisition, Modeling, and Management. Proceedings of the 10th European Workshop, EKAW '97. Lecture Notes in Artificial Intelligence 1319, Springer-Verlag (1997)

16. Fensel, D., Decker, S., Erdmann, M. and Studer, R.: Ontobroker: The very high idea. Proceedings of the 11th Annual Florida Artificial Intelligence Research Symposium (FLAIRS-98) (1998)

17. Girgensohn, A., Zimmermann, B., Lee, A., Burns, B. and Atwood, M. E.: Dynamic Forms: An Enhanced Interaction Abstraction Based on Forms. Proceedings of Interact '95 (1995) 362-367

18. Gruber, T. R.: A Translation Approach to Portable Ontology Specifications. Knowledge Acquisition, 5(2) (1993)

19. Gruber, T. R.: Toward Principles for the Design of Ontologies Used for Knowledge Sharing. International Journal of Human-Computer Studies 43(5/6) (1995) 907-928

20. Guarino, N. and Giaretta, P.: Ontologies and Knowledge Bases: Towards a Terminological Clarification. In N. Mars (editor), Towards Very Large Knowledge Bases: Knowledge Building and Knowledge Sharing. IOS Press, Amsterdam (1995) 25-32

21. Heflin, J., Hendler, J. and Luke, S.: Reading Between the Lines: Using SHOE to Discover Implicit Knowledge from the Web. AAAI-98 Workshop on AI and Information Integration (1998). Available from http://www.cs.umd.edu/projects/plus/SHOE/shoe-aaai98.ps

22. van Heijst, G.: The Role of Ontologies in Knowledge Engineering. PhD thesis, University of Amsterdam (1995)

23. HPKB: High Performance Knowledge Bases. Darpa Project. Project Description (1997). Available from http:// www.teknowledge.com:80/HPKB/

24. Krulwich, B. and Burkey, C.: The InfoFinder Agent: Learning User Interests through Heuristic Phrase Extraction. IEEE Expert Intelligent Systems and their Applications, 12(5) (1997) 22-27

25. Lenat, D.B. and Guha, R.V.: Building Large Knowledge-Based Systems: Representation and Inference in the Cyc Project. Addison-Wesley, Reading, MA (1990)

26. Lieberman, H.: Letizia: An Agent That Assists Web Browsing. International Joint Conference on Artificial Intelligence, IJCAI '95 Montreal (1995)

27. Motta E.: Reusable Components for Knowledge Models. PhD Thesis. Knowledge Media Institute. The Open University. UK (1997). Available from http://kmi.open.ac.uk/~enrico/thesis/thesis.html

28. Musen, M. A.: Automated Generation of Model-Based Knowledge Acquisition Tools. Research Notes in Artificial Intelligence, Pitman, London (1989)

29. O'Leary, D. E.: Knowledge Management Systems: Converting and Connecting. IEEE Intelligent Systems, 13(3) (1998) 30-33

30. Patman: Patient Management Workflow Systems. Telematics Applications Project HC 4017 (1998). Available from http://aim.unipv.it/projects/patman/

31. Puerta, A. R., Eriksson, H., Gennari, J. H. and Musen, M. A.: Beyond Data Models for Automated User Interface Generation. Proceedings of the HCI'94, People and Computers, The University of Glasgow, Knowledge Systems Laboratory (1994)

32. PointCast: http://www.pointcast.com/ (1998)

33. Riloff, E.: An Empirical Study of Automated Dictionary Construction for Information Extraction in Three Domains. AI Journal 85 (1996)

34. Riva, A. and Ramoni, M.: LispWeb: a Specialized HTTP Server for Distributed AI Applications, Computer Networks and ISDN Systems 28(7-11) (1996) 953-961. Available from http://kmi.open.ac.uk/~marco/papers/www96/www96.html

35. Rosch, E.: Principles of Categorisation. In E. Rosch and B. B. Lloyd (editors), Cognition and categorisation. Lawrence Erlbaum Associates, Hillsdale, NJ (1978)

36. Runkel, J. T., Birmingham, W. B. and Balkany, A.: Separation of Knowledge: a Key to Reusability. Proceedings of the 8th Banff Knowledge Acquisition Workshop. Banff, Canada (1994)

37. Schank, R. C.: Conceptual Dependency: A theory of natural language understanding. Cognitive Psychology, 3 (1972) 552-631

38. Schatz, B. R.: Information Retrieval in Digital Libraries: Bringing Search to the Net. Science 275 (1997) 327-334

39. Sowa J. F.: Top-Level Ontological Categories. International Journal on Human-Computer Studies 43(5/6) (1995) 669-685

40. Sumner, T., Domingue, J., Zdrahal, Z., Hatala, M., Millican, A., Murray, J., Hinkelmann, K., Bernardi, A., Weiss, S. and Traphoner, R.: Enriching Representations of Work to Support Organisational Learning. In Proceedings of the Interdisciplinary Workshop on Building, Maintaining, and Using Organizational Memories (OM-98). 13th European Conference on Artificial Intelligence (ECAI-98), 23-28 August, Brighton, UK (1998)

41. Uschold, M. and Gruninger, M.: Ontologies: Principles, Methods and Applications. Knowledge Engineering Review 11(2) (1996) 93-136

42. van der Vet, P. E. and Mars, N. J. I.: Bottom-up Construction of Ontologies. IEEE Transactions on Knowledge and Data Engineering 10(4) (1998) 513-526

Modeling Information Sources for Information Integration

François Goasdoué, Chantal Reynaud

LRI – Univ. De Paris-Sud – Bât. 490 – 91 405 Orsay cedex – France
{goasdoue, cr}@lri.fr
Tel: 33 (0)1 69 15 66 45 – 33 (0)1 69 15 58 46
Fax: 33 (0)1 69 15 65 86

Abstract. A critical problem in building an information mediator is to design knowledge bases describing the contents of information sources. Concepts which capture abstractions in information sources and which are usable to describe their content must be identified. This paper addresses this knowledge acquisition problem in the context of the PICSEL[1] project, when information sources are relational databases. The main contributions are (1) semi automated techniques for identifying relevant concepts from a database's conceptual schema, and (2) a set of tools for assisting database administrators in mapping these interesting concepts on to the domain model of the PICSEL mediator.

Key words. information sources modeling, identification of concepts, entity-relationship model, description logics, knowledge abstraction, support to knowledge representation.

1 Introduction

Our research works are developed in the context of the PICSEL project [14]. The aim is to build information servers over existing information sources that are distributed and possibly heterogeneous. The approach which has been chosen in PICSEL is to define an information server as a *knowledge-based* mediator between users and several information sources relative to a *same application domain*.

The idea in the knowledge-based mediator approach is to manage multiple heterogeneous information sources thanks to knowledge bases describing their contents in a logical formalism and using the same vocabulary. This provides shared access to multiple data and preserves the autonomy of each information source. The mediator plays the role of an interface between the user and the sources giving the illusion of querying a centralized and homogeneous system. The aim of this paper is

---

[1] Granted by CNET (Centre National d'Études des Télécommunications) under contract number 97 1B 378.

to present an approach and automated tools for designing the knowledge bases (KB) describing the contents of information sources in PICSEL knowledge-based mediators.

Designing such KB confronts us with a knowledge acquisition (KA) problem. We have to look for concepts which capture abstractions in information sources, usable to describe their content. In the paper, we address this KA problem when information sources are relational databases (DB). Our approach is based on Entity Relationship (ER) models used to model the schema of database applications. ER models are interesting because they are abstract representations of data. Yet, they are flat models with all concepts at the same level. Moreover, ER models are built according to modeling rules and don't necessarily represent concepts relevant for users of databases. We need abstraction mechanisms to make sets of objects really perceptible and relevant to users emerge. In our approach, we propose *semi automated techniques* to identify the main relevant concepts, called *semantic concepts*, in ER models. These techniques are based on the mechanism of aggregation to create higher level concepts from primitive ones.

Once the concepts to be described in the knowledge base of the mediator are identified, the problem is then to write their description. Statements in the PICSEL mediator knowledge bases are all represented in CARIN [12], a logical language combining description logics and Datalog rules. Moreover, the descriptions of the content of all databases must be represented using terms in the domain model of the mediator. So, we must obtain descriptions of the contents of a database, represented in CARIN and using terms in the domain model, from descriptions represented with the ER modeling language and using terms particular to a database. The problem is therefore to obtain a mapping between semantically equivalent concepts represented with different terms and different formalisms. To solve it we exploit capabilities of database administrators (DBA). DBAs know the contents of the databases they manage and the meaning of their conceptual schema. Each DBA will have to design the knowledge base referring to its own database. The identification of semantic concepts allows to organize the description of a whole conceptual schema which may be enormous. We guide then the DBA in the description of each semantic concept i.e. we have implemented automated tools to help (1) to understand the domain model, (2) to write CARIN sentences, (3) to characterize concepts represented in a database in comparison with those represented in the domain model and using terms in the domain model. Our approach and techniques have been used on a real database provided by the Web travel agent Degriftour[2].

The paper is organized as follows. In a first part, we present an architectural overview of the PICSEL mediator showing its main knowledge components. In a second part, we present the notion of semantic concept. Section 3 deals with their identification in an ER model and section 4 describes semi automated techniques to help DBA to describe semantic concepts in CARIN.

---

[2] see http://www.degriftour.fr

2 Architectural Overview

2.1 General Presentation

In PICSEL, a mediator has been designed according to a knowledge-based approach. It has two main parts: a generic query engine and KB specific to information servers. KBs contain both the model of the application domain of a server and abstract descriptions of the contents of the information sources accessible from this server. Given an information server, there are one KB to model the domain and one KB per information source to describe its contents as shown on figure 1. The domain model contains all the basic vocabulary used to ask queries. The query engine takes in charge the access to the sources in order to obtain the answers to user queries. Given a global query Q, it computes a set of local query plans which provide the set of all possible answers to Q that can be obtained by querying the different local databases. Abstract descriptions of the contents of the information sources help to localize relevant sources. They are represented in the same logical formalism as the user queries and as the sentences in the domain model. The connection making possible the correspondence between the actual database and their views in the mediator is established by interface modules called wrappers. We give a description of the main knowledge components in a PICSEL mediator in figure 1.

2.2 The Main Knowledge Components in a PICSEL Mediator

2.2.1 The Domain Model

The domain model contains all the vocabulary of an application domain used to ask queries. All the categories of objects that may be considered by users of the information server have to be represented. The domain model can be seen as a categorization of domain objects from a user-oriented point of view. It is expressed as a set of concepts, their definitions and their inter-relationships. So, the domain model is very similar to a domain ontology [8].

The domain model is represented in CARIN [12], a logical language combining description logics[3] and Datalog rules. Its semantics ensures that its exploitation at the symbol level by the engine conforms to its meaning at the knowledge level.

A domain model is built as follows. First, a basic vocabulary in terms of base predicates is acquired. New domain relations, significant for the application domain, can then be defined over the base relations using CARIN, either by rules or by concept expressions. Basic and complex relations make up a taxonomic hierarchy that can be automatically constructed.

---

[3] The DL language that we consider in the PICSEL project is referred to as core-CLASSIC. It contains the operators $\subseteq$ (inclusion) and := (definition), and the constructors $\sqcap$ (conjunction), $\forall$ (concept restriction), $(\geq n\ R)$, $(\leq n\ R)$ (number restrictions) and $\neg$ (negation on basic concepts only).

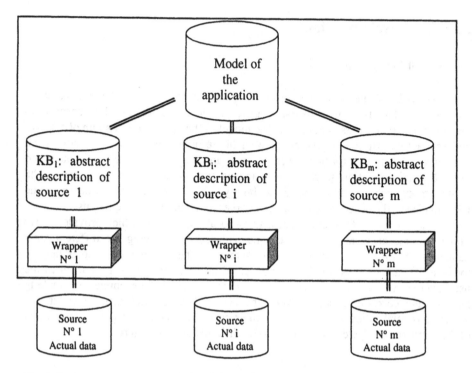

Fig. 1. The knowledge base part of the PICSEL mediator in an information server dedicated to the application domain D

For example, the hierarchy represented in figure 2 is computed from the following expressions:

Travel $\subseteq$ (= *1 DepartureDate*[4]) $\sqcap$ (= *1 ArrivalDate*),

Stay := Travel $\sqcap$ (= *1 AssBuilding*),

Journey := Travel $\sqcap$ (= *1 DeparturePlace*) $\sqcap$ (= *1 ArrivalPlace*) $\sqcap$ (= *1 MeansTransport*),

Flight := Journey $\sqcap$ (*∀MeansTransport.Plane*),

TourismFlight := Flight $\sqcap$ (*∀MeansTransport.(¬SupersonicPlane)*),

VIPFlight := Flight $\sqcap$ (*∀MeansTransport.(¬TourismPlane)*) $\sqcap$ (≥ *1 AssociatedMeal*).

These sentences define the concepts *Journey, Stay, Flight, TourismFlight* and *VIPFlight* from the primitive concept *Travel* (base predicate, unary relation) and from the primitive roles (binary relations) *DeparturePlace, ArrivalPlace, MeansTransport.* The concept *Travel* is at least characterized by a single departure date and a single arrival date. The concept *Journey* is defined as a set of travels that have exactly one departure place, one arrival place and one means of transport. The concept *Stay* is

---

[4] To simplify, we use the syntax '(= *n R*)' for '(≥*n R*) $\sqcap$ (≤*n R*)'.

defined as a set of travels that have exactly one associated building. The concept *Flight* is defined as a set of journeys which means of transport are necessarily planes. The concept *TourismFlight* is defined as a set of flights which means of transport are not supersonic planes whereas the concept *VIPFlight* is a set of flights which means of transport are not tourism planes and which have at least one associated meal.

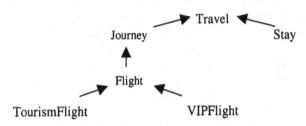

Fig. 2. A taxonomic hierarchy

Our work doesn't focus on the domain model design. We consider it already built.

2.2.2 Abstract Descriptions of the Contents of a Source

The abstract descriptions of a source consists of a set of source relations v_{S1}, v_{S2}, ..., v_{Sn} for which it is specified: (1) a one-to-one mapping with domain relations, (2) a set of constraints that are used to characterize the instances of the domain relations that can be found in a source S. For example, for a given source S, the descriptions may say that we can find instances of *Flight* and the constraints may indicate that the flight's departure places that we can find in S are all located in *Europe*, but not in *Germany*.

More precisely, each abstract description of a relational database S is a knowledge base that contains two sets of assertions: I_S and C_S.

I_S represents mappings with domain relations by logical implications. For example, $v_{S1}(x) \Rightarrow Flight(x)$, $v_{S2}(x,y) \Rightarrow DeparturePlace(x,y)$ are two elements of I_S if the source S contains instances of flights with their departure places, *Flight* and *DeparturePlace* being two relations in the domain model.

C_S indicates the constraints that are known to hold on the database relations. They are represented with core-CLASSIC inclusions or incompatibility rules. For example, let us consider that all flights in S have their departure places located in Europe, but not in Germany. This is stated by *Flight* $_{in\ S}$ $\subseteq$ ($\forall DeparturePlace$ $_{in\ S}.(Europe$ $\sqcap$ not $Germany))$, and according to the v_{Si} in I_S, the corresponding constraint that appears in C_S is v_{S1} $\subseteq$ ($\forall v_{S2}.(Europe$ $\sqcap$ not $Germany))$. That constraint can also be described thanks to (1) the inclusion statement: v_{S1} $\subseteq$ ($\forall v_{S2}.Europe$) and (2) the incompatibility rule: $v_{S1}(x) \wedge v_{S2}(x,y) \wedge Germany(y) \Rightarrow \bot$.

2.3 The Information Sources (Relational Databases) Accessible from an Information Server

In this paper, we focus on information sources which are relational DB. Relational DB developments are usually decomposed in several steps. One main step is the construction of a conceptual model. The aim is to facilitate the communication between designers and end users by providing them with a conceptual representation of an application that does not include many of the details of how the data is physically stored. One of the most popular and prominent conceptual model is the Entity Relationship (ER) model introduced by Chen [6]. Instances useful in an application are grouped into classes or concepts called entities and ER models represent entities rather than actual instances.

The approach that we propose to model the content of databases relies on the analysis of ER models. It does not exploit the data of the database at all. Given a query, the aim is to identify relevant information sources which *may* give an answer. It is not to identify the sources which, at the moment, given their data, are able to give an answer to the query. Yet, an ER model doesn't provide a conceptualization adequate to the description of the contents of a database in PICSEL mediator. ER models are quite flat. All concepts are represented at the same level. Moreover the construction of an ER model is guided by modelisation rules and the concepts that are represented are not necessarily relevant for a user of the database application. We need abstraction mechanisms to make concepts really perceptible and relevant to users emerge. (cf. section 4)

The basic primitives of an ER model are: entities, relationships, attributes. Relationships represent links between instances of differents entities and use a name to describe these links in a literal form. Attributes describe characteristics of instances of an entity or characteristics of related instances.
Cardinalities constraints $(Card(E_1,R),Card(E_2,R))$ on the participating entities (E_1, E_2) in a relationship R are given. A cardinality constraint describes a restriction on the minimum and maximum number of instances from an entity that may be associated with any one instance from the other entity.

We use these cardinality constraints to define if a relationship can be considered as a link between two entities, the first one beeing viewed as a characterization of the second one. Such links are called characterization links. We give the definition of this notion and of the different kinds of characterization links below. They are summarized in Table 1.

$Card(E_1,R)$	$Card(E_2,R)$	Strength of the characterization link
(1,1)	(1,1)	Pairable
(1,n)	(1,1)	Strong
(0,_)	(1,1)	Weak
other	other	None

Table 1. Characterization of a relationship R according to the cardinalities constraints between R and the entities E_1 and E_2

A relationship between two entities can be seen as a characterization link iff one of its cardinality constraints is equal to (1,1). This link is said pairable, strong or weak according to the cardinalities constraints of the other entity (cf. Table 1).

The characterization link between E_1 and E_2 is said pairable iff each instance from E_1 is associated with one and only one instance from E_2, and conversely. So, E_1 strictly characterizes E_2 and conversely.

It is said strong (resp. weak) iff each instance from E_1 is associated with at least one (resp. zero) instance from E_2, and E_2 strictly characterizes E_1. Here, the strength of the link indicates that E_1 is necessarily (resp. not necessarily) in relation with E_2.

3 The Notion of Semantic Concepts

In order to model relevant concepts, we defined the notion of *semantic concept*. This notion has been adapted from the *natural object* model used in the Dialog module of the CASE TRAMIS [4]. One of the aim of this model is to aggregate entities and relationships of an ER model to allow objects really perceptible to the users to emerge.

A semantic concept (SC) can be seen as a grouping of entities and relationships. Such a grouping brings to the fore one particular entity, called the *root entity* of the SC, while the other ones only characterize it.

For example, in the ER model in figure 3, only two objects are perceptible to users: Region (including data on their departments[5] and data on the towns of these departments) and Place of interest (including guided tours). That means that, in the context of the database, regions are not meaningful for a user without information on their departments and on their towns. A department is not perceptible to users apart from regions. Any department always belongs to only one region (the pair of cardinalities of (department, belongs-1) is (1,1)). Data on a department can then be seen as a characterization of the region to which it belongs. Furthermore, in the database (always according to the ER model below), some towns are not close to any place of interest and conversely, some places of interest are not close to any town. That means that the concept of town and place of interest are not dependent of each other.

To define a SC, the ER model is seen as a connected graph, where entities are vertices and relationships (characterization links) are edges or directed edges. An edge is directed only if it is a strong or weak characterization link. In this article, we only focus on strong characterization links.

Definition of a Semantic Concept: *Given a connected subgraph G of an ER model, G is a Semantic Concept iff the graph S obtained further to two operations applied on G (a grouping operation and an elimination operation, defined below) is a skeleton.*

---

[5] In France, Regions are divided in geographical areas called Departments.

Definition of a semantic concept's Skeleton: *Given a semantic concept G, it has only one skeleton S which satisfies:*

- *S is a connected directed graph.*
- *S has a single source vertex V_0 that is the root entity of the G.*
- *All the vertices of S are reachable from V_0 by following directed edges (characterization links). Reachable vertices are entities that characterize the root entity of G (V_0).*
- *Any entity of G appears in one of the skeleton's vertices. This implies that all entities of G are either the root entity, either characterizations of the root entity in S.*

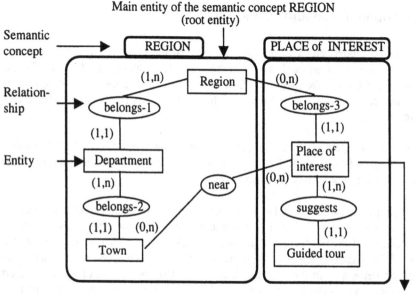

Main entity of the semantic concept REGION
(root entity)

Main entity of the semantic concept
Place of Interest

Fig. 3. An ER Model split into two semantic concepts

The grouping operation: *It consists in grouping in a vertex all entities that are indissociable i.e. vertices linked by edges that are pairable characterization links.*

The elimination operation: *It consists in eliminating all edges that aren't characterization links.*

These operations applied on a graph G ensure the resulting graph S represents groupings of indissociable entities and the characterization links that exist between those groupings. An example of these operations is given in figure 4.

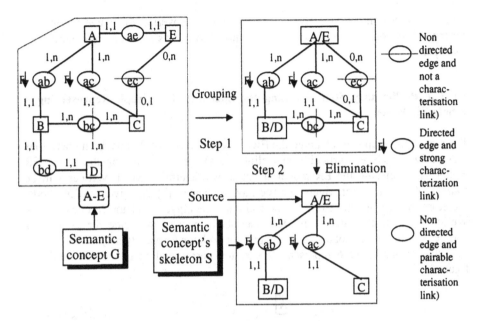

Fig. 4. The construction process of the skeleton of the SC "A/E"

In [7], we have shown that any ER model can always be split into a partition of semantic concepts (proposition 1). This first proposition led us to find an automated method to construct semantic concepts of an ER model. The method that we propose is based on the notion of skeleton. In section 4, we explain how the notion of skeleton is used and we detail the construction process.

4 Identifying Semantic Concepts

To split an ER model into SCs, we use a method based on the research of SCs' skeletons. We have shown in [7] that, given a SC' skeleton, we can find the corresponding SC on the ER model (proposition 2). Furthermore, an ER model may be enormous and complex. For example, we worked on a database containing 43 tables. In such cases, it might be hard to find relevant groupings of entities and relationships directly on the ER model. It might also be difficult to work directly on the graph representing the whole model. On the opposite, skeletons are simpler graphs than those representing an ER model or even than SCs thanks to the grouping and elimination operations.

So, to identify SCs of an ER model represented by a graph G, we have three stages. In a first preliminary step, we build the skeleton S_G of G. Second, we split S_G into different skeletons in an incremental way. Finally, according to proposition 2, we build the SCs corresponding to each different skeleton of S_G. The first two steps are described in the next sections.

In our approach, we are always interested in discovering the biggest semantic concepts. We would like to describe an ER model by means of a minimum number of concepts.

4.1 The Preliminary Step: Building the Skeleton of a Graph Representing a Whole ER Model

The aim of this step is to compute the ER model skeleton. To do this, both operations previously introduced (grouping and elimination) are performed on the whole ER model. By analysing the ER model skeleton, we determine which vertices will be sources of skeletons (cf. figure 6). We have shown in [7] that given an ER model skeleton's vertex, it can belong to one and only one biggest skeleton (proposition 3). We showed also that, given an ER model skeleton, we can decide for each of its vertices if it will be or not a source of a biggest skeleton (proposition 4).

For illustration, figure 6 represents a skeleton corresponding to the ER model in figure 5.

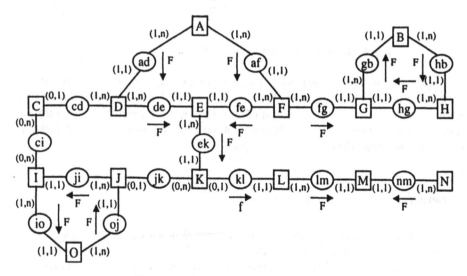

Fig. 5. An ER model represented as a graph

4.2 The Identification of Skeletons of Semantic Concepts

Our aim is to automate as much as possible this identification process. Yet, an ER model may often be split into different ways. The administrator of the database (DBA) corresponding to an ER model is the only person who can decide on the best partition. So, we propose to build at the beginning a first one in a fully-automated way. This first partition only proposes groupings which are sure in respect to our construction rules and thus, which don't need the intervention of the DBA. Then, it is shown to the DBA who can decide on further groupings.

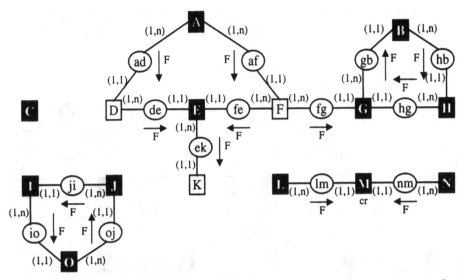

Fig. 6. The ER skeleton corresponding to the graph in figure 5 (black vertices are sources of biggest skeletons)

The identification of the most relevant concepts of a database is obviously a process which can't be performed without the contribution of a human being, the DBA. The approach that we propose is interesting because it clearly separates the process in two parts, one which can totally be automated and another more little one which needs the DBA to make choices.

To build a partition of SCs in a *deterministic way*, we showed that, given an ER model skeleton, there is only one partition of it into biggest skeletons (proposition 5). So, we developed algorithms to split an ER model skeleton into *the* partition of its biggest skeletons. The process which is performed is incremental. (Small) skeletons are built and afterwards one can decide to merge several of them.

A variant of the depth-first search algorithm is performed to build the first partition. It allows all vertices that are reachable from a source vertex and that are not sources of biggest skeletons to be grouped. A source vertex and the vertices reachable from it compose a skeleton (cf. figure 7).

Then a merging process is performed. We illustrate it on the example below. The final partition which is obtained from figure 7 is represented on figure 8.
- Let S_A and S_E be the two skeletons which source vertex is respectively A and E. We can notice that (1) E characterizes D (because of the strong characterization link "de"), (2) E characterizes F (because of the strong characterization link "fe"), (3) D and F are both characterizations of A (because of the strong characterization links "ad" and "af"). So, E and its characterizations are also characterizations of A. Since we want to build the biggest skeletons, we merge S_A and S_E.
- Let S_A, S_B, S_G and S_H be the skeletons which source vertex is respectively A, E, G and H. We can notice that (1) B, G and H characterize themselves, (2) G is a

characterization of F, (3) F is a characterization of A. So, we can deduce that B, G and H characterize A. Since we want to build the biggest skeletons, we merge S_A, S_B, S_G and S_H.

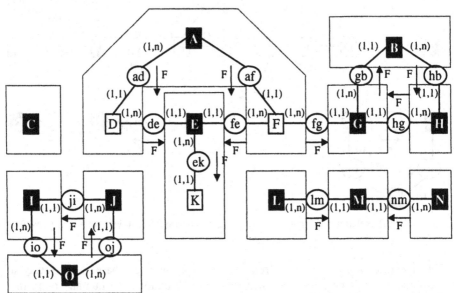

Fig. 7. A first partition of SCs obtained in an automated way (black vertices are sources of skeletons)

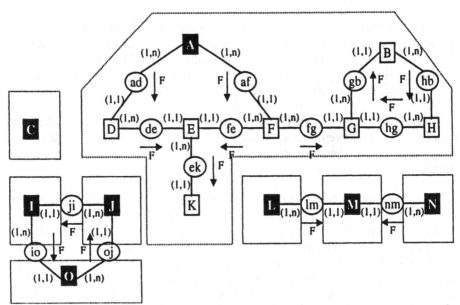

Fig. 8. The final partition of SCs obtained in an automated way (black vertices are sources of skeletons)

At the end of the identification step, we have a partition of an ER model into SCs (cf. figure 9 for example). Each one represents a semantic concept which significant entity is the root entity of the SC and which the other entities are only viewed as characterizations of the significant entity. This way, the technique described above leads to extract central concepts of a database, each concept being defined by the contents of a SC. Because these concepts are central, we assume that they are meaningful and relevant for users of a database. We have experimented the technique successfully on the conceptual schema of the database provided by Degriftour.

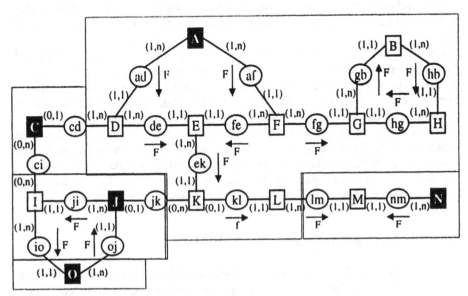

Fig. 9. A SCs partition of the ER model of figure 5 (black vertices are roots of produced SCs)

5 Describing Semantic Concepts in CARIN

Once the SCs are identified, they must be described in the terms of the domain model. To help the DBA to produce this description, we have developped three tools: a semantic concepts explorer, a domain model explorer and a CARIN sentences composer. All of them are automated supports in the description of a whole relational DB. The idea behind the approach is that the space of choices of concepts to describe can, to some extend, be controlled by the introduction of the notion of semantic concepts. That way, a DBA will have to describe its DB only part by part, each part corresponding to a SC, an abstraction representation of semantically related and indissociable data. We assume in this mapping process that the domain model in the PICSEL mediator is exhaustive. Given this assumption, except if SCs are out of the domain of the information server, all correspondences should be achieved.

5.1 The Semantic Concepts Explorer

This tool allows the administrator of a given database to browse the previously identified semantic concepts of his ER model. It is a way to recall to him the significant notions to describe.

5.2 The Domain Model Explorer

This tool displays all the hierarchies that can be computed from concept inclusions and concept declaration statements in the domain model (cf. the hierarchy presented in 2.2.1).

For each node of a hierarchy that is a base concept, a description in natural language is available. Moreover, for each node, we can retrieve all the roles that have the node type as type of one of their arguments. So, the DBA can browse the different hierarchies to learn the vocabulary defined by the domain model, or find the concept that represents the best a notion he wants to put in the knowledge base.

We can also list all the roles of the terminology, with, for each of them, their meaning in natural language. Moreover, if information is also available from domain model, we can display for each role the type of concepts that it links. For example, we can deduce that the role *DepartureDate* needs a concept of type *Date* as its second argument from the following expression: *DepartureDate(X,Y)* $\wedge \neg Date(Y) \Rightarrow \bot$.

5.3 A CARIN Sentences Composer

When a DBA decides to describe a significant notion encountered in a semantic concept of his ER model (thanks to the semantic concepts explorer), he can choose the concept of a hierarchy that represents the best that notion (thanks to the domain model explorer). The result of such an action is to produce automatically a new source relation declaration: $v_i(x) \Rightarrow C_j(x)$, where C_j is the concept that has just been selected in the domain model. The purpose of our tool is to help the DBA to characterize that source relation.

First, we try to characterize v_i using roles $R_{k\ (1 \leq k \leq n)}$ that are associated with objects of C_j. For example, the roles *DepartureDate*, *ArrivalDate*, *DeparturePlace*, *ArrivalPlace* and *MeansTransport* can be used to characterize the concept *Flight*, according to the piece of domain model presented in 2.2.1.

Possible characterizations of v_i are expressed thanks to source relation inclusions like: $v_i \subseteq C_1 \sqcap C_2 \sqcap ... \sqcap C_m$, where each $C_{1\ (1 \leq l \leq m)}$ is of the form $(\leq num\ R_k)$, $(\geq num\ R_k)$ or $(\forall R_k. C_{accepted})$. On the one hand, for a $C_{1\ (1 \leq l \leq m)}$ like $(\leq num\ R_k)$ or $(\geq num\ R_k)$, there is no particular problem. The DBA has only to select a role $R_{k\ (1 \leq k \leq n)}$ and to give the cardinality *num*. On the other hand, a $C_{1\ (1 \leq l \leq m)}$ of the form $(\forall R_k. C_{accepted})$ implies that the concept $C_{accepted}$ is compatible with R_k. To be sure that $C_{accepted}$ is compatible with a R_k selected by the DBA, let's consider the following process:

Case 1:   if $C_{accepted}$ is a concept name CN, it must appear in the domain model and CN must have the same type as the one of R_k' second argument. To do this, our tool uses the domain model explorer, pointing at the node of the hierarchy in which CN appears. Then, the DBA has to choose CN or one of its specializations for $C_{accepted}$.

Case 2:   if $C_{accepted}$ is a concept like $(\leq num\ R_l)$ or $(\geq num\ R_l)$, R_l must have as first argument's type, the same type as the R_k' second argument. To do this, our tool retrieves from the domain model all the roles R_l which satisfy this property. Then, the DBA will have to choose one of them (R_l), and to give the cardinality n.

Case 3:   if $C_{accepted}$ is a concept like $(\forall R_l. C_{accepted'})$, the choice of R_l is done as R_k's choice is. The concept $C_{accepted'}$ must be of the same type as the type of R_l' second argument. Thus, $C_{accepted'}$ is chosen like $C_{accepted}$ was (i.e. case 1,2,3 or 4).

Case 4:   if $C_{accepted}$ is a concept like C_1 and C_2 and ... and C_p, each of the $C_1...C_p$ is defined like $C_{accepted}$ is (i.e. case 1,2,3 or 4).

This way, if we want to express that we have a source relation v_i over flights which arrival places are located in Europe and which type is Tourism, we can generate the following expressions, according to the piece of domain model presented in 2.2.1.:

$$v_i(x) \quad \Rightarrow \quad Flight(x), \quad v_i \quad \subseteq \quad (\forall ArrivalPlace.Europe^6) \quad \sqcap$$
$(\forall MeansTransport.TourismFlight).$

Second, we try to characterize v_i using roles $R_{k'}$ $(1 \leq k' \leq n)$ that are known not to associate objects of C_j but objects of classes subsumed by C_j. These roles are those of the domain model that are different of the R_k above, but that accept the same concept type as the one of C_j as first argument.

Again, possible characterizations of v_i are expressed thanks to source relation inclusions like: $v_i \subseteq C_1 \sqcap C_2 \sqcap ... \sqcap C_m$, where each C_1 $(1 \leq l \leq m)$ is a $(\leq num\ R_{k'})$, $(\geq num\ R_{k'})$ or $(\forall R_{k'}. C_{accepted})$. The same process of characterization as the one described above is used.

For example, if we want to express that we have the source relation v_i over flights that propose to have diner on board, we can generate the following expression, according to the piece of domain model presented in 2.2.1.: $v_i \subseteq (\geq 1\ AssociatedMeal) \sqcap$ $(\forall AssociatedMeal.Diner^7).$

6 Related Work and Conclusion

Our aim was to obtain descriptions using terms in the domain model from representations using terms particular to a database schema. The fundamental problem

---

[6] Here, we consider that the concept *Europe* appears in the domain model.

[7] Here, we consider that the concept *Diner* appears in the domain model.

which arises is semantic heterogeneity – the fact that the same concepts are represented differently in a database schema and in the domain model.

Some issues raised by semantic heterogeneity have been studied in the database community. When two or more databases need to work together, in many cases the same data is replicated. Different database schemas and different conceptualizations are typically used to represent the replicated data.

So, in the database schema integration field which aim is to construct a global, unified schema from existing or proposed databases, the semantic heterogeneity problems to be dealt with are structural and naming conflicts [1]. Structural conflicts arise as a result of a different choice of modeling constructs or integrity constraints. Naming conflicts arise because people from different application areas refer to the same data using their own terminology and names. Thus, to make schemas compatible, one must replace terms by other ones, the new terms belonging to the same level of discourse. In both cases, conflict discovery and restructuring are generally aided by a strong interaction between the different DB designers. Techniques to solve the semantic heterogeneity problem are used prior to the integration step. It is very often a manual process, except for some kinds of structural conflicts. In any cases, the preintegration step is considered the responsability of the DB designers. Furthermore, in much works, mappings between database schemata are assumed to be provided. A solution to the semantic heterogeneity problem would be to enhance the semantic description of each schema. For that, Bonjour in [2] proposes to introduce concept bases on top of a set of schemes to integrate. These bases could help to compare concepts represented in different systems.

More recently, other database works have focused on importing and integrating selected portions of DB schemata as in federated [16] or knowledge-based mediator or data warehouses architectures [18]. A lot of problems of semantic heterogeneity which arise are the same nature as in data integration field. But they have been addressed a little. Nevertheless, in the knowledge-based mediator approaches ([11],[5]), we notice two trends. Mediator approaches have in common the use of knowledge bases which describe both the domain model and the contents of information sources. So, they don't need correspondences directly between the information sources but, instead, they need correspondences between the domain model and the descriptions of the contents of each information source. A way to make such correspondences easier is to capture the intended meaning of DB schemata using ontologies [8]. It relies on manipulation techniques coming from the fields of artificial intelligence. In Observer [13] for example, the objects in the sources are represented as intensional descriptions by pre-existing ontologies. The query engine rewrites user queries by using interontology relationships to obtain semantics-preserving translations across the ontologies. The approach is interesting but new problems arise : how to build the ontologies ? how to acquire the terminological relationships represented between terms across the ontologies ? An other approach is to use the same vocabulary to describe both the domain model and the contents of the different sources. The problem of different vocabularies disappears but we must be able (1) to describe each source with the vocabulary of the domain model, and (2) to link the descriptions of the contents of a DB to the DB itself. Our paper is relative to the first point of this second approach, when information sources are described by views.

Another related work is on the extraction of data from web sources. The focus is on building wrappers for semi structured sources. The systems use either a template-based specification of a source, as in [9], or machine-learning techniques to learn the structure of a source (cf. ARIADNE project [10]). Yet, these systems don't focus on mapping sources into a description using a "global" vocabulary.

On another hand, our problem is relative to knowledge engineering. We want to build a knowledge-based mediator. Thus, we need techniques to construct all the knowledge bases useful to the mediator. Current knowledge engineering works describe the structure of a knowledge-based system (KBS) through highly structured models [15]. The domain models which describe the specific knowledge of a domain are one of the components of such models. Recently, in the knowledge engineering community, research works have been conducted to characterize domain knowledge and to help building domain models by means of ontologies [8]. An ontology is based on the definition of a structured and formalized set of concepts. A great part of it comes from text analysis. So, one trend is to benefit from both knowledge engineering and linguistics approaches. Researchers have studied mutual contributions and this led them to elaborate the concept of Terminological Knowledge Base (TKB), first defined by Ingrid Meyer [17]. In France, the works of the TIA research group is centered on this notion too [3]. A TKB is an intermediate model which helps toward the construction of a formal ontology ; it contains conceptual data, represented in a network of domain concepts, but also linguistic data on the terms used to name the concepts. A TKB can enhance communication and be a great help to choose the names of concepts. Such research works address the problem of the identification of concepts. We deal with the same problem but we have to identify concepts from database schemata, not from text analysis. So, the techniques that we propose are specific ones, based on the notion of semantic concepts.

In conclusion, this paper deals with identifying and modeling relevant concepts. First, we have presented a way to identify them. Our aim was to automate this process as much as possible although it can't be entirely performed without the contribution of DB designers. We have identified two different parts in the process performed sequentially: one which can be totally automated and another one performed in cooperation with the DB designer. Second, we have presented techniques usable by DB designers to be guided in the description of relevant concepts in CARIN and using terms in the domain model. Most of the techniques described in the paper have been implemented in Java.

Acknowledgements.

The authors thank Marie-Christine Rousset and anonymous reviewers for helpful comments on an earlier version of this paper.

References

1   Batini, C., Lenzerini M., Navathe S.B.: A Comparative Analysis of Methodologies for Database Schema Integration". ACM Computing Surveys, Vol. 18. (1986) 323-364

2   Bonjour M., Falquet G.: Concept Bases: A Support to Information Systems Integration, CAISE 94 (1994).

3   Bourigault D., Condamines A.: Réflexions autour du concept de base de connaissances terminologiques. Dans les actes des journées nationales du PRC-IA, Nancy (1995)

4   Brès P.-A.: L'apport de l'approche objet dans la conception de systèmes d'information. AGL'93, Pact-Group (1993).

5   Chaurathe S., Garcia-Molina H., Hammer J. and al.: The TSIMMIS Project : Integration of Heterogeneous Information Sources. Proceedings of the 100th Anniversary meeting. Tokyo, Japan. Information Processing Society of Japan (1994) 7-19

6   Chen P.S.: The Entity-Relationship Model. ACM Transactions on Database Systems 1 (1976) 166-192

7   Goasdoué F.: Assistance à la conception de bases de connaissances dédiées au médiateur PICSEL. Mémoire de D.E.A. d'informatique, Université Paris 11 (1998)

8   Gruber T.R.: A translation Approach to Portable Ontology Specifications. Knowledge Acquisition 5 (1993) 199-220

9   Hammer J., Garcia-Molina H., Nestorov S. and al.: Template-based wrappers in the TSIMMIS System. In Proceedings of ACM SIGMOD 97 (1997)

10   Knoblock A., Minton S., Ambite J.L. and al.: Modeling Web Sources for Information Integration. AAAI'97 (1997)

11   Levy A., Rajaraman A., Ordille J.: Querying heterogeneous information sources using source descriptions. VLDB'96 (1996)

12   Levy A., Rousset M.-C.: Combining Horn Rules and Description Logics in CARIN. Artificial Intelligence Journal, Vol. 14 (1998)

13   Mena E., Kashyap V., Seth A., Illaramendi A.: OBSERVER: An approach for Interoperation Accross Pre-existing Ontologies. Proceedings of the first IFCIS International Conference on Cooperative Information Systems (CoopIS'96) (1996)

14   Rousset M.-C., Lattes V.: The use of CARIN language and algorithms for information Integration: the PICSEL project. Intelligent Information Integration Workshop associated with ECAI'98 Conference, Brighton (1998)

15   Schreiber A.T., Wielinga B.J., De Hoog R., Akkermans J.M., Van de Velde W.: CommonKads: a comprehensive methodology for KBS development. IEEE Expert 9(6). (1994) 28-37

16   Sheth A. P., Larson A.: Federated Database Systems for managing Distributed, Heterogeneous and Autonomous Databases. ACM Computing Surveys, Vol. 22 n°3. (1990) 183-236

17   Skuce D., Meyer I.: Terminology and Knowledge Acquisition: Exploring a Symbiotic Relationship. In Proc. 6th Knowledge Acquisition for Knowledge-based System Workshop, Banff. (1991) 29/1-29/21

18   Widom J.: Research Problems in Data Warehousing. Proceedings of Fourth International Conference on Information and Knowledge Management (CIKM'95), Baltimore, Maryland, (1995) 25-30

Ontological Reengineering for Reuse

Asunción Gómez-Pérez, Mª Dolores Rojas-Amaya
Facultad de Informática
Universidad Politécnica de Madrid
Campus de Montegancedo s/n
Boadilla del Monte, 28660. Madrid. Spain.
Tel: (34-1) 336-74-39, Fax: (34-1) 336-74-12
Email: {asun, mrojas}@delicias.dia.fi.upm.es

Abstract

This paper presents the concept of *Ontological Reengineering* as the process of retrieving and transforming a conceptual model of an existing and implemented ontology into a new, more correct and more complete conceptual model which is reimplemented. Three activities have been identified in this process: reverse engineering, restructuring and forward engineering. The aim of *Reverse Engineering* is to output a possible conceptual model on the basis of the code in which the ontology is implemented. The goal of *Restructuring* is to reorganize this initial conceptual model into a new conceptual model, which is built bearing in mind the use of the restructured ontology by the ontology/application that reuses it. Finally, the objective of *Forward Engineering* is output a new implementation of the ontology. The paper also discusses how the ontological reengineering process has been applied to the Standard-Units ontology [18], which is included in a Chemical-Elements [12] ontology. These two ontologies will be included in a Monatomic-Ions and Environmental-Pollutants ontologies.

1   Introduction

The concept of reengineering is commonly used in Software Engineering and started to move into the field of Knowledge Engineering a few years ago. When we try to define the term reengineering, other very closely related concepts emerge, such as reverse engineering, restructuring and forward engineering. The term *reverse engineering* is used to denote the process of analyzing a system to identify its components and relations and/or represent a system in another manner [5]. Therefore, the reverse engineering process could be defined as the analysis of a system/program in an attempt to create a representation of the program at a higher level of abstraction than source code. This is what Pressman refers to as design retrieval [20]. There are several definitions of the term *restructuring* [6, 8, 21]. The most representative definition was made by Chikofsky who defined restructuring as system transformation to pass from one representation to another at the same level of abstraction, conserving functionality and semantics [8]. He also defines the concept of *forward engineering* as the traditional process leading from a high level of abstraction, which is independent of implementation design, towards the physical implementation of a system [8]. Accordingly, the term *reengineering* refers to the process in which design information about the existing software is retrieved and this information is then used to alter or reconstruct the existing system in an attempt to improve overall quality [20]. The software outputted by reengineering mostly reimplements the function of the existing system; however, at the same time, the developer adds new functions and/or improves overall performance.

There are no papers on reengineering related to the field of ontological engineering, although the paper by Barley et al. [3], who show how knowledge on stillended panel layout implemented in ICAD code has been manually analyzed and transformed into production rules, which have been formalized in KIF [13] and SLANG [19], could be construed as a kind of reengineering. So, this paper presents how we have done ontological reengineering of the Standard-Units [18] ontology, which is included in a Chemicals-Elements [12] ontology. Both ontologies are reused by a Environmental-Pollutants ontology. This paper is organized as follows: Section 2 presents the need for environmental ontologies and section 3 the scope of the problem; sections 4 and 5 describe the ontological reengineering method applied to the Standard-Units ontology, and, finally, section 6 reviews the Chemical-Elements ontology.

2 Need for environmental ontologies

Specialists from different fields, such as biologists, geologists, computer scientists, chemists, lawyers, etc., are involved in the environmental sciences. Each expert uses his own vocabulary, there being no common terminology or standard to ensure that each term is used accurately. There are numerous reasons for building ontologies in the environmental field: (1) The existence of synonyms (for example, the terms "contamination" and "pollution" are used as synonyms in reference to air pollution, as are "bleaching" and "leaching" in the case of soil treatment and problems); (2) One term can be used in different sciences, where it may have a similar but not an identical meaning (for example, in the geological domain, the word "contamination" refers to the process in which the chemical composition of the magma changes due to the assimilation of rocks and, in the microbiological domain, it is defined as the biological process of bacterial alteration); and (3) there are terms that are closely related within the same science that present slight differences of meaning, (for example, within the biological sciences, "contamination" is the term used in microbiology and "pollution" is the term used in ecology).

There are a lot of possibilities for building environment-related ontologies, but we are going to center on environmental pollutants ontologies. An ontology of this type has to study the methods of detecting the different pollutants components of various media: water, air, soil, etc., and the maximum permitted concentrations of these components, taking into account all the legislation in effect (European Union regulations, Spanish, German, US legislation, etc.). Moreover, the elements that are part of compounds are ionic. Ions are, therefore, the entities to be considered when performing environmental-pollutants-related studies, as they are possible indicators of pollution, deterioration, etc. Previous knowledge about elements in their pure state and their properties, as well as the units of measure of some properties, are required to represent knowledge about ionic concentration. The Environmental-Pollutants ontology seeks to produce a unified, complete and consistent terminology that can be used consistently, precisely, unambiguously and concisely in environmental applications that employ the maximum permitted concentration of ions to detect alterations in such media.

3   Problem scope

Before developing the ontologies on monatomic-ions and environmental-pollutants, we looked for other ontologies that had already been developed to check whether any of the knowledge they contain could be reused. We looked for ontologies related to periodic system elements and containing Système International (SI) units of measure. Accordingly, we searched the ontologies in the Ontology Server[1] [9] and the Cyc[2] ontology server. Useful ontologies, like Standard-Units[3], which defines a series of base units of measure, and Chemical-Elements, which defines the chemical elements of the periodic system, were found at the Ontology Server. Definitions of some units of measure and chemical entities (atom, ion, molecule and radical) were found at the Cyc server. As the ontology describing the units of measure at the Ontology Server includes a natural language definition, physical dimension and factors of conversion to other units of the same dimension for each unit and Cyc's ontologies only include a natural language definition, we decided to use the Ontology Server ontology as it was more complete. Moreover, as Chemical-Elements was developed by our work group, we opted to take the Ontology Server ontologies as a starting point, using the Cyc ontologies as a reference point. Then, we evaluated (verify[4] and validate[5]) the Chemical-Elements and Standard-Units ontologies to assure that they were correct and complete and thus guarantee that these ontologies provided a solid basis on which new ontologies could be developed incrementally. These ontologies were analyzed bearing in mind its future use of this ontology by the Monatomic-Ions ontology. The initial analysis of Chemical-Elements revealed that: (1) it addresses the elements in their pure state, (2) it needs to be updated with new knowledge that addresses elements from the environmental viewpoint, and (3) it includes attributes (i.e., atomic-weight) that have associated SI units of measure.

In pursuit of the above-mentioned objectives, we are going to develop a new ontology on Monatomic-Ions which will be later included in an ontology on Environmental-Pollutants.

The starting point of the new ontology will be the monatomic ion, both anionic and cationic, addressed from the viewpoint of inorganic chemistry and, also, analyzed with a view to standardization in the soil and waterfields within the physical environment and in terms of human health. On the other hand, as the ontology under development covers such an extensive field, the development of an ontology of polyatomic ions has been postponed. Figure 1 shows how all these

---

[1] http://www-ksl.stanford.edu:5915 and its european mirror site at   http://www-ksl-svc-lia.dia.upm.es:5915.

[2] http://www.cyc.com.

[3] The Standard-Units used to develop this work was available at the Ontology Server in December 1997.

[4] Verification concerns with analyzing the completeness, consistency, conciseness, expandability, and robustness of the definitions and axioms that are explicitly stated in the ontology, and the inferences that can be drawn from those axioms [16].

[5] Validation refers to whether the meaning of the ontology definitions really represent the real world for which the ontology was created [16].

ontologies will be integrated in a hierarchical and distributed architecture. The ontologies at the top of this hierarchy should be interpreted as including the lower-level ontologies. Note that this hierarchical architecture facilitates ontology design, maintenance and understanding by the future user. The description of the `Monatomic-Ions` and `Environmental-Pollutants` ontologies are out of the scope of this paper.

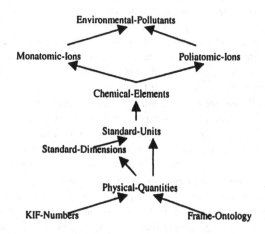

Figure 1. Relationship between the ontologies involved.

4 Ontological reengineering: method

The method for reviewing the `Standard-Units` ontology at the knowledge level is presented in Figure 2 and adapts Chikofsky's software reengineering schema [8] to the ontology domain. In this paper, we define *ontological reengineering* as "the process of retrieving and transforming a conceptual model of an existing and implemented ontology into a new, more correct and complete conceptual model, which is reimplemented". The ontological reengineering process should be carried out bearing in mind the use of the existing ontology by the system (ontology/software) that reuses it. Therefore, several ontological reengineering processes could be performed on the same ontology. If this were the case, configuration management would be required to keep a record of ontology evolution, as would strict change control.

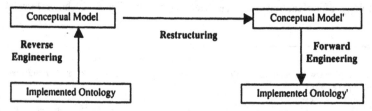

Figure 2. Ontological reengineering process.

Three activities were identified in the ontological reengineering process: reverse engineering, restructuring and forward engineering. Figure 3 pictures an organizational chart showing the activities performed during the reengineering process and the documents generated in each step.

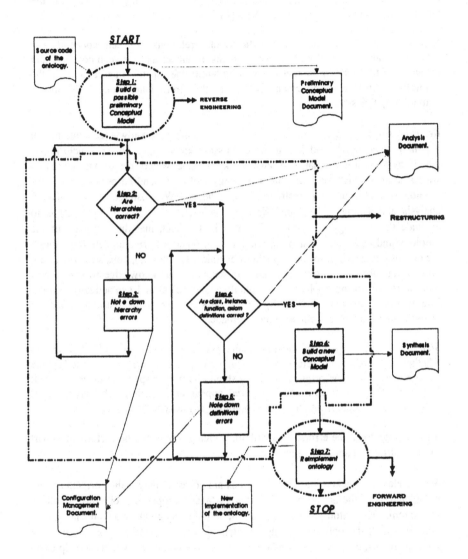

Figure 3. Ontological Reengineering activities.

Reverse Engineering: Its objetive is to output a possible conceptual model on the basis of the code in which the ontology is implemented. For the purpose of building a conceptual model, the set of intermediate representations proposed by the methodology named METHONTOLOGY [11, 12, 15] are used.

Step 1: Draw the hierarchies and taxonomic relations between concepts and instances, "ad hoc" relations between concepts, instances and between concepts and instances of the same or another hierarchy. Identify the functions and axioms of the ontology. Generate a document reflecting the preliminary conceptual model outputted by this step.

Restructuring: Its objective is to correct and reorganize the knowledge contained in an initial conceptual model, and detect missing knowledge. This restructuring is guided by the ontology that is to reuse the knowledge, which means that there is no way of assuring that the restructured ontology will be a hundred per cent valid for ontologies that reuse the restructured knowledge. We distinguish two phases: analysis and synthesis. The analysis phase goal (steps 2 to 5 of figure 3) is to evaluate the ontology technically [14], that is, to check that the hierarchy of the ontology and its classes, instances, relations and functions are complete (contain all the definitions required for the domain of chemical substances), consistent (there are no contradictions in the ontology and with respect to the knowledge sources used), concise (there are no explicit and implicit redundancies) and syntactically correct. The synthesis phase (step 6 of figure 3) seeks to correct the ontology after the analysis phase and document any changes made.

Step 2: Check the correctness and completeness of each hierarchy [14]. Analyze: a) whether the taxonomic relations between concepts are correct; b) whether the concepts present in the original hierarchy should be further specified or generalized; c) that all the concepts/instances required appear in the original hierarchy; d) if necessary, add/delete from the original ontology any concept/instance.

Step 3: Note down the errors. This will allow change control to be performed as part of configuration management process.

Step 4: Having checked that the hierarchies are correct, analyze the correctness and completeness of the definitions of classes, instances, properties, relations, functions and axioms. The ontologist will analyze the initial conceptual model attached to the code in which the ontology is implemented. Specialized material for this purpose (such as books, dictionaries, handbooks, etc.) will be required, as will the help of an expert in the domain defined in the ontology.

Step 5: Note down the errors detected in step 4 in order to perform change control as part of configuration management process.

Step 6: Having reviewed and corrected an original conceptual model, design a new conceptual model including all the above-mentioned changes, building the correct and complet hierarchies and outputting the correct and complete definitions for their later implementation. The ontologist will draw up a synthesis document specifying the actions carried out and the design criteria governing restructuring.

A series of documents will be generated, which can be divided into three groups: (1) analysis document, including a list of anomalies (problems, errors, omissions, ambiguities, etc.) encountered and detected in steps 2 and 4; (2) configuration management document, which includes reports related to the changes made in steps 3 and 5 on the basis of the set of errors identified in the analysis document. This document includes: description, need and effects of the change, possible alternatives, justification of the selected alternative, date of the change, etc.; and (3) synthesis documents, including the actions taken and criteria observed in step 6.

Forward Engineering: The objective of this step is to output a new implementation of the ontology on the basis of the new conceptual model.

Step 7: Reimplement the ontology on the basis of the new conceptual model, including all the recorded changes. This will output a document containing the code of the new ontology implementation.

The proposed work method is a sound initial approach to carrying out the above-mentioned process, although it could be improved in later studies using more complex ontologies. In order to increase the reusability of the ontology to be reengineered, guidelines and criteria to achieve a higher degree of reusability are needed in the restructuring process. Other open issue regards the relationship between the ontology that is being reengineered and top-level ontologies, if any.

5 A case study: Reengineering Standard-Units

5.1 The need of reviewing Standard Units

The Standard-Units ontology defines a series of SI units of measurement and other commonly used units that do not belong to the SI units. It includes the Standard-Dimensions ontology, which defines a series of physical dimensions (i.e., mass, time, length, temperature and electrical current) for different quantities. It also includes other dimensions, derived from the above five, including pressure, volume, etc. Depending on the system of units used, the physical quantities defined at the Standard-Dimensions ontology can be expressed in different units using the vocabulary of the Standard-Units ontology; for example, length can be expressed in meters, miles, inches, etc. Both the Standard-Units and the Standard-Dimensions ontologies include Physical-Quantities (see Figure 1), which defines the basic vocabulary for describing physical quantities in a general form, making explicit the relationship between quantities of various orders, units of measure and physical dimensions. A quantity is a hypothetically measurable amount of something. For example, the term meter, defined in the Standard-Units ontology, is an instance of the class Unit-Of-Measure defined in the Physical-Quantities ontology.

We came to revise the Standard-Units ontology because it was included in Chemical-Elements. We needed to check that the units of measurement of certain attributes in Chemical-Elements befitted the knowledge and usual practice of experts. One example of the type of check that the experts carried out was that an attribute (Semidisintegration-Period) of a concept (Elements) was filled in with a particular value type which was associated with a unit of measurement (Year). After the experts had drawn up the inspection document setting out the properties to be checked, each query was transformed into the vocabulary of the ontology. For example, check that the Semidisintegration-Period of the concept Elements of the ontology Chemical-Elements is filled in with a value type Time-Quantity and its unit of measurement is Year. This is illustrated in Figure 4.

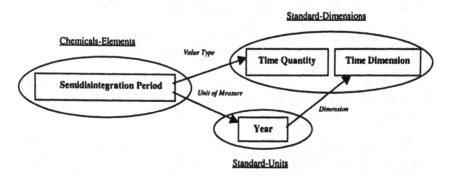

Figure 4. Relation between the Standard-Units and Standard-Dimensions ontologies.

When reviewing all the units of measure present in Chemical-Elements, we checked that they all appeared in Standard-Units. Any that were missing were added. Basically, there were two manners of reviewing the Standard-Units ontology: (1) Review the Ontolingua code of the ontology at the symbolic level, which means that the ontology has to be analyzed using Ontology Server facilities. This option was rejected as domain experts do not understand formal ontologies codified in ontology languages [1]. So, they could neither validate nor formalize knowledge without an ontologist's help; and (2) Review the ontology at the knowledge level using the work method described in section 4. This is the approach taken in this paper. The following describes how the work method was applied to the Standard-Units ontology.

5.2   Reverse engineering

The Standard-Units ontology was analyzed on the basis of its Ontolingua implementation. Figure 5 shows a preliminary conceptual model that possibly originated such implementation. It is important to note that this ontology contains neither relations, functions nor axioms. The hierarchy illustrates that there are two classes: Unit-Of-Measure and System-of-Units, both defined in the Physical-Quantities ontology. In this manner, a series of units of measure which are instances of the class Unit-Of-Measure are defined in Standard-Units, as well as a class, Si-Unit, which groups all the SI units. Additionally, Si-Unit is defined as an instance of the class System-of-Units, as there could be other systems grouping another series of units, which are also, instances of units of Unit-Of-Measure.

In the Standard-Units ontology, all the units have a property that indicates the dimension of the aforesaid unit. These dimensions are defined in the Standard-Dimensions ontology, which has two hierarchies. The hierarchy representing the definition of dimensions is shown in figure 6. In this ontology, there is a class, called Physical-Dimension, which is also defined in the `Physical-Quantities` ontology, of which all the dimensions defined are instances.

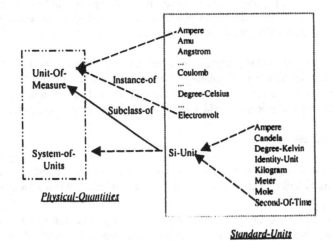

Figure 5. Preliminary hierarchy of the Standard-Units ontology.

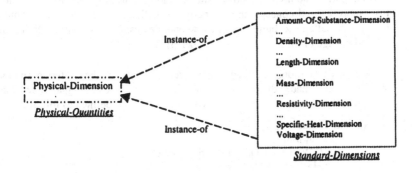

Figure 6. One of the hierarchies of the `Standard-Dimensions` *ontology.*

5.3 Restructure to create a new conceptual model

Here we summarize some design criteria and a set of principles that have proved useful in the development of ontologies. Gruber [17] identified five design criteria: *Clarity and Objectivity*, which means that the ontology should provide the meaning of defined terms by providing objective definitions and also natural language documentation; *Completeness*, which means that a definition expressed by a necessary and sufficient condition is preferred over a partial definition (defined only by a necessary or sufficient condition); *Coherence*, to permit inferences that are consistent with the definitions; *Maximize monotonic extendibility*, which means that new general or specialized terms should be included in the ontology in a such way as does not require the revision of existing definitions; and *Minimal ontological commitments*[6], which means making as few claims as possible about the world being modeled, giving the parties committed to the ontology freedom to specialize and instantiate the ontology as required. When building taxonomies, the Ontological Distinction Principle [7] proposes that classes in an ontology should be disjoint. The criterion used to isolate the core of properties considered to be invariant for an instance of a class is called the Identity Criterion.

This section presents the process used to restructure Standard-Units ontology. This ontology was restructured bearing in mind its future use by the Chemical-Elements, Monatomic-Ions and Environmental-Pollutants ontologies. It also provides a set of guidelines, which can be used, for building ontologies.

5.3.1 Analysis

Taking into account figures 5 and 6, and the Standard-Units and Standard-Dimensions Ontolingua code, the most prominent problems and faults found are:

1. There is no taxonomic organization identifying the general concepts that divide into other more specific concepts all the way down to instances. By contrast, there is a single class to which all the instances are subordinated. This is not really correct. First, the instances cannot be classified by similar characteristics. Second, part of the inference power allowing some concepts to inherit properties from more general concepts in a properly diversified hierarchy is lost. It would be more beneficial to build branched taxonomies using an identity criterion to take advantage of the above-mentioned benefits.

2. Definitions that should be made in the same manner, as they refer to similar concepts, are made differently in the implemented Ontolingua code. For example, the SI base unit of measure called Ampere was defined as follows:

```
(Define-Frame Ampere
    : Own-Slots
    (( Documentation "Si electrical current unit.")
    (Instance-Of Unit-Of-Measure)
    (Quantity.Dimension Electrical-Current-Dimension))
    : Axioms
    ((= (Quantity.Dimension Ampere) Electrical-Current-Dimension)))
```

However, the following instance definition was used to define Meter, which is another SI base unit:

```
(Define-Instance Meter (Unit-Of-Measure)
    "SI length unit. No conversion is given because this is a standard."
    : Axiom-Def
    (And (= (Quantity.Dimension Meter) Length-Dimension)
        (Si-Unit Meter)))
```

---

[6] "Ontological commitments are an agreement to use the shared vocabulary in a coherent and consistent manner. They guarantee consistency, but not completeness of an ontology" [18].

It would be advantageous to use the same pattern to make sibling definitions, thus improving ontology understanding and making it easier to include new definitions. This would improve the clarity of the ontology and its monotonic extendibility.

3. The choice of names for the different instances does not comply with a fixed standard. For example, the different multiples and divisors of Ampere are called: Milli-Amp, Nano-Ampere and Pico-Ampere. To ease ontology understanding and improve its clarity, the same naming conventions should be used to name related terms. Therefore, the above-mentioned names should be standardized and denoted as follows: Milli-Ampere, Nano-Ampere and Pico-Ampere.

4. The multiples of the base units do not appear to have been chosen systematically. For instance, Kilo-ohm and Milli-meter are omitted. Incompleteness is a fundamental problem in ontologies [14]. In fact, we cannot prove either the completeness of an ontology or the completeness of its definitions (an omission can always be found), but we can prove both the incompleteness of a definition or the incompleteness of an ontology, if at least one definition is missing with respect to the established framework of reference. When restructuring the Standard-Units ontology, our framework was the set of units of interest for the Chemical-Elements, Monatomic-Ions and Environmental-Pollutants ontologies. As Kilo-ohm and Milli-meter will not be used in these ontologies, we can say that the Standard-Units ontology is complete in this framework of reference.

5. The ontology includes factors of conversion between different units of the same dimension. However, this conversion is not always made from one particular unit to the unit that is considered as the base unit in the SI. For example, taking the base unit of time Second, each definition of its multiples (minutes, hours, etc.) and its submultiples (millisecond, microsecond, etc.) should contain the appropriate factor of conversion to seconds. However, definitions appear in the Standard-Units ontology with factors of conversion as follows:

> (Define-Frame Day
> : Own-Slots
> ((Documentation "one day, i.e. 24 hours")
> (Instance-Of Unit-Of-Measure)
> (Quantity.Dimension Time-Dimension))
> : Axioms
> ((= Day (* 24 Hours)) (= Year (* 365 Day))))

In this definition, the factors of conversion of the unit Day are established in relation to non-base units (hours and years), but not to the base unit (seconds). The following factor of conversion should be added to the formal definition:

> ((= Day (* 86400 Second-Of-Time)))

The conversion should always be made to the base unit to improve the clarity of the ontology. Other commonly used factors of conversion between units can also be added, but the conversion to the base unit should never be missing.

6. Some definitions have quite a poor informal language description, which provides the user with no information. This is the case of the natural language definition of Meter, which states: "SI length unit. No conversion is given because this is a standard." An extreme example is Kilometer, for which no informal definition is given at all. A natural language definition should be included whenever possible to give a better understanding of the more formal definition made later. In the example, " A Meter is 1650763.73 wave lengths in vacuo of the unperturbed transition $2p_{10}$ - $5d_5$ in ^{86}Kr."

7. The vocabulary of the Standard-Dimensions ontology has not been used in a standardized manner either. Thus, for example, the dimension Megapascal is defined as a Pressure-Dimension:

(Quantity.Dimension Megapascal Pressure-Dimension)

whereas the dimension Pascal is said to be:

(= (Quantity.Dimension Pascal)
(* Force-Dimension (Expt Length-Dimension -2)))

As the Pressure-Dimension definition exists in the Standard-Dimensions ontology, which is used by Standard-Units, it would be more rational and clearer to define all the units of pressure using this dimension, instead of using its equivalent in units of length and force. Therefore, the dimension Pascal should be defined as follows:

(Quantity.Dimension Pascal Pressure-Dimension)

8. In the Standard-Units ontology, the number Pi (π) is defined as an instance of the real numbers because a factor of conversion between angles and radians appears in the definition of Angular-Degree.

(Define-Instance **Angular-Degree** (Unit-Of-Measure)
"Angular measurement unit."
:= (* Radian (/ The-Number-Pi 180))
:Axiom-Def (= (Quantity.Dimension Angular-Degree) Identity-Dimension[7]))

As this is an ontology of units of measure, definitions that have nothing to do with the above units must not be included. This problem could be solved in two ways: one possible solution would be to delete the definition of the number π in the factor of conversion and enter the real number 3.1415926535897936. However, a better and modular solution is to include the real number π in the KIF-Numbers ontology, which could be included in the Standard-Units ontology and thus this definition could be used.

When an ontology is restructured, a series of criteria must be established beforehand to assess why the new ontology outputted is of higher quality than its predecessor. The following criteria were established when Standard-Units was

---

[7] Identity-Dimension is the identity element for * operator on physical-dimensions. This means that the product of identity-dimension and any other dimension is the other dimension.

restructured: (1) establish the framework of reference against which to prove the completeness of the ontology; (2) model the knowledge of the domain using the ontological distinction principle; (3) build taxonomies that allow property inheritance to be applied; (4) define terms uniformly, using the same patterns to define similar terms, which improves the clarity of the ontology, its understanding by future users and its monotonic extendibility; (5) the documentation accompanying each definition must be clear, useful and give a better understanding of the formal definition of the term; and (6) increase the information contained in the original ontology. If the original ontology was found not to contain enough domain knowledge, new classes, instances, relations, functions and axioms should be added to the new implementation.

5.3.2 Synthesis

As mentioned above, the Standard-Units ontology was analyzed because it is used in Chemical-Elements, which is used in the Monatomic-Ions, which is included in the Environmental-Pollutants ontology. After analyzing the Standard-Units Ontolingua code and obtaining a possible underlying conceptual model of the ontology and after considering the problems explained above, we modified the conceptual model of the Standard-Units ontology as follows:

Standardize naming conventions. We gave standard names to the new classes and instances. The names of the classes in the Standard-Units ontology were chosen taking into account the type of units represented and the names of the dimensions found in the Standard-Dimensions ontology.

Specialization of concepts. The goal was to identify general concepts that are specialized into more specific and disjoint concepts down to domain instances. The identity criterion used for specialization was to group units according to the base unit. Therefore, we can say that the restructured ontology complies with the Ontological Distinction Principle. For example, all the units for measuring length are grouped within the same class. The name of this class is Length-Unit, and its instances are: Meter (SI base unit), Angstrom, Centimeter, Foot, Inch, Kilometer and Mile. In this case, the new conceptual model includes one class for each type of SI base. We have created 19 new classes, and all these classes are disjoint. We also have maximized the monotonic extendibility of the Standard-Units ontology because the inclusion of classes and instances does not require the revision of existing definitions.

Branched taxonomies. Whenever possible, the hierarchy must be sufficiently branched by similar characteristics to increase the power provided by inheritance mechanisms between classes and instances. Figure 7 illustrates the new hierarchy, which should be interpreted as: all the concepts of the first branch are subclasses of the Unit-Of-Measure class, and the terms represented in boxes are instances of the concept to which they are linked by an arrow.

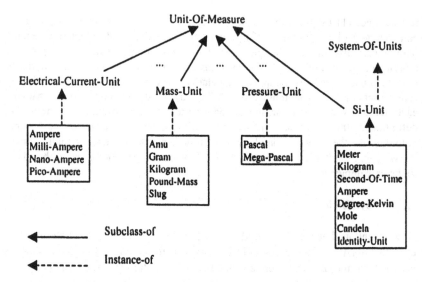

Figure 7. Taxonomy for the Modified Conceptual Model.

Inclusion of new properties and changes to existing properties. In this ontology, the property Abbreviation was added to each unit defined for the purpose of extending the use of this international standard for this attribute, ruling out widespread, though not absolutely correct, uses. In this manner, all the people who use this ontology will be accustomed to using the same standard abbreviation.

Minimize the semantic distance between sibling concepts [2]. Similar concepts are usually grouped and represented as subclasses of one class and should be defined using the same set of primitives, whereas concepts which are less similar are presented further apart in the hierarchy. All the terms in the restructured ontology have been defined using the same pattern in order to give a clearer understanding of the ontology. In this case, the factors of conversion have been expressed from any unit to its SI base unit. For any units that are not part of the SI base, the unit most commonly used by the international scientific community was chosen as the base unit used for the purpose of conversion. It is important to note that all the factors of conversion between units of the same type could be included, if considered useful, as this would not increase ontology complexity.

5.3.3   Configuration management: Standard-Units

In Software Engineering, configuration management has three objectives [20]: (1) establish and maintain the integrity of the products generated during a software development project and throughout the entire product life cycle; (2) evaluate and control the changes made to products, that is, control the evolution of the software system; and (3) ease the understanding of product evolution. Therefore, configuration management applied to the ontological engineering field can be considered as a means of assuring the quality of the ontologies and can, therefore, be included to supplement validation and verification activities [15].

For the purpose of assuring information about the evolution of the Standard-Units ontology, a rigorous change control has been performed throughout the restructuring phase. The goal is to have all the changes documented, detailing the changes made, their causes and effects. It is important to perform proficient change control of both definitions and taxonomies. In this manner, any ontologist who needs to use part of or the entire ontology can easily understand its evolution. Even if an ontology has not been fully developed, provided it is well documented, it could be finished off by another developer using the existing documentation. The configuration management documents can rule out incorrect decision making, if they state the courses of action to be taken at any time, and justify the choice of one rather than another. Change control also helps end users to determine which version of the ontology they require for their system or for the new ontology they are to develop.

Change control starts with a petition for change, followed by the classification and registration, approval or initial rejection and evaluation of the change petition, submission of the change report to the Change Control Committee, performance of the change and certification that the change was made correctly. It ends when the result is reported to the person who proposed the change. Figure 8 presents an example of a control report for a change made to the Standard-Units ontology.

Description of the Change: Modify the hierarchy of the *Standard-Units* ontology shown in figure 2, as it does not include intermediate classes that represent each type of SI base unit. In this model, all the instances of the ontology depend on one class.

Need for Change: It is not technically correct to have a class from which all the instances of the ontology hang. This structure prevents concepts being classed by similar characteristics, and some of the inference power allowing concepts to inherit properties from other more general concepts in a properly diversified hierarchy is lost.

Effects of the Change: The hierarchy has been satisfactorily branched, as shown in figure 7. In this case, one class has been created for each type of SI base unit. This change affects all the instances of the ontology, as the Unit-Of-Measure class has to be replaced in the formal definition of the instances by the new class representing the SI base unit to which they belong.

Alternatives: None.

Date of change: 27/03/98.

Change made: Changes are shown in figure 7.

Figure 8. Change control report.

5.4   Forward engineering: implementation of the new ontology

The new conceptual model of the Standard-Units ontology was reimplemented in Ontolingua using the Ontology Server editor. The new ontology has also been evaluated. In fact, (1) The ontology is syntactically correct, as it successfully passes the Ontology Server Analyze tests; (2) the ontology is complete for its use in Chemical-Elements, Monatomic-Ions and Environmental-Pollutants ontologies. The experts checked that it is possible to specify the units of measure of the properties identified in these ontologies. They also verified with ontologists that the checks identified in the inspection document have been made; (3) the ontology is internally consistent and the knowledge formalized has been checked against the above-mentioned sources of knowledge; and (4) the ontology is concise, as there is no redundant knowledge.

6   Review of Chemical-Elements

The need to use the Chemical-Elements ontology in the Monatomic-Ions and Environmental-Pollutants ontologies led us to review this ontology, as we had done for Standard-Units. The result of the review process showed that the different versions of the ontology needed to be merged to output a new unified and corrected ontology which could be extended before being included in the Monatomic-Ions ontology. The Chemical-Elements review process was divided into three clearly separate types of activities: technical evaluation, merging and configuration management.

Technical evaluation. The knowledge present in the conceptual model of the ontology was technically evaluated [14] (verified and validated) with chemical and environmental experts for the purpose of ascertaining whether the knowledge represented was correct and complete and detecting any missing knowledge. As with Standard-Units, we decided to review the conceptual model of the Chemical-Elements ontology at the knowledge level using a series of intermediate representations proposed by METHONTOLOGY. For this purpose, the conceptual model of the ontology was given to the chemical and environmental experts, along with an explanation of the meaning of the intermediate representations. The experts and ontologists verified and validated the model in 6 hours and reached the following conclusions: (1) add properties that are useful from the viewpoint of both the chemical element in its pure state and the environment; (2) retain any properties that, although they are not useful for the monatomic ions ontology, can be used to represent elements in their pure state; (3) adapt the names chosen; (4) check the values of the class and instance attributes for correctness using the sources of information recommended by the chemical and the environmental experts; and (5) validate (experts) that the definitions represented formally correspond with the knowledge that they were supposed to represent contained in books, handbooks, etc.

Merging. Development of the Chemical-Elements ontology commenced in June 1995, and a first stable version was produced in December 1996 [10]. Since then, different versions of this ontology have been created and used: (1) to extend the intermediate representations used at the conceptualization phase of METHONTOLOGY; (2) to test the usefulness and validity of the new intermediate representations proposed; (3) by the Ontogeneration system [1], which allows Spanish users to consult and access the knowledge contained in the Chemical-Elements ontology in their own language. A unified conceptual model was built merging all the releases of this ontology, and includes all the improvements.

Configuration Management was carried out according to the guidelines described in section 5.3.3 to make this new version of Chemical-Elements easier to understand for users. As a result, a Chemical-Elements configuration management document was outputted that includes a series of change control reports related to the terms modified in this ontology.

Conclusions

Although the concept of reengineering is well established in Software Engineering, the field of reengineering is totally new in the Ontological Engineering field. Therefore, the main contributions of this paper are to start up research into a process that allows any ontology to be reengineered, and configuration management and change control to be carried out on the ontology as a result of this reengineering activity. The main contributions can be summarized as a preliminary method was proposed for Ontological Reengineering, which includes three activities: Reverse Engineering, Restructuring and Forward Engineering. The *reverse engineering* activity produces a preliminary conceptual model of the ontology from its code. The *restructuring* activities involve: (1) performing a technical evaluation of the initial conceptual model with the expert; (2) reorganizing and extending the initial conceptual model to output a new conceptual model according to a series of criteria (standardize naming conventions, specialize concepts, branch taxonomies, minimize the semantic distance between sibling concepts, etc.) established beforehand. The restructuring process is carried out bearing in mind the use of the restructured ontology by the ontology/application that reuses it; (3) keep records of the changes performed; and (4) build a new, more correct conceptual model, accepted by the experts. The *forward engineering* activity produces a document containing the implementation of the new conceptual model, including the suggested changes. The reengineering process includes the evaluation of both the original and the resulting ontology, and performing configuration management to keep records of ontology evolution, the changes made, their causes and effects.

Future work will include primarily: (1) addressing in more depth the theoretical foundations of ontology reengineering, (2) extending the work method proposed after reengineering more complex ontologies that include relations, functions and axioms, apart from taxonomies of concepts and instances, and (3) developing flexible tools to automate the reengineering process.

Acknowledgements

We would like to express our thanks to the following persons: Almudena Galán and Rosario García, for their knowledge of chemistry and the environment; Mariano Fernández, for providing Chemicals and all the documentation required to understand its construction and evolution; Sofía Pinto, for her help in Chemical-Elements configuration management; and Juan Manuel García-Pinar and Mariano Fernández again, for converting the Chemicals ontologies from the earlier ODE tool format to the current version. We also thank the anonymous reviewers for their comments.

References

[1] Aguado, G.; Bañón, A.; Bateman, J.; Bernardos, S.; Fernández, M.; Gómez-Pérez, A.; Nieto, E.; Olalla, A.; Plaza, R.; Sánchez, A. *"ONTOGENERATION: Reusing domain and linguistic ontologies for Spanish text generation."* Workshop on Applications of Ontologies and Problem Solving Methods. ECAI-98. Brighton (UK). 1998. **The 13th European Conference on Artificial Intelligence.**

[2]   Arpírez, J.; Gómez-Pérez. A.; Lozano, A.; Pinto, H.S. *"(ONTO)²Agent: An Ontology-Based WWW broker to select ontologies."* ECAI-98. Brighton (UK). 1998. Workshop on Applications of Ontologies and Problem Solving Methods. **The 13th European Conference on Artificial Intelligence.**

[3]   Barley, M.; Clark, P.; Williamson, K.; Woods, S. *"The neutral Representation Project."* Boing Research and Technology. **Ontological Engineering. AAAI-97** Spring Symposium Series. March 97. Stanford University. California. 1997.

[4]   Blázquez, M.; Fernández, M.; García-Pinar, J.M.; Gómez-Pérez, A. *"Building Ontologies at the Knowledge Level using the Ontology Design Environment."* **KAW98.** Banff, Canada. 1998.

[5]   Blum, B. *"Software Engineering. A holistic view."* Oxford University Press. 1992.

[6]   Böhm, C.; Jacopini, G. *"Flow diagrams, Turing machinesd, and languages with only two formation rules."* Communications of the ACM, May 1996. PP:366-371.

[7]   Borgo, S.; Guarino,N.; Masolo, C. *"Stratified Ontologies: The case of physical objects".* **Workshop on Ontological Engineering. ECAI96.** Budapest. PP: 5-15

[8]   Chikofsky, E.J.; Cross II, J.H. *"Reverse Engineering and design recovery: A taxonomy."* Software Magazine. January 1990. PP:13-17.

[9]   Farquhar, A.; Fikes, R.; Pratt, W.; Rice, J. *"A collaborative ontology construction for information integration."* Technical Report KSL-95-63. Knowledge Systems Laboratory. Stanford University. 1995.

[10]   Fernández, M. *"CHEMICALS: Ontología de elementos químicos."* Proyecto Fin de Carrera. Facultad de Informática de Madrid. UPM. December 1996.

[11]   Fernández, M.; Gómez-Pérez, A.; Juristo, N. *"METHONTOLOGY: From Ontological Art Towards Ontological Engineering".* **Ontological Engineering. AAAI-97.** Spring Symposium Series. Stanford 1997. PP:33-40.

[12]   Fernández, M.; Gómez-Pérez, A.; Pazos, A.; Pazos, J. *"Building a Chemical Ontology using METHONTOLOGY and the Ontology Design Environment."* IEEE Intelligent Systems. Special Issue on Uses of Ontologies. January/February 1999.

[13]   Genesereth, M.R.; Fikes, R. *"Knowledge Interchange Format. Version 3.0 Reference Manual"* Tech Report Logic-92-1. Computer Science, Stanford University (CA)1992.

[14]   Gómez-Pérez, A. *"A framework to verify knowledge sharing technology".* Expert Systems with Application. Vol.11, N.4. 1996 . PP:519-529).

[15]   Gómez-Pérez, A. *"Knowledge Sharing and Reuse".* The Handbook of Applied Expert Systems. Edited by Liebowitz. CRC. 1998.

[16]   Gómez-Pérez, A.; Juristo, N.; Pazos, J. *"Evaluation and Assessment of the Knowledge Sharing Technology."* Towards Very Large Knowledge Bases. N.J.I. Mars, Ed. IOS Press, 1995.

[17]   Gruber, T. *"Towards Principles for the Design of Ontologies".* Ksl-93-04. Knowledge Systems Laboratory. Stanford University. 1993.

[18]   Gruber, T.;Olsen, G. *"An ontology for Engineering Mathematics".* **Fourth International Conference on Principles of Knowledge Representation and Reasoning.** Doyle, Torasso y Sandewall (eds.) Morgan Kaufmann. 1994.

[19]   Julling, R.; Srinivas, Y.V.; Blaine, L.; Gilham, L.M.; McDonald, J.; Waldinger, R. *"Specware language manual."* Tech Report, Kestrel Institute. 1995.

[20]   Pressman, R.S. *"Ingeniería del Software. Un enfoque práctico."* Mac-Graw Hill. 1993.

[21]   Yourdon, E. *"RE-3. Re-engineering, restructuring and reverse engineering."* American Programmer Magazine, Vol.2, Nº4, April 1989. PP:3-10.

Formally Verifying Dynamic Properties of Knowledge Based Systems

Perry Groot, Annette ten Teije*, and Frank van Harmelen

Dept. of Computer Science and Mathematics
Vrije Universiteit Amsterdam
{perry,annette,frankh}@cs.vu.nl

Abstract. In this paper we study dynamic properties of knowledge-based systems. We argue the importance of such dynamic properties for the construction and analysis of knowledge-based systems. We present a case-study of a simple classification method for which we formulate and verify two dynamic properties which are concerned with the anytime behaviour and the computation trace of the classification method. We show how Dynamic Logic can be used to formally express these dynamic properties. We have used the KIV interactive theorem prover to obtain machine-assisted proofs for all the properties and theorems in this paper.

1 Introduction

1.1 Motivation

A characteristic property of Knowledge Based Systems (KBSs) is that they deal with intractable computational tasks: diagnosis, design, and classification are all tasks for which even the simple varieties are intractable. As a result, simple uninformed search procedures cannot be used to construct realistic knowledge-based systems for complex tasks.

A traditional approach in Knowledge Engineering is to equip a KBS with strong control-knowledge that is used to guide the computation [1, 4, 12]. Such control knowledge consists of knowledge on the sequence of reasoning steps during problem solving, and is an essential part of expertise. Examples of such control knowledge are the order in which observations must be obtained during diagnostic reasoning, or the order in which components must be configured during design reasoning. Many Knowledge Engineering methodologies provide some form of expressing the control knowledge in a KBS [28, 20, 3, 27].

A more recent, and less explored approach to dealing with the intractability of KBSs is the development of anytime algorithms [19]. An anytime algorithm gradually approaches the perfect solution. As runtime increases, the quality of the solution increases. The algorithm can be interrupted at any moment, for instance when no more computation time is available, at which point the currently available solution is returned. Such methods have been employed in planning [6] and diagnosis [22] among others.

* Supported by the Netherlands Computer Science Research Foundation with financial support from the Netherlands Organisation for Scientific Research (NWO), project: 612-32-006

Both of these approaches to dealing with the intractability of KBSs (adding control knowledge and developing anytime algorithms) are concerned with *"how" solutions are computed*, and not (or: not only) with *"what" counts as a solution*. This distinction between "what" and "how" corresponds to the distinction between functional and dynamic properties of a system. Purely functional properties are concerned with the relation between inputs and outputs of the system. Dynamic properties on the other hand are concerned with the computation process itself, and not only with the final output of this process.

The typical example of a functional property is the I/O-relation of a system. Examples of dynamic properties are the number of required computation steps, the sequence in which these computation steps are taken, etc.

In this view, dynamic properties are a refinement of functional properties: two implementations of the same functional I/O-relation can have very different dynamic properties. On the other hand any two systems for which all the dynamic properties coincide necessarily have the same functional I/O-relation.

In this paper we will investigate how to formally express and verify dynamic properties of KBSs.

1.2 Approach

As stated above, we are aiming at studying the dynamic properties of KBSs: formally stating such properties, and proving whether or not such properties hold for a given KBS. In Software Engineering, many formal frameworks have been developed for a formal analysis of dynamic properties. See [24] and references included therein for a number of these approaches.

Within Knowledge Engineering formal analysis of properties has been mostly limited to functional properties ([10, 11, 26, 23], with DESIRE [5, 15] as an exception). Such functional analysis can be fruitfully formalised and carried out in Dynamic Logic [14, 17], as illustrated in [25, 7, 9].

The approach we will take in this paper is to use the same logic that has been used for analysis of functional properties (Dynamic Logic), but now for the analysis of dynamic properties. This is in contrast with work in [5, 15], where a formalism is used which is specifically designed to deal with dynamic properties. The use of Dynamic Logic has as immediate advantage that we can exploit the support offered for this formalism by interactive theorem provers like the KIV system [18], which has been used with some success before for the formal analysis of functional properties of KBSs [10, 11].

The use of Dynamic Logic for the analysis of dynamic properties is not unproblematic. In Dynamic Logic it is not possible to directly say something about an internal state of a program. In Dynamic Logic a program is seen as a pair of states: *(start, end)*. Thus programs with the same *(start,end)* state are equivalent, irrespective of the behavior that gets them from the *start* state to the *end* state. By using constructs like $\langle \alpha \rangle \phi$ we can only conclude ϕ *after* termination of program α.

We can solve this problem in the following way: given a program α, we construct a new program α' which has additional parameters. These parameters are used to encode some of the behaviour of the original program α in the I/O-relation of the program α'.

For example, we might encode the sequence of internal states of the program α in an additional output argument to α'. This additional output argument then constitutes a trace of the program α and can be used to formulate dynamic properties of α in terms of the output from α'. In effect, we are encoding some of the dynamic properties of α as functional properties of the modified program α'. This will then allow us to express and prove dynamic properties within the limitations of Dynamic Logic.

1.3 Structure and contributions of this paper

In this paper, we will take the approach outlined above and apply it to two simple case-studies. In Sect. 2 we describe a simple task-definition and problem solving method for classification. In Sect. 3 we present an anytime adaptation of this PSM. We formally express and prove a number of dynamic properties of this PSM, such as its behaviour when run-time increases, and its eventual convergence to the non-anytime PSM. In Sect. 4 we encode part of the computation trace of the classification PSM in an additional output argument, and use this to prove some properties about the control knowledge that was exploited in the PSM. In the final section, we discuss the pro's and con's of the approach taken in this paper and how well these two case-studies generalise to other dynamic properties.

This paper makes the following contributions:

Analysing dynamic properties Whereas existing literature on KBSs typically deals with functional properties, we study a number of simple dynamic properties, in particular the anytime nature of our classification algorithm and the computation trace of this algorithm.

Using Dynamic Logic We show how such dynamic properties can be formally expressed in a logical formalism, namely First Order Dynamic Logic.

Machine-assisted proofs We have formally verified these properties in machine assisted proofs using the KIV interactive verifier.

Generalisation We suggest how our analysis of the specific dynamic properties (anytime behaviour and computation trace) for a simple classification algorithm can be stated in the general case.

2 A simple Problem Solving Method

For our case study we use a very simple PSM, namely *linear filtering*. It iterates over a set of candidates to produce a set of solutions which all satisfiy a given filter criterion. This filter criterion is applied to individual candidates c_i, and will be written $correct(c_i)$. The task-definition of the PSM is then:

$$c_i \in output(cs) \leftrightarrow c_i \in cs \wedge correct(c_i), \tag{1}$$

or equivalently: $output(cs) = \{c_i | c_i \in cs \wedge correct(c_i)\}$.

This is a very generic task-definition, which comprises any task for which the output criteria can be stated in terms of individual candidates. Simple forms of classification, diagnosis and configuration can all be phrased in this format, using an appropriate definition for $correct(c_i)$ [1].

The procedural definition of our linear-filtering PSM is as follows:

```
filter#(cs; var output)
begin
  if cs = ∅ then output := ∅ else
    var candidate = select(cs) in
    if correct(candidate) then
      begin
        filter#(cs \ candidate;output);
        output := insert(candidate, output)
      end
    else
      filter#(cs \ candidate;output)
end
```

Fig. 1. PSM for classification by linear filtering

First, we check if no candidate classes are left. If so, we return the empty set, if not, we select an arbitrary candidate. If the candidate is correct it is inserted in the output set that is computed recursively. The only requirement we need to impose on the selection step is that it does indeed select one of the available classes:

$$cs \neq \emptyset \rightarrow select(cs) \in cs \qquad (2)$$

The linear filtering method that we use is quite naive. It only works for small candidate-sets, but it is adequate to demonstrate the ideas in this paper.

In terms of the specification framework of [8], formula (1) is the goal-definition. In our simple example, this goal-definition coincides exactly with the competence description of the PSM from Fig. 1. We therefore do not give a separate competence description for the above PSM. Below, we will use *filter(cs)* when we mean the competence of the filter# program.[2]

Use of KIV: The KIV interactive verifier for dynamic logic [18] was used to automatically generate the proof obligations that are required to show the termination of the PSM from Fig. 1 and its correctness with respect to its competence description (which is equal to the predicate *output* from formula (1)). Both proof obligations were proven in the KIV system. The termination proof consisted of 16 proof steps of which 8 were automatic, the correctness proof required 67 proof steps, of which 38 were automatic.

---

[1] Tasks which concern some *relation* between candidates, such as some minimality or maximality criterion, cannot be stated in this form, for example optimisation problems, or computing minimal diagnoses.

[2] Symbols ending in # are used to denote operational descriptions. The same symbol without the trailing # denotes the corresponding competence description.

3 Anytime Problem Solvers: PSMs with bounded run-Time

In this paper we are studying the dynamic properties of KBSs. In this section we will study an anytime PSM, since for such a PSM the analysis of its dynamic properties are of central importance. Remember that an anytime algorithm gradually approaches the perfect solution, and can be interrupted at any moment when no more computation time is available, at which point the currently available solution is returned.

We will be interested in dynamic properties of this PSM, such as its behaviour when run-time increases, and the gradual convergence of the anytime behaviour to the optimal solution.

3.1 Operationalisation of an anytime PSM

Our original program `filter#` returned the subset of all correct elements (solution classes) of a given input set (candidate classes) and was sound and complete w.r.t. its competence description. But this is only true under the assumption that it can have all the time it needs to compute its output. With this in mind we can adjust our program to another program, which we will call *filter-bounded*, which gets an integer as additional parameter. This integer will be a bound on the number of steps the program can do and can be interpreted as a bound on the program run-time.

This additional parameter n makes this PSM into an anytime algorithm: the method returns a sensible approximation of the final answer, even when allowed only a limited amount of run-time (i.e. when the time-bound is smaller than the number of classes that must be considered). The program terminates when n reaches zero and n decreases by one in every recursive call, and is shown in the figure below. We have indicated the differences with the original code of the `filter#` program. These differences are only: an additional parameter n, which is decreased in every recursive call, plus an additional test on $n = 0$ to prematurely end the recursion.

```
filter-bounded#(cs, n ; var output)
begin
  if cs = ∅ V n = 0 then output := ∅ else
    var candidate = select(cs) in
    if correct(candidate) then
      begin
        filter-bounded#(cs \ candidate, n-1 ;output);
        output := insert(candidate, output)
      end
    else
      filter-bounded#(cs \ candidate, n-1 ;output)
end
```

Fig. 2. Anytime version of the linear filtering PSM

3.2 Competence description of an anytime PSM

We will now give a declarative description of the competence of the anytime PSM described above. In this competence-description, we will make use of the competence-description for the non-anytime version given above in formula (1).

$$filter\text{-}bounded(cs, 0) = \emptyset \tag{3}$$

$$filter\text{-}bounded(cs, n) \subseteq filter\text{-}bounded(cs, n + 1) \tag{4}$$

$$\|filter\text{-}bounded(cs, n + 1)\| = \|filter\text{-}bounded(cs, n)\| \vee \tag{5}$$
$$\|filter\text{-}bounded(cs, n + 1)\| = \|filter\text{-}bounded(cs, n)\| + 1,$$

$$\|cs\| \leq n \rightarrow filter\text{-}bounded(cs, n) = filter(cs) \tag{6}$$

Axiom (3) states that *filter-bounded* returns the empty set when it gets no computation time. Axiom (4) states that the output set of *filter-bounded* can only increase monotonically with increasing run-time. Axiom (5) states that the number of output classes (indicated by the function $\| \cdot \|$) increases by at most one element if we allow one more computation step. Finally, axiom (6) states that if the number of allowed computation steps is at least as large as the number of candidate classes, then *filter-bounded* is identical to *filter*.

Observe that all axioms are necessary to characterize the filter-bounded# program. Omitting an axiom would allow unwanted behavior. Two simple counterexamples are given as follows:

```
filter-bounded#(cs, n; var output)
begin
   filter#(cs;output)
end
```

```
filter-bounded#(cs, n; var output)
begin
   output := ∅
end
```

Neither of these programs have anytime behaviour. The left program (which simply calls the non-anytime version of the program) satisfies the axioms (4), (5) and (6) and the right program (which always returns the empty set) satisfies the axioms (3), (4) and (5), but both violate the remaining axiom. Similar counterexamples can be found for the other cases.

Use of KIV: The termination of filter-bounded# and its correctness with respect to axioms (3)–(6) were all proven in KIV with the following statistics: termination was proven in 16 steps, of which 8 were automatic; axiom (3) only took 3 steps, axioms (4)–(6) took around 80 steps each, with an automation degree of around 30%[3].

---

[3] Because KIV is a semi-automatic tool, these and subsequent degrees of automation are to some extend dependent on the skill of the user. More sophisticated KIV users assure us that for the rather simple proofs performed for this paper, the degree of automation could have been much higher.

3.3 Anytime properties

The PSM specified above does indeed have a number of properties which are to be expected of a reasonable anytime algorithm. We have stated and proven a number of such properties in KIV, and we will discuss these properties below.

First of all, notice that axiom (6) above can be interpreted as the *adapter* [8] that is required to bridge the gap between the goal description from formula (1) and the competence of the anytime algorithm. Since *filter*(cs) = *output*(cs), axiom (6) states that *filter-bounded* does indeed achieve the classification task under the assumption of sufficient run-time (namely n at least as large as the number of classes that must be checked).

Two other properties are

$$\|\textit{filter-bounded}(cs, n)\| \leq n.$$

This states that the number of elements in the output set is bounded by the number of computation steps, and

$$n < \|\textit{filter}(cs)\| \rightarrow \textit{filter-bounded}(cs, n) \subset \textit{filter}(cs).$$

This states that given insufficient time, the anytime algorithm always computes only a strict subset of the classical algorithm.

Use of KIV: Both properties were proven in KIV with the following statistics: the first property was proven in 14 steps, of which 8 were automatic; the second property was proven in 45 steps, of which 28 were automatic.

Properties such as these guarantee that the PSM does indeed behave in a desirable anytime fashion, gradually approaching the ideal competence when run-time increases. The above results show that it is possible to use Dynamic Logic to both specify and implement such anytime behaviour, and to prove the required properties within this logic.

Notice that all of these properties are formulated in terms of the declarative competence of the anytime PSM (the function *filter-bounded*, specified in axioms (3)–(6)). Since we have proven the correctness of the operationalisation `filter-bounded#` with respect to this competence, all of these properties are also guaranteed for the operational behaviour.

3.4 General approach to specifying anytime PSMs

In this subsection we will suggest a more general characterization of programs with a bound on their computation time. If we look at the 4 axioms from the *filter-bounded* specification we can find the following underlying general conditions:

- – axiom (3): start condition,
- – axiom (4): growth direction,
- – axiom (5): growth rate,
- – axiom (6): end condition.

The first condition describes the start of the program. For the `filter-bounded#` program this was just one axiom which stated that the program returned the empty set when given no computation time. Other versions of this axiom are also possible. As an example, consider a classification algorithm that works by gradually eliminating incorrect classes from the list of candidates (instead of gradually adding candidates, as our current algorithm does). Such an alternative algorithm would return the entire set of candidates when given no computation time, instead of the empty set as our current algorithm does.

The conditions on growth direction and growth rate state what happens when the program is allowed one additional computation step. Again, other algorithms might satisfy different variations of these conditions, for example a candidate elimination algorithm would have a decreasing output with increasing computation time.

Finally, the fourth condition states that, given sufficient computation time, the program will compute exactly the desired output.

Further case-studies are required to determine if this general pattern is indeed applicable to the specification of more (and perhaps all) anytime PSMs.

4 Writing History

The first case study was concerned with a particular class of algorithms with interesting dynamic behaviour (namely anytime algorithms). Our second case study is concerned with the control knowledge of KBSs. As argued in the introduction of this paper, control knowledge is a type of knowledge that is characteristic for a KBS.

In this section we adapt the original program `filter#` from Fig. 1, such that we encode the sequence of some executed steps explicitly in a trace of the algorithm. This trace is an output parameter of the slightly adapted program `filter-trace#`. We show how we can use such a trace for proving properties of a program. As simple example of a dynamic property of `filter#` we use the order in which the candidate classes are selected by the PSM.

As already announced in our motivation in Sect. 1, these properties are functional properties of the adapted program, but dynamic properties of the original program.

4.1 Operationalisation of a PSM extended with a trace

Again, we start from the original program `filter#` (Fig. 1). The slightly adapted version of `filter#` is our new program `filter-trace#` in Fig. 3. This program has an additional output parameter, namely a list of classes. This list reflects the order in which the classes are tested by the PSM. If a class c_1 is selected before a class c_2, then this is encoded in the order of the elements in the list. The only differences with respect to the original `filter#` program are the extra parameter called `trace` and a statement that adds the selected class to the trace.

Previously, the only requirement on the class-selection step (`select`) was that it did indeed select one of the available classes (axiom (2)). In order to incorporate some meaningful control knowledge in the algorithm (about which we want to prove properties by exploiting the encoded trace), we place an additional requirement on the `select`

```
filter-trace#(cs; var  trace , output)
begin
  if cs = ∅ then
    begin output := ∅;  trace := nil  end
  else
    var candidate = select(cs) in
    begin
      if correct(candidate) then
        begin
          filter-trace#(cs \ candidate;  trace , output);
          output := insert-class(candidate, output)
        end
      else
        begin
          filter-trace#(cs \ candidate;  trace , output);
        end
       trace := candidate :: trace
    end
end
```

Fig. 3. Version of the linear filtering PSM which computes a trace

function, namely that the classes of the input are selected using a heuristic function which selects the class with the highest heuristic value.

$$(c \in cs) \rightarrow measure(c) \leq measure(select(cs)).$$

The adapted filter-trace# program has two output parameters: trace and output. However, in a specification a function can only return one output. This technical obstacle can be avoided by introducing two auxiliary programs: one program for returning the trace parameter, and one for returning the output parameter. The trivial implementation of these auxiliary programs is as follows:

```
filter-trace-1#(cs; var output)
begin
  var trace = nil in
    filter-trace#(cs;trace, output)
end

filter-trace-2#(cs; var trace)
begin
  var output = ∅ in
    filter-trace#(cs;trace, output)
end
```

4.2 Competence of PSM extended with a trace

The program `filter-trace#` performs the same task as the original `filter#` program, in the sense that the same solutions will be computed (the output parameter). Furthermore the modified program produces some extra control knowledge information in the trace parameter.

As result, the competence specification of `filter-trace#` contains the axioms of the specification of the `filter#` program plus some additional axioms to specify the trace parameter[4]:

$$filter\text{-}trace\text{-}1(cs) = filter(cs) \tag{7}$$

$$in\text{-}list(c, filter\text{-}trace\text{-}2(cs)) \leftrightarrow c \in cs \tag{8}$$

$$filter\text{-}trace\text{-}2(cs) = c_1 :: cl \wedge in\text{-}list(c_2, cl) \rightarrow measure(c_2) \leq measure(c_1), \tag{9}$$

$$filter\text{-}trace\text{-}2(cs) = c_1 :: cl \rightarrow filter\text{-}trace\text{-}2(cs \setminus c_1) = cl. \tag{10}$$

Axioms (7) specifies that the original output will not be affected by the introduction of the trace. Axiom (8) states that the trace consists only of classes that were given in the input. Axioms (9) and (10) specify that the elements in the trace are ordered: if a class c_1 precedes class c_2 in the trace, then we must have that the heuristic value of c_1 is greater than or equal to that of c_2.

Use of KIV: Again, the termination and correctness of the `filter-trace#` program has been proven with respect to this competence:

- termination in 20 steps of which 12 automatic;
- axiom (7) in 75 steps (42 automatic);
- axiom (8) in 99 steps (58 automatic);
- axiom (9) in 37 steps (21 automatic);
- axiom (10) in 30 steps (21 automatic).

These figures confirm the above mentioned statistic of ±30% proof-automation by KIV.

Notice that the trace axioms (9)–(10) were not hard to verify, because they reflect the recursive nature of the program, and lend themselves to rather easy proofs by induction. However, finding these axioms was quite difficult. We considered a number of alternative formulations of these axioms. Although these alternative formulations were all logically equivalent, they did not reflect as nicely the recursive nature of the `filter-trace#` program, and were therefore much harder to prove.

We consider this to be a general trade-off. On the one hand we would like competence formulations to be as independent as possible of the implementation (leading us in the direction of natural specifications which are hard to prove). On the other hand, the competence formulations which are easy to prove are often very unnatural, exactly because they reflect too much of the implementation. In our experience, the competence formulations which are both natural and still easy to prove are often hard to find.

Two points remain to be noticed concerning the above competence specification of *filter-trace*: first, the dynamic behaviour of the original `filter#` program has indeed

---

[4] The notation $x :: y$ denotes the list with head x and tail y.

been specified as a functional property of the `filter-trace#` program. Secondly, the specification *filter-trace* "inherits" the entire original specification of *filter* by virtue of axiom (7). This ensures that when modifying *filter* to *filter-trace* in order to capture the dynamic behaviour, we have not interfered with the solution set of the original program.

4.3 General approach to specify properties of control knowledge

From the case-study of the previous paragraphs we can again distill a general pattern for dealing with dynamic properties concerning control knowledge. Given a competence specification and an operationalisation of a PSM, the steps involved in formulating and proving such dynamic properties are as follows:

1. **Choose the "trace semantics":** First of all, we must of course decide which aspects of the control knowledge must be captured. In our example this concerned the use of the heuristic function in determining the sequence of candidate classes. Another possibility in the above would have been to restrict the trace to only the sequence of solution classes (instead of the sequence of all considered candidate classes). Alternatively, we could have chosen a more refined trace, for instance modelling for every failed candidate class the observations that caused it to be excluded from the final solution. In general, the "grain size" of the trace is one of the important choices that must be made.

   A second choice concerns the ordering of the trace. In our example we have chosen to model the sequence of the intermediate states. An alternative choice would have been to abstract from the sequence of the intermediate states, treating all histories that go through the same set of states as equivalent. This latter option would have prevented us from stating (let alone proving) the required property expressed in axiom (9)-(10). This illustrates that in general, these choices are determined by the dynamic properties that one would like to prove.

2. **Introduce additional output parameter(s) for the trace:** The semantic choice made in the previous point must be encoded syntactically by modifying the original program. This amounts to adding code to the original algorithm plus additional output parameters to return the results of this extra code. In our example, the boxed line in Fig. 3 reflects the decision to model only the class-selection step. The choice of modelling the history-sequence is reflected by the use of a list for the `trace` parameter (instead of a set).

3. **Introduce auxiliary programs for additional output parameters:** As explained above, auxiliary programs are needed to side-step the technical limitations that specifications are expressed in functional terms, and therefore allow only one output parameter (in our example the programs `filter-trace-1#` and `-2#`).

4. **Introduce conservation axioms:** New axioms are required to enforce that the original output will not be affected by the additional code (axiom (7) above).

5. **Introduce behaviour axioms:** As a final step, add axioms that represent the dynamic properties of the original program. In our example these were axioms (8)–(10): the original `filter#` program considers the candidate classes in decreasing order of their heuristic value. This property is expressed as a functional property of the modified program `filter-trace#`.

5 Discussion, summary and conclusion

5.1 Discussion of our approach

Encoding dynamic properties as functional properties. The limitation of Dynamic Logic that any two programs with the same input and output states are equivalent forced us to encode dynamic properties of one program as functional properties of a modified program.

Our experiences with this encoding "trick" in Dynamic Logic have been surprisingly positive. The original structure of the program could easily be preserved while making the required modifications: the differences between the modified code in Figs. 2 and 3 and the original code in Fig. 1 are very small. This preservation of the original program structure was essential because it enabled us to reuse proofs of the original program to obtain proofs for the adjusted programs. Using the proof-reuse facilities of KIV, many of the termination and correctness proofs could be obtained rather easily.

Automatic PSM transformations. In fact, the differences in program code are so small that one could easily imagine an automatic transformation from the original program (Fig. 1) to the adjusted anytime and tracing programs (Figs. 2 and 3). Furthermore, it should be not too difficult to prove some meta-theorems that such transformations are correctness preserving[5], thereby obviating the proof obligations for the modified programs.

Using Dynamic Logic. Instead of Dynamic Logic, we could have chosen to use an alternative logic in which we could have directly expressed the dynamic properties in which we are interested. In particular, languages such as TR [2] and TROLL [16], and languages with a temporal semantics like DESIRE [27] and METATEM [13] have a trace-semantics, in which program-equivalence is determined not just by pairs of input-output states, but by the entire behavioural trace of the program. We see an important trade-off here. On the one hand such trace -logics would seem to require no additional encoding dynamic information. However, this is only the case if the trace-semantics provided by the logic is exactly what is needed to express the specific properties of interest. On the other hand, logics such as Dynamic Logic require additional encoding effort, but at the same time this allows us to determine exactly which dynamic information is required. Thus, the trade-off is between ease of use and flexibility.

Non-terminating programs. A potentially serious critique is that we can only deal with terminating programs, since non-terminating programs do not give rise to an output state. Important examples of such non-terminating programs are agent-systems, and KBS applications such as monitoring. A possible way around this problem resembles our approach to anytime algorithms. Instead of dealing with a non-terminating program α, we would prove properties about a modified program $\alpha'(n)$ that terminates after n steps. If we can then prove that this property holds for arbitrary values of n, we can think of α as running for an arbitrarily long time. In effect, we have replaced the notion of infinite run-time with that of arbitrarily long run-time.

---

[5] Such theorems are indeed meta-theorems: they cannot be expressed in Dynamic Logic itself because they require quantification over programs.

Toy nature of our PSM*s*. Our examples are unrealistically small, and cannot be used in realistic applications. For example, in multi-class classification (where an answers contains n classes, instead of just one), the number of answer-candidates growths exponentially with n. In such a case, our linear filtering PSM would not be very attractive. Nevertheless, we believe that the same results as presented in this paper can be obtained for more realistic PSM's. We are currently working on obtaining anytime-results for a collection of more realistic methods taken from a standard KBS textbook [21]

5.2 Evaluation of KIV

Our case-study was not meant as a serious evaluation study of KIV. Nevertheless, our experiences with KIV have been quite positive, for the following reasons. Firstly, KIV allows the hierarchical decomposition of the software system (both specifications and implementations). This achieves the usual advantages of modularity. Furthermore, KIV allows us to prove properties of higher level functions and programs (such filter#) without having to provide implementations of lower level programs, such as insert which is used by filter#. Instead, only a specification of these lower-level functions is required, abstracting from their implementation details.

Secondly, KIV performs correctness management, keeping track of which proofs are dependent on which others (the so-called lemma-graph). KIV also keeps track of which proof obligations have already been fulfilled or not, taking these dependencies into account. Furthermore, it calculates which proofs must be redone when parts of specifications and implementations are changed.

Thirdly, KIV is very user-friendly and easy to learn (certainly in comparison with other interactive theorem provers). Important features are its graphical user-interface (e.g. proofs displayed as trees, which can be used for proof-navigation, proof-replay and re-use, proof-cut-and-paste), its use of natural mathematical notation in both editing and displaying formulae, and the production of pretty-printed specifications, programs and proofs.

5.3 Summary and conclusions

In this paper we have shown how despite its limitations, Dynamic Logic can be fruitfully used to express and prove dynamic properties of problem solving methods. This could be done by encoding dynamic properties of these methods as functional properties of slightly modified methods. These modifications were small and systematic, so that the additional encoding effort remained small.

We have illustrated our approach in two case studies. In the first we proved anytime behaviour of a simple linear filtering method, and in the second we analysed its behaviour during computation when a heuristic candidate-selection function was employed.

All the proof obligations for these methods (termination, correctness, dynamic behaviour) have been fulfilled via machine assisted proofs using the KIV interactive verifier for Dynamic Logic.

Finally, for both case studies we have suggested a general approach that could be applied to other problem solving methods in order to obtain the same results for those methods.

References

1. J. S. Aikins. Representation of control knowledge in expert systems. In *Proceedings of AAAI'80*, pages 121–123, 1980.
2. A.J. Bonner and M. Kifer. Transaction logic programming. In *Proceedings of the Tenth Internat. Conf. on Logic Programming (IPLP'93)*, pages 257–279, 1993. MIT Press.
3. B. Chandrasekaran. Generic tasks in knowledge based reasoning: High level building blocks for expert system design. *IEEE Expert*, 1(3):23–30, 1986.
4. W. Clancey. The advantages of abstract control knowledge in expert system design. In *Proceedings of AAAI'83*, pages 74–78, 1983. 1983.
5. F. Cornelissen, C. Jonker, and J. Treur. Compositional verification of knowledge-based systems: a case study for diagnostic reasoning. In E. Plaza and R. Benjamins, editors, *Proceedings of EKAW'97*, number 1319 in Lecture Notes in Artificial Intelligence, pages 65–80, 1997. Springer-Verlag.
6. T. Dean and M. Boddy. An analysis of time-dependent planning problems. In *Proceedings of AAAI'88*, pages 49–54, 1988.
7. D. Fensel. *The Knowledge-Based Acquisition and Representation Language KARL*. Kluwer Academic Pubblisher, 1995.
8. D. Fensel and R. Groenboom. A software architecture for knowledge-based systems. *The Knowledge Engineering Review* , 1999. To appear.
9. D. Fensel, R. Groenboom, and G. R. Renardel de Lavalette. Modal change logic (MCL): Specifying the reasoning of knowledge-based systems. *Data and Knowledge Engineering*, 26(3):243–269, 1998.
10. D. Fensel and A. Schönegge. Using KIV to specify and verify architectures of knowledge-based systems. In *Proceedings of the 12th IEEE International Conference on Automated Software Engineering (ASEC'97)*, 1997.
11. D. Fensel and A. Schönegge. Inverse verification of problem-solving methods. *International Journal of Human-Computer Studies*, 49:4, 1998.
12. D. Fensel and R. Straatman. The essense of problem-solving methods: Making assumptions for gaining efficiency. *International Journal of Human-Computer Studies*, 48(2):181–215, 1998.
13. M. Fisher and M. Wooldridge. On the formal specification and verification of multi-agent systems. *International Journal of Cooperative Information Systems*, 6(1):37–65, January 1997. World Scientific Publishers.
14. D. Harel. Dynamic logic. In D. Gabbay and F. Guenthner, editors, *Handbook of Philosophical Logic, Vol. II*, pages 497–604. Reidel, Dordrecht, The Netherlands, 1984.
15. C. Jonker, J. Treur, and W. de Vries. Compositional verification of agents in dynamic environments: a case study. In *Proceedings of European V&V Workshop at KR'98*, june 1998.
16. R. Jungclaus, G. Saake, Th. Hartmann, and C. Sernades. TROLL- a language for object-oriented specification of information systems. *ACM Transactions on Information Systems*, 14(2):175–211, April 1996.
17. V.R. Pratt. Semantical considerations on Floyd-Hoare logic. In *IEEE Symposium on Foundations of Computer Science*, pages 109–121, October 1976.
18. W. Reif. The KIV-approach to Software Verification. In M. Broy and S. Jähnichen, editors, *KORSO: Methods, Languages, and Tools for the Construction of Correct Software*. Springer LNCS 1009, 1995.

19. S. J. Russell and S. Zilberstein. Composing real-time systems. In *Proceedings of IJCAI'91*, pages 212–217, 1991.
20. L. Steels. Components of expertise. *AI Magazine*, Summer 1990.
21. M. Stefik. *Introduction to Knowledge-Based Systems*. Morgan Kaufmann, 1995.
22. A. ten Teije and F. van Harmelen. Exploiting domain knowledge for approximate diagnosis. In *Proceedings of IJCAI'97*, pages 454–459, 1997.
23. J. Treur and Th. Wetter, editors. *Formal Specification of Complex Reasoning Systems*, Workshop Series. Ellis Horwood, 1993.
24. P. van Eck, J. Engelfriet, D. Fensel, F. van Harmelen, Y. Venema, and M. Willems. Specification of dynamics for knowledge-based systems. In B. Freitag, H. Decker, M. Kifer, and A. Voronkov, editors, *Transactions and Change in Logic Databases*, volume 1472 of *Lecture Notes in Computer Science*, pages 37–68. Springer Verlag, 1998.
25. F. van Harmelen and J. R. Balder. $(ML)^2$: a formal language for KADS models of expertise. *Knowledge Acquisition*, 4(1), 1992.
26. F. van Harmelen and A. ten Teije. Characterising approximate problem-solving by partial pre- and postconditions. In *Proceedings of ECAI'98*, pages 78–82, 1998.
27. I. A. van Langevelde, A. W. Philipsen, and J. Treur. Formal specification of compositional architectures. In B. Neumann, editor, *Proceedings ECAI'92*, pages 272–276, 1992.
28. B. J. Wielinga, A. Th. Schreiber, and J. A. Breuker. KADS: A modelling approach to knowledge engineering. *Knowledge Acquisition*, 4(1):5–53, 1992.

Integration of Behavioural Requirements Specification within Knowledge Engineering

Daniela E. Herlea[1], Catholijn M. Jonker[2],
Jan Treur[2], Niek J.E. Wijngaards[1,2]

[1] University of Calgary, Software Engineering Research Network
2500 University Drive NW, Calgary, Alberta T2N 1N4, Canada
Email: {danah, niek}@cpsc.ucalgary.ca

[2] Vrije Universiteit Amsterdam, Department of Artificial Intelligence
De Boelelaan 1081a, 1081 HV, Amsterdam, The Netherlands
Email: {jonker, treur, niek}@cs.vu.nl
URL: http://www.cs.vu.nl/{~jonker,~treur,~niek}

Abstract. It is shown how specification of behavioural requirements from informal to formal can be integrated within knowledge engineering. The integration of requirements specification has addressed, in particular: the integration of requirements acquisition and specification with ontology acquisition and specification, the relations between requirements specifications and specifications of task models and problem solving methods, and the relation of requirements specification to verification.

1 Introduction

Requirements Engineering (RE) addresses the development and validation of methods for eliciting, representing, analysing, and confirming system requirements and with methods for transforming requirements into more formal specifications for design and implementation. Requirements Engineering is one of the early but important phases in the software development life cycle and numerous studies have revealed the misidentification of requirements as one of the most significant sources of customer dissatisfaction with delivered systems [10], [22], [28]. However, it is a difficult process, as it involves the elicitation, analysis and documentation of knowledge from multiple stakeholders of the system. There is an increased need to involve the users at this stage of the development life-cycle [8], 29]. It is recognised that the users are the experts in their work and a thorough understanding of the requirements is achieved only by promoting effective communication with them during the requirements engineering process [3]. It is also argued that an effective requirements definition requires involvement and mutual control of the process by all players, and that a good partnership between users and designers enables a high quality of the system being developed [19].

Requirements express intended properties of the system, and scenarios specify use-cases of the intended system (i.e., examples of intended user interaction traces), usually employed to clarify requirements. The process of requirements engineering within software development is an iterative process, in which a sharp borderline between defining requirements and constructing the system design is not always easy to draw. When an effective stakeholder-developer communication link is in place, on the basis of a (partially) constructed design description of the system, additional information may be elicited from the stakeholders (i.e., domain experts, users, system customers, managers), and more detailed requirements and scenarios can be developed which refer to this design description. Requirements can be expressed in various degrees of formality, ranging from unstructured informal representations (usually during initial requirements acquisition) to more structured semi-formal representations and formal representations.

The interleaving of the process of requirements engineering and the process of design is emphasised in current research in the area of AI & Design (e.g., [16], [17]), in which it is put forward that realistic design processes include both the manipulation of requirement specifications and the manipulation of design object specifications, resulting in a detailed description of a design object and a good understanding of the requirements. This perspective on design, applied in particular to the design of knowledge-intensive software, is employed throughout the paper. This is in contrast with the tradition in software engineering to separate the activity of manipulating software requirements from the 'design of software', the actual construction of the system design [4], [20], [25], [26].

Principled model-based methodologies for knowledge engineering, such as DESIRE (cf. [6], [7]), CommonKADS (cf. [27]) or MIKE (cf. [1]), the emphasis is on specification of the (conceptual) model of the system being developed and not on specification of required behaviour properties of a system to be developed. A transparent distinction between specification of the structure of a system (or task or problem solving method) and its (behavioural) properties is not made. For example, in the AI and Design community a specification of the *structure* of a design object is often distinguished from a specification of *function* or *behaviour*; e.g., [16], [17]. In recent research in knowledge engineering, identification and formalisation of properties of knowledge-intensive systems is addressed, usually in the context of verification or competence assessment [2], [9], [14], [15]. Such properties can be used as a basis for requirement specifications. In this paper it is shown how specification of behavioural requirements from informal to formal can be integrated within knowledge engineering.

From the basic ingredients in knowledge engineering methodologies the following are especially relevant to the integration of requirements specification: knowledge level approaches to *problem solving methods* (e.g., [14]), *ontologies* (e.g., [23]) and *verification* (e.g., [9]). It has to be defined how requirements specification relates to these basic ingredients. Therefore, integration of requirements specification within a principled knowledge engineering methodology has to address, in particular:

- integration of requirements acquisition and specification with ontology acquisition and specification
- relations between requirements specifications and specifications of task models with tasks at different levels of (process) abstraction, or problem solving methods
- relation of requirements specification to verification

These aspects are addressed in this paper. The different forms of representation of requirements and scenarios are presented in Section 2, for reasons of presentation illustrated by a simple example. In Section 3 refinement of requirements related to different proces abstraction levels (e.g., as in task or task/method hierarchies) is addressed. Section 4 briefly summarizes the relations between requirements and scenarios. Section 5 concludes the paper with a discussion.

2 Representation of Requirements and Scenarios

In the approach presented in this paper, the processes of requirements engineering and system development are integrated by a careful specification of the co-operation between the two. The manipulation process of a set of requirements and scenarios, and the manipulation process of a design object description (i.e., a description of the system) are intertwined in the following way: first the set of requirements and scenarios is made as precise as possible. This requires multiple interaction with and among the stakeholders. Based on that set a possible (partial) description is made of the system. The description of the system is used not only to validate the understanding of the current set of requirements and scenarios, but also to elicit additional information from the stakeholders. This leads to more requirements and scenarios and to more detailed requirements and scenarios. The process continues, alternating between manipulating a set of requirements and scenarios, and manipulating a description of a system. Adequate representations of requirements and scenarios are required for each part of the overall process, and, therefore, the relations between the different representation forms of the same requirement or scenario need to be carefully documented.

One of the underlying assumptions on the approach presented in this paper is that a compositional design method will lead to designs that are transparent, maintainable, and can be (partially) reused within other designs. The construction of a compositional design description of the system that properly respects the requirements and scenarios entails making choices between possible solutions and possible system configurations. Such choices can be made during the manipulation of the set of requirements and scenarios, but also during the manipulation of the design object description. Each choice corresponds to an abstraction level. For each component of the system design further requirements and scenarios are necessary to ensure that the combined system satisfies the overall system requirements and scenarios. The different abstraction levels in requirements are reflected as levels of process abstraction in the design description during the manipulation of the compositional design description.

Different representations of requirements and scenarios are discussed in Sections 2.1 to 2.3. The use of process abstraction levels is explained further in Section 3. An overview of the relations between representations of requirements and scenarios, and different levels of process abstraction is presented in Section 4.

In Requirements Engineering the role of scenarios, in addition to requirements, has gained more importance, both in academia and industry practice [13], [30]. Scenarios or use cases are examples of interaction sessions between the users and the system [24], [30]; they are often used during the requirement engineering, being regarded as effective ways of communicating with the stakeholders (i.e., domain experts, users, system customers, managers, and developers). The initial scenarios can serve to verify (i.e., check the validity in a formal manner) the requirements specification and (later) the system prototypes. Evaluating the prototypes helps detecting misunderstandings between the domain experts and system designers if, for example, the system designers made the wrong abstractions based on the initial scenarios. In our approach requirements and scenarios both are explicitly represented, and play a role of equal importance. Having them both in a requirements engineering process, provides the possibility of mutual comparison: the requirements can be verified against the scenarios, and the scenarios can be verified against the requirements. By this mutual verification process, ambiguities and inconsistencies within and between the existing requirements or scenarios may be identified, but also the lack of requirements or scenarios: scenarios may be identified for which no requirements were formulated yet, and requirements may be identified for which no scenarios were formulated yet.

To enable effective ways of communicating with the stakeholders, requirements and scenarios are to be represented in a well-structured and easy to understand manner and precise and detailed enough to support the development process of the system. Unfortunately, no standard language exists for the representation of requirements and scenarios. Formats of varying degrees of formality are used in different approaches [25]. Informally represented requirements and scenarios are often best understood by the stakeholders (although also approaches exist using formal representations of requirements in early stages as well [11]). Therefore, continual participation of stakeholders in the process is possible. A drawback is that the informal descriptions are less appropriate when they are used as input to actually construct a system design. On the other hand, an advantage of using formal descriptions is that they can be manipulated automatically in a mathematical way, for example in the context of verification and the detection of inconsistencies. Furthermore, the process of formalising the representations contributes to disambiguation of requirements and scenarios (in contact with stakeholders). At the same time however, a formal representation is less appropriate as a communication means with the stakeholders. Therefore, in our approach in the overall development process, different representations and relations between them are used: informal or structured semi-formal representations (obtained during the process of formalisation) in contact with stakeholders and designers of the system, and related formal representations to be used by the designers during the construction of the design.

Independent of the measure of formality, each requirement and each scenario can be represented in a number of different ways, and/or using different representation languages. Examples are given below. When manipulating requirements and scenarios, different activities can be distinguished (see Fig. 1):

- requirements and scenarios are elicited from stakeholders, checked for ambiguities and inconsistencies, reformulated in a more precise or more structured form, and represented in different forms (informal, semi-formal, and formal) to suit different purposes (communication with stakeholders, verification of a design description)
- they are refined across process abstraction levels (which is addressed in Section 3).

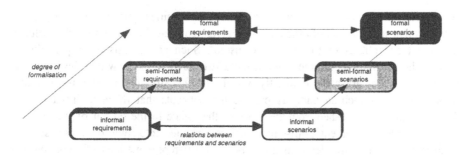

Fig. 1. Representations from informal to formal

2.1 Informal representations

Different informal representations can be used to express the same requirement or scenario. Representations can be made, for example, in a graphical representation language, or a natural language, or in combinations of these languages. Scenarios, for instance, can be represented using a format that supports branching points in the process, or in a language that only takes linear structures into account. A simple example of a requirement R1 on a system to control a chemical process is the following:

> *Requirement R1*
> *For situations that the temperature and pressure are high the system*
> *shall give a red alert and turn the heater off.*

A requirement is a *general* statement about the (required) behaviour of the system to be designed. This statement is required to hold for *every* instance of behaviour of the system. In contrast to this, a scenario is a description of a behaviour instance (e.g., to be read as an instance of a system trace the system has to show, given the user behaviour in the scenario). An example of an informal representation of a scenario is:

> *Scenario S1*
> *The temperature and pressure are high.*
> *A red alert is generated and the heater is turned off.*

Note that this scenario describes one of the behaviour instances for which requirement R1 holds.

2.2 Structured semi-formal representations

Both requirements and scenarios can be reformulated to more structured and precise forms.

Requirements. To check requirements for ambiguities and inconsistencies, an analysis that seeks to identify the parts of a given requirement formulation that refer to the input and output of the system is useful. Such an analysis often provokes a reformulation of the requirement into a more structured form, in which the input and output references are made explicitly visible in the structure of the formulation. Moreover during such an analysis process the concepts that relate to input can be identified and distinguished from the concepts that relate to the output of the system. Possibly the requirement splits in a natural manner into two or more simpler requirements. This often leads to a number of new (representations of) requirements and/or scenarios. For example, the following requirement may be found as a result of such an analysis:

> *Requirement R1.1:*
> *at any point in time*
> *if the system received input that the temperature is high and the pressure is high*
> *then the system shall generate as output a red alert and an indication that the situation is explosive, and after the user gives an input that it has to be resolved, the system gives output that the heater is turned off*

A reformulation can lead to structured requirements in a semi-formal form that provide more detail, for example R1 can be reformulated to R1.1, but also to two parts:

> *Requirement R1a.1:*
> *at any point in time*
> *if the system received **input** that the temperature is high and the pressure is high*
> *then the system shall generate as **output** a red alert and an indication that the situation is explosive*

> *Requirement R1b.1:*
> *at any point in time*
> *if the system provided as **output** an indication that the situation is explosive and after this the user gave an **input** that it has to be resolved,*
> *then the system shall generate **output** that the heater is turned off*

Requirement R1a.1 can also be represented graphically, for example, by (here each of the pairs of arrows means that both arrows of the pair occur at the same time):

As a specific case, also requirements referring only to input or only to output can be encountered. For requirements formulated in such a structured manner the following classification can be made:

- requirements on input only, independent of output (*input requirements*),
- requirements on output only, independent of input (*output requirements*), and
- requirements relating output to input

The latter type of requirements can be categorised as:

- output is dependent on input (input-output-dependency): *function or behaviour requirement*,
- input is dependent on output (output-input-dependency): *environmental requirement or assumption*

When stating properties of the environment (which includes users) of the system (output-input-dependency), the term 'requirement' is avoided and the term 'assumption' is used: the environment is not within the scope of the software development; it cannot be 'tuned' to exhibit particular properties. As such, only assumptions can be made on its behaviour and properties. The term 'requirements' is used for those parts of the system that are within the scope of designable parts of the system.

In addition, requirements can be categorised according to the kind of properties they refer to: static requirements, or requirements. For nontrivial dynamic requirements a temporal structure has to be reflected in the representation. This entails that terms such as 'at any point in time', 'at an earlier point in time', 'after', 'before', 'since', 'until', 'next' are used to clarify the temporal relationships between different fragments in the requirement.

The input and output terms used in the structured reformulations form the basis of an ontology of input and output concepts. Construction of this ontology takes place during the reformulation of requirements: acquisition of a (domain or task or method) ontology is integrated within requirements engineering (requirements engineering contributes at least to part of the ontology acquisition). For the requirements engineering process it is very useful to construct an ontology of input and output concepts. For example, in R1b.1 the concepts indicated below in bold can be acquired.

> *Requirement R1b.1:*
> *at any point in time*
> *if the system provided as output an indication that the **situation is explosive**,*
> *and after this the user gave an input that it has **to be resolved**,*
> *then the system shall generate output that the **heater is turned off***

This ontology later facilitates the formalisation of requirements and scenarios, as the input and output concepts are already defined.

In summary, to obtain a structured semi-formal representation of a requirement, the following is to be performed:

- explicitly distinguish *input and output* concepts in the requirement formulation
- define (domain and task/method) *ontologies* for input and output information

- *classify* the requirement according to the categories above
- make the *temporal structure* of the statement explicit using words like, 'at any point in time', 'at an earlier point in time', 'after', 'before', 'since', 'until', 'next'.

Scenarios. For scenarios, a structured semi-formal representation is obtained by performing the following:
- explicitly distinguish *input and output* concepts in the scenario description
- define (domain) *ontologies* for the input and output information
- represent the temporal structure described implicitly in the sequence of events.

The scenario S1 shown earlier is reformulated into a structured semi-formal representation S1.1:

> *Scenario S1.1*
> - input: *temperature is high, pressure is high*
> - output: *red alert, situation is explosive*
> - input: *to be resolved*
> - output: *heater is turned off*

Notice that from this scenario, which covers both requirements given above, it is not clear whether or not always an input *to be resolved* leads to the heater being turned off, independent of what preceded this input, or whether this should only happen when the history actually was as described in the first two lines of the scenario. If the second part of the scenario is meant to be history independent, this second part is better specified as a separate scenario. However, we assume that in this example at least the previous output of the system *situation is explosive* on which the user reacts is a condition for the second part of the scenario (as also expressed in the requirements above). These considerations lead to the splitting of scenario S1.1 into the following two (temporally) independent scenarios S1a.1 and S1b.1:

> *Scenario S1a.1*
> - input: *temperature is high, pressure is high*
> - output: *red alert, situation is explosive*
>
> *Scenario S1b.1*
> - output: *situation is explosive*
> - input: *to be resolved*
> - output: *heater is turned off*

2.3 Formal representations

A formalisation of a scenario can be made by using formal ontologies for the input and output, and by formalising the sequence of events as a temporal trace. Thus a formal temporal model is obtained, for example as defined in [7] and [9]. To obtain formal representations of requirements, the input and output ontologies have to be chosen as formal ontologies. In the example this can be done, for example by formalising a conceptual relation of the form A is B, with as meaning that the object A has property B, in a predicate form: B(A); for example 'the situation is explosive' is formalised by explosive(situation), where situation is an object and explosive a predicate. This format can be used within an appropriate subset or extension of predicate logic. For example, requirement R1a.1 can also be represented formally in combined symbolic and graphical form by the following:

In addition, the temporal structure, if present in a semi-formal representation, has to be expressed in a formal manner. Using the formal ontologies, and a formalisation of the temporal structure, a mathematical language is obtained to formulate formal requirement representations. The semantics are based on compositional information states which evolve over time. An *information state* M of a component D is an assignment of truth values {true, false, unknown} to the set of ground atoms that play a role within D. The compositional structure of D is reflected in the structure of the information state. The set of all possible information states of D is denoted by IS(D). A *trace* $\mathcal{M}$ of a component D is a sequence of information states $(M^t)_{t \in \mathbf{N}}$ in IS(D). Given a trace $\mathcal{M}$ of component D, the information state of the input interface of component C at time point t of the component D is denoted by $state_D(\mathcal{M}, t, input(C))$, where C is either D or a sub-component of D. Analogously, $state_D(\mathcal{M}, t, output(C))$, denotes the information state of the output interface of component C at time point t of the component D. These formalised information states can be related to statements via the formally defined satisfaction relation $\models$. Behavioural properties can be formulated in a formal manner, using quantfiers over time and the usual logical connectives such as not, &, $\Rightarrow$. An alternative formal representation of temporal properties (using modal and temporal operators) within Temporal Multi-Epistemic Logic can be found in [12]. For example, requirement R1b.1 can be represented formally by:

> *Requirement R1b.2:*
> $\forall \mathcal{M}, t$ [$state_S(\mathcal{M}, t, input(S)) \models$ to_be_resolved &
> $\exists t' < t$ $state_S(\mathcal{M}, t', output(S)) \models$ explosive(situation) $\Rightarrow$
> $\exists t'' > t$ $state_S(\mathcal{M}, t, output(S)) \models$ turn_off(heater)]

In this formalisation of R1b.1 the word "after" is represented by indicating that the time point t at which to_be_resolved appeared on the input is greater than some time point t' at which the system reported that the situation is explosive on its output.

   Scenario S1.1 can be represented formally by the temporal model that is defined as follows:

Scenario S1.2:

state$_S$($\mathcal{M}$, 1, input(S))	⊨	high(temperature)
state$_S$($\mathcal{M}$, 1, input(S))	⊨	high(pressure)
state$_S$($\mathcal{M}$, 2, output(S))	⊨	explosive(situation)
state$_S$($\mathcal{M}$, 2, output(S))	⊨	red_alert
state$_S$($\mathcal{M}$, 3, input(S))	⊨	to_be_resolved
state$_S$($\mathcal{M}$, 4, output(S))	⊨	turn_off(heater)

To summarise, formalisation of a requirement or scenario on the basis of a structured semi-formal representation is achieved by:

- choosing *formal ontologies* for the input and output information
- formalisation of the *temporal structure*

This results in a temporal formula F for a requirement and in a temporal model $\mathcal{M}$ for a scenario.

Checking a temporal formula, which formally represents a requirement, against a temporal model, formally representing a scenario, means that formal verification of requirements against scenarios can be done by model checking. A formal representation $\mathcal{M}$ of a scenario S and a formal representation F of a requirement are compatible if the temporal formula is true in the model. For example, the temporal formula R1b.2 is indeed true for the model S1.2: the explosive situation occurred at time point 2 in the scenario, at time point 3 (which is later than 2) the system received input to_be_resolved, and at time point 4 (again later than 3), the system has as output turn_off(heater).

However, requirement R1b.2 would also be true in the following two scenarios. Scenario S2 is an example of a situation in which the system turns off the heater when this is not appropriate, scenario S3 is an example of a situation in which the system waits too long before it turns off the heater (which might lead to an explosion).

Scenario S2
The temperature and the pressure are high
The system generates a red alert and turns off the heater,
The temperature and the pressure are medium
The temperature is low and the pressure is medium
The system turns off the heater

Scenario S3
The temperature and the pressure are high
The system generates a red alert and turns off the heater,
The system increases the heater
The system increases the heater
An explosion occurs
The system turns off the heater

Furthermore, the requirement would also be true in a scenario in which the system waited with turning off the heater, maybe even first increasing the heat for some time. This last scenario is formalised as scenario S3.1:

Scenario S3.1:

$state_S(\mathcal{M}, 1, input(S))$	$\models$	high(temperature)
$state_S(\mathcal{M}, 1, input(S))$	$\models$	high(pressure)
$state_S(\mathcal{M}, 2, output(S))$	$\models$	explosive(situation)
$state_S(\mathcal{M}, 2, output(S))$	$\models$	red_alert
$state_S(\mathcal{M}, 3, input(S))$	$\models$	to_be_resolved
$state_S(\mathcal{M}, 4, output(S))$	$\models$	increase(heater)
$state_S(\mathcal{M}, 5, output(S))$	$\models$	increase(heater)
$state_S(\mathcal{M}, 6, input(S))$	$\models$	occurred(explosion)
$state_S(\mathcal{M}, 7, output(S))$	$\models$	turn_off(heater)

In other words, requirement R1b.2 leaves too many possibilities for the system's behaviour, and, being a formalisation of R1b.1, so do the requirements that form the reason for formulating R1b.1, i.e., R1a.1, and R1.1. During the requirement engineering process this has to be resolved in contact with the stakeholders. In this case, the semi-formal R1.1 and R1a.1, and the formal R1a.2 have to be reformulated: after a discussion with the stakeholders, R1.1 is reformulated into:

Requirement R1.2:
at any point in time
if the system received input that the temperature is high and the pressure is high
then at the next point in time the system shall generate as output a red alert and an indication that the situation is explosive, and at the next point in time after the user gives an input that it has to be resolved, the system gives output that the heater is turned off

Requirement R1b.1 is reformulated into:

Requirement R1b.3:
at any point in time
if the system provided as output
        *an indication that the **situation is explosive**,*
and at the next time point after the user gave an input
        *that the situation has **to be resolved**,*
then the system shall generate output
        *that the **heater is turned off***

Based on these reformulations (that also affect the ontologies), the requirement engineers choose a different representation of R1b.2:

Requirement R1b.3:

$\forall \mathcal{M}, t \quad [\quad \text{state}_S(\mathcal{M}, t, \text{input}(S)) \quad \models \quad \text{to_be_resolved(situation)} \quad \& $
$\text{state}_S(\mathcal{M}, \text{prev}(t), \text{output}(S)) \quad \models \quad \text{explosive(situation)} \quad \Rightarrow$
$\text{state}_S(\mathcal{M}, \text{succ}(t), \text{output}(S)) \quad \models \quad \text{turn\_off(heater)} \,]$

Requirement R1b.3 is true in scenario S1.2 (let prev be the function: n -> n-1 and succ: n -> n+1), but not in the sketched unwanted scenarios like S3.1.

3 Requirements Refinement and Process Abstraction Levels

The requirements engineering process considers the system as a whole, in interaction with its stakeholders. However, during a design process, often a form of structuring of the system is used: sub-processes are distinguished, for example in relation to development or selection of a task or task/method hierarchy. For the processes at the next lower process abstraction level, also requirements can be expressed. Thus a distinction is made between *stakeholder requirements* and *stakeholder scenarios* (for the top level of the system, elicited from stakeholders, such as users, customers) and *designer requirements* and *designer scenarios* (for the lower process abstraction levels, constructed by requirement engineers and designers). Designer requirements and scenarios are dependent on a description of the system. Requirements on properties of a sub-component of a system reside at a next lower level of process abstraction than the level of requirements on properties of the system itself; often sets of requirements at a lower level are chosen in such a way that they realise a next higher level requirement. This defines a process abstraction level refinement relation between requirements. These process abstraction refinement relationships can also be used to validate requirements: e.g., if the refinements of a requirement to the next lower process abstraction level all hold for a given system description, then the refined requirement can be proven to hold for that system description. Similarly, scenarios can be refined to lower process abstraction levels by adding the interactions between the sub-processes. At each level of abstraction, requirements and scenarios employ the terminology defined in the ontology for that level. In the example used above, for the structured semi-formal requirements two processes can be distinguished:

> *interpret process info*
> > input information of type: temperature is high, pressure is high
> > output information of type: situation is explosive

> *generate actions*
> > input information of type: situation is explosive
> > output information of type: red alert, heater is turned off

At the next lower abstraction level of these two processes the following requirements can be formulated, as a refinement of the requirements given earlier:

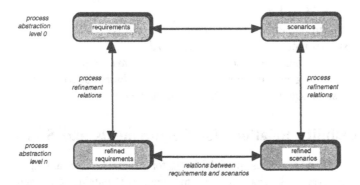

Fig. 2. Process abstraction level refinements

interpret process info

> *Requirement R1int.1:*
> *at any point in time*
> *if the component received **input** that the temperature is high and the pressure is high*
> *then the component shall generate as **output** an indication that the situation is explosive*

generate actions

> *Requirement R1acta.1:*
> *at any point in time*
> *if the component received **input** that the situation is explosive ,*
> *then the component shall generate as **output** a red alert*

> *Requirement R1actb.1:*
> *at any point in time*
> *if the component received **input** that the situation is explosive,*
> *and after this it received an **input** that it has to be resolved,*
> *then the component shall generate **output** that the heater is turned off*

Furthermore, scenarios S1a.1 and S1b.1 given earlier can be refined to

> *Scenario S1inta.1*
> - system input: *temperature is high, pressure is high*
>   - interpret process info input: *temperature is high,*
>   *pressure is high*
>   - interpret process info output: *situation is explosive*
>   - generate actions input: *situation is explosive*
>   - generate actions output: *red alert*
> - system output: *situation is explosive, red alert*

Scenario S1intb.1
- system output: *situation is explosive*
- system input: *to be resolved*
    - generate actions input: *to be resolved*
    - generate actions output: *heater is turned off*
- system output: *heater is turned off*

4 Traceability Relations for Requirements and Scenarios

As requirements and scenarios form the basis for communication among stakeholders (including the system developers), it is important to maintain a document in which the requirements and scenarios are organised and structured in a comprehensive way. This document is also important for maintenance of the system once it has been taken into operation. Due to the increase in system complexity nowadays, more complex requirements and scenarios result in documents that are more and more difficult to manage. The different activities in requirements engineering lead to an often large number of inter-related representations of requirements and scenarios.

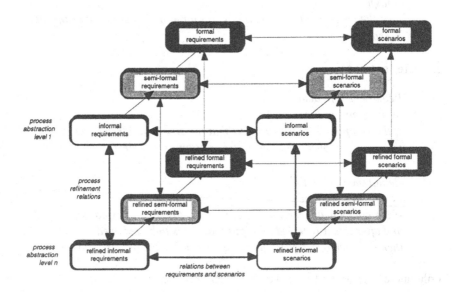

Fig. 3. Traceability relations

The explicit representation of these *traceability relations* is useful in keeping track of the connections; traceability relationships can be made explicit:

- among requirements at the same process abstraction level (Fig. 1),
- between requirements at different process abstraction levels (Fig. 2),

- among scenarios at the same process abstraction level (Fig. 1),
- between scenarios at different process abstraction levels (Fig. 2),
- between requirements and scenarios at the same process abstraction level (Figs 1, 2 and 3)
- among requirements at the same level of formality (Fig. 3)
- between requirements and scenarios at the same level of formality (Fig. 3).

These relationships are often adequately specified using hyperlinks. This offers traceability; i.e., relating relevant requirements and scenarios as well as the possibility to 'jump' to definitions of relevant requirements and scenarios. Thus requirements and scenarios resulting from an extensive case-study have been placed in a hyperlinked structure [18]; see Fig. 3, which combines Figures 1 and 2.

5 Discussion

Requirements describe the required properties of a system (this includes the functions of the system, structure of the system, static properties, and dynamic properties). In applications to agent-based systems, the dynamics or behaviour of the system plays an important role in description of the successful operation of the system. Requirements specification has both to be informal or semi-formal (to be able to discuss them with stakeholders) and formal (to disambiguate and analyse them and establish whether or not a constructed model for a system satisfies them). Typical software requirements engineering practices are geared toward the development of a formal requirements specification.

The process of making requirements more precise is supported by using both semi-formal and formal representations for requirements. Part of this process is to relate concepts used in requirements to input and output of the system. Since requirement specifications need system-related concepts, it has been shown how the acquisition and specification of requirements goes hand in hand with the acquisition and specification of *ontologies*.

The formalisation of behaviour requirements has to address the semantics of the evolution of the system (input and output) states over time. In this paper the semantics of properties of compositional systems is based on the temporal semantics approach, which can be found in the development of a compositional verification method for knowledge-intensive systems; for diagnostic process models see [9]; for co-operative information gathering agents, see [21]; for negotiating agents, see [5]. By adopting the semantical approach underlying the compositional verification method, a direct integration of requirements engineering with the specification of properties of *problem solving methods* and their *verification* could easily be established.

For some example systems requirements and scenarios have been elicited, analysed, manipulated, and formalised. The lessons learned from these case studies are:

- The process of achieving an understanding of a requirement involves a large number of different formulations and representations, gradually evolving from informal to semi-formal and formal.
- Scenarios and their formalisation are, compared to requirements, of equal importance.

- Categorisation of requirements on input, output and function or behaviour requirements, and distinguishing these from assumptions on the environment clarifies the overall picture.
- Keeping track on the various relations between different representations of requirements, between requirements and scenarios, and many others, is supported by hyperlink specifications within a requirements document.

In current and future research, further integration of requirements engineering in the compositional development method for multi-agent systems, DESIRE and, in particular, in its software environment is addressed.

References

1. Angele, J., Fensel, D., Landes, D., and Studer, R., Developing Knowledge-based Systems with MIKE. *Journal of Automated Software Engineering*, 1998

2. Benjamins, R., Fensel, D., Straatman, R. (1996). Assumptions of problem-solving methods and their role in knowledge engineering. In: W. Wahlster (Ed.), *Proceedings of the12th European Conference on AI, ECAI'96*, John Wiley and Sons, pp. 408-412.

3. Beyer, H.R. and Holtzblatt, K. (1995). Apprenticing with the customer, *Communications of the ACM*, vol. 38(5), pp. 45-52.

4. Booch, G. (1991). *Object oriented design with applications*. Benjamins Cummins Publishing Company, Redwood City.

5. Brazier, F.M.T., Cornelissen, F., Gustavsson, R., Jonker, C.M., Lindeberg, O., Polak, B., and Treur, J. (1998). Compositional Design and Verification of a Multi-Agent System for One-to-Many Negotiation. In: *Proceedings of the Third International Conference on Multi-Agent Systems, ICMAS'98*. IEEE Computer Society Press, pp. 49-56.

6. Brazier, F.M.T., Jonker, C.M., and Treur, J. (1998). Principles of Compositional Multi-agent System Development. In: J. Cuena (ed.), *Proceedings of the 15th IFIP World Computer Congress, WCC'98, Conference on Information Technology and Knowledge Systems, IT&KNOWS'98*, pp. 347-360.

7. Brazier, F.M.T., Treur, J., Wijngaards, N.J.E. and Willems, M. (1999). Temporal Semantics of Compositional Task Models and Problem Solving Methods. *Data and Knowledge Engineering*, vol. 29(1), 1999, pp. 17-42.

8. Clavadetscher, C. (1998). User involvement: key to success, *IEEE Software*, Requirements Engineering issue, March/April, pp. 30-33.

9. Cornelissen, F., Jonker, C.M., and Treur, J. (1997). Compositional verification of knowledge-based systems: a case study in diagnostic reasoning. In: E. Plaza, R. Benjamins (eds.), *Knowledge Acquisition, Modelling and Management, Proceedings of the 10th European Knowledge Acquisition Workshop, EKAW'97*, Lecture Notes in AI, vol. 1319, Springer Verlag, Berlin, pp. 65-80.

10. Davis, A. M. (1993). *Software requirements: Objects, Functions, and States*, Prentice Hall, New Jersey.

11. Dubois, E., Yu, E., Petit, M. (1998). From Early to Late Formal Requirements. In: Proc. IWSSD'98. IEEE Computer Society Press.

12. Engelfriet, J., Jonker, C.M. and Treur, J., Compositional Verification of Multi-Agent Systems in Temporal Multi-Epistemic Logic. In: J.P. Mueller, M.P. Singh, A.S. Rao

(eds.), *Pre-proc. of the Fifth International Workshop on Agent Theories, Architectures and Languages, ATAL'98*, 1998, pp. 91-106. To appear in: J.P. Mueller, M.P. Singh, A.S. Rao (eds.), *Intelligent Agents V*. Lecture Notes in AI, Springer Verlag, 1999

13. Erdmann, M. and Studer, R. (1998). Use-Cases and Scenarios for Developing Knowledge-based Systems. In: J. Cuena (ed.), *Proceedings of the 15th IFIP World Computer Congress, WCC'98, Conference on Information Technology and Knowledge Systems, IT&KNOWS'98*, pp. 259-272.

14. Fensel, D. (1995). Assumptions and limitations of a problem solving method: a case study. In: B.R. Gaines, M.A. Musen (Eds.), *Proceedings of the 9th Banff Knowledge Acquisition for Knowledge-based Systems Workshop, KAW'95*, Calgary: SRDG Publications, Department of Computer Science, University of Calgary.

15. Fensel, D., Benjamins, R. (1996) Assumptions in model-based diagnosis. In: B.R. Gaines, M.A. Musen (Eds.), *Proceedings of the 10th Banff Knowledge Acquisition for Knowledge-based Systems workshop, KAW'96*, Calgary: SRDG Publications, Department of Computer Science, University of Calgary, pp. 5/1-5/18.

16. Gero, J.S., and Sudweeks, F., eds. (1996) *Artificial Intelligence in Design '96*, Kluwer Academic Publishers, Dordrecht.

17. Gero, J.S., and Sudweeks, F., eds. (1998) *Artificial Intelligence in Design '98*, Kluwer Academic Publishers, Dordrecht.

18. Herlea, D., Jonker, C.M., Treur, J. and Wijngaards, N.J.E. (1998). *A Case Study in Requirements Engineering*. Report, Vrije Universiteit Amsterdam, Department of Artificial Intelligence. URL: http://www.cs.vu.nl/~treur/pareqdoc.html

19. Holzblatt, K. and Beyer, K.R. (1995). Requirements gathering: the human factor, *Communications of the ACM*, vol. 38(5), pp. 31.

20. Jackson, M.A. (1975). *Principles of Program Design*, Academic Press.

21. Jonker, C.M. and Treur, J. (1998). Compositional Verification of Multi-Agent Systems: a Formal Analysis of Pro-activeness and Reactiveness. In: W.P. de Roever, H. Langmaack, A. Pnueli (eds.), *Proceedings of the International Workshop on Compositionality, COMPOS'97*. Lecture Notes in Computer Science, vol. 1536, Springer Verlag, 1998, pp. 350-380

22. Kontonya, G., and Sommerville, I. (1998). *Requirements Engineering: Processes and Techniques*. John Wiley and Sons, New York.

23. Musen, M. (1998). Ontology Oriented Design and Programming: a New Kind of OO. In: J. Cuena (ed.), *Proceedings of the 15th IFIP World Computer Congress, WCC'98, Conference on Information Technology and Knowledge Systems, IT&KNOWS'98*, pp. 17-20.

24. Potts, C., Takahashi, K. and Anton, A. (1994). Inquiry based requirements analysis, *IEEE Software*, 11(2), March.

25. Pressman, R.S. (1997). *Software Engineering: A practitioner's approach*. Fourth Edition, McGraw-Hill Series in Computer Science, McGraw-Hill Companies Inc., New York.

26. Sage, A.P., and Palmer, J.D. (1990). *Software Systems Engineering*. John Wiley and Sons, New York.

27. Schreiber, A.Th., Wielinga, B.J., Akkermans, J.M., Velde, W. van de, and Hoog, R. de (1994). CommonKADS: A comprehensive methodology for KBS development. In: *IEEE Expert*, 9(6).

28. Sommerville, I., and Sawyer P. (1997). *Requirements Engineering: a good practice guide*. John Wiley & Sons, Chicester, England.

29. The Standish Group, (1995) *The High Cost of Chaos*: http://www.standishgroup.com

30. Weidenhaupt, K., Pohl, M., Jarke, M. and Haumer, P. (1998). Scenarios in system development: current practice, *IEEE Software*, pp. 34-45, March/April.

Towards an Ontology for Substances and Related Actions

Björn Höfling[1], Thorsten Liebig[2], Dietmar Rösner[1], and Lars Webel[1]

[1] Otto-von-Guericke-Universität Magdeburg,
Institut für Wissens– und Sprachverarbeitung,
P.O.Box 41 20, D-39016 Magdeburg, Germany,
(hoefling,roesner,webel)@iws.cs.uni-magdeburg.de
[2] Abteilung Künstliche Intelligenz, Fakultät für Informatik,
Universität Ulm, D-89069 Ulm, Germany
liebig@ki.informatik.uni-ulm.de *

Abstract. Modelling substances in knowledge representation has to be different from the treatment of discrete objects. For example liquids need a different approach to individuation. We propose an ontology which represents physical states and other properties of substances in a uniform way. Based on this we describe how to model a hierarchy of actions that can deal with such substances. For these actions a general distinction is made with respect to the type of properties the actions are changing. Further we describe an implementation in description logic allowing especially the definition of actions by specialization of more abstract actions and the inheritance of pre- and postconditions.

1 Introduction

When knowledge in a technical application area is made explicit, i.e. represented formally in a computer readable way, substances often play an important role, e.g. to have a detailed model of the material a technical part is made of, or the substances which are necessary for its use. It would be helpful to have this knowledge available in a sharable and reusable way suitable for different purposes. One way to do this is by specifying an *ontology* for this domain. Such an explicit specification of a conceptualization ([Gru95]) helps to clarify the meaning of relevant entities in the domain and therefore allows a shared understanding between different applications.

We are modelling knowledge about products, e.g. for the automatic generation of multilingual technical documentation from a language independent representation of the relevant domain knowledge. For some technical devices the relevant domain knowledge may be completely represented through a model comprising the resp. object, their parts and actions for manipulating those parts (e.g. checking, replacing). In this case modelling discrete objects is sufficient.

* Part of this author's contribution was funded by a PhD scholarship of the program "Graduiertenförderung des Landes Sachsen-Anhalt".

But in many realistic applications we have to adequately model substances that are part of a product and play a functional role there (e.g. engine oil, coolant, ...). In addition related maintenance actions operating with these substances need to be modeled (e.g. checking an appropriate substance level, adding some fluid, replacing a fluid, ...).

A traditional way of representing substances is as properties of concrete objects. For well delimited objects made of solid material this might be a sufficient approach. But it will run into problems when trying to take into account the physical state of liquids. For this state one has to decide which amount of a substance may be called an instance or object, because every part of a liquid also fulfills the necessary and sufficient conditions for being an object. This *individuation problem* has to be handled in a uniform way in order to be able to represent all kinds of substances independent of their physical state or other properties in a single ontology.

As objects and their substances may change some of their properties over time, like e.g. the physical state as a consequence of a rising or lowering of temperature, it becomes also necessary to decide upon the behaviour of the individuated substances. Some of the questions that arise include: What happens to two substances when they are mixed together? What happens when a liquid is distributed over several containers? These questions belong to a general category of the modelling of *actions* which are related to substances.

We should clarify the role of our application in the design decisions which have been made in the ontology: Our goal, the automatic generation of multilingual technical documentation, requires a language independent representation of the domain knowledge (due to multilinguality) and reusability via specialization of general concepts (in order to be able to adapt the generated documents to different kinds of users, levels of detail or discourse situations). In addition the qualitative simulation of the represented actions is a requirement, as it allows the testing of feasibility and completeness of sequences of actions and can even lead to the automatic generation of warning instructions when possible dangerous events are detected. Nevertheless we believe that our approach is a general one which can be reused in cases where the modelling of non-discrete objects and related actions is necessary.

The paper is structured as follows: Section 2 analyses in more detail the domain of substances and related actions. Originating from this analysis a toplevel ontology for substances is presented in section 3 which has been implemented in description logic. Next, a taxonomy for actions related to this ontology is introduced in section 4. The consequences which follow for the implementation of action hierarchies in description logics are the topic of section 5. The paper concludes with remarks on related work, a summary and outlook.

2 Domain analysis

A substance can be defined as a physical material from which something is made or which has a discrete existence. To illustrate major problems in the modelling of substances we give a simple example: A cup of water, standing in front of someone. What are the substances which are of importance in this situation and how should the be represented? The object referred to by the first noun 'cup' is made of a certain material (e.g. china), which could for example be represented as a property of the instance 'cup'. The second noun 'water' directly describes some amount of a substance. Is this to be modelled as an instance as well?

In linguistics a disctinction is made between *count expressions*, which refer to a discrete, well-delineated group of entities and *mass expressions*, which refer to something without making it explicit how its referent is to be individuated or divided into objects [PS89]. Mass and count expressions are in most cases nouns, but some authors classify also other expressions (like verbs) as count or mass expressions. Even if in natural language the type of referent of mass expressions can be left unspecified, for explicit representations in ontologies or knowledge bases one has to solve this individuation problem. For the cup we can say there is a cup-object, but can we say that there is a water-object (i.e. the amount of water in the cup)? Such a water-object is a fundamentally different kind of object because any part of it is also a water-object, which is not the case for the cup.

To create an ontology and to be able to distinguish between individuals and their categories we have to examine properties of substances. The question arises whether a property belongs to the material or the object made of the material. The following definitions manifest this distinction ([RN95]): *Intrinsic properties* belong to the very substance of the object rather than to the object as a whole (examples: density, boiling point, composition of its chemical elements). *Extrinsic properties* are specific for an indivualised object (examples: volume, weight, shape). Intrinsic properties remain the same for every part of an object because it is made of the same material. On the other hand extrinsic properties are not retained under subdivision.

In the following we will discuss only those properties of substances which we consider important enough to be represented at a very high level in a substance ontology, which help to solve the individuation problem and which are essential for categorizing operations on substances. One important distinction is *pure* vs. *mixed substances*. For pure substances general properties like composition of its chemical elements, melting point and boiling point are important. Mixed substances should be represented as a list of the included pure substances. Unfortunately many properties of mixed substances cannot be deduced from the properties of its (pure) components. Since the components may also be in different physical states (example: sparkling water as a mixture of a liquid and a gaseous substance) it can even be difficult to specify the physical state of a mixed substance.

Nevertheless the *physical state* is a very important distinctive attribute, because in physics most other properties of substances are related to whether they are in a solid, liquid or gaseous state. In which physical state an object of a specific substance manifests itself depends on its temperature and on its pressure which we neglect here for the sake of simplicity. A general difference between most solid substances on the one hand and liquid and gaseous substances on the other hand is that the latter are not bound to a certain shape and may require a container to avoid dispersion. For all three physical states there are other possible distinctions or types of appearance [Web98]:

solid: depending on cohesive and adhesive forces
- powderous substances (like flour); no identifiable shape, so mass or volume or an embracing container have to be specified
- granular substances (like sugar); either like powderous substances, or by external influence or forces pressed into a shape (lump sugar)
- substances with tight connection (like iron); shape plays an important role, can only be changed by external forces
- malleable substances (like plasticine); hold together but their shape can be easily modified

liquid: [Hay85] distinguishes 15 possible states of liquid substances categorized along the following dimensions: (lazy still, lazy moving, energetic moving); (bulk, divided);(on surface, in space, unsupported)

gaseous: Like liquid substances they do not have a predefined shape and require a container to be kept together. To specify a certain amount of a gas one has to mention pressure and temperature (or to use normalized values for both) in addition to volume.

These top-level distinctions are sufficient to solve the individuation problem for substances in a general way and to be able to model related actions. In this context an *action* can be defined as the discrete change of one or more properties of an object or a substance. In this paper we will not describe continous processes for substances (like flowing of water), instead we restrict ourselves to discrete states of substances and to actions where the state changes can be modelled in a discrete way. As with substances we will not be able to make a complete classification of actions but will analyse some major categories.

We distinguish between the following categories of actions based on the type of properties of substances that they are changing:

Substance-preserving actions: Only extrinsic properties of the objects are changed. The intrinsic properties of the related substances are preserved.

Substance-changing actions: Intrinsic (i.e. substance-specific) properties are changed, which means that the participating substances before and after the execution of the action differ (examples: mixing of different substances, chemical reaction between substances).

Instance-preserving actions: In these actions the participating instances remain the same before and after the execution of the action (examples: movement of an object, or pouring of a liquid into another container).

Instance-changing actions: They modify essential properties of an object and also result in the destruction or creation of instances (examples: division or putting together quantities of substances).

The last distinction between instance-changing and instance-preserving actions is also motivated by a distinction of the extrinsic properties changed. Those extrinsic properties which are essential for an object (i.e. when they are changed, the instance will not remain the same; we will call them *existential properties*) must be distinguished from those which have no fundamental influence on the existence of an instance (we will call them *non-existential properties*). It ist dependent on the context whether a substance property is existential or not. In solid or liquid substances changing the property 'volume' is normally an instance-changing action because some part of it has been separated from the original object. As gases can be easily compressed changing the volume can also be an instance-preserving action for gaseous substances. In the former case the volume would be an existential in the latter case a non-existential property.

3 An ontology for substances

In this section we will propose a toplevel ontology for substances. Before describing our major distinctions and the reasons for these decisions we should clarify the requirements which lead to our ontology. They can be summarized as follows:

- Discrete objects and those for which an individualization is not obvious should be handled in a uniform way.
- For discrete objects the traditional way of instantiation and reference to a substance must be supported in order to be able to reuse existing representations.
- The ontology should be usable in dynamic contexts (i.e. the change of substance-related properties during actions).

The first requirement needs additional explanation. Intuitively people often treat all kinds of substances the same way. Therefore a separation of discrete objects and other kinds of substances seems artificial. Especially when not only static aspects but also dynamic changes are relevant. Why should an ice cube only begin to exist in the moment when the water freezes? Although the physical state has changed the individuated substance remains the same. In addition the modelling of e.g. a liquid only as a property of its container together with the degree of filledness (similar to other properties of the container) would complicate the treatment of transfering this liquid to another container or its identification in relation to a substitute (e.g. the oil in a motor before and after a change).

An ontology may be defined in an abstract way without using a concrete knowledge representation mechanism. However, since we want to be able to make actions related to substances executable we need an implementation basis. For this reason we chose POWERLOOM, which is a very expressive description logic system. POWERLOOM accepts expressions using the full predicate calculus, extended with sets, cardinality, equality, and predicate variables [Mac94].

In the traditional approach to abstraction and inheritance there is the basic distinction between instances, i.e. the individual objects (e.g. my car – identified by its type and license number – or my dog, identified by its owner and name), and concepts, i.e. the collection or class of all objects sharing certain properties (e.g. the concept CAR as the class of all cars or the class DOG). Individual objects or instances are elements of their concepts (seen as sets); specialisation is a subset relation between classes.

For a uniform treatment of both discrete objects and substances we first have to work out a generalized concept of what may constitute an 'instance' and how it relates to the resp. concept (the individuation problem). A solution can be summarized as follows: The concept of a substance e.g. the concept 'water' is the abstraction comprising all occurrences of this substance in the universe which share their intrinsic properties. Substances are instantiated by specifying their extrinsic properties like a definite amount of the substance or by relating it to some container that contains the substance and thus implicitly restricts its amount.

This approach to the individuation of substances is in accordance with the linguistic treatment of the phenomena, especially the use of definite referring expressions:

- In a recipe you may e.g. first introduce the amount of ingrediences needed (e.g. 250 cl of milk, 25 gramm of butter, ...) and later use definite noun phrases to refer to these substances as if they were instances (e.g. Melt the butter ... Pour the milk ...).
- As soon as a container is introduced into a discourse, an amount of substance contained in it behaves as an instance (e.g. Warm up the engine ! CAUTION: The oil gets hot!)

We will call the most general substance concept which specifies only intrinsic properties *stuff* and the most general concept specifying only extrinsic properties *thing*. A category with both intrinsic and extrinsic properties has to be defined using (sub)concepts from both. The advantages of this factorisation of our ontology are:

- It is possible to augment already existing discrete objects with information about their substance by referring to the stuff hierarchy only.
- If one is interested only in intrinsic properties of a substance, for example to decide which material is particularly well suited for a certain function of an object, this can be described without using the thing-part of the ontology.
- A combination (through inheritance) of both hierarchies allows the uniform modelling of individuals for all kinds of substances.

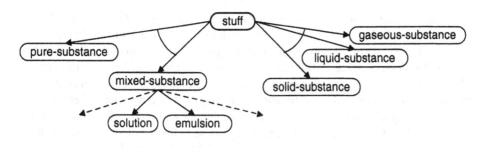

Fig. 1. *stuff hierarchy*

The stuff hierarchy[1] (cf. Figure 1) distinguishes at the toplevel between the following subconcepts: Pure and mixed substances are important for being able to model actions where more than one substance participate and because of the mentioned problem of not being able to make general inferences from properties of the components. For mixed substances only two examples are given, emulsion and solution. The distinction between three physical states is made because typical intrinsic properties often depend on their physical state (e.g. colour, conductivity, chemical reactivity, etc.). The divisions in the abstract ontology have been useful in modelling examples from specific technical domains [Web97].

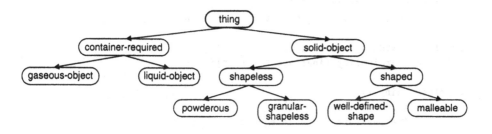

Fig. 2. *thing hierarchy*

Within the thing hierarchy (cf. Figure 2) a distinction is made between objects that require a container and those which do not. The former are specified by their mass or volume and can inherit properties like shape from their container. The temperature of an object (cf. Figure 3) is modelled as an extrinsic property

---

[1] We use the following notational conventions: Normal arrows describe a class/subclass relation (in the sense of subset of the instances). Arrows connected by an arc describe a disjunctive partition. For the concept `mixed-substance` we only mention two subconcepts as examples, the dashed arrows indicate that there exist other subconcepts which are not shown.

(it is only relevant for concrete instances) and as the physical state depends on this fact (in relation to the intrinsic properties melting point and boiling point) the latter may also be seen as an extrinsic property. Therefore we decided to model the physical state in the thing hierarchy, too but as a direct consequence of the extrinsic property temperature. Solid objects that do not require a container can be subdivided into shapeless and shaped which are generalizations of the four categories powderous, granular, malleable and well defined shape (cf. section 2). We do not consider shapeless objects as being inevitably container dependent because we should also be able to model a pile of sand without needing a container. A container is an example of an object with well defined shape.

Figure 3 shows the definition of some of the upper concepts of the stuff and thing hierarchy (figure 1 and 2 resp.) in POWERLOOM. The syntax of POWER-LOOM is a variant of KIF3.0 [GF92]. ?self is the default variable used to refer to the concept itself.

```
(defclass stuff ()
  :slots ((melting-point :type Integer)
          (boiling-point :type Integer)
          (ingredients :type (set of chemical-substance)))))

(defclass pure-substance (stuff)
  :<=> (= (cardinality (ingredients ?self)) 1))

(defclass mixed-substance (stuff)
  :<=> (> (cardinality (ingredients ?self)) 1))

(defclass thing ()
  :slots ((made-of :type stuff)
          (temperature :type Integer)))

(defclass solid-object (thing)
  :<=> (> (melting-point (made-of ?self)) (temperature ?self)))

(defclass gaseous-object (container-required)
  :<=> (< (boiling-point (made-of ?self)) (temperature ?self)))

(defclass liquid-object (substance-thing)
  :<=> (and (> (boiling-point (made-of ?self)) (temperature ?self))
            (< (melting-point (made-of ?self)) (temperature ?self))))
```

Fig. 3. *Excerpts from the thing and stuff ontology in* POWERLOOM.

4 Towards a taxonomy for substance-related actions

Based on the ontology for substances and its factorisation into the stuff and thing hierarchy we can now describe how actions related to substances can be modelled. The main distinction for actions (cf. section 2) is between substance-preserving actions (where intrinsic properties remain the same and extrinsic may change) and substance-changing actions (where intrinsic properties can change). Concerning the extrinsic properties a change of existential properties leads to instance-changing actions and if only non-existential properties are changed to instance-preserving actions.

Figure 4 shows the general taxonomy for substance related actions and an example for each type of action. There may exist several intermediate action categories between the top-level action categories and the examples (indicated by pointed arrows).

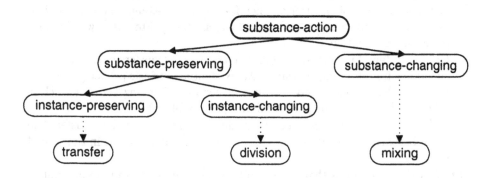

Fig. 4. *taxonomy for substance related actions*

In addition to this top-level taxonomy for actions we want to illustrate how actions on substances can be represented by giving a more specific example. It describes the different kinds of transfer of liquids from one container into another (cf. figure 5). How this can be implemented in PowerLoom is described in the following section.

The resp. concepts in the hierarchy for transfer actions are the following:

transfer: represents the transportation of a substance from one container into another. The second container may be filled partially with the same type of substance before the action has been carried out. This is a substance-preserving action (the same holds for all other subtypes) because only extrinsic properties like the referred container and potentially the volume are changed but the substances remain the same.

complete-transfer: specializes transfer in the aspect that the whole quantity of the first container is transferred to the second.

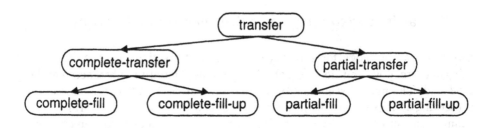

Fig. 5. *taxonomy for transfer actions*

complete-fill: has the additional constraint that the second container must be empty before the transfer. Since only non-existential properties of the substance (container) are changed, this is an instance-preserving action.

complete-fill-up: requires that the second container is filled by an amount of the same type of substance. Therefore it is an instance-changing action, because the substances in both containers are merged to one new substance in the second container.

partial-transfer: In contrast to complete-transfer it transfers only part of the substance from the first container. An existential extrinsic property (amount or volume) is changed and we have an instance-changing action (which is inherited by the actions partial-fill and partial-fill-up).

partial-fill: requires that the second container is empty before the transfer. The old substance is divided into two parts, one in the first and one in the second container.

partial-fill-up: requires that the second container must contain an amount of the same substance.

To illustrate the structure and the naming conventions of this taxonomy: The distinctive property for the first level is whether the first container is empty after the action has been carried out (named `complete-...`) or not (named `partial-...`). The distinction at the second level depends on the filledness of the second container before the action. If it has been empty it is named `...-fill`, in the other case `...-fill-up`. More complex actions like the distribution a substance into several empty new containers can be composed starting from these actions.

5 Action hierarchies in description logics

There are many different approaches for representing actions in object centered systems. For example, there are hierarchically organized action descriptions in systems for natural language processing (e. g. PENMAN Upper Model [BKMW90]). These descriptions classify actions by focusing mainly on the verb as the relevant object for classification. Action descriptions of this kind are well suited for natural language processing, but not sufficient for simulated execution. Other action descriptions in AI are related to the field of planning or plan recognition (e. g. RAT [HKNP92], T-REX [WL92]) and follow the STRIPS [FN71] approach. There, actions are interpreted as operators, mapping one world description into another. As a result of their operational description, actions can be executed for planning or simulation purposes. But there is no satisfying approach for defining actions by specializing more abstract actions.

In order to support the qualitative simulation of actions and to fulfill the requirements of object–centered languages, which are reusability, extensibility and understandability [Mey88], we propose an action representation which

- is *declarative* and *executable* (operational),
- allows *action* definitions by *specialization*,
- supports the *inheritance of pre- and postconditions* and
- results in a *hierarchical organization* of action descriptions.

Such an action representation allows the underlying inference mechanism to reason about actions in multiple dimensions. Performable actions, for example, are those which have a precondition which is true with respect to the current state of the world. Or one could ask for all those actions which fulfill a particular goal. All those answers are implicitly encoded in the action hierarchy and can be inferred by the classifier without much additional effort.

Consider the following fraction of a simplified action hierarchy as shown graphically in figure 5. Let us assume that all `transfer` actions change the location attribute of their action object[2], referenced here by the function `has-action-object`. The action `complete-transfer` inherits all properties (slots, pre- and postcondition, etc.) of `transfer`. The most relevant difference between these actions is, that the latter is defined to perform a complete transfer of the action object while specializing the former one. `complete-fill` is again more specific because this action assumes that the target container is empty.

Our work showed that one should be able to express conditions about attributes which are not known explicitly at time of description. This is useful in order to express abstract knowledge (consider an action `change` for example), shared by many different actions, but reified by different attributes (e. g. `transfer`, `change-temperature`). At the hierarchical level of `change` we have to abstract from the attribute we want to change because this could be either `has-location`, `has-temperature` or others. Nevertheless we want to specify pre- and postconditions for this abstract action. However, this requires second order features because we need to work with referenced relations, which are predicates in fact.[3] Second order features are not present in ordinary description logic sys-

---

[2] An action object, i.e. the object whose property is changed by an action, should not be confused with an instance of the category 'action'.

[3] What we actually need is unqualified existential quantification on predicates.

tems. In POWERLOOM (as well as in KIF [GF92]) this can be done via the holds predicate[4]. The abstract action change could then look as in figure 6.[5]

```
(defaction change (action)
 :slots ((affected-attribute :type RELATION)
         (has-new-value :type UNKNOWN)
         (has-old-value :type UNKNOWN))
 :precondition (holds (affected-attribute ?self)
                      (has-action-object ?self)
                      (has-old-value ?self))
 :postcondition (holds (affected-attribute ?self)
                       (has-action-object ?self)
                       (has-new-value ?self)))
```

Fig. 6. Definition of change

The action transfer could then be defined as a specialization of change inheriting all slots, pre- and postconditions of change. According to the action hierarchy of figure 5 we define complete-fill (which is itself an indirect descendant of transfer) in figure 7.

```
(defaction transfer (change)
 :constraints (= (affected-attribute ?self) has-location))

(defaction complete-fill (complete-transfer)
 :slots ((has-new-value :type container)
         (has-old-value :type container))
 :precondition (and (empty (has-new-value ?self))
                    (>= (capacity (has-new-value ?self))
                        (amount (has-action-object ?self)))))
 :postcondition (empty (has-old-value ?self)))
```

Fig. 7. Definition of transfer and complete-fill

Due to the inheritance of the action parameter, pre- and postcondition and concretion of the affected attribute in transfer, the action complete-fill has actually the internal definition, given in figure 8 for the sake of completeness.

---

[4] The semantics of holds is defined in KIF and POWERLOOM in the following way: If τ denotes a relation, then the sentence (holds τ τ_1 ... τ_k) is true if and only if the list of objects denoted by $\tau_1,...,\tau_k$ is a member of that relation.

[5] For sake of simplicity we omit all potential actions which may exist in the hierarchy between action and change.

```
(defaction complete-fill (complete-transfer)
  :slots ((has-action-object :type (and stuff thing))
          (has-new-value :type container)
          (has-old-value :type container))
  :precondition (and (empty (has-new-value ?self))
                     (has-location (has-action-object ?self)
                                   (has-old-value ?self))
                     (>= (capacity (has-new-value ?self))
                         (amount (has-action-object ?self))))
  :postcondition (and (empty (has-old-value ?self))
                      (has-location (has-action-object ?self)
                                    (has-new-value ?self))))
```

Fig. 8. Actual definition of `complete-fill`

Intuitively, the semantics of actions in general, and pre- and postconditions in particular, are straightforward with respect to PowerLoom semantics. Pre- and postconditions are semantically different from ordinary slots or relations for at least two reasons. First, there is an inherent relationship between them in the sense of a temporal ordering. Second, they characterize the action concept by expressing conditions about an instance (the action object) different from the action concept itself. Consequently the relationship between two actions has more dimensions than the relation between ordinary concepts. As a result, there are different subsumption relations between actions conceivable [LRn97]. The keywords `:precondition` and `:postcondition` were introduced in order to express these differences syntactically.

6 Related work

With respect to the analysis of *substances*, the distinction between count and mass expressions has for a long time been a subject in linguistic and philosophical literature (for an overview cf. [PS89]). The ontological distinction between thing and stuff motivated by intrinsic and extrinsic properties is adopted by many authors, for instance in the AI textbook of [RN95]. There exist many approaches for modelling special kinds of substances for domains which are motivated by the role substances play in certain application areas (e.g. the Plinius ontology for ceramic materials [vdVSM94]).

Concerning the *modelling of actions*, a system for the representation of actions and plans in a description logic (RAT – representation of actions using terminological logics, [HKNP92]) was developed in the WIP project [WAB+92]. Pre- and postconditions of atomic actions are described by using a subset of the underlying description logic. They define conjunctions of feature restrictions, agreements, and disagreements. However, RAT does not support the specialization of actions, as it is not possible to define similar actions as special cases of a general action. In contrast to the RAT sytem, actions in CLASP [DL91] as well as in T-REX [WL92] are primitive non-decomposable units. Yet, their language for composing plans is much richer. Another approach using Allen's temporal constraints is proposed in [AF97]. Action specialization is not possible in any of these systems.

The modelling of *actions related to substances* has been investigated by [Ter95] in the broader context of ontologies concerning processes or causes and effects. Especially the production or consumption of stuff has been treated but without considering the individuation problem for all physical states. Patrick Hayes was the first to define a detailed ontology for liquids [Hay85]. He solved the individuation problem for liquids by referring to a container and discussed actions by defining functions for modelling change and movements. He did, however, only consider what we call substance-preserving actions. [Dal92] analyses actions related to substances in the context of recipes. He argues that any mass object can be converted into a countable object by packaging operations. Further he proposes a representation for actions which admit decomposition and planning. [NH98] have created an ontology for the domain of experimental molecular biology where both substances and processes play a major role. In this domain, it is necessary to track substances through a series of experimental processes including transformations, which are modelled with the help of object histories.

None of the proposals just mentioned is able to define actions as a specialization of abstract actions. For the individuation of substances we have shown that all kinds of substances (especially in different physical states) can be treated uniformly in an ontology by a factorisation into an 'intrinsic' part (the stuff hierarchy) and an 'extrinsic' part (the thing hierarchy). One might not need this general approach for specific application domains but ignoring it could make extensions to include other kinds of substances very difficult.

7 Summary and outlook

In this paper we have described a proposal for the individuation of substances and for the modelling of actions in dynamic contexts. Due to technical reasons (the implementation status of PowerLoom is still very unstable and incomplete) up to now we have not been able to fully implement our ideas in a more or less complete ontology especially with respect to actions. Nevertheless we consider our approach an important step towards an ontology for substances and related actions.

Aspects similar to the individuation problem for substances can be found in other domains. The action of assembling a (technical) object from its parts will result in the creation of a corresponding instance. On the other hand, disassembling an object – e.g. for recycling – has the effect that the lifecycle of the object ends and the instance of the composite object ceases to exist.

There are some subtle issues related to the questions of what constitutes the identity of an instance and when the identity of an instance should change. Some even lead to paradoxa. For example we probably do not want to give up the identity of a non-trivial object (e.g. a car) when we replace a minor part of it (e.g. a spark-plug). But what about the case – already discussed by Greek philosophers – where we would step by step replace all parts that make up a compound object?

A related question with respect to instances of a substance: Assume that a fluid in a container continuously looses small amounts of substance. Will we create a new instance when we refill the more or less insignificant amount lost? Is there a difference to doing a significant fill-up (e.g. when more than half of the required amount has to be refilled)?

As often in issues of modelling there is no single and simple answer to these questions. The adequacy of the chosen granularity of a model has to be judged from the perspective of the application and the inferences needed. For the more abstract levels of an ontology this gives support for a 'strategy of least commitment', i.e. only those decisions should already be fixed on the ontological level that will not vary between different applications.

References

[AF97]   Alessandro Artale and Enrico Franconi. A temporal description logic for reasoning about action and plans. In *Journal of Artificial Intelligence Research*, 1997.

[BKMW90] J. Bateman, R. Kasper, J. Moore, and R. Whitney. A general organization of knowledge for natural language processing: the penman upper model. Technical report, USC/ISI, 1990.

[Dal92]   Robert Dale. *Generating Referring Expressions, Constructing Descriptions in a Domain of Objects and Processes.* MIT Press Cambridge, Massachusetts, 1992.

[DL91]   Premkumar T. Devanbu and Diane J. Litman. Plan-based terminological reasoning. In J. F. Doyle, R. Files, and Erik Sandewall, editors, *Principles of Knowledge Representation and Reasoning, Proceedings of the Second International Conference (KR '91)*, pages 128 – 138, Cambridge, MA, April 1991. Morgan Kaufmann Publishers, Inc., San Francisco, CA.

[FN71]   Richard E. Fikes and Nils J. Nilsson. STRIPS: A new approach to the application of theorem proving to problem solving. *Artificial Inteligence*, 2(3-4):189 – 208, 1971.

[GF92]   Michael R. Genesereth and Richard E. Fikes. *Knowledge Interchange Format, V. 3.0, Reference Manual.* Stanford University, June 1992.

[Gru95]   Thomas R. Gruber. Towards principles for the design of ontologies used for knowledge sharing. *International Journal of Human Computer Studies*, 43:907 – 928, 5/6 1995. Also available as Technical Report KSL 93-04, Knowledge Systems Laboratory, Stanford University.

[Hay85]   Patrick J. Hayes. *Formal theories of the commensense world*, chapter Naive physics I: Ontology for Liquids, pages 71–107. Ablex Publishing Corporation, 1985.

[HKNP92] J. Heinsohn, D. Kudenko, B. Nebel, and H. Profitlich. RAT: representation of actions using terminological logics. Technical report, DFKI, Saarbrücken, 1992.

[LRn97]   Thorsten Liebig and Dietmar Rösner. Action hierarchies for the automatic generation of multilingual technical documents. In Rémi Zajac, editor, *IJCAI-97 Workshop Ontologies and Multilingual NLP*, Nagoya, Japan, August 1997. International Joint Conference on Artificial Intelligence.

[Mac94]   Robert M. MacGregor. A description classifier for the predicate calculus. In *Proceedings of the Twelfth National Conference on Artificial Intelligence*, pages 213 – 230, 1994.

[Mey88]   Bertrand Meyer. *Object-oriented Software Construction*. Prentice Hall, New York, 1988.

[NH98]   Natalya Fridman Noy and Carole D. Hafner. Representing Scientific experiments: Implications for Ontology Design and Knowledge Sharing. In *15th National Conference on Artificial Intelligence (AAAI98)*, Madison Wisconsin, July 1998. AAAI Press.

[PS89]   Francis Jeffry Pelletier and Lenhart K. Schubert. *Handbook of philosophical logic*, chapter Mass Expressions, pages 327–407. D. Reidel Publishing Company, 1989.

[RN95]   Stuart Russel and Peter Norvig. *Artificial Intelligence: A Modern Approach*, pages 241 – 243. Prentice Hall, 1995.

[Ter95]   Paolo Terenziani. Towards a causal ontology coping with the temporal constraints between causes and effects. *International Journal for Human-Computer Studies*, 43(5/6):847–863, 1995.

[vdVSM94] Paul E. van der Vet, Piet-Hein Speel, and Nicolaas J. I. Mars. The plinius ontology of ceramic materials. *Workshop Notes ECAI'94 in Amsterdam, Workshop Comparison of Implemented Ontologies*, pages 187 – 205, 1994.

[WAB+92] W. Wahlster, E. André, S. Bandyopadhyay, W. Graf, and T. Rist. WIP: The Coordinated Generation of Multimodal Presentations from a Common Representation. In A. Ortony, J. Slack, and O. Stock, editors, *Communication from an Artificial Intelligence Perspective: Theoretical and Applied Issues*, pages 121 – 144. Springer-Verlag, New York, Berlin, Heidelberg, 1992.

[Web97]   Lars Webel. Modellierung eines Teilgebiets der Domäne Werkstoffe für technische Produkte und Implementation in LOOM. Technical report, Otto-von-Guericke Universität Magdeburg, Institut für Informations- und Kommunikationssysteme, 1997.

[Web98]   L. Webel. Untersuchungen zur Modellierung von Substanzen. Diplomarbeit, Otto-von-Guericke Universität Magdeburg, 1998.

[WL92]   R. Weida and D. Litman. Terminological reasoning with constraint networks and an application to plan recognition. In Nebel, Swartout, and Rich, editors, *Proceedings of Principles of Knowledge Representation and Reasoning (KR'92)*, 1992.

Use of Formal Ontologies to Support Error Checking in Specifications

Yannis Kalfoglou and David Robertson

School of Artificial Intelligence,
Institute for Representation and Reasoning,
Division of Informatics, University of Edinburgh,
80, South Bridge, Edinburgh EH1 1HN,
Scotland
{yannisk,dr}@dai.ed.ac.uk

Abstract. This paper explores the possibility of using formal ontologies to support detection of conceptual errors in specifications. We define a conceptual error as a misunderstanding of the application domain knowledge which results in undesirable behaviour of the software system. We explain how to use formal ontologies, and in particular ontological constraints, to tackle this problem. We present a flexible architecture based on meta interpretation in logic programming in which the specification is viewed as a multilayer design. We illustrate the significance of this approach for the software and ontology engineering community via an example case in the domain of ecological modelling.

1 Introduction

1.1 Specifications

The use of blueprints for guiding the development process of projects is common in many disciplines. In particular, in the field of software development, these blueprints are precise and independent descriptions of the desired program behaviour. They are crucial for the success of projects since they guide the way in which programmers will construct the desirable software. This has lead to the adoption of formal descriptions expressed in logic as a medium of blueprint, the purpose of which is to [9] "define all required characteristics of the software to be implemented, and thus form the starting point of any software development process". However, the precise role of formality in software development is a matter of debate([4]).

Formal methods support tests for some forms of completeness and consistency and there exist methods for methodological refinement of some types of formal specification into executable form, via appropriate interpreters. This provides an additional advantage, an executable specification represents not only a conceptual but also a behavioural model of the software system to be implemented [10], allowing early validation. Moreover, execution of the specification supplements inspection and reasoning as a means of validation. This might increase the correctness and the reliability of the software, and reduce development costs and time.

1.2 Conceptual errors

When describing a chosen domain we can make mistakes related to the mathematical language underpinning the formal model, like writing a non-terminating recursion using a logic programming language, or we can make mistakes in describing the domain, like defining an ecological model in which animals photosynthesise. The latter type of mistake is difficult to detect because it requires subjective knowledge about correct forms of domain description to be applied to the model description. We call this sort of mistake a conceptual error.

It is difficult, even with executable formal languages, to make models error free. In fact, it is easy(maybe easier) to make errors in this phase with pernicious side-effects for the remainder of the life cycle. This is because they may not be detected by those who use the formal model in subsequent design and may affect the functionality of entire systems by being propagated to subsequent design phases. The earlier the errors are detected the less serious are their consequences.

1.3 Our solution

Ontologies, which forge agreements on the use of terminology for particular domains are, potentially, a way of reducing this problem. Ontological engineers are beginning to supply information which helps in detecting conceptual errors. This information accompanies the formal ontology to which the specification should conform to and is often expressed in the form of axioms whose role is to restrict all possible interpretations of the ontology's constructs. In this paper we present a mechanism that makes the most of this information to allow us perform checks for conceptual errors in specifications.

1.4 Organisation of this paper

This paper is organised as follows: section 2 describes the field of formal ontologies with respect to ontological constraints, the core of our mechanism. In section 3 we present our detection mechanism and on section 4 we illustrate an example of its use. We elaborate further on a different use of the mechanism on section 5 where we conclude our work.

2 Formal ontologies

Ontologies have become popular in the recent years in the field of artificial intelligence. There exist different types of ontologies and numerous ways of constructing them ([8],[27]). The interpretation of the term varies across different communities and [15],[14] elaborates on terminological clarifications. The engineering community, and particular the KBS community has adopt a definition proposed by [11] and further elaborated by [27] and [24]. The type of ontologies in which we are interested in are the formal ontologies. A formal ontology is a language with a precisely defined syntax and semantics(which may be determined via model theory, proof theory or in terms of another formal ontology).

The inferences permitted in the language are constrained by one or more sets of proof rules accompanied by appropriate proof strategies. The forms of description allowed by those using the ontology are required to be consistent with a set of axioms limiting its use, which we call 'ontological constraints'. The aim of the ontology is to provide a language which allows a stipulated group of people to share information reliably in a chosen area of work.

A variety of ontologies have been reported in the literature with emphasis to their intended use in the area of knowledge sharing and reuse. There exist tools for browsing and editing ontologies(e.g.Ontolingua) as well as guidelines and methodologies to be followed on constructing them([27],[6],[2]). Although there have been efforts in applying ontologies(e.g.[5],[28],[21],[26],[16],[1]) as pointed out in [25] there is a dearth of well-developed applications based on formal ontologies. This contradiction is visible in the field of AI where the few applications that are discussed are intended applications which are yet to be built, or small research prototypes. According to [25] the reason for this is the lack of a rich representation of meanings which is contrary to the traditionally formal knowledge representation adopted by the AI ontology community.

Ontologies provide a set of characteristics that can be used in various ways. Apart from their intended purpose of knowledge sharing and reuse, we advocate that ontologies can be used in software design and in particular to support verification and formal evaluation of the early phases of it. This approach, although in its infancy, has already been explored in research experiments ([26]). Other researchers have used similar techniques([20]) and pointed out the benefits of using an ontology as a starting point in the design of a software product([19]).

By using ontologies as a starting point of software development we hope to gain a higher level of assurance that the specification is well defined and evaluated with respect to the real world it represents. This assumes that the syntax and semantics of an ontology can be checked and verified(arguably) against axioms. Note that, should one choose to follow this path it is not necessary strictly to use only the ontology's constructs in the specification. In fact, it is normally impractical to construct an executable specification by using only the ontology's constructs. Other constructs should be included as well, which do not directly benefit from the presence of ontological constraints but will be checked for errors using normal debugging techniques.

2.1 Ontological constraints

These are usually have the form of ontological axioms. We describe in textual form an axiom of a formal ontology, the PIF ontology [1] as presented in [21]:

> "The *participates-in* relation only holds between objects, activities, and timepoints, respectively"

This axiom can be formalised in first order theory as follows:

---

[1] more on PIF can be found on [17]

$$participates\_in(X, A, T) \leftarrow object(X) \wedge activity(A) \wedge point(T).$$

The purpose of having formally defined this axiom is to allow reason about the various definitions of *participates-in* relation. So, whenever someone using the PIF ontology describes the relation in a way which does not conform to its axiomatised definition, this will reveal a potential discrepancy. For example, the following erroneous definition:

$$participates\_in(O1, O2, T) \leftarrow object(O1) \wedge object(O2) \wedge point(T).$$

is difficult to detect since it conforms to the ontology's syntax but reflects a misunderstanding of ontology's semantics [2].

The ontological axioms can be enhanced by adding more axioms or by introducing domain specific error conditions [3]. An error condition, which could be domain specific and added later on by the 'error checker' or software tester of the specification, is an erroneous condition which exhibits some undesired behaviour of the specification. Once this condition is satisfied during the error checking phase it will demonstrate an error occurrence in the specification. The erroneous definition of *participates-in* relation given above is an example of error condition. This technique will make the error checking domain specific and result in a customisation of the error detection process.

We call this sort of axiomatisation along with the domain specific error conditions, ontological constraints. Our approach explores a different angle in the use of ontological constraints. Moreover, it has been written that ontological constraints apart from the practical benefit of formal evaluation they provide([13]), they also verify that the ontology is consistent with respect to its conceptual coverage. This may facilitate mapping of ontologies that exhibit the same conceptual coverage of the real world([12],[3]), though conflicts may arise due to lack of correspondence on their top level division ([8]).

3 Error detection mechanism

Our mechanism, which is based on meta-interpretation, uses the products of ontological engineering such as ontological constraints to detect conceptual errors in specifications that are based on ontologies. The internals of the meta-interpreter will be described in detail at section 3.1. In this section we will focus on the general architecture we are adopting and the invention of a multilayered approach for error checking in specifications. The diagrammatic version of the mechanism is illustrated on Figure 1.

Specification construction starts by adopting the syntax and semantics of the ontology. We use Horn clause logic as a specification construction formalism [4],

---

[2] although this example is a typing error, not all ontological errors are simply defined in terms of types

[3] [26] elaborates on the need of additional axioms tailored to domain specific applications

[4] refer to [10] for the value of using declarative specifications

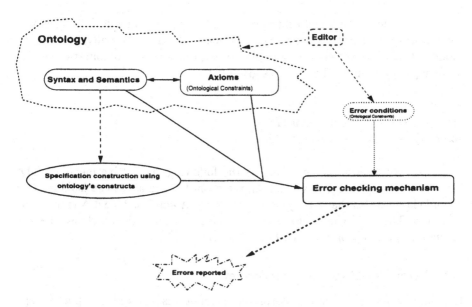

Fig. 1. Multi-layer architecture

with the normal Prolog execution model. To this we apply our checking mechanism and thus prevent the occurrence and propagation to subsequent phases of software development of harmful conceptual errors.

Few conventional ontological constraints are defined in this form so a transformation of them to the appropriate format is required. Although, the transformation could be done manually, we used an editor to facilitate the task of writing the constraints in the format manipulated by the meta-interpreter.

Additional domain specific error conditions can be defined to facilitate customised error checking. Assuming that an exhaustive check is required, then the ontological axioms will be the focal point of the mechanism. Whenever a statement in our specification will not satisfy the ontological axioms an error will be reported. Our mechanism can utilise both approaches to error detection, ontological axioms and error conditions, simultaneously and thus raise our confidence that the specification which will pass the test will be error-free.

3.1 Meta-interpreters

A meta interpreter is an interpreter for a language written in the language itself [23]. It gives access to the computation process of the language and enables the building of an integrated programming environment. In the domain of Prolog programming, a meta interpreter is program written in Prolog which interprets Prolog programs. This makes it possible to represent in Prolog the search strategy used by Prolog interpreter and to adopt that strategy in various ways, which are often different from the standard interpreter. Among the best known and widely used meta interpreters is the 'vanilla' model. It models the computation model of logic programs as goal reduction. Actually, the vanilla model reflects Prolog's choices of implementing the abstract computation model of logic programming. The model is given below:

$solve(true).$
$solve(A, B) \leftarrow solve(A) \wedge solve(B).$
$solve(A) \leftarrow clause(A, B) \wedge solve(B).$

This meta-interpreter program has the following declarative meaning: The first clause states that, by convention, the atom true is always satisfiable. The second clause states that a conjunction of literals A and B is true if A is true and B is true. The third clause states that A is true if there exists a clause $A \leftarrow B$ in the interpreted program such that B is true.

3.2 Error checking meta interpreter

Our aim in using the meta-interpreter technique is not only to purely replicate the computational model of Prolog. We are interested in utilising the products of ontological engineering - ontological constraints - to augment the meta-interpreter. This, in turn, will enable us to perform specific tests on selected goals of the specification with regard to the ontological constraints. The basis of the meta-interpreter is the standard vanilla model. In doing this we can explore the whole search space for a proof in the specification exactly in the normal way. So, the specification is actually executed in the normal way and checking for conceptual errors is performed on goals which have succeeded in the proofs. Thus, the maximum possible information is supplied for testing making sure that we wont loose crucial information on intermediate results.

The error checking is recursive, so the proof that an error exists may itself generate errors. Those are checked against the ontological constraints exhaustively. We cumulate all the errors that are detected on given goals for testing as well as on their subgoals. We also cumulate information regarding the execution path that has been followed by the inference mechanism in proving a goal, the type of ontological constraint that has not been satisfied - axiom or error condition - and the layer that the error has occur. This notion will be explored in detail on section 5.1, we ignored for the time being since it does not affect the understanding of the algorithm.

We draw the attention of the reader to the specific format we are using for expressing specification statements as well as axioms and error templates. We use the standard logic notation $A \leftarrow B$, to denote that A is satisfiable if there exists a literal B which is satisfiable as follows:

$specification(Index, (A \leftarrow B))$

where *Index* stands for the index of specification layer that the clause $A \leftarrow B$ belongs to. In cases where we have ground terms (clauses without subgoals) we use, by convention, the $A \leftarrow true$ notation. As far as concern the axioms and/or error conditions the format is:

ConstraintType(Index,Axiom,Condition)
where *ConstraintType* stands for either ontological axiom or error condition and denote the property that should hold, *Index* has the same meaning as before, and *Condition* is a condition(s) that has to be satisfiable in order for the ontological axiom to be satisfiable. The same format applies for error condition with the only difference being that the condition(s) must not be satisfiable.

The error checking meta-interpreter is given in Prolog notation at appendix A. We illustrate below in a pseudo-language the algorithm we apply:

for the given goal, **G**, *for testing*
> *while its layer,* **L**, *is not the last one*
> > *1. prove* **G** *by applying the 'vanilla' model exhaustively and check for conceptual error occurrences on goal* **G** *with respect to ontological constraints of layer* **L+1**
> > *2. prove subgoal,* **Gn**, *if any, of* **G**, *by applying the same strategy*
> *exit while loop and cumulate information regarding execution path, conceptual errors found as well as the goal that are contained along with the ontological constraints that has not been satisfied*

4 Error detection demonstration

In this section we will present, briefly, the practical use of our mechanism in an example case: an error detection in the ecological modelling domain. We use the following pattern in describing the case: an introductory part stating the problem description and relative domain knowledge opens the description which is followed by the specification of the problem. The ontological constraints are described in the sequel. This will help the reader to follow the test query and the conceptual errors detected based on the ontological constraints given, which close the case description.

4.1 Ecological model error checking

We have chosen ecology domain because in ecological modelling, being concerned with complex biological systems, it is difficult to decide how to represent the observed systems in a simplified form as simulation models. Furthermore, they are fraught with uncertainty and are prone to errors, especially conceptual errors. We demonstrate how our mechanism can alleviate this situation.

We have used a simple ecological model described in detail on [22]. The representation of this model in Prolog is given in the appendix B. We describe here the model in textual form: The model uses a "State Transition" approach to represent the passage of time during simulation. Suppose that we have 3 different animals(call them *a,b* and *c*) and that *a* prey on *b*; *b* prey on *c*; and *c* will prey on *a*. The area on which these animals live is represented by a grid with 3 squares along each side(thus 9 grid square grids in all). Animals move by shifting from the square in which they are currently situated to adjoining square. Each animal moves in the direction of potential prey(e.g. they actively hunt rather than browsing at random) but will not visit a square which it has occupied previously. If an animal is ever in the same square as its prey, the prey is eaten and thus removed from the simulation.

The specifier chooses to represent the states as follows: the initial state is named s0. New states of the system will be obtained whenever some aspect of the system changes so we require some way of linking the changes imposed on the system to the events which impose those changes. This could be achieved by the use of a nested term of the form:

`do(Action,State)`

where `Action` is a term representing some action which has been performed. `State` is either the initial state s0 or another term of the form:

`do(PreviousAction,PreviousState)`

The only action which it is necessary to represent in this model is the movement of an animal from one grid square to another. The specifier represents this action using the term `move(A,G1,G2)` where A is the name of some animal; G1 is the location of the grid square at which the animal was located in the previous state and G2 is its new location. Figure 2 illustrates a diagrammatic version of a move of animal a from square (1,1) which triggers a move of animal b to square (3,2).

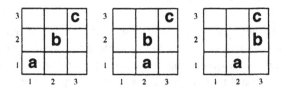

Fig. 2. State transition model - sequence of moves

Specification Although the model can generate any valid state of the system based on the constraints stipulated in the previous section for brevity and clarity we will focus on a fragment of the model that represents the treatment of locations for each animal in the system. However, before describing this chunk of code we will see how system generates the valid states: [5]:

```
1 specification(0,(possible_state(State) ←
              possible_state(s0,State))).
2 specification(0,(possible_state(State,State) ← true)).
3 specification(0,(possible_state(State,FinalState)←
4              possible_action(do(A,State)) ∧
5              possible_state(do(A,State),FinalState))).
```

---

[5] the whole model is included at appendix B

For convenience of reading we have numbered the lines in correspondence with the code of appendix B. The declarative meaning of this top level goal of the specification is as follows: State must be a valid state of the system and this is defined by stating that possible_state(s0,State) must be true. This has effect of producing a valid State, starting with s0 as in initial state(line 1). This is true if FinalState is a valid state of the system which can be reached from State. In the simplest case, this is true if FinalState=State(line 2). Otherwise, it will be true if there is a possible action, A, which can be applied to State and the new state described by do(A,State) leads to FinalState.

In order to reason about the validity of various states of the system the specifier introduces a predicate, holds(C,S), where condition C holds in state S. Three conditions are modelled: the location of an animal; whether it has been eaten; and which squares it has visited. For the purpose of demonstrating the error detection, we list here chunks of the specification that include potential error occurrences in describing the condition of animal location:

```
11 specification(0,(holds(location(a,(1,1)),s0) ← true)).
12 specification(0,(holds(location(b,(2,2)),s0) ← true)).
13 specification(0,(holds(location(c,(3,3)),s0) ← true)).
14 specification(0,(holds(location(A,G),State) ← ¬ State=s0 ∧
15               animal(A) ∧
17               last_location(A,State,G))).
```

At lines 11-13, the specifier defines the locations of the animals in the initial state, s0. In lines 14-17 defines the location of any animal in states other than s0. In such states an animal has a location determined by its most recent position in the sequence of actions. However, as we will see below there is a serious omission in this representation which will lead to undesirable behaviour of the model. This is detectable with the use of domain knowledge as expressed by the ontology.

Ontological constraints Although the specification is constructed based on the ontology's syntax and semantics, it should conform to various domain-specific constraints on the use of the ontology. For example, in order for an animal to exist at a particular location on the system it should not have been eaten in the meantime. Thus, a predator and a prey cannot be at the same square at the same state. We represent this constraint as follows:

```
60 axiom(1,holds(location(A,G),S),
61      (predator(A,B),
62      ¬ holds(location(B,G),S))).
```

Lines 60-62 represent the ontology's axiom. As we will see the specifier will have to redefine the holds/2 clause with respect to animals location in order to conform to the ontological axiom given above.

Test query Assume a specification which has no errors, we can use the model by asking: 'Is there a state of the system in which animal, *a*, gets eaten?' giving the Prolog goal:

```
| ?- onto_solve((possible_state(S),holds(eaten(a),S)),[]).
```

The Prolog interpreter would then use the definitions of model structure [6] to solve this goal, instantiating S to a sequence of potential moves. The result is given below diagrammatically in figure 3 and in Prolog form:

```
S = do(move(c,(2,3),(2,2)),do(move(c,(3,3),(2,3)),
     do(move(a,(2,1),(2,2)),do(move(a,(1,1),(2,1)),s0)))))
```

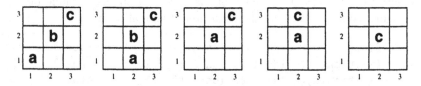

Fig. 3. Sequence of moves

As we can see, animal *a* has moved from its initial position (1,1) to (2,2) through square (2,1). Animal *c*, which preys on *a*, has moved from its initial position (3,3) to (2,2) and this satisfied the condition of holds(eaten(a),S). Note that animal *b* has removed from the simulation since its predator, animal *a* occupies the same square in the grid, that is (2,2).

However, assume the specification of our case(lines 14-17), on backtracking an erroneous answer will be returned to the same query. The Prolog answer is given followed by an illustration in Figure 4:

```
S = do(move(a,(3,2),(3,3)),do(move(b,(3,2),(3,3)),
     do(move(a,(2,2),(3,2)),do(move(b,(2,2),(3,2)),
     do(move(a,(2,1),(2,2)),do(move(a,(1,1),(2,1)),s0))))))
```

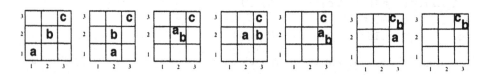

Fig. 4. Erroneous sequence of moves

---

[6] refer to appendix B for the representation of the model in Prolog

It is obvious that there is a problem with this answer. We observe a contradiction with the problem constraints: animal *b* continues to exist and actively moves although its predator, animal *a*, has visited its location to the grid, that is (2,2). This discrepancy is detected from the ontological axiom given above and explained in the next section.

Errors detected The error is detectable by the ontological axiom of lines 60-62. We illustrate the result diagrammatically in the form of a proof tree as shown in figure 5.

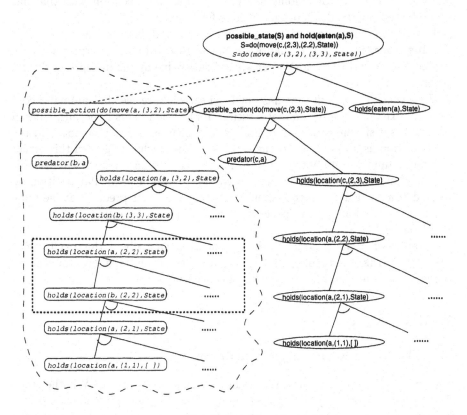

Fig. 5. Proof trees

The right part of the tree is the correct one while the left one is the ontologically erroneous path that has been followed. State variable S is instantiated to two values: the correct one is in plain font while the erroneous is in italics. In the right tree we have place in ellipses the goals that has been satisfied conjunctive arcs connecting them. The erroneous tree which is surrounded by a dashed line shows the correspondent satisfied goals within rectangle boxes. The rectangle box with a dashed line border represents the goal that does not conform to the axiom. This is reported by the mechanism as follows:

```
|?-onto_solve((possible_state(S),holds(eaten(a),S)),[]),report_errors.
axiom_violated(1,holds(location(a,(2,2)),do(move(a,(2,1),(2,2)),
                do(move(a,(1,1),(2,1)),s0)))),
                (predator(a,X),
                ¬ holds(location(X,(2,2)),
                do(move(a,(2,1),(2,2)),do(move(a,(1,1),(2,1)),s0)))))
```

we are using the reporting goal, report_errors/5(appendix A) to provide information concerning the axiom violated as well as the execution path that has been followed but we don't present it here for brevity.

In terms of meta-interpreter the discrepancy found, because the ¬ holds(location(B,G),S) clause was not satisfiable by the interpreter. As we pointed out earlier(3.1) axioms that are not satisfiable by the interpreter denote an error occurrence.

If we check the axiom that has not been satisfied we see that animal b continues to exists even after animal a visited its location. This is because animal b failed to satisfy the condition of line 62, in which 'an animal cannot hold the same position as its predator at the same state'. But what triggered this error?

If we examine carefully the specification of location condition we will discover an important omission: In order for an animal to keep a particular position on the grid at a particular State it should not get eaten by its predator at the same State. This could added to the specification by the statement:
$\neg holds(eaten(A), State)$
This statement, which is added to the specification manually by the specifier as a subgoal of holds(location(A,G),State) resolves the discrepancy. Our system, currently, does not support correction of conceptual errors.

5 Discussion

5.1 Checking the ontological constraints

How we can be sure that the ontological constraints are correct? Whether they are provided by ontological engineers in the form of ontological axioms or are domain specific error conditions they may be erroneously defined. This could lead to an erroneous error diagnosis with pernicious side effects. However, our proofs that error exist are done using the same mechanism as for specifications, making it possible to define constraints on error ontologies.

The advantage of this approach is that we can use the some core mechanism, the meta interpreter program, to check many specifications and their ontological constraints simultaneously. A key decision we made here is to use the same kind of augmentations to our meta interpreter model so that it can be used in many layers without the need of amendments. A diagrammatic version of the mechanism is given on Figure 6.

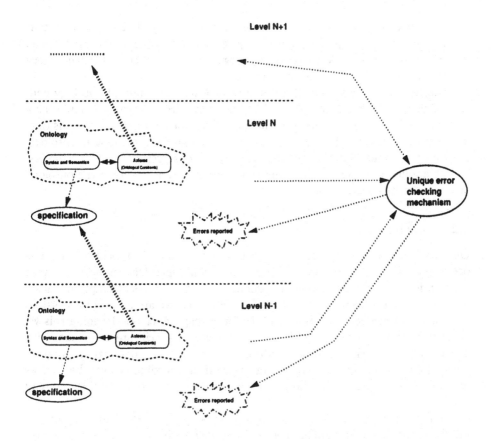

Fig. 6. Multi-layer architecture

This multi layered architecture is used as follows: assume that at the lower layer a specifier constructs the specification which we hope conforms to the syntax and semantics of the chosen ontology. The specification should also conform to the ontological constraints provided by the ontology - which can be checked with our mechanism as shown in the examples on a previous section(4). This will guarantee that the specification is correct with respect to the parts of it that conform to the ontological constraints.

However, if ontological constraint has been erroneously defined we can check this for error with our flexible mechanism. Ontological constraints are checked for errors against another set of constraints which can be viewed as meta-level constraints. They are part of the ontology and their use is to verify the correctness of the constraints. The result of this check will be the detection of an error, if any, in the ontological constraints. Ultimately, this layer checking can be extended to an arbitrary number of layers upwards, until no more layers can be defined.

The advantage is that we can capture a wide variety of errors occurring at different layers of the specification. It is possible to view the axioms introduced at each layer of error checking as an ontology and to check these for each query of the program by using the same mechanism.

Another use of this multi-layer architecture is in the area of ontology construction. It is often stated ([2]) that ontology construction can be viewed as a software design process. Moreover, the lack of rigorous evaluation methods during their construction will make prospective users reluctant to adopt an ontology. Assuming a middle-out or a bottom-up way of construction [7] this mechanism can be applied in order to detect discrepancies at various layers of the ontology or phases of its construction.

5.2 Conclusions

Our work contributes to existing work in error checking in specifications. The occurrence of conceptual errors which plague the specifications is of a great concern for the software engineering community and various attempts to tackle the problem have been made([20],[18],[7]). However, we are aware of no system that deploys ontological axioms to check for conceptual errors. In doing this we connect domain knowledge with the specification to facilitate error check for conceptual errors whereas other traditional techniques(e.g. debugging, program tracers) fail to reveal those errors. Our mechanism is flexible and can be used as a supplement to normal checking procedure without affecting the test strategy used.

Our work also contributes to ongoing work in the area of applications of ontologies. It proposes a different use of ontologies which diverge from the traditional ones(reuse, knowledge sharing). This use is(arguably) easier to apply since it relies on selective usage of ontological constraints tailored to domain specific problem descriptions. Furthermore, the multilayered approach we present is flexible to assist ontological engineers perform specific tests during the various phases of ontology construction with respect to domain knowledge.

Acknowledgements

The research described in this paper is supported by a European Union Marie Curie Fellowship(programme: Training and Mobility of Researchers) for the first author and a EPSRC IT Advanced Fellowship for the second author.

References

1. R. Benjamins and D. Fensel. The Ontological Engineering Initiative-KA2. In N. Guarino, editor, *Proceedings of the 1st International Conference on Formal Ontologies in Information Systems, FOIS'98, Trento, Italy*, pages 287–301. IOS Press, June 1998.

---

[7] see [8] and [27] for a discussion on various ways of ontology construction

2. M. Blazquez, M. Fernadez, J.M. Garcia-Pinar, and A. Gomez-Perez. Building Ontologies at the Knowledge Level using the Ontology Design Environment. In *Proceedings of the 11th Knowledge Acquisition Workshop, KAW98, Banff, Canada,* April 1998.
3. P. Borst, H. Akkermans, and J. Top. Engineering Ontologies. In *Proceedings of the 10th Knowledge Acquisition for Knowledge Based Systems Workshop,Banff, Canada,* 1996.
4. G. Cleland and D. MacKenzie. Inhibiting Factors, Market Structure and the Industrial Uptake of Formal Methods. In *Proceedings of Workshop on Industrial-Strength Formal Specification Techniques,* pages 47–61, Orlando(Florida) USA, April 1995. Boca Raton, Florida, USA.
5. Enterprise Integration Laboratory, University of Toronto, Canada. TOVE Project. available from http://www.ie.utoronto.ca/EIL/tove/ontoTOC.html, July 1995.
6. M. Fernandez, A. Gomez-Perez, and N. Juristo. METHONTOLOGY: From Ontological Arts Towards Ontological Engineering. In *Proceedings of the AAAI-97 Spring Symposium Series on Ontological Engineering, Stanford, USA,* pages 33–40, March 1997.
7. A. Finkelstein. Reviewing and Correcting Specifications. *Instructional Science,* 21:183–198, 1992.
8. N. Fridman Noy and C.D. Hafner. The State of the Art in Ontology Design: A Survey and Comparative Review. *AI Magazine,* pages 53–74, 1997.
9. N. Fuchs. Specifications are (preferably) executable. *Software Engineering Journal,* pages 323–334, September 1992.
10. N. Fuchs and D. Robertson. Declarative Specifications. *The Knowledge Engineering Review,* 11(4):317–331, 1996.
11. T.R. Gruber. A Translation Approach to Portable Ontologies. *Knowledge Acquisition,* 5(2):199–220, 1993.
12. M. Gruninger. Designing and Evaluating Generic Ontologies. In *Proceedings of the 12th European Conference of Artificial Intelligence,* August 1996.
13. M. Gruninger and M.S. Fox. Methodology for the Design and Evaluation of Ontologies. In *Proceedings of Workshop on Basic Ontological Issues in Knowledge Sharing, Montreal, Quebec,Canada,* August 1995.
14. N. Guarino. Formal Ontology and Information Systems. In N. Guarino, editor, *Proceedings of the 1st International Conference on Formal Ontologies in Information Systems, FOIS'98, Trento, Italy,* pages 3–15. IOS Press, June 1998.
15. N. Guarino and P. Giaretta. Ontologies and Knowledge Bases: Towards a Terminological Clarification. *Towards Very Large Knowledge Bases,* 1995. IOS Press, Amsterdam.
16. Z. Jin, D. Bell, F.G. Wilkie, and D. Leahy. Automatically Acquiring Requirements of Business Information Systems by Reusing Business Ontology. In Gomez-Perez,A. and Benjamins,R., editor, *Proceedings of Workshop on Applications of Ontologies and Problem Solving Methods, ECAI'98, Brighton, England,* August 1998.
17. J. Lee, M. Gruninger, Y. Jin, T. Malone, A. Tate, G Yost, and other members of the PIF working group. The PIF Process Interchange Format and framework. *Knowledge Engineering Review,* 13(1):91–120, February 1998.
18. Luqi and D. Cooke. How to combine nonmonotonic logic and rapid prototyping to help maintain software. *International Journal of Software Engineering and Knowledge Engineering,* 5(1):89–118, 1995.
19. W. Mark. Ontologies as Representation and Re-Representation of Agreement. In *Proceedings of the 5th International Conference on Principles of Knowledge*

Representation and Reasoning, KR'96, Massachusetts, USA, 1996. Position paper presented on the panel: *Ontologies: What are they and where's the research.*

20. W. Mark, S. Tyler, J. McGuire, and J. Schossberg. Commitment-Based Software Development. *IEEE Transactions on Software Engineering*, 18(10):870–884, October 1992.

21. S. Polyak, J. Lee, M. Gruninger, and C. Menzel. Applying the Process Interchange Format(PIF) to a Supply Chain Process Interoperability Scenario. In A. Gomez-Perez and R. Benjamins, editors, *Proceedings of Workshop on Applications of Ontologies and Problem Solving Methods, ECAI'98, Brighton, England*, August 1998.

22. D. Robertson, A. Bundy, R. Muetzefeldt, M. Haggith, and M. Uschold. *ECOLOGIC Logic-Based Approaches to Ecological Modelling.* MIT Press, 1991. ISBN: 0-262-18143-6.

23. L. Sterling and E. Shapiro. *The Art of Prolog.* MIT Press, 4th edition, 1994. ISBN: 0-262-69163-9.

24. M. Uschold. Knowledge level modelling: concepts and terminology. *The Knowledge Engineering Review*, 13(1):5–29, February 1998.

25. M. Uschold. Where are the Killer Apps? In Gomez-Perez,A. and Benjamins,R., editor, *Proceedings of Workshop on Applications of Ontologies and Problem Solving Methods, ECAI'98, Brighton, England*, August 1998.

26. M. Uschold, P. Clark, M. Healy, K. Williamson, and S. Woods. An Experiment in Ontology Reuse. In *Proceedings of the 11th Knowledge Acquisition Workshop, KAW98, Banff, Canada*, April 1998.

27. M. Uschold and M. Gruninger. Ontologies: principles, methods and applications. *The Knowledge Engineering Review*, 11(2):93–136, November 1996.

28. M. Uschold, M. King, S. Moralee, and Y. Zorgios. The enterprise ontology. *Knowledge Engineering Review*, 13(1), February 1998. Also available as AIAI-TR-195 from AIAI, University of Edinburgh.

A Error checking meta interpreter

```
1 onto_solve(Goal,Path):- solve(Goal,Path,0).
2 solve((A,B),Path,Level):- solve(A,Path,Level),
3         solve(B,Path,Level).
4 solve((A;B),Path,Level):- solve(A,Path,Level) ;
5         solve(B,Path,Level).
6 solve(\+ X,Path,Level):- \+ solve(X,Path,Level).
7 solve(X,Path,Level):- \+ logical_expression(X),
8         predicate_property(X,(meta_predicate _Z)),
9         solve_metapred(X,Call,Path,Level),!,
10        Call.
11 solve_metapred(findall(X,Z,L),
12        findall(X,solve(Z,Path,Level),L),Path,Level).
13 solve_metapred(setof(X,Z,L),
14        setof(X,solve(Z,Path,Level),L),Path,Level).
15 solve(X,_,_) :- \+ logical_expression(X),
16        predicate_property(X, built_in),
17        X.
18 solve(X,Path,Level) :-
19 \+ (logical_expression(X); predicate_property(X,built_in)),
```

```
20          specification(L, (X :- Body)),
21          L =< Level,
22          solve(Body,[X|Body],Level),
23          NextLevel is Level + 1,
24          detect_errors(X,Path,NextLevel).
25 detect_errors(X,Path,Level):- error(Level,X,Condition),
26          solve(Condition,Path,Level),
27          record_error(Level,X,Condition,Path,error),
28          fail.
29 detect_errors(X,Path,Level):- axiom(Level,X,Condition),
30          \+ solve(Condition,Path,Level),
31          record_error(Level,X,Condition,Path,axiom),
32          fail.
33 detect_errors(_,_,_).
34 record_error(Level,X,Condition,Path,Type):-
35          \+ found_ontological_error(Level,X,Condition,Path,Type),
36          assert(found_ontological_error(Level,X,Condition,Path,Type)).
37 report_errors:- show_errors,
38          clear_errors.
39 show_errors:- found_ontological_error(L,X,C,P,T),
40          ((T=error,
41          write(error_condition_satisfied(L,X,C)),nl,
42          write('path: '),write(P),nl);
43          (T=axiom,
44          write(axiom_violated(L,X,C)),nl,
45          write('path: '),write(P),nl)),
46          fail.
47 show_errors.
48 clear_errors :- retractall(found_ontological_error(_,_,_,_,_)).
49 logical_expression((_,_)).
50 logical_expression((_;_)).
51 logical_expression(\+ _).
```

B   State Transition model

```
1 specification(0,(possible_state(State):-possible_state(s0,State))).
2 specification(0,(possible_state(State,State):-true)).
3 specification(0,(possible_state(State,FinalState):-
4              possible_action(do(A,State)),
5              possible_state(do(A,State),FinalState))).
6 specification(0,(possible_action(do(move(A,G1,G3),State)):-
7              predator(A,B),
8              holds(location(A,G1),State),
9              holds(location(B,G2),State),
10             move_in_direction(A,G1,G2,State,G3))).
11 specification(0,(holds(location(a,(1,1)),s0):-true)).
12 specification(0,(holds(location(b,(2,2)),s0):-true)).
13 specification(0,(holds(location(c,(3,3)),s0):-true)).
14 specification(0,(holds(location(A,G),State):- \+ State=s0,
```

```
15              animal(A),
16              \+ holds(eaten(A),State),
17              last_location(A,State,G))).
18 specification(0,(holds(eaten(A),do(move(A,_,G),State)):-
19              predator(P,A),
20              holds(location(P,G),State))).
21 specification(0,(holds(eaten(A),do(move(P,_,G),State)):-
22              predator(P,A),
23              holds(location(A,G),State))).
24 specification(0,(holds(visited(A,G),s0):-holds(location(A,G),s0))).
25 specification(0,(holds(visited(A,G),do(move(A,_,G),_)):-true)).
26 specification(0,(holds(Condition,do(move(_,_,_),State)):-
27              \+ Condition=location(_,_),
28              holds(Condition,State))).
29 specification(0,(move_in_direction(A,(X1,Y1),(X2,Y2),State,(X3,Y3)):-
30              (X1<X2,X3 is X1+1,Y3=Y1;
31              X1>X2,X3 is X1-1,Y3=Y1;
32              Y1<Y2,Y3 is Y1+1,X3=X1;
33              Y1>Y2,Y3 is Y1-1,X3=X1),
34              \+ holds(visited(A,(X3,Y3)),State))).
35 specification(0,(last_location(A,do(move(A,_,G),_),G):-true)).
36 specification(0,(last_location(A,do(move(A1,_,_),State),G):-
37              \+ A=A1,
38              last_location(A,State,G))).
39 specification(0,(last_location(A,s0,G):-
40              holds(location(A,G),s0))).
41 specification(0,(animal(a):-true)).
42 specification(0,(animal(b):-true)).
43 specification(0,(animal(c):-true)).
44 specification(0,(predator(a,b):-true)).
45 specification(0,(predator(b,c):-true)).
46 specification(0,(predator(c,a):-true)).
47 specification(0,(adjoining_square((X1,Y1),(X2,Y2)):-
48              max_x_square(MaxX),
49              max_y_square(MaxY),
50              min_x_square(MinX),
51              min_y_square(MinY),
52              (X2 is X1+1,X2=<MaxX,Y2=Y1;
53              X2 is X1-1,X2>=MinX,Y2=Y1;
54              X2=X1,Y2 is Y1+1,Y2=<MaxY;
55              X2=X1,Y2 is Y1-1,Y2>=MinY))).
56 specification(0,(max_x_square(3):-true)).
57 specification(0,(max_y_square(3):-true)).
58 specification(0,(min_x_square(1):-true)).
59 specification(0,(min_y_square(1):-true)).
60 axiom(1,holds(location(A,G),S),
61              (predator(A,B),
62              \+ holds(location(B,G),S))).
```

The Ontologies of Semantic and Transfer Links

Mourad OUSSALAH   Karima MESSAADIA

LGI2P/EMA-EERIE
Parc scientifique Georges Besse - 30000 Nimes, France
Email : oussalah@eerie.fr, messaadi@eerie.fr.

Abstract. Constructing Knowledge Base Systems using pre-existing generic components rather than from scratch is a promising way of minimising development time and facilitating evolution and maintenance. The concepts commonly used in describing KBS are tasks, PSMs (problem solving methods) and domain knowledge. Developers have to select them from a library, then adapt and link them so that they fit their specific needs. In order to help developers to quickly understand, find, and configure the components[1] best suited to their applications, we need to specify languages for describing the tasks, PSMs and domains[2] plus the different interactions between them. In this paper, we describe a methodology for structuring a library which has different components and relationships defined through levels of description: meta- ontology, ontology library and application. We propose the use of semantic and transfer links - often applied in databases systems and object modelling - to specify the relationships between tasks, PSMs and domain knowledge and to use ontologies to describe these concepts, improving thus their reusability and shareability.

1. INTRODUCTION

Constructing an application using a library of reusable components is a promising way to minimise development time and facilitate evolution and maintenance. In order to help developers to quickly understand, find, and configure the components best suited to their applications, component-oriented approaches need to specify first languages for describing components, second reuse methodologies standardising the construction of reusable components and their structuring and indexing in libraries. Existing knowledge engineering (K.E) approaches often use task, PSM and domain knowledge concepts to describe a knowledge base system (KBS) at a knowledge level (as opposed to implementation or symbol level [15]). This separation between the task to achieve, the reasoning used to achieve it and the knowledge specific to the domain allows viewing the construction of an application as an adaptation and a connection of these three components.

---

[1] We use components referring to the concepts task, PSM, domain, and links and for their specialisation

[2] We use the term domain referring to the domain knowledge statement.

Different libraries, generally PSM ones, have been described in the literature, among them: Generic Task and Task Structure[5], CommonKADS library [3], the diagnosis library of Benjamins [1]. PSMs in these libraries are often described using either task-specific terms like the CommonKADS library or the Benjamins diagnosis library, or domain-specific terms like the Generic Task library. Task specific and domain-specific PSMs are less reusable than generic ones. This is known as the usability/reusability trade-off [10]. Other studies focus on ontology portability in order to construct libraries of reusable PSMs, tasks and domains [6][2][13]. An ontology is an explicit, partial account of a conceptualisation [7]. It provides a vocabulary of terms and relations initially used to formally describe generic models of domains so that they can be reused to describe different specific domains sharing the same structure. As we can reuse tasks and PSMs, the notion of task ontology and PSM ontology has appeared in recent works [2][6] referring to independent descriptions of them. Comparative studies can be found in [13] and [23].

We think that a library should possess different sorts of components defined at different levels of description, like modelling-, generic- or application specific- components, so that users can use/reuse a component at the appropriate level of specialisation. We have described in [14] the structure of a KBS model incorporating the three main concepts - task, PSM, and domain knowledge. In addition, we introduce the *inter-concept link* and the *intra-concept link* in order to clarify the different interactions between tasks, PSMs and domain knowledge. These links are represented using object modelling concepts: *semantic* [11] and *transfer* [17] *links* commonly applied in data base systems and object modelling like OMT or UML.

In this paper, we will first see a KBS described incrementally – at the knowledge level - through different levels of abstraction: *meta- ontology*, *ontology library* and *application* levels. Second we will see that the implementation (symbol) level we use is an object one where the *meta- ontology level* is implemented as *meta- classes* while the *ontology library level* and *application level* are implemented as *classes*. Then we will concentrate on the library ontologies of semantic and transfer links. Finally, we will introduce a way of reusing a component identifying: first the different library users; second, the different steps needed to construct reusable components; finally a way of constructing an application which (re)uses components from the library.

2. KNOWLEDGE ABSTRACT LEVELS

We can use different abstract levels to describe a KBS at the knowledge level [8] [9]. For our case we have identified three levels of abstraction (fig. 1): meta- ontology, ontology library and application.

1. The *meta- ontology level* describes the basic concepts needed to describe a KBS. Thus, at this level, we identify generic types of concept: task, PSM, domain knowledge plus inter- concept link and intra- concept link (fig.2.C).

2. The *ontology library level* enables the description of different sorts of ontology - task, PSM, domain and links. It can be decomposed into different layers according to their degree of specialisation.

3. The *application level* is concerned with describing applications. An application is constructed using task-, PSM- and domain-ontologies specialised, if needed, using intra-concept links, and linked using inter-concept links (fig. 12). We will see these levels in more detail in the next sections.

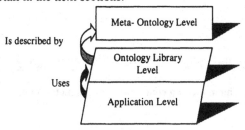

Fig. 1. Abstract levels

3. THE META- ONTOLOGY LEVEL

The meta- ontology level permits a precise description of the main components needed to model a KBS for purposes of sharing and reuse. This meta- ontology level corresponds to the *representation level* in [24].

Fig. 2.a The concepts of the Y- model　　　**Fig.2.b The modelling components**

The three concepts used in constructing a KBS - task, PSM and domain - give this model a characteristic Y-shape. In order to clarify the different kinds of relationship between these three concepts, we use two sorts of link - inter-concept and intra-concept. An inter-concept link describes relationships between concepts of different sorts: task/PSM, PSM/domain or task/domain. An intra-concept link describes the ones between two concepts of the same sort: task/task, PSM/PSM or domain/domain. These links are bi-directional but, for simplification, we use undirected links, considering for example task/PSM and PSM/task links as being the same (fig. 2.a). An inter-concept link is used to link two different concepts and can transfer information between them; examples are mapping or transferring information between tasks and PSMs. We describe this link using *semantic* and *transfer* links. Intra-concept links are described the way inter-concept ones are, using *semantic* and *transfer* links, but the concepts they link are of similar sort (fig 2.b).

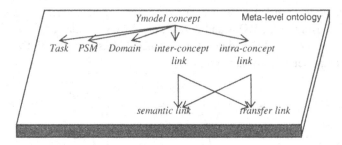

Fig.2.c The modelling components at the meta- ontology level

3.1 TASK META- ONTOLOGY LEVEL

A task at the meta-ontology level is specified by its *name*, which is a unique term designating it, its *input/output*, the *goal* it is to reach and the *semantic* and *transfer* links attached to it.

name	<task-name>
goal	<task-goal>
input	<input-concepts>
output	<output-concepts >
semantic	<semantic-names >
transfer	<transfer-names>

The attributes are in italics while their value types are enclosed in angle brackets "<" ">". We do this for simplicity but we can also describe them using formal languages like ontolingua, loom, etc.

3.2 PSM META- ONTOLOGY LEVEL

A PSM meta-ontology level is specified by its *name*, its *input/output*, its *competence* to achieve tasks, and the *semantic* and *transfer* links attached to it.

name	<PSM-name>
input	<input-concepts>
output	<output-concepts >
competence	<assumptions>
semantic	<semantic-names>
transfer	<transfer-names >

3.3 DOMAIN META- ONTOLOGY LEVEL

The domain meta- ontology level can be specified by the *concepts* of domain, the *relations* between these *concepts* and their *characteristics* allowing a leveraged domain description, plus the different links attached to it. The reader can refer to the work done in [24] for a categorisation of domain ontology levels.

name	<domain-name>
Domain_Concepts	<domain-concepts>
Domain_Relations	<domain_concept x domain_concept>
Characteristics	
semantic	<semantic-names>
transfer	<transfer-names >

3.4 SEMANTIC LINK META- ONTOLOGY LEVEL

The definition of a semantic link: A semantic link as it is defined in object modelling describes a relation between two or more concepts. Its semantics can express an association (logical, physical, etc.), a composition, a specialisation, etc. It has its own semantics and behaviour - allowing the concepts it relates together to communicate and collaborate [11]. It is often used in data modelling (data base systems, or CAD) so that semantic information is not distributed among related concepts but defined in an entity of its own, thus enabling modularity and reusability. In our model, we use binary semantic links (fig.3) because studies in object modelling demonstrate that it's easier to manipulate them, and tuple relations can be represented as a number of binary relations.

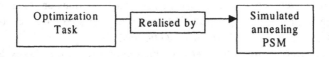

Fig. 3. . Example of a semantic relation

In our model, we describe a semantic link using the attributes:
1. *from* and *to* links defining the source and destination concepts.
2. *roles* determining the roles the source and the destination play in the link. These roles can help to identify the semantic link best suited to a specific case.
3. *semantic attributes* describing the semantic properties of the links. These properties allow improving their representation while simplifying their handling [11]. These properties are:
   □ *Exclusivity/ sharing*: *Exclusivity* expresses the limitation that a concept referenced by an exclusive semantic link of any one family cannot be referenced by further semantic links of the same family. Links of other, different, families however are permitted - examples of families being composition and association. If, for instance, a component is referenced by an *exclusive* composition link, it cannot be referenced by another composition (*part of*) link but it can be referenced by say an association link. The *sharing* property specifies the converse.
   □ *Dependence/ independence* : *Dependence* specifies that a destination component is dependent for its existence on its source component. If a source component of a semantic link is destroyed, that implies the destruction of the destination component referenced by the same link. *Independence* is the opposite of dependence.

☐ *Predominance / non-predominance* : The semantics of predominance and non-predominance is symmetric to dependence and independence. *Predominance* specifies the case where the source concept is dependent on the destination one. *Non-predominance* is the converse.

☐ *Cardinality/ Inverse cardinality*: *Cardinality* is defined as an interval *[card min, card max]* where *card min (card max)* expresses the minimal (maximal) number of target concepts that can be associated with a source concept. *Inverse cardinality* is defined the same but for a target concept.

4. *Transfer link* : defines the transfer link associated with the semantic link.

---

name : <semantic-link-name>
from : <from-concepts>
to : < to-concepts>
Roles: <from-role; to-role>
Transfer < associated transfer name>
Semantics attributes

3.5 TRANSFER LINK META-ONTOLOGY

Definition of a transfer link : A transfer link [17] expresses the transferability of information between concepts. It may in addition have transfer functions for transforming the information it transports between source and target concepts. A transfer link (fig. 4)may be associated with a semantic link.

Translator definition: A transfer is composed of a set of translators describing information propagation between related concepts. Each translator defines information propagation between the attributes of linked concepts and specifies the transfer function used to translate the information being sent.

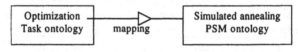

Fig. 4. Transfer link example

Name : <transfer-name>
Semantics : <associated semantic link name>
source : <source-concepts>
destination : <destination-concepts>
translator : <translator-names>

Name <translator-name>
Input < source -attributes >
output < destination-attributes >
Transfer-functions

Reusing transfer links for different semantic links: A question that springs to mind is: why separate transfer link from semantic link?. The answer is that it enhances reusability as the same transfer link can serve two different semantic links. An example we give for this is the *derivation link* used for evolution management in object design. This link permits linking versions of a class (component) to the initial one. A version can be derived by deletion of, addition to, or modification of an existing component. Many methodologies have confused derivation link with inheritance (since inheritance permits addition and modification). Some alter the inheritance link so that it fits derivation, using inheritance with exceptions or adding constraints. We can reuse the transfer applied for inheritance, adapt it so that it can support information-deletion and reuse it for this link.

4. ONTOLOGY LIBRARY

At this level, we can describe a number of different sorts of ontology, among them: task, PSM, domain, semantic link and transfer link (fig. 5).

Task ontologies PSM ontologies   Domain ontologies   Semantic link ontologies   Transfer link ontologies

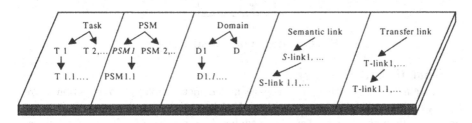

Fig. 5. The different ontologies of the library

4.1 TASK, PSM, AND DOMAIN KNOWLEDGE ONTOLOGIES

Tasks, PSMs and domains can be seen at this level as an extended Y-shape with several branches - as in fig. 6. Task branches describe types of task such as: *diagnosis, configuration, and conception.* PSM branches describe PSM types such as*: classification, abduction, qualitative simulation;* domain branches describe domains like: *networks, medicine, cardiology.* Task T_1 for instance is specialised into T'_1 as design and parametric design; D_1 is specialised into D'_1 such as : *networks* and *telecommunication networks* ; and PSM_2 is specialised into PSM'_2 as : *union of n sets* and *union of two sets.* Examples of such ontologies can be found in [18]. Following the example in fig. 9, we have the example of an optimisation task.

Optimisation_Task ontology

name	optimisation

goal	find the best realisable solution among a set of possible ones
input	the cost function ; set of constraints; set of realisable solutions
output	the best solution
realised-by	optimisation-realisation link
association	optimisation-association link
transfer	optimisation-transfer link
strategy	optimisation-strategy

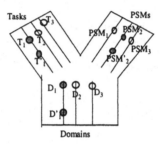

Fig. 6. Library : the extent Y model

4.2 Semantic Link Ontology

The semantic link definition we gave at the meta-ontology level section corresponds to the studies in object modelling [11] but what about the other disciplines?. Semantic relations (or links) have been studied by a number of different disciplines - among them linguistics, logic, psychology, information systems, and artificial intelligence (Winston et al. 88, Herrmann & Chaffin 87, Iris et al. 88, Woods 91, Dahlberg 94, Priss 96). The reader can find a comparison of these studies in [20]. For ontology design, reader can refer to [16] for a comparison of some ontologies and their different use of relations. For our case, we have focused our work on two large, well-known categories, often used in object modelling, and used in the Y-model. These two categories are inclusion - where inheritance and composition (*part of*) are frequent - and association.

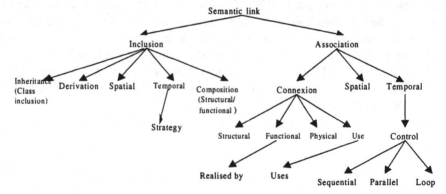

Fig. 7. Some semantic links (relations)

In fig.7 we have listed our hierarchy of semantic links, based on the different linguistic studies we have mentioned [21] [26]. For reasons of space, we haven't listed all the hierarchy classes.

Inclusion

The inclusion link specifies that a concept includes other concepts. This inclusion is then refined as structural, functional, spatial, temporal and class inclusion.

```
name :   <Inclusion-name>
sort of:  <semantic relation>
from     <from-concept>
to :     <to-concept>
Roles:   < sub set, set>
Transfer <transfer- inclusion>
```

Inheritance (Class inclusion)

This link defines the inheritance link. Its main characteristic is similarity, permitting differentiation from other sorts of inclusion link (we refer to the work done on similarity of inheritance links in [21]). The source concept should then be similar to the destination concept.

```
name :      <sort-of>
sort of:    <inclusion>
from   :    <from_concept>
to :        <to_concept>
Roles:      <subtype , super-type >
Transfer    <transfer sort-of>
```

Composition (structural and functional inclusion)

The composition link connects a source concept called composite to another concept called component. This link is known as *"part of"* in ontology design. Readers can refer to [16] for a comparison of the use of the *part of* link in ontology design.

```
name :      <Composed of-name>
sort of:    <inclusion>
from   :    <from_concept>
to :        <to_concept>
Roles:      < composite, component >
Transfer    <transfer composition>
```

Derivation

Often confused with inheritance, this link states that a destination concept is derived from a source concept. It is often used for evolution management in object design.

name :	<sort-of>
sort of:	<derivation>
from :	<from_concept>
to :	<to_concept>
Roles:	<versioned, version >
Transfer	<transfer version>

Association

The association link relates two concepts. It contrasts with inclusion which consists of constructing a concept from other concepts. The association can be structural, functional, spatial, or temporal.

name	<association-name>
Sort of	<semantic link>
from	<from-concept>
to	<to-concept>
Roles	< from-role; to-role >
Transfer	<transfer- association>

Functional Connection

This link defines a functional connection where the linked concepts are associated together to realise a specific function. The realised-by link used in the Y-model is a sort of functional connection.

name :	<realised by-name>
sort of:	<functional-connection>
from :	<from-concept>
to :	<to-concept>
Roles :	< problem type; resolution method>
Transfer	<transfer-functional>

Control link

This link is used in the Y-model for specifying the order of the components invocation. It is a sort of temporal connection

Name	< control-name>
sort of	<temporal association >
from	<from-concept>
to	<to-concept>
Roles	<scheduler; schedules>
Transfer	<transfer name>

4.3 Transfer links Ontology

Transfer link defines a transfer of information between the concepts it relates. We have defined a hierarchy of some of the common transfer links we can use in our model (fig.8). An example of mapping transfer might be renaming - where the source-attribute is renamed to the destination-attribute name.

> *Name* \<translator-rename-name\>
> *Sort of* \<translator\>
> *input* \<attribute-source\>
> *output* \<attribute-destination\>
>   *transfer function* \<rename(attribute-source, attribute- destination)\>

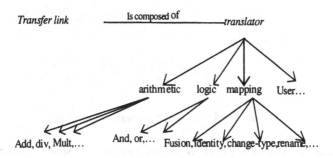

Fig. 8. Different sort of transfer links

4.4 SEMANTIC AND TRANSFER LINKS ONTOLOGIES OF THE Y-MODEL

Now that we have defined a generic ontology of semantic links, we will see in this section the ones we use in the Y model.

Inter concept- semantic and transfer links: the various sorts of inter-concept semantic links used in the Y-model are:

- PSM/domain link: The association of a PSM with a domain describes the knowledge that the former requires from the latter. In order to consider a PSM as a black box, its knowledge requirements are specified using *assumptions*. We use *association link* to represent it. Data transfers between tasks and PSMs, as well as their inter-ontology mapping [22], are defined using *mapping* transfer links.

- Task/domain link: This link describes the association of a task with a domain in terms of knowledge requirements. We use an *association link* as defined below to specify it. The transfer can be defined using *mapping* transfer links.

- Task/PSM link : A task can be *realised-by* (achieved) either one or several PSMs and each PSM can *decompose* a task into sub-tasks. These in their turn, are *realised-by* sub-PSMs, until reaching terminal and non-decomposable PSMs. We define two *new* semantic links expressing the task/PSM relations. We refer to them as: *realised-by* and *composed-of* (fig. 9). The associated transfer link allows for, amongst other things, inter-ontology mapping.

  □ The *Realised-by link*: It allows relating a task to the different PSMs helping to achieve it.

  □ The *Composed-of link*: It expresses the decomposition of the PSM into different sub-tasks.

User inter-concept link: In the generic semantic link hierarchy defined in fig. 7, the user can define their own inter-concept semantic link.

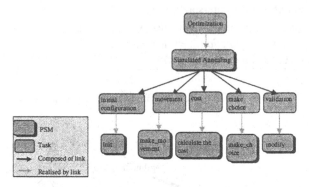

Fig. 9. The decomposition/realisation graph

The figure above gives the Task/PSM decomposition of a specific and real case. It concerns the optimisation of concentrator locations in an access network. The concentrator location problem aims to find the number of concentrators, their locations, and the connection of terminals to concentrators. We can use a simulated annealing algorithm (PSM) to find the optimal configuration. As this PSM is often used for many other problems, we need to describe a generic simulated annealing and optimisation task using terms such as realisable solution, optimal solution - rather than concentrators, terminals; etc (see the example of optimisation task ontology in section 4.1). Then transfer links can be used for terminology mapping.

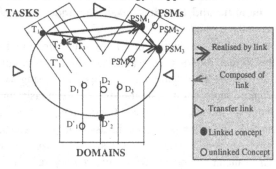

Fig. 10. The different types of inter-concept links : The extended Y model

In fig. 10, the full circle represents a chosen task T_1 which is *realised-by* PSM_1 and PSM_3 following a specific control in the domain D'_2. In this extended Y model, we can take various entry points: for a given task T_1, we can find : the PSMs which can carry it out - through the task/PSM *realised-by* link; the domains where it can be applied - through the task/domain association link (fulfilling its knowledge requirements). We can also take a given PSM such as PSM_1, and find its sub-tasks through the *composed-of* link and the domains to which it applies (in this example, T_2, T_3 and D'_2). We can also take a domain as an entry point (D'$_2$) and find the tasks and PSMs where it can be used (in this example T$_1$, PSM$_1$ and PSM$_2$).

Intra-concept semantic links : we have identified the various sorts of intra-concept semantic links (fig. 11) used in the Y-model as:

- *Specialisation link*: it is used to specialise a task, a PSM, a domain or a link.
- *Instantiation link* : it is used to instantiate a concept. The concept can be a task, PSM, or domain, or a link.
- *Control link*: it specifies the order of invocation of tasks or PSMs, or the union of two domains.
- *Strategy link*: this specifies the strategic knowledge used when there is a choice to be made among PSMs, tasks, or domains.
- *User intra-concept link*: as for inter-concept links, the user can extend the links we have identified by defining his/her own intra-concept link.

Intra-concept transfer links : Transfer links allow the propagation of information between related concepts: task/task and PSM/PSM used in the decomposition/realisation graph (fig. 9); and domain/domain for a mapping between domains sharing common structures such as electrical and telecommunication networks.

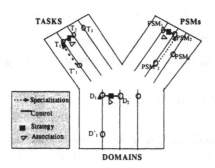

Fig. 11. Intra-task, intra-PSM and intra-domain links

5. THE APPLICATION LEVEL

Our library is composed of: task, PSM, domain, semantic link and transfer link ontologies. Applications are collections of related task, PSM, domain knowledge components using inter-concept – like the realised-by - and intra-concept links - like the specialisation link. The related components making up applications are like 'Lego' bricks. Such a structure allows swapping one component with another without generating a knock-on series of changes in the overall application. This is in contrast to the more common glue architectures, where components are glued together into more rigid applications in which small changes can have numerous and large repercussions. In the figure below, we can see an example of an application for planning an access network domain. We take a telecommunication domain ontology from the library. We assume that this component has been already created. We specialise this component -

using the *specialisation* intra-concept link - into an access network domain. We see that linking the optimisation task with the simulated annealing PSM is done using the *realised by* semantic inter-concept link and the *mapping* transfer inter-concept link.

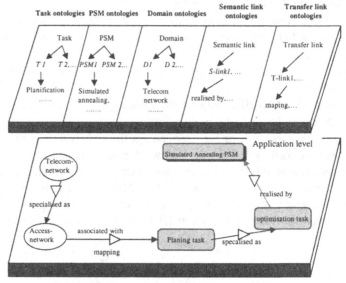

Fig. 12. Library and application ontologies

6. IMPLEMENTATION LEVEL

The different hierarchies of the Y-model are represented as objects using meta-class and class hierarchies (Fig. 13). The construction of the instantiation graph permits to create classes and instances.

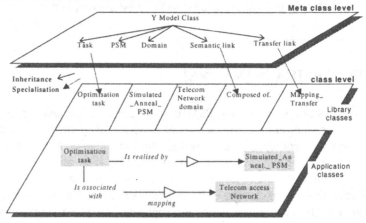

Fig. 13. Implementation level

1. The *meta- ontology level* is represented at the *meta-class level*: Task, PSM, domain, semantic links and transfer link meta-ontologies are represented as meta-classes.
2. The *ontology library* level is defined by instantiating the meta-classes listed above - for representing the different sorts of task, PSM, domain, semantic link and transfer link ontologies as *classes*. The inheritance graph enables us to maintain the levels of abstraction of the different sorts of semantic and transfer link and the specialisation degree (generic or more specific) of task, PSM and domain ontologies.
3. The *application level* is also at the *class level* where an application uses the different classes of the library.

7. HOW TO REUSE A COMPONENT?

Before talking about ways of reusing components, we have to know something about the different sorts of users of the Y-model. In order to construct and manage the Y-model library, we distinguish four different ones, each having a specific function in the overall development:

1. The infrastructure builder (I.B) has to define the modelling components used to build the infrastructure. In the Y-model, the I.B will define the meta-classes.
2. The application builder (A.B) is the domain expert and will instantiate the meta-classes for describing his/her specific components. The A.B is concerned by the library ontologies level.
3. The Reuse Engineer (R.E) or library manager will construct and manage the library. This is composed of generic parts: generic meta-class components defined by the infrastructure builder and reusable components and reusable applications defined by the application builder (see fig 14). Before accepting a component or application into the library, the R.E has to verify if:
   - the components are well documented and well tested;
   - the standards are respected;
   - the components are well used in the applications;
   - we are not developing already existing components and applications.
4. The End User (E.U) instantiates specific applications in order to solve real problems (feeding in the initial values of the problem).

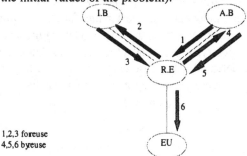

1,2,3 for reuse
4,5,6 by reuse

Fig. 14. Reuse methodology

In fig 14, we can see an example of the different interactions between the 4 Y-model users. The reuse methodology is divided into two stages. The first one, called for-reuse, concerns the construction of the components; the second, called by-reuse, concerns the construction of the application by reuse and the adaptation of these ready-made components.

1 : the application builder (A.B) identifies the components s/he needs and asks the reuse engineer.

2 : the reuse engineer (R.E) asks the infrastructure builder (I.B) to represent the needed components.

3 : the infrastructure builder gives the components to the R.E who will organise them.

4 : the R.E will find and select the needed components and gives them to the application builder.

5 : the application builder has to adapt and integrate them.

6 : finally, the End User will instantiate and use the applications.

The Reuse Engineer plays the pivotal role between the different users. By-reuse and for-reuse stages can be seen as two process reuse engineering stages.

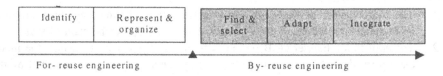

Fig 15 Reuse process

A REUSE SCENARIO

Lot of works has been done concerning PSM, task and domain reuse. For our scenario, we will take a transfer link as an example for the reuse-process (Fig 15):

1. The for-reuse stage concerns the library components construction. At this stage, if an inheritance semantic link component is needed, the infrastructure builder will use the transfer and translator meta classes to represent it. This link has to be organised later in the structured library.

2. By-reuse stage concerns the next step where we have existing reusable components. If the application builder needs a transfer link for an *evolution* semantic (see section 3.5) s/he will ask for it from the library. Getting the inheritance transfer component from the library, s/he will adapt it for his evolution link (adding the ability for information deletion). The reuse engineer can take this new evolution transfer link and make the necessary testing and verifications listed above. Then, s/he can integrate it to the library for future (re)use.

8. CONCLUSION

We have described in this article a library which can model any task-oriented knowledge base whilst offering the re-use of tasks, PSMs, domains, and their different links. This library is structured in a multi-hierarchical model allowing the integration of reusable components described at different levels of specification. Our work approaches that in [6] in its reuse of tasks, PSMs and domains by means of ontologies to describe them and adapters to refine and glue the components. The semantic and transfer links can represent the different sort of *adapters*.

Concerning the task/PSM decomposition, and the use of ontology, our work has some similarities with protégéII [12]. It differs from it in its use of an explicit control, rather than, as in protégéII, a hard-wired one and the use of semantic and transfers links. The main contribution of our work is the explicit description it offers of the different concept interactions (relationships) by means of two concepts, intra- and inter-concept links defined through different levels of description; secondarily, the use of object modelling concepts for representing them. The semantic link ontology can be used in the KA-2 project to represent the different relations. Our purpose was to give a simple description of the modelling components and not a completely formal language. This will be our next concern. The meta-model we have used can be reflective. Our future work will concentrate on defining such a reflection and formalising concepts and links. This work is under development for an application concerning the re-use of tasks and PSMs in the telecommunications domain.

Bibliography

[1] Benjamins, R. Problem Solving Methods for diagnosis. PhD Thesis, Department of social Science Informatics, University of Amsterdam, The Netherlands, 1993.

[2] Benjamins, R., Plaza, E., Motta, E., Fensel, D., Studer, R., Wielinga, B.J, Shreiber, G. Zdarahal, Z., -IBROW3- An intelligent Brokering Service for Knowledge –Component Reuse on the World-Wide-Web. In Proceedings of KAW'98, Banff, Canada.

[3] Breuker J. A. & Van de Velde, W. CommonKADS library for expertise modelling. IOS Press, Amsterdam, The Nederlands (1994).

[4] Chandrasekaran B., Josephson J. R. & Benjamins, V.R., The Ontology of Tasks and Methods. In Proceedings of KAW'98. Banff, Canada, 1998.

[5] Chandrasekaran B. & Al. Task-Structure Analysis for Knowledge Modelling, Communication of the ACM, 35(9) :124-137, 1992.

[6] Fensel D. The tower of adapters method for developing and reusing problem solving methods. In Plaza 1 Benjamins, V. R. Edts, Knowledge Acquisition, Modelling and Management, pp 97—112. Springler-Verlag 1997.

[7] Gruber, T.R. A Translation Approach to Portable Ontology Specifications, Knowledge Acquisition, 5: 199-220, 1993.

[8] Guarino, N. The ontological level, In R. Casati, B. Smith and G. White (eds.), Philosophy and the Cognitive Sciences, Vienna, 1994.

[9] Guarino, N., Understanding, Building, And Using Ontologies A Commentary to "Using Explicit Ontologies in KBS Development", by van Heijst, Schreiber, and Wielinga. International Journal of Human and Computer Studies vol. 46 n.2/3, pp. 293-310, 1997.

[10] Klinker, G. & Al, Usable and Reusable Programming Constructs, Knowledge Acquisition, 3:117-136, 1991.

[11] Magnan, M. Oussalah, C. Multiple Inheritance Systems with Exeptions. In Artificial Intelligence Review, Volume 6, Kluwer Acad. Pub. Pp 31-44, 1995.

[12] Molina, M. Shahar Y., Cuena, J.& Musen, M. A Structure of problem-Solving Methods for Real-time Decision Support : Modelling Approaches Using PROTEGE-II and KSM. proceedings of (KAW'96), Banff Alberta, Canada, November 9-14, 1996.

[13] Motta, E. Trends in knowledge modelling: Report on 7th KEML Workshop. The Knowledge Engineering Review, Volume 12/Number 2/June 1997.

[14] Messaadia, K.& Oussalah, M. Using Semantic links for reuse in KBS; In Proc. of Database and Expert Systems Applications, DEXA'98, Vienna, Austria, 1998.

[15] Newel, A., The knowledge level, artificial Intelligence 18, 1982, 87-127.

[16] Noy, N.F., Hafner, C.D. The State of the Art in Ontology Design, AI Magazine, Volume 18(3): Fall 1997, 53-74

[17] Oussalah & al, A framework for modelling the structure and behaviour of a system including multi level simulation, IASTED INT. Symp. On Applied Simulation an Modelling, ASM, Grindelwald, Switzerland, February 1988.

[18] Oussalah, C.& K. Messaadia; An architecture for solving complex tasks, in Proc. of Nimes'98, Complex Systems, Nimes, France 1998

[19] Pierret-Golbreich,C. TASK MODEL: A Framework for the Design of Models of Expertise. and Their Operationalisation. KAW'96. Banff, Alberta, Canada 1994.

[20] Priss, U. Relational Concept Analysis: Semantic Structures in Dictionaries and Lexical Databases. Dissertation, TH-Darmstadt, october 96.

[21] Storey V.C. Understanding Semantic Links, VLDB Journal 2, 455-488, 1993.

[22] Studer, R. Eriksson, H. Gennari,J.H., Tu,S.W., Fensel, D. & Musen, M. Ontologies and the Configuration of Problem-Solving Methods, proceedings of (KAW'96), 9-14, 1996.

[23] Uschold, M. & Tate, A. Putting ontologies to use .The Knowledge Engineering Review, Volume 13/ Number 1/ March 1998.

[24] Van Heijst, G. Shreiber, A. Th. & Wielinga, B.J. Using explicit ontologies in KBS development, International Journal of Human-Computer Studies, 46(2/3):128-292, 1997.

[25] Wielinga, B. Schreiber.A. & Breuker, J. KADS: A Modelling Approach to Knowledge Engineering. Knowledge Acquisition. 4, 5-53. 1992.

[26] Winston, M.E, Chaffin, R. Herrmann, D.J. A Taxonomy of Part – Whole Relations, Cognitive Science 11, 417-444, (1987).

Distributed Problem Solving Environment Dedicated to DNA Sequence Annotation

Thibault Parmentier[1], Danièle Ziébelin[1]

[1] Projet Sherpa, INRIA Rhône-Alpes, 655 Avenue de l'Europe, F-38330 MONTBONNOT - FRANCE.
{Thibault.Parmentier, Daniele.Ziebelin}@inrialpes.fr
http://www.inrialpes.fr/sherpa/

Abstract. Genomic sequence analysis is a task using techniques coming from different fields in order to extract biologically relevant objects (genes, regulatory signals...) from rough DNA sequences. Analysis methods, coming from domains like statistics, sequence alignment or pattern matching, have been developed and regrouped into program libraries. These libraries aim at helping biologists to manipulate data. However their use revealed itself being too difficult as it requires the user to have background knowledge to be handled efficiently. In order to tackle this problem, the ImaGene system has been proposed. ImaGene is a system built upon a generic task model allowing to model methods of DNA sequence analysis and to execute them thanks to shell scripts, binaries and specific libraries already developed. This system makes it possible to manipulate these methods and present a synthesis of the obtained results in a cartographic interface allowing the biologist to evaluate the biological pertinence of the results and to annotate DNA sequences. In order to profit from analysis methods and specialized libraries and to simplify their accesses, we have provided ImaGene with the possibility of using distributed methods and binaries. The solution chosen consists in transferring task code from server sites to client sites; but, unlike the solution adopted in Java, the data is computed at the server site if necessary. This distribution of the system has highlighted some problems like managing different versions of methods and dealing with tasks that have been recently decomposed into new sub-tasks.

1 Introduction

The use of specialized libraries of programs is not always easy: to choose, connect and carry out the suitable modules during the resolution of a problem often requires, the user to have an excellent control of the field concerned and a good knowledge of the organization of the libraries. This is for example true in domains like automobile or plane design, in which competences from several disciplines are requested. It is also true in genomic sequence analysis where computer science techniques used to manipulate genomic sequences meet techniques from statistics and pattern matching used to locate and extract biologically relevant objects. These techniques and methods are regrouped in software libraries or binaries. Though biologists are able to set parameters of the distinct methods selected from the libraries, they need more competences to select the right modules of a library or to link them up.

In order to help users with these difficulties, Problem Solving Environments (PSEs) have been developed which offer automatic supervision of software libraries and binaries. To do that, the PSEs are based on solving strategies (methodological knowledge) easily comprehensible by users. The PSEs use this methodological knowledge to identify, specialize and execute the modules best adapted to the current problem. Users can control the solution process by means of graphical interfaces allowing them to visualize all stages of the execution of a strategy and the results.

The objective of designing a PSE is to provide an integrated environment and to supervise programs [18] coming from different specialized domains. A PSE proposes a model of each domain through knowledge bases representing [19]:

- on the one hand, domain entities (cf. Fig. 1) which we will call them domain knowledge. They represent the concepts being handled (variable, domain of definition, scatter plot, grid,...),
- on the other hand, problem solving strategies modeling different ways to solve problems (cf. Fig. 1). This methodological knowledge expressed thanks to strategies allows an evaluation of the problem to be solved. They lead to the selection, the sequence and the execution of the modules or programs of a library in the most relevant way [19][22][14].

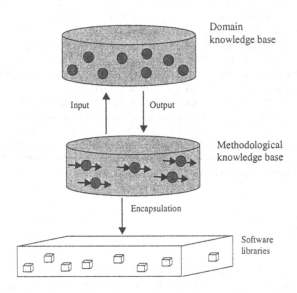

Fig. 1. The PSE is built around two kinds of knowledge which are used to pilot, in a suitable way, software libraries: the methodological knowledge contains problem solving strategy, and the domain knowledge base contains the input needed by the tasks and the output produced during the resolution processes (programs are encapsulated and controlled by the PSE thanks to the methodological knowledge).

The Sherpa project at INRIA Rhone-Alpes developed in collaboration with the company Ilog a generic PSE PowerTasks [17] whose knowledge base is built on an objects model. Domain knowledge is represented by means of classes and instances, methodological knowledge is described using particular classes and instances: tasks [4][5]. A task allows a compact and structured representation of a problem and knowledge necessary to its resolution with regard to the description of its data and results, as well as a strategy for solving the problem (cf. section 2).

PowerTasks was used for the task of genome annotation, within a framework involving several biology laboratories. This work was financed by a French organism, the G.R.E.G. ("Groupement de Recherche et d'Études sur les Génomes"). The system obtained, ImaGene, allows the analysis and the annotation of complete bacterial genoms [15][16]. It gives a biologist the possibility of exploiting and carrying out in a transparent way methods for DNA sequence analysis obtained from several libraries offering complementary methods. These methods seek and identify, on a DNA sequence, biological objects of interest, such as genes, signals of regulation... To this end, ImaGene uses three distinct windows allowing to manage the biological objects, the solution strategies and the solution processes (for the first two ones) and to visualize the DNA map including the biological objects resulting from the different solution processes (in the last window).

The installation and use of a PSE provides a satisfactory response to the problem of managing programs libraries. Nevertheless, some difficulties remain, like for example the installation and the updates of libraries. The code of these libraries used to be not portable, and difficult to install (split into several parts, calls to other tool libraries, incompatibilities of compilers versions...) and often involves the purchase of hardware or specialized software (required computing power, uses of specific databases). To illustrate this last difficulty, we briefly present the case of two strategies included in ImaGene, which, in its current version, encapsulates twelve libraries, eight of which require specialized resources.

Before explaining the way this strategy works, the biological background of DNA sequence analysis needs to be briefly reviewed/explained. A DNA sequence is a sequence built from four letters A, T, C, G which represent a nucleotide acid or nucleotide. A group of three nucleotides can be translated into an amino acid thanks to a translation table. In the case of bacteria, a DNA sequence is about 10^6 nucleotides long. But the major part of the process of nucleotides is never translated into amino acid: they do not code for proteins. The DNA sequence annotation consists in finding the coding sequences. There are different ways of selecting the interesting part of a DNA sequence.

One of these consists in comparing sequences coming from similar organisms starting from the position of the relevant biological objects on an analyzed sequence of a similar organism. This method is contained in a library that uses a database with sequences of several partially or completely analyzed organisms. During the installation of this library, it is necessary to have a copy of the complete database which must be upgraded regularly (every week). Another solution is to access the initial database remotely.

Another method is based on statistical search. The corresponding library uses the frequency of appearance of nucleotides in genes or other relevant biological objects. The installation of this method is thus linked to the installation, at the same time, of statistical programs and to the data relating to partially or completely analyzed organisms, and finally to the procedures of error tolerance in sequence analysis. The installation of the three parts of this library, and the updating of one of them independently from the others two, is not go without difficulties, in particular for non-specialists in computer science.

In order to remove these difficulties of installation and maintenance [13], we propose an extension of the PSE PowerTasks towards a distributed problem solving environment (DPSE). Thanks to this distributed version of PowerTasks, the sites using this DPSE, on the one hand, become customers of competences of others sites and, on the other hand, carry out the modules and library programs. In this way, each site is server of its own competencies, ensures the maintenance of the modules and libraries which are under its control, gives total or partial access to them, and allows other sites to use its specialized software and hardware with its own licenses of use.

The distribution of domain and methodological knowledge bases across several sites presents many advantages and provides a solution to the problems mentioned in the preceding paragraph. In section 3, we will present the architectural choices of the DPSE PowerTasks, and particularly the technological alternatives that have guided us in this realization (cf. sections 3.1 and 3.2). The development of such a distributed architecture required an extension of the tasks model (cf. section 2), in the sense that new attributes were introduced and various communication protocols added (cf. section 4). Lastly, we present a way to adapt solution strategies allowing themselves to use tasks developed later in the distributed environment (cf. section 5).

2 Expressing Methodological Knowledge

In order to allow a representation of knowledge with a high level of abstraction [4], to give an easy access to this knowledge and to facilitate its maintenance, we chose to represent knowledge by means of object-oriented models. This choice makes it possible to describe domain knowledge and methodological knowledge in a similar way.

The knowledge representation within the PowerTasks environment is realized out using two different types of entities:

- the domain description is expressed in terms of classes and instances; (cf. Fig. 2)
- the solution strategies are built over programs libraries using tasks in order to allow a suitable use of those.

As defined in section 1, a task associates the description of a problem and its solving strategy. This strategy is represented, in our task model, by means of two graphs representing the specialization or decomposition of a task into more elementary subtasks. At the lower level, the description of an elementary problem is reduced to a task and its solving strategy to a call for the execution of a library program. The PSE methodological knowledge base thus consists in tasks hierarchies. They are constructed in declarative way using a graphic editor, with a explicit links of specialization and decomposition between tasks and sub-tasks.

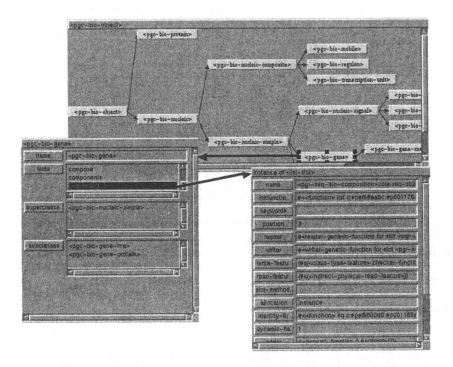

Fig. 2. In ImaGene, the domain knowledge base contains biological objects described by means of a hierarchy of classes. The editor at the left allows the user to visualize the class "gene" and the editor at the right-hand side allows the user to visualize the attribute "sequence" representing the DNA sequence associated with this gene. For a given instance of a gene, the values of the attributes are specified. In particular, the sequence is explicitly described by means of an alphabet of 4 symbols (A, T, G, C).

We can distinguish two categories of tasks: complex tasks which break up into sub-tasks and elementary tasks which refer to a program of library. Complex tasks allow users to approach problems via their strategies, i.e. specialization, sequence or iteration of sub-tasks (cf. Fig. 3). On the opposite, elementary tasks play the role of "black box". Their role is limited to encapsulating a library program and providing access to its functionality. An elementary task thus contains the most powerful up-to-date version of the encapsulated program.

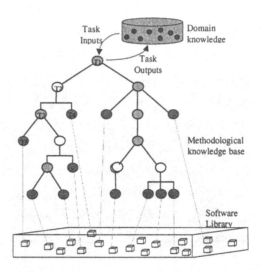

Fig. 3. Detailed description of links between the three main components of PowerTasks (methodological knowledge, domain knowledge and programs). For example, during a resolution based on the task T1, the T1 solution process uses inputs provided by the domain knowledge base. T1 can be specialized into two sub-tasks. If one of these subtasks T2 is selected, inputs necessary to the execution of T2 are transmitted to T2 via T1; T2 breaks up into two other tasks: an elementary task T4, which encapsulates a program and a complex task T3 which can be further specialized.

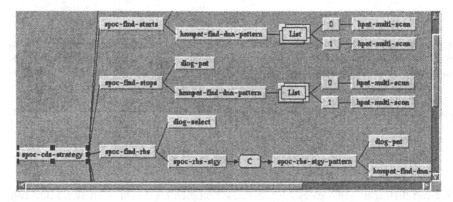

Fig. 4. In this graphic editor, we visualize the result of the execution of the "spoc-cds-stategy" which is a strategy included in ImaGene. "spoc-cds-stategy" allows the user to identify interesting patterns on genome sequences starting from patterns supplied by users. The task "spoc-cds-stategy" is broken up into three tasks "spoc-find-starts, spoc-find-stop, spoc-find-rbs", and these sub-tasks are decomposed into loops on lists ("List"), sequences or specialization ("C").

The internal task representation (cf. Fig. 5) is a class made up of two sets of attributes which describe:

- the problem by means of the data manipulated and the expected results. Each data element or result corresponds to an attribute, whose type can be simple (real, integer, chain...) or refer to a class of the knowledge base;
- the solution strategy by means of sub-tasks (cf. Fig. 4). A task is associated with a decomposition and/or specialization. Decomposition uses a list of sub-tasks and operators (sequence, choice, iteration) which will be interpreted during the solution process. Specialization consists in specifying inputs and the task application conditions in order to particularize the solving strategy according to these conditions.

```
(defctlgoal spoc-rbs-stgy (<ctl-task>)
   context: ((lst-adr-seq set-of: <address>)
             (sym-mode type: <symbol>
                       domain: ('pattern 'consensus)))
   goal-state: ((cons-parm type: <list>)
                (lst-rbs    set-of: <list>)))
```

Fig. 5. Code of the task spoc-cds-stgy (from ImaGene). The attribute "context" contains task inputs, "goal state" outputs. This task will solve thanks to a specialization, it is thus defined as a goal (defctlgoal).

During the problem resolution process, PowerTasks inferences engine chooses the solving strategy best adapted to the context. In order to achieve this, task execution is carried out two phases:
- the specialization phase uses a mechanism which classifies a task according to its data and to its conditions describing the context. This classification makes it possible to select the sub-task that suits best to the characteristics of the current problem;
- the decomposition phase uses choice, sequence or iteration operators. This makes it possible to decompose a task into simpler sub-tasks.

The alternation of these two phases (specialization and decomposition) results in an opportunistic resolution approach since the sequence of tasks is chosen only during execution [14] according to problem characteristics. For each resolution, the system selects the most suitable strategy. (cf. Fig. 6)

The task model of PowerTasks has the advantage of allowing a declarative expression of the problem solving strategies [10]. This characteristic differentiates it from the approaches adopted in the knowledge acquisition domain [5] [8], and is closely related to the way tasks are used in program supervision [7] [9] [23] [16]. This knowledge representation by means of objects and tasks is based upon several tasks models and PSEs [3] [19] [24] developed within the Sherpa project in the last five years. It gave rise to a number of collaborations for programs supervision in several domains like data analysis [2], signal processing and genomic sequences analysis [15].

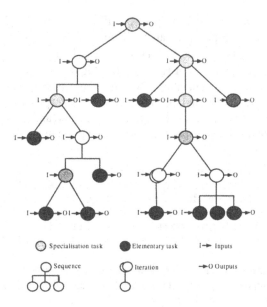

Fig. 6. problem solving strategy built above a specialization. The inference engine will start by specializing the problem according to its characteristics. Then, it will alternate between specialization and decomposition phases until it reaches the appropriates elementary tasks which are executed...

3 Distributed Environment

The PSE make it possible to use specialized libraries in an optimal way. The system allows the user to develop various strategies based on several distinct domains, creating in this way a list of problem solving strategies. For ImaGene, the application of PowerTask to the problem of DNA sequence annotation, a lot of strategies have been developed and integrated into the environment. However, their maintenance remains a problem because each strategy can be modified to take into account new discoveries like of course annotation of new genes, i.e. update of databases; but also some modifications more important. On the other hand, the installation of libraries themselves is a demanding problem, both in time and competence. These libraries require in addition resources which are not always available, like special compilers or expensive hardware configurations. In addition, the sites which use PowerTasks create methodological knowledge bases and therefore develop a private competence which could be put at the disposal of the community. We have thus extended the environment so as to allow a distributed use of methodological knowledge bases and specialized libraries. This choice enables one to reduce the costs of installation and maintenance of libraries to a minimum: only one server site is responsible for each strategy. We thus provide access to these libraries for sites having insufficient hardware or software configurations and propose using distant knowledge bases to client sites.

The options chosen for the distribution of PowerTask can be separated into two points: on the one hand the network configuration and on the other hand the code mobility. These choices were made to solve the different problems expressed above.

3.1 Network Configuration.

In biology like in several other experimental domains, research is carried out in different laboratories: each one working on a specific part of a global problem and proposing solutions based on its own speciality. Thus the network configuration most adapted to this collaborative way of working is made up of several server sites providing their own competencies. Each site maintains the libraries which are local for him, and the strategies of resolution which it created. The DPSE allows the code of each module to remain in its original environment with specialized software/hardware and required databases or knowledge bases. This configuration avoids rewriting some code, having to upgrade every strategy or library coming from a distinct domain, and problems of software/hardware compatibility. This choice of distributed architecture thus authorizes the coexistence of different hardware and software configurations.

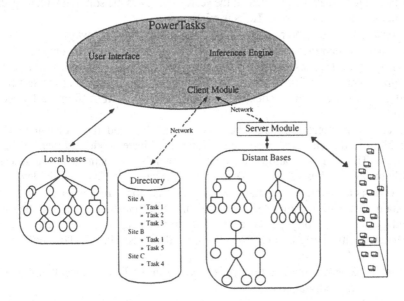

Fig. 7. Communications between elements of the DPSE. Network communications are indicated by arrows in dotted line. PowerTasks is localized at each user site. There is a server module at each site containing public tasks. This server also provide access to programs encapsulated in elementary public tasks.

Further, it allows the availability of all solution strategies whatever their localizations. Each server site thus contributes, according to its competence field, to design a single methodological knowledge base, multi localized. To do that, it develops single or multi-localized strategies and allows other sites to access these strategies while making them public. Just as the WWW makes it possible to see a multitude of distant documents like a single hyper-document, the goal here is to see a multitude of strategies developed and maintained at various sites as constituting a single methodological base.

Accessing distant methodological knowledge bases is allowed by server modules. At the opposite, using local methodological knowledge bases remains directly controlled by PowerTasks (cf. Fig. 7).

3.2 Code Mobility.

Few years ago, Java proposed a new approach towards compilation and distributed architectures. The code is semi-compiled into byte code and this byte code is then executed on each hardware configuration thanks to the Java Virtual Machine. Our vision of the distribution of PowerTasks has been nearly the same: the methodological knowledge, i.e. the tasks, are similar to the byte code in that they are valid in each architecture (comprising PowerTasks). Tasks can be easily transferred through networks from server sites to client sites and then be used to solve problems. The main difference comes from the execution of library modules used to solve elementary tasks: they are executed at the server site. Thus the solution with respect to code mobility adopted in PowerTasks is mixed.

Using distant software library code can be done in three different ways:

- the code is untransportable due to hardware or software incompatibility of environments. This case is the most frequent because a lot of libraries for scientific programming are in Fortran or C. Then executions are launched at the server site and results transferred to client sites as in the case of RPC (Remote Procedure Call);
- the code can migrate through the network and be used on a distant machine (mobile). In this case, the client can transfer the selected code and then execute it locally. This solution allows a significant number of simultaneous accesses, without slowing down servers responses. It is the case of a language like Java;
- the code is available for several hardware configuration. In this case, server sites contain different versions of the same modules depending on the hardware configuration; mobility policy consists in transferring to client sites a version adequate to its configuration. Executions are then, also, local. These possibilities are offered, for example, by ActiveX or Ilog products.

In terms of the above classification, code mobility in the DPSE PowerTasks depends on its nature (task/program/data):

- tasks code is mobile: tasks language is interpreted. On the other hand, an interpreter module is included in PowerTasks allowing each client site to understand and use distant tasks;
- on the other hand, software library modules used to solve elementary tasks are generally executed at their server site;
- data used or produced by external programs or library modules are moved from client to server before execution and from server to client after execution. Each site keeps its own data it uses to work on, i.e. DNA sequences in the biological application.

Tasks transfer makes it possible to solve problems locally thanks to classification and/or decomposition and thus allows one to preserve user interactions present in the single-site model. Users can thus intervene interactively during a resolution. This approach gives the impression to users that all problem solving resources (i.e., methodological knowledge, binaries, databases,...) are available on their own computers, but binaries, databases and specific resources are only virtual since they remain on their original site.

All these choices affect the task model and imply some modifications, in order to:
- define accessible competencies localization,
- allow interaction between distributed tasks,
- give access to all the tasks in an identical way, independently of their localization,
- propose new techniques to deal with strategy actualization,
- check coherence between both domain and methodological knowledge bases.

These various points involve a modification of the task model (cf. section 4), the definition of mechanisms concerning task use and modification, the creation of new entities facilitating the adaptability of strategies (cf. section 4.1).

4 Distributed Tasks Model

The tasks model described in section 2, supports well the distribution (cf. Fig. 8). The distribution has only a minor effect on the whole system, since the tasks are transferred. Once the answers are returned, resolution proceeds locally until calls to binaries or modules. Nevertheless, the evolution towards a distributed tasks language led us, on the one hand, to add a status attribute in order to characterize distant authorization access, and, on the other hand, to propose protocols to manage tasks versions.

4.1 Tasks Status and Availability.

To be accessed and used from a distant site, a task must be declared as being *public*. This publication generates a submission process to a directory which centralizes each available task (i.e. public). Another alternative to this publication exists. It consists in providing the client only the task functionality without visualization of the strategy, this kind of tasks is declared as *blind*. This status is used in two distinct cases: to protect the methodological knowledge because it contains secret into, or to hide this knowledge because it is too complex and without any interest for the client (e.g. a low level of tasks decomposition due to the software library configuration). In ImaGene, some annotation methods come from private laboratories which just give permission to execute them without explaining their working, e.g. the use of the method based on nucleotide appearance frequency is restricted to execution.

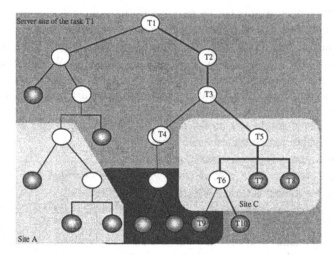

Fig. 8. Example of strategy localization. Strategy T1 is based upon strategies of site A, B and C. For example, during a resolution, task T1 specializes in T2, next in T3; T3 specialization is done towards a task of the site C (T5). This task T5 breaks up into three sub-tasks whose first (T6) specializes in T10, an elementary task (in gray) which is located at the first site.

Any site can publish a task to make it available to others. Doing this, it becomes server of the task with respect to the others sites, the strategy and the different resources used to solve this task (databases, binaries and calculation time). A site publishing or proposing public tasks remains client for distant tasks already used. Each site is thus potentially client and server. A site can even be server of a strategy whose elementary tasks are distant, it is then only server of tasks hierarchies. On the opposite, it is possible that the methodological base of a site is empty if the users just use public and blind tasks. The consequences of this status is that methodological knowledge bases of other sites are not seen in full, but only through their public tasks, sub-tasks of public tasks and blind tasks.

4.2 Publication Protocol.

To publish a task, a site must send to a directory (i) the name of the task, (ii) its signature (description of the inputs and outputs), (iii) its functional description and (iv) a number of version (identification of the last update). This publication is validated by the directory which checks that there is no name conflict. Setting a public status to a task leads to setting this status to all its sub-tasks except if they are already in a blind status. On the opposite, setting a blind status does not modify the status of the subtasks.

4.3 Modification Protocol.

Modifications on public/blind tasks are possible. They can be more or less complex depending on their type (cf. Fig. 9). These modifications may concern the signature (input/output description), the solution strategy or the encapsulated module used to solve the elementary task.

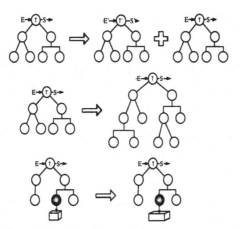

Fig. 9. Different kinds of modification: signature, strategy and programs.

Each of these modifications is briefly described in the paragraphs below.

- The task whose signature is changed must take another name. Indeed, there cannot be two different tasks having the same name and distinct signatures at the same site. This constraint is justified by the fact that the change of signature of a task, after its publication, would involve inconsistencies in the strategies using this task, making them thus unusable. Each server site publishing a task must ensure its persistence.

- The modification of a strategy which does not affect the signature of a public/blind task is considered as a change of version of this task. The strategies based on this task can use the old version or the new one. Forward planning, the old version will be replaced by the new one. But, making the change immediate would perturb users. Indeed, solving strategies of tasks act upon the way users apprehend the domain in question and an automatic change would disturb them even if the functionality of the new strategy is similar to the previous one.

- On the opposite, the modification of an elementary task solution resources is automatic. Indeed, the update of the binary/module encapsulated in an elementary task is totally transparent for users. The only difference is that the version number in the directory is incremented in order to be able to inform users of possible causes of an problem, if one occurs.

4.4 Use Protocol.

Client sites can consult the directory and use any of the described tasks. Public task use is similar to local task use: once the strategy has been transferred, the resolutions based on it are local, the only difference being that elementary tasks are solved at the server site (cf. Fig. 10). Blind task use is slightly different since they are not decomposed during the resolution. Thus, users can not make any difference between blind tasks and elementary tasks. But inside the system, exactly the same process of classification/decomposition phases is carried out.

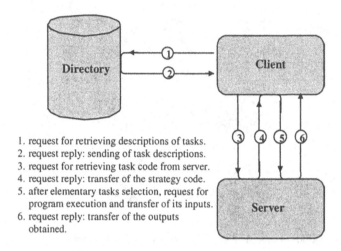

1. request for retrieving descriptions of tasks.
2. request reply: sending of task descriptions.
3. request for retrieving task code from server.
4. request reply: transfer of the strategy code.
5. after elementary tasks selection, request for program execution and transfer of its inputs.
6. request reply: transfer of the outputs obtained.

Fig. 10. Description of the communications during a resolution employing a distant task.

5 Perspectives: Adaptability of Solving Strategies

The new opportunities offered by the distribution of PowerTasks have highlighted an important problem: task solution strategy are fixed. There is no dynamic process to include new available tasks. This problem can be illustrated by means of a simple example in DNA sequence annotation. Suppose that a laboratory has a task consisting in launching several annotation methods one after another in order to compare results and find sequencing errors. Later on, a laboratory proposes a very interesting method through a public task. The first laboratory is not informed that a new method is available and it keeps using its old task. This is due to the fact that all the tasks available to solve a problem are explicitly declared as sub-tasks of the task containing the problem. To solve this problem, we propose to generate a *request* able to find in the directory the tasks that could solve the current task [21] [1]. This request would be based on the task functionality and its data signature. In order to include this request, the inference engine of PowerTasks will be modified: the request will be executed before specialization in order to find new possibilities to solve a task. The tasks obtained will be proposed to the user and eventually included in the task solving strategy.

6 Conclusion

PowerTasks is a generic problem solving system designed around an object model developed by Ilog software company and a task model resulting from our preceding experiments. It makes available through a single user interface:
- the description of tasks in a suitable language allowing the expression of a problem solving strategy,
- to control the execution of tasks, to control and set parameters to programs encapsulated in elementary tasks,
- to start the execution of these programs,
- to describe problems and to visualize resolution results,
- to intervene directly during the solving process by changing a value, adding a parameter or choosing a solving strategy.

The PSEs developed on top of PowerTasks include all these functionalities in a homogeneous environment. This one thus allows users a simple use of software libraries and an access to methodological knowledge without requiring them to be an expert in the different techniques used.

The PSEs permit experts to work on their specific domain while using knowledge developed by others. In addition, PowerTasks authorizes the use of distant problem solving strategies or programs. This contribution facilitates the diffusion of competences. Thus users of various domains can work in partnership through networks. This possibility represents a major asset in the resolution of problems, since it enables each task to be based on the last strategy developed by experts of the concerned domain and each elementary task to encapsulate the most recent and high-performing program. The strategies are written in a mobile code and are interpreted locally; this allows users to preserve the same interactions with the system as in a not distributed environment.

As the distributed model makes it possible to have several strategies solving the same problem, we are introducing rationality criteria into the choice of the tasks. These choices will not only be based on the input characteristics, but also on the geographical localization of the task, its execution time [11], and the quality of the solutions provided. Moreover, the possibility of launching parts of the resolution on a distant site allows one to launch them in parallel [6] [12]. Distributed problem solving environments thus generate new opportunities which are still to be investigated.

References

1. Bisson, G., Botraud, J-C.: A proposal to improve information retrieval on WEB sites, http://nangaparba.inrialpes.fr/, 1998.
2. Chevenet F., Jean-Marie, F., Willamowski, J.: SLOT: a cooperative problem-solving environment in explanatory data analysis. Proceedings 49th session of the International Statistical Institute, pp. 255-256, Firenza (IT), September 1993.
3. Chaillot M.: Une architecture de contrôle réactif pour la résolution coopérative de problèmes, PH.D Thesis, INPG, Grenoble (Fr), 1993.
4. Chandrasekaran B.: Generic tasks in knowledge based reasoning high level building blocks for expert system design, IEEE Expert, 1986.

5. Chandrasakaran, B., Johnson, T.R., Smith, J.W.: Task-structure analysis for knowledge modelling, Communication of the ACM, 35(9), pp. 124-137, 1992.
6. Charpillet F., Boyer, A.: Progress : un modèle d'agent pour la conception de systèmes multi-agents temps réel, Journées Francophones IA distribuée et Systèmes Multi-agents, 1997.
7. Clément V.: Raisonnements cognitifs appliqués au pilotage d'algorithmes de traitement d'images, PH.D Thesis, Université de Nice Sophia-Antipolis, Nice (Fr), 1990.
8. Delouis I.: LISA, un langage réflexif pour la modélisation du contrôle dans les systèmes à bases de connaissances. Application à la planification de réseaux électriques, PH.D Thesis, Université de Paris Sud centre d'Orsay, Paris (Fr), 1993.
9. Demazeau Y., Ferber, J.: Actes de la 1ère Journée Nationale sur les Systèmes Multi-Agents, ed. PRC-GDR IA MARCIA CRIN, France, LIFIA Publication, Grenoble, France, December 1992.
10. Erickson et al: Task modeling with reusable problem solving method, AI 2(79), p. 293-326, 1995.
11. Fink E., Statistical Selection Among Problem-Solving Methods, Research Report CMU-CS-97-101, 1997
12. Fujita S., V.R. Lesser, Centralized Task Distribution in the Presence of Uncertainly and Time Deadlines, Proceeding of ICAMS, Japan, 1996.
13. Gallopoulos E. et al.: Future Research Directions In Problem Solving Environments For computational Science, CSRD Report, N°1259, 1992.
14. KbuP'95, First international workshop on Knowledge-Based systems for the (re) Use of Program Libraries, INRIA, Sofia Antipolis, France, 1995.
15. Médigue, C., Vermat, T., Bisson, G., Viari, A., Danchin, A.: Cooperative computer system for genome sequence analysis, Proceedings of 3rd ISMB, Cambridge, United Kingdom, pp249-258, 1995.
16. Moszer I., Kunst, F., Dachin, A.: The European Bacillus subtilis genome sequencing project : current status and accessibility of the data from a new World Wide Web site, Microbiology 142, p. 261-268, 1996.
17. Rechenmann F.: Knowledge bases and computational molecular biology, In Nicolaas Mars (ed.), Towards very large knowledge bases (proceedings 2nd international conference on building and sharing very large-scale knowledge bases (KBKS), Enschede (NL), IOS press, Amsterdam, Pays Bas, pp. 7-12, 1995
18. Rice J. R., R. F. Boisvert, From Scientific Software Libraries to Problem-Solving Environnements ", IEEE Computational Science & Engineering, pp. 44-53, 1996.
19. Rousseau B., Vers un environnement de résolution de problèmes en biométrie, PH.D Thesis, Université C. Bernard, Lyon, France, 1988.
20. Schreider, A.Th., Wielinga, B.J., de Hoog, R., Akkermans, J.M., Van de Velde, W.: CommonKADS: A Comprehensive Methodology for Knowledge Based Systems Development, IEEE Expert, 9(6), pp. 28-37, 1994.
21. Thonnat, M., Clément, V., Van den Elst, J.: Supervision of perception tasks for autonomous systems: the OCAPI approach. J. of Information Science and Technology, Vol. 3(2), pp. 140-162, 1994.
22. Thonnat, M., Moisan, S.: Knowledge-based systems for program supervision, KbuP'95, First international workshop on Knowledge-Based systems for the (re) Use of Program Libraries, Sofia Antipolis, France, 1995.
23. Van Den Elst, J., Modélisation de connaissances pour le pilotage de programmes de traitement d'images, Ph.D. Thesis, Université de Nice Sophia Antipolis, Nice, France, 1996.
24. Willamowski J.: Modélisation de tâches pour la résolution de problèmes en coopération système-utilisateur, Ph.D. Thesis, Université Joseph Fourier, Grenoble, France, 1994.

Knowledge Acquisition from Multiple Experts Based on Semantics of Concepts

Seppo Puuronen[1], Vagan Terziyan[2]

[1] University of Jyväskylä, P.O.Box 35, FIN-40351 Jyväskylä, Finland
sepi@jytko.jyu.fi
[2] Kharkov State Technical University of Radioelectronics, 14 Lenin Avenue,
310166 Kharkov, Ukraine
vagan@kture.cit-ua.net

Abstract. This paper presents one approach to acquire knowledge from multiple experts. The experts are grouped into a multilevel hierarchical structure, according to the type of knowledge acquired. The first level consists of experts who have knowledge about the basic objects and their relationships. The second level of experts includes those who have knowledge about the relationships of the experts at the first level and each higher level accordingly. We show how to derive the most supported opinion among the experts at each level. This is used to order the experts into categories of their competence defined as the support they get from their colleagues.

1 Introduction

When an expert system is being built, knowledge is usually acquired from multiple knowledge sources. This knowledge usually includes inconsistencies, incompleteness, and incorrectness. These difficulties are often solved either by selecting some part of knowledge as the only one to be saved or by adding up some extra knowledge into the knowledge base.

Distributed AI can be exploited in knowledge acquisition to modell cooperation and conflicts of experts, the knowledge acquisition process, and especially cooperation during knowledge acquisition from a group of experts. Knowledge acquisition from several experts is an extremely difficult task. Turban and Tan [24] review the difficulties as well as the benefits involved. Research has been carried on about knowledge acquisition from multiple experts [9] as constructive modelling and elicitation [14], models of cognitive agents [10] for guiding knowledge acquisition [7], management and comparison of multiple viewpoints [20, 3], detection and solving of conflicts among several expertise models [16], comparison of knowledge graphs [6], generation of consensual rules among experts [18], architecture of a cognitive agent [7], extension of CommonKADS [25, 5] for multi-expertise [8] and for multi-agent systems [3], and cooperative knowledge evolution [22]. The type of cooperation depends on the organization of the agents where horizontal and vertical organization structures can be distinguished. In a non hierarchical society, cooperation is based on sharing of tasks and results, while in a hierarchical society, commands, bids, and competition is relied on [19].

Gappa and Puppe [11] discuss an application of the construction of knowledge-based systems. The task description was prepared and the knowledge sources were made available via the World Wide Web. The common knowledge material consisted of the transcripts of various reports and interviews of domain experts, partly formalised relational knowledge, pictures of the domain objects, and a database containing descriptions of the domain objects' samples. The essential knowledge engineering problem how to deal with conflicting knowledge from the experts was discussed. The authors tried to resolve the differences based on the consistency and frequency of the different expert opinions to result one authoritative knowledge base. Another approach would be to build a special knowledge base for each expert and then to integrate the solutions they produce for example by a majority vote or by a weighted majority vote.

The area of eliciting expertise from one or more experts in order to construct a single knowledge base is still under great research interest. Taylor et al [23] argue that the overlapping knowledge obtained from multiple knowledge sources cannot be described in a context or even process independent way. They claim that even when there have been inference engines that were subsequently applied to related domains, the sets of rules have been different generally. According to Mak et al [15] the other researchers have found that if more than one expert are available, then one must either select the opinion of the best expert or pool the experts' judgements. It is assumed that when experts' judgements are pooled, collectively they offer sufficient cues leading to the building of a comprehensive theory. Medsker et al [17] distinguish three practical strategies for knowledge acquisition: 1) use only the opinion of one expert, 2) collect the opinions of several experts, but use only one at a time, and 3) integrate the opinions of several experts. It was assumed that the acquired knowledge has more validity if it is obtained as a consensus of several experts. Mak et al [15] discuss about five knowledge classification techniques and make experimental evaluation of them. The elicited knowledge was aggregated using classical statistical methods, the ID3 pattern classification method, the k-NN technique, and neural networks. They found that the neural net method outperformed the other methods in robustness and predictive accuracy.

Arens et al [1] have described an approach which exploits the semantic model of a problem domain to integrate the information from various knowledge sources. In the SIMS project they have created a complete semantic model for data retrieval and integration from multiple dispersed knowledge sources. Roos [21] has described a logic for reasoning with inconsistent knowledge coming from different and not fully reliable knowledge sources. Inconsistency may be resolved by considering the reliability of the knowledge sources used. Since the relative probability is conditional on inconsistencies, information from one reliable source cannot be overruled by information from many unreliable knowledge sources. Goto et al [12] discuss the three level structure of information distribution. Their levels are brains, gatekeepers, and end users. A brain has expertise in a specific area and a gatekeeper has geeneral information but not special expertise of any area. Each brain recognizes the other brains and they create the structure of knowledge by interacting with each other. The necessity to several brains appears only if the area of knowledge is too wide to be covered by a single brain. The gatekeepers may be interpreted as an intelligent interface between the brains and the end users. A gatekeeper knows to which brain or group of brains to address user's question and so he has in multi brain human society a key role.

Current books in formal semantics widely use approaches based on fundamental conceptual research in philosophy and cognitive psychology. For example Larsen and Segal [13] study a particular human cognitive competence governing the meanings of words and phrases. The authors argue that speakers have unconscious knowledge of the semantic rules of their language. The knowledge of meanings is both in the semantics of domain attributes, i.e. properties and relations, and in learning technology how to derive the semantics of inconsistent and incomplete meanings. A knowledge base is built upon the definition of a structured set of concepts, derived, for a large part, by the knowledge engineer from text analyses of the transcriptions of discussions with an expert or written documents. The focus of knowledge acquisition is the conceptual organisation of knowledge areas from the study of terms representing concepts in texts as it was mentioned in a methodological issue of Aussenac [2].

One goal of our research is to develop formalisms for representation and reasoning with knowledge obtained from several knowledge sources. In this paper we present one formalism that is based on a matrix representation of semantic networks. The knowledge structure has several levels and the upper levels include knowledge about the relationships of the experts and the domain objects, too.

We use our formalism to handle three types of problems:

1) How to derive the most supported knowledge about the basic domain objects and their relations among the experts? This gives a user a possibility to use "consensus" knowledge during reasoning process.

2) How to order the experts according to their supported competence concerning each domain relation and each domain object? This order helps a user to select the most "competent" expert of each domain relation and object. We name this as deriving the *horizontal order of the experts* according to their competences.

3) How to use the opinions of the experts about the relations between the experts and the domain objects and between each other to group the experts into different levels? This helps a user both to evaluate the subjectivity of each expert and to select an expert whose knowledge he wants to be used during the reasoning process. We name this as deriving the *multilevel vertical structure of the experts*.

The rest of the paper is organised as follows. Section 2 introduces the basic concepts with an example that is used across the whole paper. Section 3 presents how to derive the most supported knowledge about the objects and their relations from the opinions of the experts. In Section 4 we introduce our method to derive the horizontal order of the experts according to their supported competence concerning each piece of knowledge. In section 5 we present the derivation of the vertical structure of the experts. Section 6 concludes with a few future research topics.

2 Basic concepts

In this chapter, we introduce the basic concepts and the notation used thorought the paper. We introduce also the example used across the whole paper.

In this paper we interpret *knowledge* to be composed of information about the *objects*, and their *properties* and *relations* which we present as a set of *semantic predicates*.

Each object has an unique *identifier* (for an object we use the notation A with an index) and zero, one, or more *properties*.

A *Relation* has four attributes: the two objects between which the relation holds, the name of the relation (we use the notation L with an index), and a *source* from which the information about this relation was acquired (we use notation Ex with an index). The name of the relation indicates the *semantic contents* of the relation. For example, the fact "Mary told that Bill contacted his friend Tom by phone", is presented using the two objects <Bill> and <Tom> , the two relations defined by the concepts <to be friend> and <to contact by phone>, and the source <Mary>.

A *property* describes an object separately from the other objects. It may be interpreted as a special relation where the two objects between which the relation holds are the same object. A *concept* in such relation is the name of property. For example, the fact: "Bill is forty years old black man", is described using one object <Bill> with three properties: <to be male>, <to be black>, <to be 40 years old>.

We will index objects using $s, t = 1,...,n$ (n objects), concepts - using $i, j = 1,...,r$ (r concepts), and sources using $k, l = 1,...,m$ (m sources) with notation of sources.

Semantic predicate describes a piece of knowledge (relation or property) by expression: $P(A_s, L_i, A_t, Ex_k) = true$, if there is knowledge, acquired from the knowledge source Ex_k, that a relation with concept L_i holds between objects A_s and A_t, and $P(A_s, L_i, A_t, Ex_k) = false$, if there is knowledge acquired from source Ex_k that a relation with concept L_i does not hold between objects A_s and A_t.

For example knowledge about the statement: *"Pete says that Bill hates poor Mary"* can be formally represented as follows: Ex_1: <Pete> is the source of knowledge; A_1: <Bill> and A_2: <Mary> are the objects; L_1: <to hate>, L_2: <to be poor> are the concepts; $P(A_1, L_1, A_2, Ex_1)- < Bill\ hates\ Mary >$ is the relation; $P(A_2, L_2, A_2, Ex_1)- < Mary\ is\ poor >$ is the property.

We present the *semantics* of certain concept L_i acquired from the knowledge source Ex_k as a matrix $(L_i^k)_{n \times n}$ (n is number of objects), where:

$$(L_i^k)_{s,t} = \begin{cases} 1, & if\ P(A_s, L_i, A_t, Ex_k) = true; \\ -1, & if\ P(A_s, L_i, A_t, Ex_k) = false; \\ 0, & otherwise. \end{cases}$$

Let us consider, as an example, some of the characters and their relationships in the film "Santa-Barbara". The characters and concepts to be considered are presented in Figure 1.

Objects and their ids.	Concepts and their ids.
<Mejson> - A_1	<to respect> - L_1
<Iden> - A_2	<to help> - L_2
<Julia> - A_3	<to love> - L_3
<Victoria> - A_4	<to envy> - L_4

Fig. 1. Objects and concepts in "Santa-Barbara" example

Let us suppose that three spectators express their opinions about relationships in this domain in the following way:

Spectator 1: "Mejson loves, respects and envies Victoria. Iden respects, helps and envies Mejson. Iden envies Victoria. Julia loves Mejson, and she helps Victoria and Iden. Victoria loves and envies Mejson and she respects Julia."

Spectator 2: "Mejson envies Iden, he respects Iden and Victoria and loves Julia. Iden helps Mejson and Julia and envies Victoria. Julia helps Iden. Victoria loves Mejson, respects Julia, and envies Iden."

Spectator 3: "Mejson loves Julia. Iden respects Mejson and Victoria and she helps Julia. Julia helps Iden, and she helps, loves and envies Victoria. Victoria respects Mejson and Iden and envies Iden."

The knowledge expressed by the semantic networks in Figure 2 a-c.

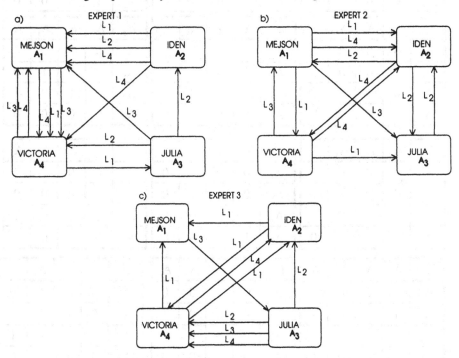

Fig. 2. Opinions of experts in the example presented by semantic networks

3 Deriving the most supported knowledge

In many cases as, in previous example, each expert interprets domain area by his own way. Without any co-ordination between experts, it is difficult to acquire useful information from their opinions. It is usual that information about one domain attribute is more in the area of expertise of one expert and another attribute is more in the expertise area of another expert. If one does not have such additional knowledge about expertise, then he has to select opinion of some of the experts. Another way is to use those pieces of knowledge that receive most support among all the experts.

In this chapter, we present the way to derive the most supported knowledge and then we show how to discover knowledge sources that have given the pieces of knowledge included to the most supported knowledge.

In our example the semantics $L_1^k - L_4^k$ of concepts L_1 - L_4 according to the knowledge sources $k = 1,2,3$ is presented in Figure 3.

L_1^1	A_1	A_2	A_3	A_4		L_1^2	A_1	A_2	A_3	A_4		L_1^3	A_1	A_2	A_3	A_4
A_1	0	0	0	1		A_1	0	1	0	1		A_1	0	0	0	0
A_2	1	0	0	0		A_2	0	0	0	0		A_2	1	0	0	1
A_3	0	0	0	0		A_3	0	0	0	0		A_3	0	0	0	0
A_4	0	0	1	0		A_4	0	0	1	0		A_4	1	1	0	0

L_2^1	A_1	A_2	A_3	A_4		L_2^2	A_1	A_2	A_3	A_4		L_2^3	A_1	A_2	A_3	A_4
A_1	0	0	0	0		A_1	0	0	0	0		A_1	0	0	0	0
A_2	1	0	0	0		A_2	1	0	1	0		A_2	0	0	1	0
A_3	.0	1	0	1		A_3	0	1	0	0		A_3	0	1	0	1
A_4	0	0	0	0		A_4	0	0	0	0		A_4	0	0	0	0

L_3^1	A_1	A_2	A_3	A_4		L_3^2	A_1	A_2	A_3	A_4		L_3^3	A_1	A_2	A_3	A_4
A_1	0	0	0	1		A_1	0	0	1	0		A_1	0	0	1	0
A_2	0	0	0	0		A_2	0	0	0	0		A_2	0	0	0	0
A_3	1	0	0	0		A_3	0	0	0	0		A_3	0	0	0	1
A_4	1	0	0	0		A_4	1	0	0	0		A_4	0	0	0	0

L_4^1	A_1	A_2	A_3	A_4		L_4^2	A_1	A_2	A_3	A_4		L_4^3	A_1	A_2	A_3	A_4
A_1	0	0	0	1		A_1	0	1	0	0		A_1	0	0	0	0
A_2	1	0	0	1		A_2	0	0	0	1		A_2	0	0	0	0
A_3	0	0	0	0		A_3	0	0	0	0		A_3	0	0	0	1
A_4	1	0	0	0		A_4	0	1	0	0		A_4	0	1	0	0

Fig. 3. Semantics of concepts in the example

Deriving the most supported semantics of concepts. We build a matrix $(CL)_{n \times m}$ by a following way:

$$(CL)_{i,k} = \sum_{s,t}^{n} ((L_i^k)_{s,t} \times \sum_{j,j \neq k}^{m} (L_i^j)_{s,t}).$$

The formula gives to each element of the *CL* matrix an integer value that summarises the support that knowledge source gets among the experts using the concept to describe the relation. When the formula is applied to the example, we obtain the matrix in Figure 4. It shows that expert 1 gets most support among experts to the use of concept "to respect". It also shows that experts get equal support using the concept "to help".

CL	Ex$_1$	Ex$_2$	Ex$_3$
L$_1$	3	2	1
L$_2$	4	4	4
L$_3$	1	2	1
L$_4$	1	2	1

Fig. 4. Support to use concepts

The most supported knowledge about concepts is derived by selecting only knowledge of most supported knowledge sources. We will use the concept *competent* and it is presented by matrix $(L_i^{msup})_{n \times n}$:

$$(L_i^{m\,sup})_{s,t} = sign(\sum_{\substack{k \\ \forall k(CL)_{i,k}=max(CL)_{i,l}}} (L_i)_{s,t}^k).$$

When the formula is applied to the example, we obtain the matrixes of Figure 5.

L$_1^{msup}$	A$_1$	A$_2$	A$_3$	A$_4$
A$_1$	0	0	0	1
A$_2$	1	0	0	0
A$_3$	0	0	0	0
A$_4$	0	0	1	0

L$_2^{msup}$	A$_1$	A$_2$	A$_3$	A$_4$
A$_1$	0	0	0	0
A$_2$	1	0	1	0
A$_3$	0	1	0	1
A$_4$	0	0	0	0

L$_3^{msup}$	A$_1$	A$_2$	A$_3$	A$_4$
A$_1$	0	0	1	0
A$_2$	0	0	0	0
A$_3$	0	0	0	0
A$_4$	1	0	0	0

L$_4^{msup}$	A$_1$	A$_2$	A$_3$	A$_4$
A$_1$	0	1	0	0
A$_2$	0	0	0	1
A$_3$	0	0	0	0
A$_4$	0	1	0	0

Fig. 5. The most supported opinion about each concept in the example

These matrixes of Figure 5 together present the most supported knowledge about concepts that describe domain relations. The semantic network presentation of it is in Figure 6.

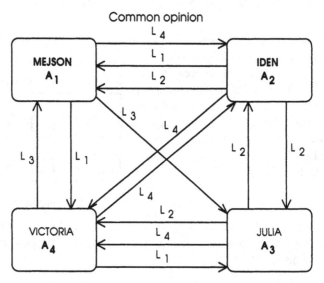

Fig. 6. The semantic network presentation of the most supported knowledge

4 Deriving horizontal order of experts

In this chapter we present how to order the experts according to their competence concerning each relation and object. This ordering is based on the most supported knowledge among the experts about concepts used to describe of domain relations. The amount of competence of an expert is measured by the support he receives to his opinions among experts. This is surely no absolute evaluation of competence and the result depends on the group of experts selected. In deriving expert's competence we firsts derive a numerical value for expert's competence concerning each possible relation and then use these values to order the experts according to their competence. After that, we order the experts according to their competence about objects using their competence about relations connected to each object.

The numerical value for expert's competence concerning each possible relation is derived as $(CR)_{n \times n \times m}$ array using the formula:

$$(CR)_{s,t,k} = \sum_{\substack{i, \\ (L_i^k)_{s,t}=(L_i^{m\,sup})_{s,t}}}^{r} (L_i^{m\,sup})_{s,t}, \text{ where } s, t = 1, ..., n; k = 1, ..., m.$$

Experts are grouped into categories of competence, relation by relation, according to the corresponding values of the CR-array. This can be described by the algorithm A:

Step 1: For each pair of objects A_s and A_t, (s, t = 1,...n) do step 2.

Step 2: Group the experts Ex_k, (k = 1,...,m) into categories $CEx_{s,t,l}$, (l = 1,..., n) so that the experts who have the same highest value of $CR_{s,t,k}$, (k = 1,...,m) belong to the first category $CEx_{s,t,1}$, the experts who have the same second highest value of $CR_{s,t,k}$, (k = 1,...,m) belong to the second category $CEx_{s,t,2}$, and so on until all experts have assigned into some category.

Step 3: Return the grouping of experts into categories as the result of this algorithm.

In our example above we receive CR-array presented in Figure 7.

CR	Ex$_1$				Ex$_2$				Ex$_3$			
	A$_1$	A$_2$	A$_3$	A$_4$	A$_1$	A$_2$	A$_3$	A$_4$	A$_1$	A$_2$	A$_3$	A$_4$
A$_1$	0	0	0	1	0	1	1	1	0	0	1	0
A$_2$	2	0	0	1	1	0	1	1	1	0	1	0
A$_3$	0	1	0	1	0	1	0	0	0	1	0	1
A$_4$	1	0	1	0	1	1	1	0	0	1	0	0

Fig. 7. CR-array for the example

The categories, obtained with algorithm *A*, are shown in Figure 8.

CEx	First category				Second category				Third category			
	A$_1$	A$_2$	A$_3$	A$_4$	A$_1$	A$_2$	A$_3$	A$_4$	A$_1$	A$_2$	A$_3$	A$_4$
A$_1$	Ex$_1$ Ex$_2$ Ex$_3$	Ex$_2$	Ex$_2$ Ex$_3$	Ex$_1$ Ex$_2$	∅	Ex$_1$ Ex$_3$	Ex$_1$	Ex$_3$	∅	∅	∅	∅
A$_2$	Ex$_1$	Ex$_1$ Ex$_2$ Ex$_3$	Ex$_2$	Ex$_1$ Ex$_2$	Ex$_2$ Ex$_3$	∅	Ex$_1$ Ex$_3$	Ex$_3$	∅	∅	∅	∅
A$_3$	Ex$_1$ Ex$_2$ Ex$_3$	Ex$_1$ Ex$_2$ Ex$_3$	Ex$_1$ Ex$_2$ Ex$_3$	Ex$_3$	∅	∅	∅	Ex$_1$	∅	∅	∅	Ex$_2$
A$_4$	Ex$_1$ Ex$_2$	Ex$_2$ Ex$_3$	Ex$_1$ Ex$_2$	Ex$_1$ Ex$_2$ Ex$_3$	Ex$_3$	Ex$_1$	Ex$_3$	∅	∅	∅	∅	∅

Fig. 8. The experts categories in the example

We group experts into categories according to their competence about objects using their categories according to their competence about relations connected to each object. For each object and expert, we calculate the *sum* of the numbers of categories, they are included to, concerning the connected relations. The more competent experts have smaller sum. This can be described by the algorithm B:

Step 1: For each object A_s, (s, = 1,...n) do step 2.

Step 2: For each expert Ex_k, (k = 1,...,m) do step 3.

Step 3: Calculate sum of the numbers 1 of the categories $CEx_{s,t,l}$, (t = 1,...,n) where the expert Ex_k belongs to and add up into the sum the numbers 1 of the categories $CEx_{t,s,l}$, (t = 1,...,n) where the expert Ex_k belongs to.

Step 4: Group the experts Ex_k, (k = 1,...,m) into categories $COEx_{s,l}$, (l = 1,..., n) so that the experts who have the same smallest value of sum calculated in the step 3 belong to the first category $COEx_{s,1}$, the experts, who have the same second smallest value of the sum, belong to the second category $COEx_{s,2}$, and so on until all experts have assigned into some category.

Step 5: Return the grouping of experts into categories as the result of this algorithm.

In the example above, we receive sum values and categories, that are presented in Figure 9.

Sum	Ex_1	Ex_2	Ex_3	COEx	First category	Second category	Third category
A_1	10	9	12	A_1	Ex_2	Ex_1	Ex_3
A_2	11	9	12	A_2	Ex_2	Ex_1	Ex_3
A_3	11	10	10	A_3	Ex_2, Ex_3	Ex_1	Ø
A_4	9	9	12	A_4	Ex_1, Ex_2	Ex_3	Ø

Fig. 9. Sum values and expert categories concerning objects of the example

Results of knowledge attributes' distribution among experts accordingly to their competence are presented as a graph in Figure 10.

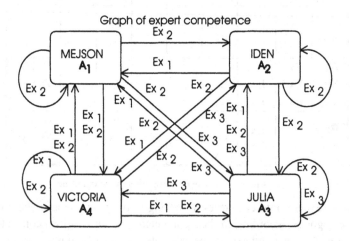

Fig. 10. Graph of horizontal competence of experts in the example

5 Multilevel vertical structure of experts

In this chapter we describe how to derive vertical hierarchy of experts. In our approach we suppose that experts give statements about the other experts (and even themselves) using the same relations as the basic level. We use the content of these statements to locate experts (and their statements) in different levels. The experts who give statements are both the experts who have given basic level knowledge of the domain area and experts who give only statements about the relations of the other experts. Figure 11 presents an example of cross-expertise professor-student. Student has his own opinion (a) about his own level of learning some course of lectures given by professor. Professor contacting with student forms his opinion (b) about student's level. Student has an opinion (c) about quality of lectures. Professor gives his own appreciation (d) of himself as lecturer. It seems reasonable to take into consideration all (a-d) opinions to derive resulting opinion concerning student. Experts in such situation represent multilevel structure of expertise. It is possible that some of the experts are present at the different levels in the same structure. We can be at one level of competence when we are evaluating a student and we are certainly at another level when we discussing the policy of a president.

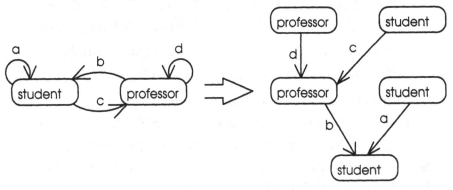

Fig. 11. Vertical hierarchy of competence

We introduce a new relation *Exp* that can exist between any two experts and it has the meaning that the first expert in the relation has expressed a statement about the second expert's relation with domain objects or himself. When the notion of object is allowed to represent also an expert then this can be described by formula:

$$\forall k, \exists i, t(P(Ex_l, L_i, A_t, Ex_k) \vee P(A_t, L_i, Ex_l, Ex_k) \vee$$
$$\vee P(Ex_l, L_i, Ex_l, Ex_i)) \Rightarrow P(Ex_k, Exp, Ex_l, Ex_k).$$

We construct a multilevel structure of experts in the following way. The zero level of the structure, marked D^0, includes only basic domain objects and their relations. The first level of the structure includes *Exp*-relations that are statements of experts about the other experts and/or their relations at the zero level D^0. The next level of the structure includes *Exp*-relations that are statements about experts that gave statement at the previous level and so on. There is a need to prevent infinite formation of levels in the case when statements form a circular structure. The formation of the upper levels of the structure can be described by:

$$\forall q(0 < q < 3)\forall A_k \exists A_l ((A_l \in D^{q-1}) \wedge P(A_k, Exp, A_l, A_k)) \Rightarrow (A_l \in D^q), \text{ and}$$

$$\forall q(q \geq 3)\forall A_k \exists A_l ((A_l \in D^{q-1}) \wedge P(A_k, Exp, A_l, A_k) \wedge \neg \exists p((0 \leq p \leq q-2) \wedge$$

$$\wedge Connect(A_l, q-1, A_k, p))) \Rightarrow (A_k \in D^q),$$

where *Connect* is a predicate that defines connection between the objects of different levels of the structure through circular chain of *Exp*-relations as:

$$\forall p \forall A_l (A_l \in D^p)\forall q(q \leq p-2)\forall A_k (A_k \in D^q)\exists A_{d_1}, A_{d_2}, ..., A_{d_{p-q-1}}(((A_{d_1} \in$$

$$\in D^{p-1}) \wedge (A_{d_2} \in D^{p-2}) \wedge ... \wedge (A_{d_{p-q-2}} \in D^{q+2}) \wedge (A_{d_{p-q-1}} \in D^{q+1})) \wedge$$

$$\wedge (P(A_l, Exp, A_{d_1}, A_l) \wedge P(A_{d_1}, Exp, A_{d_2}, A_{d_1}) \wedge ...$$

$$... \wedge P(A_{d_{p-q-1}}, Exp, A_k, A_{d_{p-q-1}}))) \Rightarrow Connect(A_l, p, A_k, q).$$

To continue our previous example we assume that the three experts have expressed their statements about competence of each other in the following way:

$$P(Ex_1, L_1, Ex_1, Ex_1) \wedge P(Ex_1, L_2, Ex_2, Ex_1) \wedge P(Ex_1, L_3, Ex_2, Ex_1) \wedge$$

$$\wedge P(Ex_2, L_1, Ex_1, Ex_1) \wedge P(Ex_2, L_3, Ex_2, Ex_1) \wedge P(Ex_3, L_3, Ex_3, Ex_2) \wedge$$

$$\wedge P(Ex_3, L_1, Ex_3, Ex_2) \wedge P(Ex_1, L_1, Ex_1, Ex_3) \wedge P(Ex_1, L_3, Ex_3, Ex_3) \wedge$$

$$\wedge P(Ex_3, L_1, Ex_1, Ex_3) \wedge P(Ex_3, L_1, Ex_3, Ex_3) \wedge P(Ex_3, L_3, Ex_3, Ex_3) = 1.$$

Using definition of *Exp*-relation it is possible to write:

$$P(Ex_1, Exp, Ex_1, Ex_1) \wedge P(Ex_1, Exp, Ex_2, Ex_1) \wedge P(Ex_2, Exp, Ex_3, Ex_2) \wedge$$

$$\wedge P(Ex_3, Exp, Ex_3, Ex_3) \wedge P(Ex_3, Exp, Ex_1, Ex_3) = 1.$$

These relations form the graph of cross-expertise in the way that is shown in Figure 12. Arrows mean *Exp* - relations.

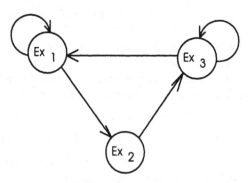

Fig. 12. Graph of cross-expertise

Using the above description, it is possible to unfold this graph into the multilevel vertical structure of experts presented in Figure 13.

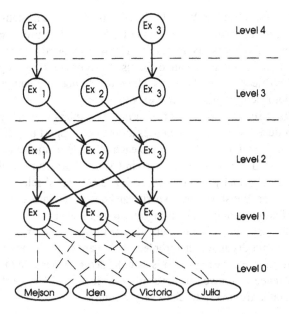

Fig. 13. Multilevel vertical structure of experts in the example

The method of deriving horizontal order of experts can be used to derive the most supported knowledge at each level. In the example the levels 1, 2 and 3 are as in Figure 14.

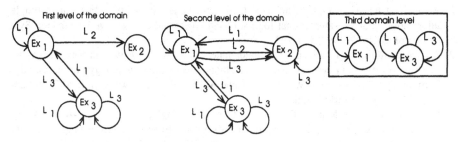

Fig. 14. Horisontal ordering for domain levels 1, 2, and 3 in the example

6 Conclusion

In this paper, we have presented a matrix-based way to process knowledge acquired from multiple knowledge sources. The basic representation of knowledge behind is semantic network presentation with objects and their relations. Concepts are used to define semantics of relationship and they are interpreted in a very broad way. Concept includes the name of relation, all necessary attributes of the relation and certain values of the attributes. We discussed about three problems.

First, how to derive the most supported (common) knowledge from knowledge sources. Knowledge obtained from different sources can include different and even conflicting pieces of knowledge. We introduced a method of calculating the amount of support to relations between any two pairs of objects and its use to select the most supported relations. It is necessary to note that most supported knowledge is not always the best one and sometimes cannot be used as correct knowledge. We accept most supported knowledge in applications which use democratic voting-based principle of acquiring knowledge from multiple experts.

Second, we discussed the problem of ordering the experts into categories of competence. We introduced a method which uses amount of support to locate each expert into one competence category with respect to each possible relation and object.

Third, we discussed the problem of deriving vertical structure in the case when there exist statements given by experts concerning also experts' relations with domain objects and each other. We show how experts can be grouped into a multiple structure and can be classified into competence categories at each level.

There are some restrictions in the methods used to describe experts' opinions. In this paper, we have not discussed the problem of semantics from the individual interpretation point of view. Further research is also needed to generalize the results to the cases where ignorance is allowed to have different levels, and support is allowed to be partly (for example from very weak to very weighty).

Acknowledgments. This work has been partly supported by the grant from the Academy of Finland.

References

1. Arens, Y., Chee, C., Hsu, C., Knoblock, C.: Retrieving and Integrating Data from Multiple Information Sources. International Journal of Intelligent and Cooperative Information Systems, Vol. 2, No. 2 (1993) 127-158.
2. Aussenac-Gilles, N., Bourigault, D., Condamines, A., Gros, C.: How Can Knowledge Acquisition Benefit from Terminology? In: A. Nuopponen (ed.), Terminology Forum, Library: Terminology Science and Work, Available in WWW: http://www.irit.fr/ACTIVITES/ EQ_SMI/ PUBLI/banff95.html.
3. Cointe, C.: Guide to Manage Conflicts in Concurrent Engineering: A Multi-Agent Architecture. In: K.Reger (ed.), Building Tomorrow's Virtual Enterprise: Proceedings of the 4th European Conference on Concurrent Engineering - CEE'97, SCS, Germany (1997).
4. Cointe, C., Matta, N., Ribiere, M.: Design Propositions Evaluation: Using Viewpoint to manage conflicts in CREOPS2. In: S. Ganesan, B. Prasad (eds.), Advanced in Concurrent Engineering, Proceedings of ISPE 4th International Conference on Concurrent Engineering Research and Applications (CE'97), Rochester, Michigan, USA (1997) 336-343.
5. Corby, O., Dieng, R.: Cokace: a Centaur-Based Environment for CommonKADS Conceptual Modelling Language. In: W. Wahlster (ed.), Proceedings of the 12th European Conference on AI - ECAI'96, Budapest, Hungary (1996) 418-422.
6. Dieng, R.: Comparison of Conceptual Graphs for Modelling Knowledge of Multiple Experts. ISMIS (1996) 78-87.
7. Dieng, R., Corby, O., Labidi, S.: Agent-Based Knowledge Acquisition. In: L. Steels, G. Schreiber, W. de Velde (eds.), A Future for Knowledge Acquisition: Proceedings of the 8th European Knowledge Acquisition Workshop - EKAW'94, Hoegaarden, Belgium (1994) 63-82.

8. Dieng, R., Hug, S.: Comparison of "Personal Ontologies" Represented through Conceptual Graphs. In: H. Prade (ed.), Proceedings of the 13th European Conference on Artificial Intelligence - ECAI'98, Brighton, UK (1998) 341-345.

9. Dieng, R.: Knowledge Acquisition for Explainable, Multi-expert, Design Systems. Available in WWW: http://www.inria.fr/acacia/present-Acacia.html.

10. Franklin, S.: Autonomous Agents as Embodied AI. Cybernetics and Systems, Vol. 28, No. 6 (1997) 499-520.

11. Gappa, U., Puppe, F.: A Study in Knowledge Acquisition - Experiences from the Sisyphus III Experiment for Rock Classification, to appear in Proceedings of KAW-98: 12th Banff Knowledge Acquisition for Knowledge-Based Systems Workshop (1998), Available in WWW: http://ki-server.informatik.uni-wuerzburg.de/forschung/publikationen/lehrstuhl/Sisy-III-98/sisy-III-98.html

12. Goto, S., Nojima, H.: Equilibrium Analysis of the Distribution of Information in Human Society. Artificial Intelligence, Vol. 75, No. 1 (1995) 115-130.

13. Larson, R., Segal, G.: Knowledge of Meaning. An Introduction to Semantic Theory. A Bradford Book (1995).

14. Leroux, B., Laublet P.: An approach to knowledge acquisition combining alternate steps of constructive modelling and elicitation. In: P. Brezillon et V. Stefanuk (Eds), East-West Artificial Intelligence Conference, Moscow (1993) 138-143.

15. Mak, B., Bui, T., Blanning, R.: Aggregating and Updating Experts' Knowledge: An Experimental Evaluation of Five Classification Techniques. Expert Systems with Applications, Vol. 10, No. 2 (1996) 233-241.

16. Matta, N., Cointe, C.: Concurrent Engineering and Conflicts Management Guides. In: A. Riitahuhta (ed.), World Class Design by World Class Methods, Proceedings of the 11th Int. Conference on Engineering Design (ICED97), Tampere, Finland (1997) 761-766.

17. Medsker, L., Tan, M., Turban, E.: Knowledge Acquisition from Multiple Experts: Problems and Issues. Expert Systems with Applications, Vol. 9, No. 1 (1995) 35-40.

18. A Protocol for Building Consensual and Consistent Repositories: INRIA research report RR-3260, available in WWW: http://www.inria.fr/RRRT/RR-3260.html.

19. Readings in Distributed Artificial Intelligence, A. H. Bond and L. Gasser (eds.), Morgan Kaumann, 1988.

20. Ribiere, M., Dieng, R.: Introduction of Viewpoints in Conceptual Graph Formalism. In: D. Lukose, H. Delugach, M. Keeler, L. Searle, J. Sowa (eds.), Conceptual Structures: Fulfilling Peirce's Dream, Fifth International Conference on Conceptual Structures (ICCS'97), LNAI, 1257 (1997) 168-182.

21. Roos, N.: A Logic for Reasoning with Inconsistent Knowledge. Artificial Intelligence, Vol. 57, No. 1 (1992) 69-103.

22. Schmalhofer, F., Tschaitschian, B.: Cooperative Knowledge Evolution for Complex Domains. In: Tecuci, G. and Kodratoff, Y., (eds.), Machine Learning and Knowledge Acquisition: Integrated Approaches. London: Academic Press (1995) 145-166.

23. Taylor, W., Weimann, D., Martin, P.: Knowledge Acquisition and Synthesis in a Multiple Source Multiple Domain Process Context. Expert Systems with Applications, Vol. 8, No. 2 (1995) 295-302.

24. Turban, E., Tan, M.: International Journal of Applied Expert Systems. Vol. 1, No. 2 (1993) 101-119.

25. Wielinga, B., Van de Velde, W., Schreiber, A., Akkermans, J.: Towards a Unification of Knowledge Modelling Approaches. In: J. David, J. Krivine, and R. Simmons (eds.), Second Generation Expert Systems,. Springer-Verlag, Berlin Heidelberg, Germany (1993) 299-335.

Acquiring Expert Knowledge for the Design of Conceptual Information Systems

Gerd Stumme

Technische Universität Darmstadt, Fachbereich Mathematik
Schloßgartenstr. 7, D–64289 Darmstadt, stumme@mathematik.tu-darmstadt.de

Abstract. Conceptual Information Systems unfold the conceptual structure of data stored in relational databases. In the design phase of the system, conceptual hierarchies have to be created which describe different aspects of the data. In this paper, we describe two principal ways of designing such conceptual hierarchies, *data driven design* and *theory driven design*, and discuss advantages and drawbacks. The central part of the paper shows how *Attribute Exploration*, a knowledge acquisition tool developed by B. Ganter can be applied for narrowing the gap between both approaches.

1 Introduction

Conceptual Information Systems ([20], [21]) unfold the conceptual structure of data stored in relational databases. A *Conceptual Information System* consists of the relational database together with conceptual hierarchies. These hierarchies, called *conceptual scales*, are used to support navigation through the data. Conceptual Information Systems are based on the mathematical theory Formal Concept Analysis ([10]). The management system TOSCANA visualizes arbitrary combinations of conceptual scales and allows on-line interaction with the database to analyze and explore data conceptually. TOSCANA has been developed at the Technische Universität Darmstadt and is, for four years now, also marketed by NAVICON GESELLSCHAFT FÜR BEGRIFFLICHE WISSENSVERARBEITUNG MBH. There are more than 30 Conceptual Information Systems implemented up to now, including an information system about laws and regulations in civil engineering ([7]), a library retrieval system ([14]) and an information system about flight movements ([12]). The use of Conceptual Information Systems gave rise to new theoretical questions which now dominate the research in Formal Concept Analysis. The demand of integrating knowledge acquisition tools in the design process of Conceptual Information Systems appeared for instance during the development of a Conceptual Information System about IT security.

For most applications, the Conceptual Information System is designed in a discursive process involving a domain expert and a knowledge engineer. Beside the database design, the conceptual scales have to be generated. Both steps require knowledge about the domain and about the structure of conceptual scales. In order to obtain interesting and non-trivial insights from the data, it is crucial that the domain expert is intensively involved in the design process. On the other hand, it has been observed that the time a domain expert is expected to spend for the design is one of the most critical factors for the decision of a company whether to implement a Conceptual Information System. Hence, one important requirement is to make the knowledge acquisition from the domain expert more efficient.

In order to keep the scales in a suitable size, they are, in some applications, designed to fit the actual data, and are not conform to all possible updates of the underlying database. These scales are derived semi-automatically from the actual data, thus their design needs less expertise — and time — from the domain expert. If an update violating the structure of the scale happens, then the user is warned, and he has to redraw the scale. If there are only small changes, the re-drawing can be done automatically, but due to the lack of acceptable drawing algorithms for lattices, large changes cannot be recovered automatically, and have to be effectuated by the knowledge engineer. If the latter is not part of the company in which the system is implemented, then these eventualities should be covered in advance. Hence, a second requirement is the stability of the conceptual scales against all possible updates of the underlying database. This requirement will be obsolete when acceptable drawing algorithms for lattices are developed, but this evolution is not in sight in the next future.

In this paper, we describe two principal ways of designing conceptual scales, *data driven design* and *theory driven design*, and discuss advantages and drawbacks with respect to the two requirements. The central part of the paper shows how *Attribute Exploration*, a knowledge acquisition algorithm developed by B. Ganter, can be applied in order to narrow the gap between both approaches. Attribute Exploration determines implications (functional dependencies) between attributes in an interactive session. Its typical application is in Mathematics, where mathematical theorems or counter-examples, resp., are asked from the mathematician in a systematic way in order to obtain a complete theory about specific mathematical structures.

In the next section, we describe the basics of Conceptual Information Systems and illustrate them by means of examples. Section 3 discusses the two principal ways of preparing a Conceptual Information System: theory driven design and data driven design. The design of the underlying database scheme is not topic of this paper. In Section 4, we describe the algorithm of Attribute Exploration and show by means of an example how it can be applied to the design of Conceptual Scales.

2 Conceptual Information Systems

Conceptual Information Systems provide a multi-dimensional conceptually structured view on data stored in relational databases. Conceptual Information Systems are similar to On-Line Analytical Processing (OLAP) tools, but focus on qualitative (i. e. non-numerical) data. The analog to OLAP dimensions are hierarchies of concepts. They are based on Formal Concept Analysis ([23], [10]), a mathematical theory modeling the concept of 'concept' as discussed in Philosophy since the logic of Port Royal ([3]) and described in the German Industrial Standards DIN 2330 and DIN 2331. There, a concept is understood as a unit of thought consisting of two parts: its extension and its intension ([22]). The extension consists of all objects belonging to the concept, and the intension of all attributes common to all the objects. In OLAP terminology, intensions of concepts correspond to coordinates addressing a cell, and extensions to entries of cells of a data cube. *Formal concepts* as defined below act as knots tying together the extensional and the intensional aspect of the data.

Each conceptual scale is generated from a *formal context*, a binary relation which allocates subsets of the attribute domains of the database to attributes which are meaningful to the analyst. The derived conceptual hierarchy can be an arbitrary lattice. It is displayed by a *Hasse diagram* which provides a universal and intuitively readable visualization of the data. By combining Hasse diagrams and zooming into them, operations similar to slicing, pivoting, drill-down and drill-up are supported ([17]). In the next section, we provide the mathematical background. Readers not familiar to mathematical notation may directly skip to the example.

2.1 The Mathematical Background: Formal Concept Analysis

Definition. A *(formal) context* is a triple $\mathbb{K} := (G, M, I)$ where G and M are sets and I is a relation between G and M. The elements of G and M are called *objects* and *attributes*, respectively, and $(g, m) \in I$ is read *"the object g has the attribute m"*.

For $A \subseteq G$, we define $A' := \{m \in M \mid \forall g \in A\colon (g, m) \in I\}$. For $B \subseteq M$, we define dually $B' := \{g \in G \mid \forall m \in B\colon (g, m) \in I\}$. Now a *(formal) concept* is a pair (A, B) such that $A \subseteq G$, $B \subseteq M$ and $A' = B$, $B' = A$. (This is equivalent to A and B being maximal with $A \times B \subseteq I$.) The set A is called the *extent* and the set B the *intent* of the concept.

Each formal context gives rise to a conceptual hierarchy, called *concept lattice* of $\mathbb{K}$ and denoted by $\mathfrak{B}(\mathbb{K})$. The hierarchical subconcept–superconcept–relation of concepts is formalized by

$$(A, B) \leq (C, D) : \iff A \subseteq C \quad (\iff B \supseteq D) .$$

Theorem 1 (cf. [10]). The set of all concepts of the context $\mathbb{K}$ together with this order relation is a complete lattice. I. e., for each set (A_t, B_t), $t \in T$, of concepts, a least common superconcept and a greatest common subconcept exist. They are computed as follows:

$$\bigvee_{t \in T} (A_t, B_t) = \left(\left(\bigcup_{t \in T} A_t\right)'', \bigcap_{t \in T} B_t\right) , \qquad \bigwedge_{t \in T} (A_t, B_t) = \left(\bigcap_{t \in T} A_t, \left(\bigcup_{t \in T} B_t\right)''\right)$$

The first equation describes the aggregation along the subconcept-superconcept-hierarchy: The extent of the least common superconcept is the closure by $''$ of the set union $\bigcup_{t \in T} A_t$. Because of the symmetry of the definition, attributes

M 3.8	M 3.7	M 3.6	M 3.5	M 3.4	M 3.3	M 3.2	M 3.1	
						X		Personalausfall
							X	Unzureichende Kenntnis über Regelungen
			X				X	Vertraulichkeits-/Integritätsverlust von Daten durch Fehlverhalten der IT-Benutzer
X	X		X	X		X	X	Fahrlässige Zerstörung von Gerät oder Daten
	X		X			X	X	Nichtbeachtung von IT-Sicherheitsmaßnahmen
			X	X			X	Fehlerhafte Nutzung des IT-Systems
X	X	X	X			X		Manipulation/Zerstörung von IT-Geräten oder Zubehör
X	X	X	X			X		Manipulation von Daten oder Software
			X				X	Social Engineering

M 3.1: Geregelte Einarbeitung/Einweisung neuer Mitarbeiter

M 3.2: Verpflichtung der Mitarbeiter auf Einhaltung einschlägiger Gesetze, Vorschriften und Regelungen

M 3.3: Vertretungsregelungen

M 3.4: Schulung vor Programmnutzung

M 3.5: Schulung zu IT-Sicherheitsmaßnahmen

M 3.6: Geregelte Verfahrensweise beim Ausscheiden von Mitarbeitern

M 3.7: Anlaufstelle bei persönlichen Problemen

M 3.8: Vermeidung von Störungen des Betriebsklimas

Fig. 1. Formal context about perils and counter-measures concerning IT security in Human Resources

can be aggregated in an analogous way by *descending* the hierarchy (cf. second equation). Again, the appropriate aggregation is not set union, but its closure by ''. This allows the investigation of *implications (functional dependencies)* between the attributes:

Definition. For two sets $X, Y \subseteq M$ of attributes, *the implication $X \to Y$ holds* in a formal context, if each object having all attributes in X also has all attributes in Y (i.e., $X' \subseteq Y'$, or equivalently $Y \subseteq X''$).

These implications play an important role in data analysis, and are also crucial for knowledge acquisition by Attribute Exploration (cf. Sect. 4). [1]

Example: The following example is taken from an information system about IT security ([16]). In the 'IT–Grundschutzhandbuch' of the Bundesamt für Sicherheit in der Informationstechnik ([4]), perils to certain objects, such as e.g. infra structure, telecommunication, human resources, are listed, and counter-measures are discussed. The presented information system is for demonstration purpose only, but a similar, more praxis oriented system with a higher level of detail is offered by NaviCon. The design of conceptual scales for the latter gave rise to this paper.

---

[1] A remark for readers who are familiar with association rules ([1]): Implications are association rules with minsupp=0 and minconf=1. In the framework of this paper, other association rules than implications are of no importance, because the concep-

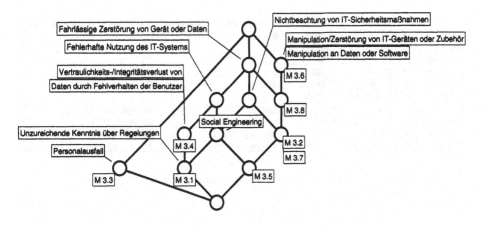

Fig. 2. Hasse diagram of the formal context in Fig. 1

The table for human resources from [4] is given in Fig. 1. It can be understood as a formal context, where the perils 'Personalausfall' (Staff drop out), ..., 'Social Engineering' are the attributes, and the counter-measures M 3.1, ..., M 3.8 are the objects. The relation assigns to each peril possible counter-measures. The context has 13 formal concepts. For instance, there is one concept having M 3.2, M 3.5, M 3.7, and M 3.8 in its extent, and 'Fahrlässige Zerstörung von Gerät oder Daten' (negligent destruction of machines or data), 'Manipulation/Zerstörung von IT-Geräten oder Zubehör' (manipulation of IT tools or accessories), and 'Manipulation an Daten oder Software' (manipulation on data or software) in its intent.

The concept lattice of that formal context is shown in Fig 2. Each circle stands for a formal concept, and the subconcept-superconcept hierarchy can be read by following ascending paths of straight line segments. The intent [extent] of each concept is given by all labels reachable from that context by ascending [descending] paths of straight line segments. For instance, the concept mentioned above is the one labeled by M 3.8.

In such a diagram, we can read the implications between the attributes. For determining the conclusion of an implication, one determines the greatest common subconcept of the premise (the concept where "the attributes of the premise first meet" by descending the diagram), and collects all attributes listed above. I. e., the implication $X \to Y$ holds if and only if $\bigvee_{m \in X}(\{m\}', \{m\}'') \leq (\{n\}', \{n\}'')$ for all $n \in Y$. The concept $(\{m\}', \{m\}'')$ is the concept which is labeled by the attribute m. For instance, we have that each counter-measure against both 'Fehlerhafte Nutzung des IT-Systems' (misuse of the IT system)

---

tual scales to be created shall cover *all* possible combinations, not only the frequent ones.

Bauteil	Bauteileart	Nennweite	DichtWerkst	Wanddicke
Rohr DIN 2448- 13 CrMo 4 4 -355,6x8,0	Rohr	350		8
Rohr DIN 2448- 13 CrMo 4 4 -355,6x8,8	Rohr	350		8,8
Rohr DIN 2448- 13 CrMo 4 4 -355,6x11,0	Rohr	350		11
Rohr DIN 2448- 13 CrMo 4 4 -406,4x8,8	Rohr	400		8,8
Rohr DIN 2448- 13 CrMo 4 4 -406,4x11,0	Rohr	400		11
Rohr DIN 2448- 13 CrMo 4 4 -406,4x14,2	Rohr	400		14,2
Flansch C 15x21,3 DIN 2631 - St 37-2	Vorschweißflansch	15	Weichgumm	2
Flansch C 20x26,9 DIN 2631 - St 37-2	Vorschweißflansch	20	Weichgumm	2,3
Flansch C 25x33,7 DIN 2631 - St 37-2	Vorschweißflansch	25	Weichgumm	2,6
Flansch C 32x42,4 DIN 2631 - St 37-2	Vorschweißflansch	32	Weichgumm	2,6

Fig. 3. Part of a many-valued context

and 'Manipulation an Daten oder Software' (the only counter-measure against both perils simultaneously is M 3.5) is also a counter-measure against the perils 'Manipulation/Zerstörung von IT-Geräten oder Zubehör', 'Nichtbeachtung von IT-Sicherheitsmaßnahmen' (ignoring of IT security measures), and 'Fahrlässige Zerstörung von Gerät oder Daten'.

2.2 The conceptual data model of Conceptual Information Systems: Many-valued contexts and conceptual scales

Often attributes are not one-valued as in the previous example, but allow a range of values. This is modeled by a *many-valued context*. In order to obtain a concept lattice, a many-valued context is 'translated' into a one-valued context by *conceptual scales*. (Remark that 'conceptual' is used in two different meanings in the heading!)

Definition 2. A *many-valued context* is a tuple $(G, M, (W_m)_{m \in M}, I)$ where G and M are sets of *objects* and *attributes*, resp., W_m is a set of *values* for each $m \in M$, and $I \subseteq G \times \bigcup_{m \in M}(\{m\} \times W_m)$ such that $(g, m, w_1) \in I$ and $(g, m, w_2) \in I$ imply $w_1 = w_2$. A *conceptual scale* for an attribute $m \in M$ is a context $\mathbb{S}_m := (G_m, M_m, I_m)$ with $W_m \subseteq G_m$. The context (G, M_m, J) with $gJn :\iff \exists w \in W_m : (g, m, w) \in I \land (w, n) \in I_m$ is called the *realized scale* for the attribute $m \in M$.

Example: Figure 3 shows a part of a many-valued context about pipes. The total context consists of 240 pipes, 2428 curved pipes, 560 T-parts, 348 flanges, and 385 restricted fittings, and of 54 attributes. The objects are listed in the column 'Bauteil' (Part). In Fig. 4, the realized scale for the attribute 'Bauteileart' (Part type) is given. Since there are almost 4000 objects, the diagram does not display their names, but contingents only.

Conceptual Information Systems consist of a many-valued context together with a collection of conceptual scales. The many-valued context is implemented

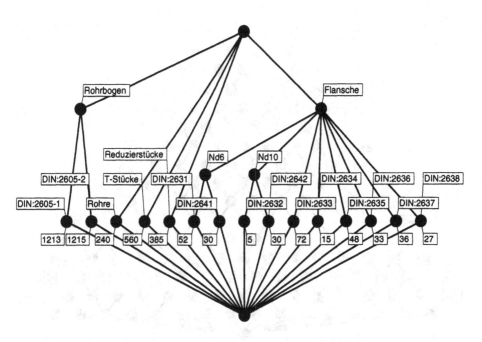

Fig. 4. Realized scale 'Part type'

as a relational database. The collection of the scales is called *conceptual scheme* ([20], [15]). It is written in the description language CONSCRIPT ([19]). Beside the contexts of the conceptual scales, the conceptual scheme also contains the layout of their line diagrams. The layout has to be provided in advance, since, in general, well readable line diagrams cannot be generated fully automatically.

For Conceptual Information Systems, the management system TOSCANA ([13], [21]) has been developed. Based on the paradigm of conceptual landscapes of knowledge ([24]), TOSCANA supports the navigation through the data by using the conceptual scales like maps designed for different purposes and in different granularities. We illustrate the navigation procedure by the pipeline system.

Example: The context in Fig. 3 and the conceptual scale in Fig. 4 are part of a Conceptual Information System on pipelines ([18]). It shall support the engineer by choosing suitable parts for a projected pipeline system. Let us assume that he needs a pipe which has an inner diameter of about 100 mm and a wall thickness of about 4 mm. Starting with the scale 'Part type' in Fig. 4, he finds the concept labeled with the attribute 'Rohre' (Pipes), and sees that he can choose among 240 different pipes. By *zooming into* that context with the scale 'Inner diameter', see Fig. 5), he can see the distribution of the 240 pipes according to their inner diameter. Each concept stands for an interval. Since the engineer is interested in pipes with about 100 mm inner diameter, he chooses the 8th concept from the right at the bottom level, which stands for the interval 90–110 mm. By taking a

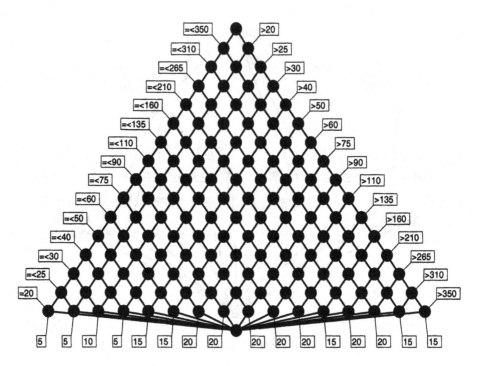

Fig. 5. Realized scale 'Inner diameter' after zooming into the concept labeled by 'Rohre' in Figure 4

concept which is higher in the hierarchy, he could have continued with an interval of larger width. By zooming into the chosen concept with the next conceptual scale (e. g.'Wall thickness'), the engineer can drill-down further until he obtains a small number of parts which are suitable for the projected pipeline system. By clicking on the numbers, he can obtain the names of the parts, and can then drill-down to the original data given in the database or to additional information such as DIN standards.

3 Preparation of Conceptual Information Systems

The preparation of a conceptual information system consists basically of two steps. First, the underlying many-valued context has to be designed and implemented as a database system. Second, the conceptual scales have to be created. Both are non-trivial tasks which require expertise in the domain of interest as well as in the knowledge representation techniques of formal concept analysis. Hence conceptual information systems are usually.designed in a discursive process involving both domain experts and knowledge engineers ([2]). This process is described in detail in [7] for a system about laws and regulations in civil engineering.

In this paper, we focus on the second step of the preparation. We assume that the many-valued context is already given. The task is then to design adequate conceptual scales. We discuss the two basic ways.

3.1 Theory Driven Design

The first step in designing scales driven by theory is to choose attributes meaningful to the user. They need not to be the domain values of the database, but are usually on a more general level. For instance, the user is often not interested in exact numerical values but only in certain ranges: In a medical application, the physician is not interested in the exact pH level of the blood, but only if the pH level is pathological or even dangerous.

The second step is to assign the domain values to the attributes. Here, the knowledge engineer has to bring in his expertise about conceptual hierarchies, since domain experts always tend to scale nominally. In the medical example, for instance, a longer discussion revealed that a dangerous pH level is also understood as pathological, hence a bi-ordinal scale (with a third attribute 'pH level normal') was chosen.

Figures 4 and 5 show two theory driven scales. While the scale in Fig. 4 is specially designed for the application, the inter-ordinal scale in Fig. 5 is a standard scale that is used in many applications. Typically, database attributes of type **string** need an individual design, while numerical types as **integer** or **real** allow the use of standard scales. There is a broad variety of standard scales that can be used, e. g., nominal scales, ordinal scales, and inter-ordinal scales. In the latter case, only the number of intervals to be considered and the interval boundaries have to be fixed. It is planned to release the knowledge engineer from implementing such standard scales by implementing *parametrized scales* which adopt themselves to the actual range of the values. Naturally this approach fails for free-text entries such as those in 'Bauteileart' in Fig. 3. Here the conceptual structure in the data has to be determined in a discursive process.

3.2 Data Driven Design

While theory driven design is typically (but not exclusively) applied to many-valued attributes, data driven design is only possible for the data type **boolean**. In that case, the attributes of the database are usually also the attributes of the conceptual scale. While there is normally one conceptual scale for each many-valued attribute, some one-valued (i. e., Boolean) attributes are grouped together in order to form one conceptual scale. The task for knowledge engineer and domain expert is to find a suitable grouping of the attributes. Groups should not be too large since the size of the scale may be exponential to the number of attributes; neither too small in order not to hide dependencies between the attributes. Typically there are between five and ten attributes. But before all, it is important that attributes addressing similar topics are grouped together. Therefore it is possible that attributes appear in more than one scale.

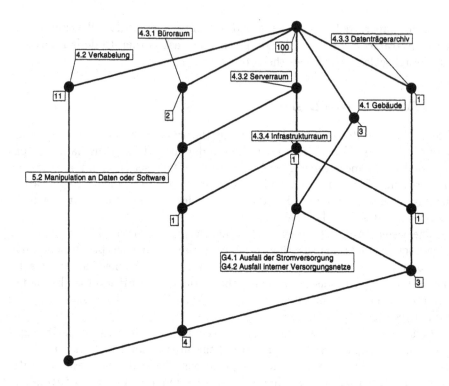

Fig. 6. Realized scale 'Rooms' for the IT Security System

Having obtained a suitable grouping, a conceptual scale has to be designed for for each of the sets of attributes. In a first approach, one could assume that there are no valid implications between the attributes. This leads to a scale that is conform to all possible updates of the database. However, this scale will be too large for more than five attributes, since for n attributes the number of concepts of such a *Boolean scale* scale is 2^n. Therefore, *data driven design* takes into account all implications which hold for the actual entries in the database. It is supported by DOKUANA, a tool developed by NAVICON. An example for a data driven scale is the scale 'Rooms' of the IT security system (Fig. 6). It shows the distribution of perils according to locations. Instead of $2^6 = 64$ possible concepts it only consists of 14 concepts.

When knowledge engineer and domain expert agreed on a data driven design process, then the design can be performed by the former without any support by the latter, once the grouping of the attributes is decided. Hence data driven design is efficient for the client in the way that he does not have to invest much time of the domain expert. This is an important argument in marketing Conceptual Information Systems.

The big disadvantage of this approach however is that scales need not be consistent with updates of the database. New entries can contradict to the functional dependencies used for the design of the conceptual scales. If there are not too many new concepts (up to ten at the moment), and if the structure of the new scale does not differ too much from the original scale, then the diagram can be re-drawn automatically. However, if the change is more complex, then the layout has to be done manually, which usually requires the expertise of the knowledge engineer. Hence, an important research task is the development of fully automatic lay-out algorithms for lattices. Unfortunately, satisfying answers are not in sight in the next future.

For applications provided to a remote client or for time critical applications it is therefore important to prepare the scales such that future updates of the database are covered. Hence all possible combinations of attributes have to be determined before handing over the information system. In the next section we discuss how this task can be performed in a systematic way by involving the domain expert as less as possible.

4 Extending Scales by Attribute Exploration

The data driven design of a conceptual scale provides us with all combinations of attributes which occur as concept intents for the actual data. Then the question arises which combinations may occur additionally. As we pointed out in the last section, the powerset of the attribute set would cover all eventualities, but is in general too large for practical applications. Hence we have to find a subset of the powerset, which contains all possible combinations, by systematically inquiring the domain expert.

The solution to that problem is *Attribute Exploration* ([8], [10]), an interactive knowledge acquisition algorithm developed by B. Ganter. The algorithm is implemented in the program ConImp ([5]) of P. Burmeister. It benefits from the fact that the requested set of intents must be closed under set intersection (cf. to first equation in Theorem 1). The knowledge is acquired from the domain expert in a dialogue in which he has to answer questions of the form "Does each possible object in the database having attributes $x_1, \ldots x_n$ necessarily have the attributes $y_1, \ldots y_m$ as well? (I.e., "Does the implication $\{x_1, \ldots, x_n\} \to \{y_1, \ldots, y_m\}$ hold?") Either the expert confirms the implication, or he has to provide a counter-example.

Details about Attribute Exploration can be found in [8] and [10]. Here, we only give a short summary: The algorithm uses the fact that, for a given formal context, the implications $P \to P''$, where P is a *pseudo-intent* (see below), are sufficient (and even minimal) for describing the structure of the concept lattice. This set of implications is called the *Duquenne-Guigues-basis* ([6], [11]).

The algorithm asks the implications in such a sequence that pseudo-intents determined once remain pseudo-intents even after adding the counter-examples to the context:

Definition. A set $P \subseteq M$ of attributes is called a *pseudo-intent*, if $P \neq P''$ and if for each pseudo-intent $Q \subset P$ the inclusion $Q'' \subseteq P$ holds.

For a set $X \subseteq M$ and a set $\mathcal{L}$ of implications, we define $\mathcal{L}^*(X)$ as the closure of X under repeated application of $X \mapsto X \cup \bigcup \{B \mid A \to B \in \mathcal{L}, A \subset X, A \neq X\}$.

For sake of simplicity, we assume now that $M = \{1, 2, \ldots, n\}$. For $i \in M$, we define $X <_i Y : \iff i \in Y \setminus X$ and $X \cap \{1, \ldots, i-1\} = Y \cap \{1, \ldots, i-1\}$. Furthermore we define a *lectic order* on the subsets of M by $X < Y : \iff \exists i \in \{1, \ldots, n\}: X <_i Y$.

Algorithm: Let (G, M, I) be the formal context determined by data driven design. The set M contains the attributes that are used as labels in the diagram. The set G contains strings which are used as **where**-parts of SQL-statements which TOSCANA generate in order to query the database.

1. The first intent or pseudo-intent is the empty set.
2. For a given intent or pseudo-intent X one obtains the next intent or pseudo-intent in the lectic order by letting $i := n$, and decreasing i until $X <_i X^* := \mathcal{L}^*((X \cap \{1, 2, \ldots, i-1\} \cup \{i\})$ holds. X^* is then the next intent or pseudo-intent in the lectic order.
3. IF $X^* = M$ then Stop.
4. If X^* is an intent, then let $X := X^*$ and go to 2).
5. If X^* is a pseudo-intent, then ask the user "Does the implication $X^* \to X^{*''}$ hold?" If the answer is "Yes", then add the implication to $\mathcal{L}$. Let $X := X^*$ and go to 2). If the answer is "No", then the user has to provide a counter-example. Add the counter-example to G and go to 4).

The dialogue is optimal in the sense that the number of confirmed implications is minimal. The complexity of the algorithm is, for each concept, cubic in the number of attributes and objects. As the number of the concepts can grow exponentially in the number of attributes, the overall complexity of the algorithm is exponential. However, as the number of attributes for one scale is usually between five and ten, and the attributes are normally not totally independent, the number of questions is tolerable in all practical applications.

Attribute Exploration can handle the answer "I don't know", but for designing a conceptual scale, finally each of the implications has to be either confirmed or rejected. As "I don't know" indicates that there *may be* objects that violate the implication, only the interpretation of these answers as "no" assures that the scale will be consistent for all possible updates of the database.

Example: The 'IT-Grundschutzhandbuch' provides for each object the relationship between its related perils and counter-measures. The relationship between objects and perils is not given explicitly in the handbook. Since the data tables are designed locally — for each single object — only, there may be groups of objects sharing the same perils which are not identified in the book. Figure 6 provides us with the scale considering only the actual entries in the handbook.

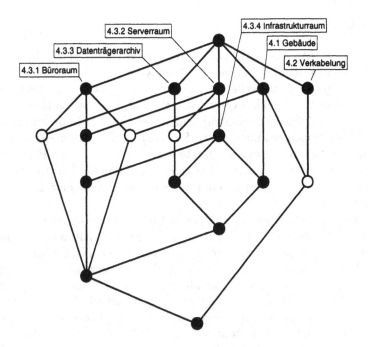

Fig. 7. The scale 'Rooms' extended by Attribute Exploration

For determining all possible combinations of objects, we applied Attribute Exploration to that scale. The exploration dialogue consisted of twelve questions, starting with:

> "Is each possible peril for 'Gebäude' (building) and 'Archiv' (archive) necessarily a peril for 'Serverraum' (server room) and 'Infrastrukturraum' (infrastructure room)?" — "Yes" — "Is each possible peril for 'Infrastrukturraum' necessarily a peril for 'Serverraum?'" — "Yes" — "Is each possible peril for 'Infrastrukturraum' necessarily a peril for 'Serverraum?'" — "Yes" — "Is each possible peril for 'Serverraum' and 'Archiv' necessarily a peril for 'Infrastrukturraum?'" — "No." ...

For the last question, one can e. g. provide the attribute 'Datenträgervernichtung' (destruction of storage media) as counter-example. In this example, nine of the twelve implications were accepted, and three denied. The resulting scale is shown in Figure 7. It consists of 18 concepts, while the 'worst case', the Boolean scale, has $2^6 = 64$ concepts and is too large for a useful visualization. The black circles indicate how the data driven scale is embedded in the scale determined by Attribute Exploration. This example also shows that the diagram has to be re-layouted for remaining readable.

5 Outlook

We have shown how the gap between data driven and theory driven design can be bridged (or at least narrowed) by applying Attribute Exploration. This knowledge acquisition process serves three purposes. Firstly, it makes knowledge acquisition from the domain expert more efficient, since it starts with the actual data (instead from the scratch) and solves the remaining questions in a systematic and somehow minimal way. Secondly, it allows to prepare the scales so that all eventual updates of the database are covered a priori. Hence the system can be run without support of the knowledge engineer. Thirdly, the process provides to the domain expert a better understanding of the data by making his knowledge explicit.

A restraint for the approach is however that a certain knowledge about the dependencies between the attributes must be present. Although the answers during the dialogue do not have to be infallible (since TOSCANA provides a warning if an accepted implication is violated), they must however be confident to a certain degree. For instance, the Library Retrieval System at the 'Zentrum für interdisziplinäre Technikforschung' at the Technische Universität Darmstadt ([14]) is also based on a data driven design. In that application, books and journals are objects, and catchwords are attributes. The conceptual scales produced by data driven design are almost all near to Boolean scales, i. e., almost all combinations of catchwords are possible. In this application, the experts were not able to answer the questions with a certain confidence, since for each remaining combination of catchwords one could imagine a book having exactly those catchwords. Such applications would profit enormously from automatic layout algorithms for lattices.

An automatic layout algorithm would also provide the possibility to choose on-line Boolean attributes (e. g., catchwords) of the database and to let the resulting conceptual scale be drawn on the fly. The development of layout algorithms is one of the most urgent research tasks for advancing the commercial application of conceptual knowledge processing.

Attribute Exploration determines the structure of the conceptual scale only; but it does not indicate which concepts may be labeled by objects. Each concept which potentially is labeled gives rise to a SQL-query. Hence it may be of interest for time-critical applications to minimize the number of these concepts. For determining them, a variation of Attribute Exploration called *Clause Exploration* ([9]) can be applied. As this knowledge acquisition procedure generates more questions than Attribute Exploration, it has to be examined for each application if the extra work during the design phase is really necessary.

References

1. R. Agrawal, T. Imielinski, A. Swami: Mining association rules between sets of items in large databases. *Proc. ACM SIGMOD*, 1993
2. U. Andelfinger: *Diskursive Anforderungsanalyse: ein Beitrag zum Reduktionsproblem bei Systementwicklungen in der Informatik*. Peter Lang, Frankfurt 1997.

3. A. Arnauld, P. Nicole: La logique ou l'art de penser — contenant, outre les règles communes, plusieurs observations nouvelles, propres à former le jugement. 3° édit. reveüe & augm. P., Ch. Saveux, 1668

4. Bundesamt für Sicherheit in der Informationstechnik: *IT-Grundschutzhandbuch 1996. Maßnahmenempfehlungen für den mittleren Schutzbedarf.* Bundesanzeiger, Köln 1996

5. P. Burmeister: ConImp - Programm zur formalen Begriffsanalyse einwertiger Kontexte. TH Darmstadt 1987 (latest version 1995)

6. V. Duquenne:Contextual implications between attributes and some properties of finite lattices. In: B. Ganter, R. Wille, K.E. Wolff (eds.): *Beiträge zur Begriffsanalyse.* B. I.-Wissenschaftsverlag, Mannheim 1987, 213–239

7. D. Eschenfelder, W. Kollewe, M. Skorsky, R. Wille: Ein Erkundungssystem zum Baurecht: Methoden der Entwicklung eines TOSCANA-Systems. In: G. Stumme, R. Wille (eds.): *Begriffliche Wissensverarbeitung: Methoden und Anwendungen.* Springer, Heidelberg 1998 (to appear)

8. B. Ganter: Algorithmen zur Begriffsanalyse. In: B. Ganter, R. Wille, K. E. Wolff (eds.): *Beiträge zur Begriffsanalyse.* B. I.-Wissenschaftsverlag, Mannheim, Wien, Zürich 1987. 241–254

9. B. Ganter, R. Krauße: *Pseudo models and propositional Horn inference.* (in preparation)

10. B. Ganter, R. Wille: *Formal Concept Analysis: Mathematical Foundations.* Springer, Heidelberg 1999 (Translation of: *Formale Begriffsanalyse: Mathematische Grundlagen.* Springer, Heidelberg 1996)

11. J.-L. Guigues, V. Duquenne: Familles minimales d'implications informatives resultant d'un tableau de données binaires. *Math. Sci. Humaines* **95**, 1986, 5–18

12. U. Kaufmann: *Begriffliche Analyse von Daten über Flugereignisse — Implementierung eines Erkundungs- und Analysesystems mit TOSCANA.* Diplomarbeit, TU Darmstadt, 1996

13. W. Kollewe, M. Skorsky, F. Vogt, R. Wille: TOSCANA — ein Werkzeug zur begrifflichen Analyse und Erkundung von Daten. In: R. Wille, M. Zickwolff (eds.): *Begriffliche Wissensverarbeitung — Grundfragen und Aufgaben.* B. I.-Wissenschaftsverlag, Mannheim 1994

14. T. Rock, R. Wille: Ein TOSCANA-System zur Literatursuche. In: G. Stumme and R. Wille (eds.): *Begriffliche Wissensverarbeitung: Methoden und Anwendungen.* Springer, Berlin-Heidelberg (to appear)

15. P. Scheich, M. Skorsky, F. Vogt, C. Wachter, R. Wille: Conceptual data systems. In: O. Opitz, B. Lausen, R. Klar (eds.): *Information and classification.* Springer, Heidelberg 1993, 72–84

16. H. Söll: *Begriffliche Analyse triadischer Daten: Das IT-Grundschutzhandbuch des Bundesamtes für Sicherheit in der Informationstechnik.* Diplomarbeit, TU Darmstadt 1998

17. G. Stumme: On-Line Analytical Processing with Conceptual Information Systems. *Proc. 5th Intl. Conf. on Foundations of Data Organization,* 12.–13. November 1998, 117–126 (to be published by Kluwer)

18. N. Vogel: *Ein Begriffliches Erkundungssystem für Rohrleitungen.* Diplomarbeit, TH Darmstadt 1995

19. F. Vogt: *Datenstrukturen und Algorithmen zur Formalen Begriffsanalyse: Eine C++-Klassenbibliothek.* Springer, Heidelberg 1996

20. F. Vogt, C. Wachter, R. Wille: Data analysis based on a conceptual file. In: H.-H. Bock, P. Ihm (eds.): *Classification, data analysis, and knowledge organization.* Springer, Heidelberg 1991, 131–140

21. F. Vogt, R. Wille: TOSCANA – A graphical tool for analyzing and exploring data. In: R. Tamassia, I. G. Tollis (eds.): *Graph Drawing '94*, Lecture Notes in Computer Sciences **894**, Springer, Heidelberg 1995, 226–233

22. H. Wagner: Begriff. In: H. M. Baumgartner, C. Wild (eds.): *Handbuch philosophischer Grundbegriffe.* Kösel Verlag, München 1973, 191–209

23. R. Wille: Restructuring lattice theory: an approach based on hierarchies of concepts. In: I. Rival (ed.): *Ordered sets.* Reidel, Dordrecht–Boston 1982, 445–470

24. R. Wille: Conceptual landscapes of knowledge: A pragmatic paradigm of knowledge processing. In: *Proceedings of the international conference on knowledge retrieval, use, and storage for efficiency*, Vancouver, Kanada, 11.–13. 8. 1997, 2–13

A Constraint-Based Approach to the Description of Competence

S. White and D. Sleeman

Department of Computing Science,
King's College, University of Aberdeen,
Aberdeen, AB24 3UE
Scotland, UK.

Tel.: +44 (0)1224 272296; Fax.: +44 (0)1224 273422
Email: <swhite, dsleeman>@csd.abdn.ac.uk

Abstract. A competency description of a software component seeks to describe what the artefact can and cannot do. We focus on a particular kind of competence, called *fitness-for-purpose*, which specifies whether running a software component with a supplied set of inputs can satisfy a given goal. In particular, we wish to assess whether a chosen problem solver, together with one or more knowledge bases, can satisfy a given (problem solving) goal. In general, this is an intractable problem. We have therefore introduced an effective, practical, *approximation* to fitness-for-purpose based on the *plausibility* of the goal. We believe that constraint (logic) programming provides a natural approach to the implementation of such approximations. We took the Common LISP constraints library SCREAMER and extended its symbolic capabilities to suit our purposes. Additionally, we formulated an example of fitness-for-purpose modelling using this enhanced library.

1 Introduction

A competency description of a software component seeks to describe what the artefact *can* do, and what it *cannot* do. In addition, it *may* choose to describe the methods that are applied by the software artefact to achieve its results, although our work focuses on the questions of *what* rather than *how*.

Competency descriptions can enable human- or machine agents to assess the suitability of application of the described component for some particular task. This assessment of suitability, which we also refer to as *fitness-for-purpose analysis*, is becoming increasingly important for two main reasons. Firstly, as the range and sophistication of software increases, it becomes difficult for a human user to make an informed choice of the best software solution for any particular task. The same point applies equally to domain independent reasoning components, such as the problem solving methods (PSMs). We believe that novice users, in particular, could benefit greatly from *advice* generated as a result of a fitness-for-purpose analysis. Secondly, we observe a demand for *software brokers*, which, given some software requirements, return either the software itself, or a pointer. In the knowledge acquisition community, the IBROW3 project [3] intends to build such a broker for the distribution of problem solving components.

In this paper, we present a general approach to fitness-for-purpose analysis which was developed to assist in the generation of advice for novice users of knowledge acquisition tools (KA tools) and problem-solvers in the MUSKRAT system [10], [24], [27]. MUSKRAT is a MUltiStrategy Knowledge Refinement and Acquisition Toolbox which makes it easier for novice users to apply and combine the incorporated software tools to solve some specific task. When generating advice on the application of a chosen problem-solver, MUSKRAT should be able to differentiate between the following three cases for the knowledge bases available to the problem-solver.

Case 1: The problem-solver can be applied with the knowledge bases already available, i.e., no acquisition or modification of knowledge is necessary.

Case 2: The problem-solver needs knowledge base(s), not currently available; therefore these knowledge base(s) must be first acquired.

Case 3: The problem-solver needs knowledge base(s), not currently available, but the requirements can be met by modifying existing knowledge base(s).

The phrase 'fitness-for-purpose' and the computational approximation to it, as described in this paper, arose out of the need for a test for case 1. We expect subsequent research to investigate issues relating to cases 2 and 3.

Issues related to the description of competence are also being investigated by others in the field, notably Benjamins *et al.* in the context of the IBROW3 project [3], [4], Fensel *et al.*, as part of an ongoing investigation into the role of *assumptions* [6], [7], and Wielinga *et al.*, as a methodological approach to the operationalisation of knowledge-level specifications [30]. We consider Fensel's approach to be the nearest to our work, because it investigates the *context dependency* of an existing problem solver/PSM through the discovery of assumptions. We are also investigating the context dependency of problem solvers, but through the question of task suitability with the *available* knowledge. Thus, whilst Fensel investigates a problem solving method in isolation of its inputs in order to *derive* suitability conditions, we take a problem solver together with its inputs and *test* their combined suitability for solving a specific task. Both lines of inquiry are intractable, and therefore demand some compromise(s) in any implementation. Fensel's compromise concerns the level of automation of his proof mechanism, which is an *interactive* verifier, rather than a fully automated proof mechanism. Since we would like to generate advice at *run-time* for the potential user of a problem solver, we compromise instead with the deductive power of our proof mechanism. We believe, however, that what our constraint satisfaction mechanism may lack in expressive power, it gains in its abilities to combine the results of multiple problem solvers (through propagation mechanisms), and run as a batch process. Figure 1 compares Fensel *et al.*'s process of assumption hunting with our approach to matching a problem solver to a toolkit user's goal.

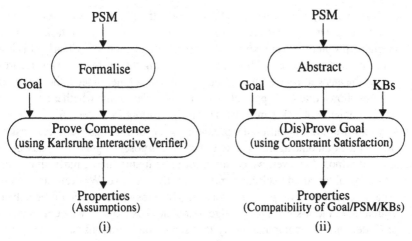

Figure 1. Comparison of the Fensel approach (i), and our approach (ii), to the discovery of problem solving properties

In the following section, we define more exactly what we mean by fitness-for-purpose, and explain the computational difficulties which arise in its analysis. In section 3, we describe how we approach these difficulties by considering an *approximation* of fitness-for-purpose, rather than the *actual* fitness-for-purpose. In section 4, we explain how we are implementing these ideas using constraint logic programming in Common LISP. Finally, in section 5 we summarise the ideas, relate them to other work in the field, and indicate some possible directions for future work.

2 Fitness-for-Purpose

In the previous section, we defined a competency description of a software component as a description of what the artefact can do, and what it cannot do. Since a fitness-for-purpose analysis considers the suitability of some component for a particular task *instance*, it concerns not only the 'absolute' competence of that component for contributing to the solution, but also any other inputs which the component, or the task, might have. So, for example, a kettle undoubtedly has a competence for boiling water, but it is nevertheless not fit for the purpose of making a cup of tea unless water, tea and (optionally) milk and sugar are also available. Fitness-for-purpose therefore represents a specific interpretation of 'competence', because it expresses the contribution to the solution of the problem instance *with regard to the current state of the containing system*. In the tea-making example, the 'current state' concerned the availability of ingredients in the kitchen; in the context of knowledge acquisition and problem solving, the current state refers to the availability and nature of the system's knowledge.

When the advisory subsystem of MUSKRAT addresses the problem of fitness-for-purpose, it is in effect posing the question "Is it possible to solve the given task instance with the available problem-solver[1], knowledge bases, and KA tools?". Clearly, this is a very difficult question to answer without actually running the problem-solver, regardless of whether the answer is generated by a human or a machine. Indeed, the theory of computation has shown that it not possible, in general, to determine whether a program (in this case, a problem-solver) terminates. This is the *Halting Problem* [25]. Therefore the only way to affirm the suitability of a problem-solver for solving a particular task is to run it and test the outcome against the goal. For the purposes of generating advice in a multistrategy toolbox, however, we cannot afford this luxury, particularly since running the problem-solver could itself be computationally intensive. We prefer instead to pose the weaker question "Is it *plausible* that the given task instance could be solved with the available problem-solver, knowledge bases, and KA tools?". We believe that it is possible to demonstrate computationally that some configurations of a task, problem-solver, existing knowledge bases and KA tools cannot, even *in principle*, generate an acceptable solution to the task. Such situations form a set of *recognisably implausible* configurations with respect to the problem at hand. Furthermore, the computational cost associated with recognising this implausibility is, in many cases, far less than that associated with running the problem-solver.

For example, consider a question from simple arithmetic: is it true that $22 \times 31 + 11 \times 17 + 13 \times 19 = 1097$? Rather than evaluate the left hand side of the equation straight away, let us first inspect the problem to see if it is reasonable. We know that when an even number is multiplied by an odd number, the result is always even; and that an odd number multiplied by an odd number is always odd. Therefore the left hand side of the equation could be rewritten as <even> + <odd> + <odd>. Likewise, an even number added to an odd number is always odd, and the sum of two odd numbers is always even. Then evaluating left to right, we have <odd> + <odd>, which is <even>. Since 1097 is not even, it cannot be the result of the evaluation. We have thus answered the question without having to do the 'hard' work of evaluating the actual value of the left hand side.

As another example, consider the truth of the statement 'If **Pigs** can fly, then I'm the Queen of Sheba', which we write as $P \Rightarrow Q$. Given our background knowledge that the premise P is false, we can use the truth table for logical implication[2] to derive that the whole statement is true, since any implication with a false premise is true. Notice that we derived our result *without having to know* the truth of the consequent Q. In a similar way, it is possible to investigate the outputs of programs (in particular, problem

---

1. For simplicity, we currently assume the application of a single, chosen problem-solver.

2.

P	Q	$P \Rightarrow Q$
T	T	T
T	F	F
F	T	T
F	F	T

solvers) without needing complete information about their inputs. This issue becomes important if running a problem solver has a high cost associated with it, such as the time it takes to perform an intensive search[3]. In such cases, a preliminary investigation of the plausibility of the task at hand could save much time if the intended problem solver configuration can be shown to be unsuitable for the task. We consider such an investigation to be a kind of 'plausibility test' which should be carried out before running the actual problem solver. The idea was suggested as part of a general problem solving framework by Polya [19]. In his book 'How to Solve It', he proposed some general heuristics for tackling problems of a mathematical nature, including an initial inspection of the problem to understand the condition that must be satisfied by its solution. For example, is the condition sufficient to determine the problem's "unknown"? And is there redundancy or contradiction in the condition? Polya summarised by asking the following:

'Is our problem "reasonable"? This question is useful at an early stage of our work *if* we can answer it easily. If the answer is difficult to obtain, the trouble we have in obtaining it may outweigh the gain in interest.' (Polya, 1957).[4]

It is interesting to note that the arithmetic example given above first abstracts the problem instance to a different 'space' (i.e., from real numbers to that of odd and even numbers), to which a simpler algebra can be applied. We note that much of the problem instance detail has been ignored to keep the plausibility test simple. On the other hand, enough detail has been retained for the test to reflect the current problem instance and for it to be useful. In this sense, the plausibility test has *approximated* the task. In the next section, we define a more precise notion of plausibility approximation, and explain how it can be applied to problem-solvers.

3 The Plausibility Approximation to Fitness-for-Purpose

We classify proposed solutions to a problem as either *plausible values*, *candidate values*, or *actual values*. Informally, a *plausible value* is any solution which cannot be ruled out by applying such reasoning as that in the arithmetic or logical examples above. A *candidate value* can be a solution to the problem in some cases. An *actual value* is the solution in a given case. It is worth noting that all *candidate* solutions are also *plausible*, and any *actual* solution is always a *candidate* solution (see Figure 2).

---

3. Many AI programs perform searches of problem spaces which grow exponentially with the size of the problem.

4. One way to determine whether the plausibility test is useful is to compare the computational complexities of the problem solver and the plausibility test. If the order of complexity of the plausibility test is lower than that of the problem solver, we might assume it is reasonable to apply the plausibility test first. Unfortunately, this model takes no account of the *utility* of the information gained from the plausibility test.

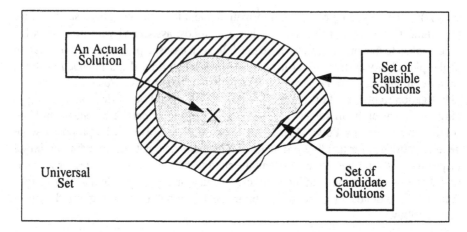

Figure 2. Venn Diagram showing the relationships between plausible, candidate, and actual solutions

As an example of this classification, consider the formula for the area of a circle, πr^2. Suppose that we know r, the radius, to be larger than 1, but no greater than 10, i.e., $r \in [1, 10]$ and $r^2 \in [1, 100]$. Now we should like to define ranges of plausibility and candidacy for the value of the circle's area. The range of candidate values is $[\pi, 100\pi]$, but since π is rather a difficult number to deal with, the calculation of plausibility might approximate it to 3 for estimating the lower bound of the range, and 3.5 for estimating the upper bound of the range. The lower bound of the range is therefore $lower\_bound(r^2) \times 3 = 3$; and the upper bound is $upper\_bound(r^2) \times 3.5 = 350$. This gives the range of plausibility as $[3, 350]$. Note that we were careful to *underestimate* the lower bound of the plausibility range, and *overestimate* the upper bound, so that the range of candidate values lies completely within the range of plausible values (*c.f.* the theory of errors used in the empirical sciences). When evaluating the expression, an *actual value* might be 78.54.

The set of plausible solutions is an approximation to the set of candidate solutions, but we define it such that *the set of candidate solutions is always contained within the set of plausible solutions*. This guarantees that an implausible solution is not a candidate solution, so we can approximate the test for candidacy with a test for plausibility. Note that a plausible solution may not necessarily be a candidate – plausible, but non-candidate, solutions are the 'small fish' that slip through the net! Note also that for any gain in computational effort, testing an element for membership of the set of plausible solutions must be in some sense less expensive than testing it for membership of the set of candidate solutions.

We are applying these ideas to problem solving scenarios in which a number of knowledge bases (KB_1, KB_2, ..., KB_n) are assigned input roles (R_1, R_2, ..., R_n) to a problem-solver, and a desired goal G is stated. We call this a *problem-solver configuration* (left hand side of Figure 3). Note that at this stage we have made no assumptions about the representation of the knowledge; when we say 'knowledge base' we do not imply a set of rules. Neither do we make any assumptions about the specificity of the knowledge bases with respect to the given problem instance. (That is, a knowledge base might remain constant over all problem instances, it might change occasionally, or it might change with every instance.) In essence, any input to the problem-solver has been labelled as a knowledge base. We use the knowledge obtained from these inputs and a plausibility 'description' of the behaviour of the problem-solver to generate an output space of plausible values. Note that under this scheme, a problem-solver 'description' is itself a *program* which implicitly describes another program by generating its plausible output. The description therefore represents a kind of model of the problem solving task; it is a *meta*problem-solver (right hand side of Figure 3). The aim of the model is to determine whether the goal G is consistent with the plausible space generated by the metaproblem-solver, because if G is *not* consistent with this space, then it will also not be satisfied by the output of the problem-solver itself. In such cases, we need not run the problem-solver to test its outcome.

But how can this functionality be implemented? In a naive *generate-and-test* approach, we might answer the plausibility question by testing every point in the plausibility space against the goal G. Unfortunately, this is both computationally inefficient [13], and enables only the modelling of spaces of finite size. For a more flexible and computationally more efficient version, we prefer a *constraint-based* approach[5]. The idea is that a plausibility space is expressed as a set of constrained entities. This set could be of infinite, or indefinite, size, such as the set of even counting numbers, or the set of all persons whose surname begins with 'W'. To test the plausibility of a given goal, its features are applied as further constraints to the plausibility space generated by a metaproblem-solver. If the resulting space is empty, then the goal was not plausible; if the resulting space is non-empty (or cannot easily be demonstrated to be empty), then the goal remains plausible. Furthermore, unlike the meta-level reasoning required for the halting problem, the question of plausibility, if defined appropriately, can be guaranteed to terminate within a finite number of program steps, because the meta-level need only be an *approximation* to the problem solving level[6].

---

5. Consider the whimsical analogy of a man wishing to buy a pair of shoes: he does not walk into a bookshop, pick up every book, and inspect it for its shoe-like qualities (the generate-and-test approach). Instead, he recognises from the outset that bookshops sell books (i.e. the plausibility space is a set of books), and that this is not consistent with his goal of buying shoes.

6. Consider the case of the halting problem, in which we should like to determine whether a program runs forever or halts. At the meta-level, we may choose to run the program for some given length of time to see what happens. If the program halts within the allotted time, then we know that it halts. Otherwise it remains plausible that it runs forever.

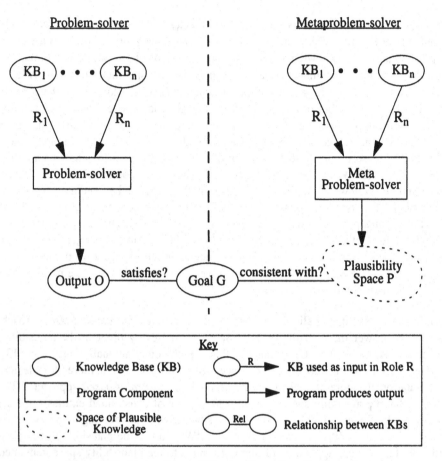

Figure 3. Problem-solver and Metaproblem-solver Configurations

Note that the plausibility refers to the combination of knowledge bases, their problem-solving roles and the specific goal. In principle, a reassignment of knowledge bases to different problem-solving roles could transform an implausible configuration into one which is plausible. To avoid such anomalies, we also assign preconditions to each problem solving role, and check that these are fulfilled by a knowledge base before conducting a plausibility test.

More general scenarios are also possible, since plausibility spaces can also be used as *inputs* to further metaproblem-solvers. Such an input space could describe the plausible output of another problem-solver, or even a knowledge acquisition tool. By cascading descriptions in this way, plausibility spaces are combined. When plausibility spaces are used as inputs to metaproblem-solvers, the plausible output space produced is necessarily more general than when specific knowledge bases are used as inputs.

Nevertheless, the output space may still contain enough knowledge to answer some interesting questions.

4 Implementation Approach

We mentioned earlier that we prefer a constraint-based approach to answering the question "Is the goal G contained in the plausibility space P ?". In fact, it is crucial to the implementation that constraints derived from the goal can be used to reduce the size of the plausibility space *without enumerating it*. This technique makes the plausibility test less expensive than running the problem-solver because the whole search space does not have to be explored to determine whether a goal is implausible. It also leads one naturally to consider an implementation using constraint (logic) programming. Indeed, we can rephrase the plausibility question in the terminology of constraint programming: "Is the goal G consistent with the domain of the constraint variable P ?". Since the tools we wished to model and the rest of the MUSKRAT framework were already implemented in Common LISP, we sought to implement the plausibility approximation to fitness-for-purpose using SCREAMER, a constraint logic programming library for Common LISP [22], [23].

4.1 A Brief Introduction to SCREAMER and SCREAMER+

SCREAMER introduced two paradigms into Common LISP: firstly, it introduced a non-determinism similar to the backtracking capabilities of PROLOG. Secondly, and more importantly for our purposes, it used these backtracking capabilities as the foundation for a *declarative constraints* package. The SCREAMER constraints package provides LISP functions which enable a programmer to *create constraint variables*, (often referred to simply as *variables*), *assert constraints* on those variables, and *search for assignments of values to variables* according to the asserted constraints.

Although SCREAMER[7] forms a very good basis for solving numeric constraint problems in Common LISP, we found it less good for tackling problems based on constraints of a more symbolic nature. We therefore extended the SCREAMER library in three major directions: firstly, to improve the expressiveness of the library with respect to constraints on lists; secondly, to introduce higher order[8] constraint functions such as constraint-oriented versions of the LISP functions `every`, `some`, and `mapcar`; and thirdly, to enable constraints to be imposed on CLOS[9] objects and their slots. We called the extended library SCREAMER+. A detailed discussion of SCREAMER+ is

---

7. Version 3.20; available at the time of writing from `http://www.cis.upenn.edu/~screamer-tools/home.html`

8. A 'higher order function' is a function which accepts another function as an argument.

9. CLOS is the *Common LISP Object System*, a specification of functions to enable object-oriented programming in LISP which was adopted by the ANSI committee X3J13 in 1988 as part of the Common LISP standard.

outside the scope of this paper; the interested reader is referred to our recent technical report [28]. In the next section, we provide an example of the usage of the SCREAMER+ library to model the fitness-for-purpose of two problem-solvers applied to the domain of meal preparation.

4.2 A Problem Solving Scenario

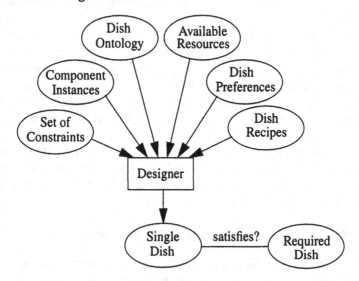

Figure 4. Problem Solving in the Domain of Meal Preparation

Suppose we are applying a problem-solver which constructs solutions consistent with some given domain and temporal constraints (a design task)[10]. We have chosen to apply the problem-solver to the domain of meal preparation because the domain is rich and challenging, but also easily understood. Furthermore, the problem-solving task is analogous to flexible design and manufacturing, also called *just-in-time manufacturing*. In the domain of meal preparation, the *designer* is used to compose (or 'construct') a dish which is consistent with culinary, temporal, and resource constraints, also taking a set of dish preferences into consideration (see Figure 4).

Now suppose that we would like to use plausibility modelling on this problem-solver by constructing its corresponding metaproblem-solver. A *meta-designer* is easy to construct if we neglect the constraints, dish preferences, and the available resources. The meta-designer produces a space of plausible dishes, together with their plausible preparation times. These times are represented as upper and lower bounds on the preparation of whole dishes, and are derived from knowledge of the preparation times of dish

---

10. The task is also soluble by two separate problem solvers: the domain constraints are solved by the first, and the temporal constraints satisfied by the second [29]. A detailed discussion of the cascading of problem solvers is outside the scope of this paper.

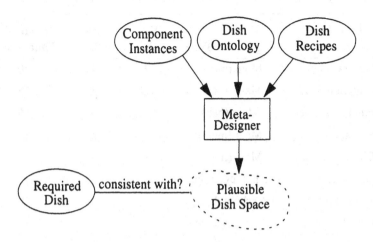

Figure 5. Plausibility Reasoning in the Domain of Meal Preparation

components. The upper bound of the dish preparation time is set as the sum of the durations of the composite tasks; the lower bound is the duration of the lengthiest task. Constraints from the goal can then be applied to the space of plausible scheduled dishes to see if inconsistencies can be detected (see Figure 5). Note that although we advocate the use of the constraint satisfaction paradigm for the implementation of the meta-level, this choice is independent of the implementation method used by the problem solver itself. The independence arises because the meta-layer treats the problem solver as a black box, describing only its input/output relationship and not how it works internally.

4.3 An Implementation of Plausibility

We have implemented a prototype of plausibility reasoning by using the knowledge provided in Table 1: a list of dish components, together with their component type, a measure of their dietary value, their cost and preparation time. In addition, the designer must be told what it should construct from this knowledge. This information is provided by a dish ontology which states that a dish consists of a main component, together with a carbohydrate component and two other vegetables. Likewise, the cost of a dish is defined to be the sum of the costs of its component parts, and the number of diet points associated with a dish is the sum of the diet points of its components. The meta-designer generates upper and lower bounds for the preparation time of a dish, as described in the previous section.

The SCREAMER+ implementation makes use of the CLOS facilities offered by defining the space of plausible dishes as a *single object* in which each *slot* (such as the main component of the dish, the preparation time, dietary points value, and cost) is constrained to be plausible. In practice, this means that constraints are expressed across

Ingredient Name	Ingredient Type	Diet points[a]	Cost (£)	Preparation Time (mins)
Lamb Chop	Main (meat)	7	4	20
Gammon Steak	Main (meat)	10	4	15
Fillet of Plaice	Main (fish)	8	4	15
Sausages	Main (meat)	8	2	10
Chicken Kiev	Main (meat)	8	3	30
Quorn Taco	Main (vegetarian)	6	3	10
Jacket Potato	Carbohydrate	5	1	60
French Fries	Carbohydrate	6	1	15
Rice	Carbohydrate	6	1	15
Pasta	Carbohydrate	2	1	10
Runner Beans	Vegetable	1	1	10
Carrots	Vegetable	1	1	15
Cauliflower	Vegetable	1	1	10
Peas	Vegetable	2	1	3
Sweetcorn	Vegetable	2	1	5

a. Points schemes like these are commonly used by slimmers as a simplification of calorific value. When using such schemes, slimmers allow themselves to consume no more than, say, 40 points worth of food in a single day (the actual limit usually depends on the slimmer's sex, height, and weight).

Table 1. Meal Preparation Knowledge Used in Plausibility Space Generation

the slots within a single object. If the domain of one of the slot's constraint variables changes, then this causes propagation to the other related slots.

For example, let us inspect some plausible dish preparation times and costs:

```
;;; Create an instance of the object
;;; An after method asserts the appropriate constraints across
;;; the object's slots at object creation time.
USER: (setq my-dish (make-instance 'plausible-dish))
#<PLAUSIBLE-DISH @ #x99c86a>

;;; Retrieve the value of the duration slot
USER: (slot-value my-dish 'duration)
[774 integer 10:120]
```

```
;;; Retrieve the value of the cost slot
USER: (slot-value my-dish 'cost)
[769 integer 5:7 enumerated-domain:(5 6 7)]
```

This tells us that a plausible dish takes between ten minutes and two hours to prepare, and costs £5, £6, or £7. Now let us restrict our search to a fish dish, and again inspect the plausible values:

```
USER: (assert! (typepv (slot-valuev my-dish 'main) 'fish))
NIL

USER: (slot-value my-dish 'duration)
[774 integer 15:105]

USER: (slot-value my-dish 'cost)
7
```

The plausible range size for the preparation time of the dish has decreased, and the cost of the dish has become bound without having to make any choices of vegetables. If the goal were to have such a fish dish ready in less than quarter of an hour, it would fail without having to know the details of the dish preferences or kitchen resources used by the actual problem-solver, and without needing to run the problem-solver:

```
USER: (assert! (<v (slot-valuev my-dish 'duration) 15))
Error: Attempt to throw to the non-existent tag FAIL
   [condition type: CONTROL-ERROR]
[1] USER:
```

In a similar way, if we define a quick dish to be one that takes less than half an hour to prepare, and a 'healthy' dish to be one that has a dietary points count of 16 or less, then it is easy to discover that there is no such thing as a quick dish that includes a jacket potato, or a 'healthy' dish that includes gammon and french fries!

5 Summary and Discussion

In this paper, we defined the *fitness-for-purpose* of a problem solving configuration which consists of a problem-solver, knowledge bases, and a goal. We argued that fitness-for-purpose is a particular kind of competence, and that the *plausibility* of a configuration is a tractable approximation to fitness-for-purpose. We noted that any test for the plausibility of a configuration should be in some sense 'easier' than running a problem-solver. Constraint logic programming offers a promising approach to the implementation of plausibility tests because it enables a knowledge engineer to write a declarative *meta*problem-solver, which makes statements about the relationship between the inputs and outputs of the actual problem-solver. When this knowledge is coupled with the knowledge of some goal which the user is trying to achieve, it reduces the space of plausible results in a way that can lead to early failures. A failure denotes the *implausibility* of the task. In addition, we believe that metaproblem-solvers can deal with plausibility spaces as *inputs*, propagating this knowledge to a plausible output space. This ability would allow us to reason about the plausibility of a goal which is to be solved using a *combination* of problem-solvers.

Finally, we discuss the contributions which MUSKRAT is making. These include the following:

1. A notation for representing the competencies of methods and the content of knowledge sources.

2. The further development of the technology of constraint satisfaction through our extension to the SCREAMER package.

3. Formulation of the idea of 'economical' problem solving and the investigation of its relationship to the description of problem solving methods.

4. The provision of a framework which unifies problem solving, knowledge acquisition and knowledge transformation/refinement.

5. The development of a method to determine whether it is plausible/likely that knowledge bases can be reused by a particular problem solver.

Our notation for representing the competencies of problem solvers, and the technology we have chosen for proving their properties differs considerably from the related works of Wielinga *et al.* [30], Fensel *et al.* [6], [7], and Pierret-Golbreich [18]. The differences have evolved because we have been working towards a different, but associated, objective. Unlike the methodology of Wielinga *et al.*, for example, we assume our problem solvers exist and seek to describe them as they are, rather than attempting to construct them as we would like them to be. Furthermore, since we are building an advisory system for novice users of problem solvers, we have strong requirements for *operational* descriptions, and a fully *automatic* proof technique. Pierret-Golbreich argues that formal methods should be used to describe problem-solving methods and that this offers a means to decide on a component's reusability. Since such methods are not operational, however, this approach cannot be applied to our problem. Fensel & Schönegge have operationalised their proof technique, but its powerful proof mechanisms are necessarily interactive [6], and not suitable to be driven by novices. Our notation, on the other hand, is declarative, operational, and sufficiently expressive to enable the automatic derivation of interesting properties of a problem solver and the knowledge it employs.

Our extension to the SCREAMER package, driven by our requirement for a declarative and operational description of problem solvers and knowledge sources, has reached a level of expressiveness that contributes to the field of constraint technology. SCREAMER+ can be used to provide elegant solutions to many of the non-trivial problems cited as soluble by commercially available systems such as CHIP [21] and ECLIPSE [26]. The LISP-based nature of SCREAMER+, however, has also helped it to gain advantages over its PROLOG-based counterparts, such as the ability to assert constraints on expressions which take *functions* as arguments. This is important in the current context when one considers that a function might be the realisation of a PSM.

Our ideas of economical problem solving have been motivated by the requirement to generate advice on the suitability of problem solvers 'on the fly' at run-time. Conceptually, some of the techniques applied can be seen variously as applications of abstraction [9], or special cases of generalisation transformations within the plausibility framework of Collins and Michalski [5], [17]. In contrast to these approaches, which classify their methods according to the morphology of their mappings, we are investigating the knowledge-level dependencies of each technique in terms of domain, task, and method.

The fourth contribution of MUSKRAT is to create a unified framework for problem solving, directed knowledge acquisition, and knowledge transformation. This aim is shared by the generalised directive models (GDM) work of O'Hara, Shadbolt and van Heijst [14], but there are significant differences as their work takes place in the context of analysing source materials and attempting to co-evolve domain ontologies as well as the appropriate model for the task; in some cases a KA task is activated. In the case of MUSKRAT, the task to be solved and the problem solver to be used have already been identified. MUSKRAT seeks to discover whether an existing knowledge base can be used without change with the identified problem solver, whether it can be transformed before use, or whether it is necessary to acquire a completely new knowledge base using a KA tool. Other work which has sought to provide a common framework for problem solving and KA includes MOBAL [15], VITAL [16], and NOOS [1], [2].

Our contribution to the topic of knowledge base reuse is most closely related to Puppe's work [20] and the Protégé project [8]. Puppe has realised, as do O'Hara *et al.* [14] that as experts learn more about the domain, their perspectives on the task may change, and hence it is highly desirable that acquired knowledge can be used with a different algorithm from the one for which it was initially acquired. Puppe confines his attention to classification tasks, and notes that there are a number of different classification algorithms which process the same information in different ways. He discusses a number of algorithms including CATEGORICAL (which produces decision trees/tables), heuristic classifiers (which use heuristic rules) and case-base reasoners. Puppe's important insight was to reimplement several classifiers so that they have common data files which can be readily reused. In MUSKRAT, however, we have set up a more general framework in which a knowledge base initially used with a PSM for a classification task might be reused with a different PSM for synthesis or planning.

Protégé's long term goal is to build a tool-set and methodology for the construction of domain-specific KA tools and knowledge-based systems from reusable components. The project plans to develop a variety of methods and knowledge bases, all packaged as CORBA (Common Object Request Broker Architecture) components. Knowledge bases are made available on a server which uses the OKBC (Open Knowledge Base Connectivity) protocol, enabling developers to query the frame-based knowledge with functions such as `get-class-all-subs` to retrieve classes, `get-frame-slots` to retrieve slots, and `get-class-all-instances` to retrieve the instances of a class. A single method, *propose-and-revise*, is available within the framework to date, but there are several knowledge bases which have been used for the VT (elevator-configuration) task, U-Haul (truck selection), as well as the Ribosome and tRNA configuration tasks. In order for a particular method to reuse knowledge from a particular knowledge base a mediator must be manually encoded for each method/KB pair. However, Gennari *et al.* [8] argue that given the similarities in the representations of the knowledge bases, there will be many commonalities between the various mediators needed. This already reduces the workload required to produce the mediators, and the Stanford group envisages partially automating mediator production in the future. MUSKRAT's third case (see section 1) corresponds to the situation for which Protégé currently creates mediators. Whilst Protégé *assumes* that a mediator is necessary, MUSKRAT has evolved a test to determine whether an available knowledge base might be *directly* reusable for the given task. If this is the case, no mediation or adaptation is required.

Complementary to the competence description of problem-solvers, we believe that the plausibility approach can also be used to describe the competence of knowledge acquisition tools. We have already made some progress on the plausible outputs of a repertory grid tool, and also believe that we can similarly describe plausible decision trees [29]. Using these techniques, we believe it will be possible to show that a given knowledge acquisition tool cannot produce a required knowledge base. If this research direction is successful, knowledge acquisition will become more efficient because questions could still be answered about the plausibility of the task at hand *without carrying out the details of the knowledge acquisition task.*

Acknowledgements

This work is financially supported by an EPSRC studentship. The MUSKRAT framework was initially conceptualised by Nicolas Graner; further inspiration came from the Machine Learning Toolbox Project (ESPRIT project 2154). We are very grateful to the anonymous referees who helped to improve this paper by providing useful comments on an earlier draft.

References

1. Arcos, J. L., Plaza, E., (1994), "Integration of Learning into a Knowledge Modelling Framework", in Proceedings of the Eighth European Knowledge Acquisition Workshop (EKAW '94), LNCS, Springer Verlag.
2. Arcos, J. L., Plaza, E., (1997), "Noos: An Integrated Framework for Problem Solving and Learning", Research Report 97-02, Institut d'Investigació en Intelligència Artificial (IIIA), Barcelona, Spain.
3. Benjamins, V. R., Plaza, E., Motta, E., Fensel, D., Studer, R., Wielinga, B., Schreiber, G., Zdrahal, Z., Decker, S., (1998), "IBROW3 – An Intelligent Brokering Service for Knowledge Component Reuse on the World-Wide Web", in proceed-

ings of the Eleventh Banff Knowledge Acquisition for Knowledge-Based Systems Workshop (KAW98), Banff, Alberta, Canada.

4. Benjamins, V. R., Wielinga, B., Wielemaker, J., Fensel, D., (1999), "Brokering Problem Solving Knowledge on the Internet", in the proceedings of the Eleventh European Workshop on Knowledge Acquisition, Modeling, and Management (EKAW '99), LNCS, Springer Verlag.

5. Collins, A., Michalski, R. S., (1989), "The Logic of Plausible Reasoning: A Core Theory", Cognitive Science, Vol. 13, pp. 1-49.

6. Fensel, D., Schönegge, A., (1997), "Using KIV to Specify and Verify Architectures of Knowledge-Based Systems", in Proceedings of the Twelfth International Conference on Automated Software Engineering (ASEC-97), Incline Village, Nevada.

7. Fensel, D., Schönegge, A., (1998), "Inverse Verification of Problem Solving Methods", International Journal of Human-Computer Studies, Vol. 49, No. 4, pp. 339-361.

8. Gennari, J. H., Cheng, H., Altman, R. B., Musen, M. A., (1998), "Reuse, CORBA, and Knowledge-based Systems", International Journal of Human-Computer Studies, Vol. 49, No. 4, pp. 523-546.

9. Giunchiglia, F., Walsh, T., (1992), "A Theory of Abstraction", Artificial Intelligence, Vol. 56, No. 2-3, pp. 323-390.

10. Graner, N., Sleeman, D., (1993), "MUSKRAT: A Multistrategy Knowledge Refinement and Acquisition Toolbox", in proceedings of the Second International Workshop on Multistrategy Learning, R. S. Michalski and G. Tecuci (Eds.), pp. 107-119.

11. Imielinski, T., (1987), "Domain Abstraction and Limited Reasoning", in Proceedings of the Tenth International Joint Conference on Artificial Intelligence, pp. 997-1003.

12. Johnson, J., (1997), "Mathematics, Representation, and Problem Solving", Mathematics Today (Bulletin of the Institute of Mathematics and its Applications), Vol. 33, No. 3., pp. 78-80.

13. O'Hara, K., Shadbolt, N., (1996), "The Thin End of the Wedge: Efficiency and the Generalised Directive Model Methodology", in Shadbolt, N., O'Hara, K., Schreiber, G., (Eds), *Advances in Knowledge Acquisition*, proceedings of the 9th European Knowledge Acquisition Workshop (EKAW '96), Nottingham, UK, pp. 33-47.

14. O'Hara, K., Shadbolt, N., van Heijst, (1998), "Generalised Directive Models: Integrating Model Development and Knowledge Acquisition", International Journal of Human-Computer Studies, Vol. 49, No. 4, pp. 497-522.

15. Morik, K., Wrobel, S., Kietz J-U., Emde, W., (1993), "Knowledge Acquisition and Machine Learning: Theory, Methods and Applications", Academic Press, London.

16. Motta, E., O'Hara, K., Shadbolt, N., (1996), "Solving VT in VITAL: A Study in Model Construction and Knowledge Reuse", International Journal of Human-Computer Studies, Vol. 44, No. 3, pp. 333-371.

17. Oroumchian, F., (1995), "Theory of Plausible Reasoning", in *Information Retrieval by Plausible Inferences: An Application of the Theory of Plausible Reasoning of Collins and Michalski*, PhD Thesis, School of Computer and Information Science, Syracuse University, New York.

18. Pierret-Golbreich, C., (1998), "Supporting Organization and Use of Problem-solving Methods Libraries by a Formal Approach", International Journal of Human-Computer Studies, Vol. 49, No. 4, pp. 471-495.

19. Polya, G., (1957), "How To Solve It: A New Aspect of Mathematical Method", Doubleday Anchor Books, New York.

20. Puppe, F., (1998), "Knowledge Reuse among Diagnostic Problem-Solving Methods in the Shell-Kit D3", International Journal of Human-Computer Studies, Academic Press, Vol. 49, No. 4, pp. 627-649.

21. Simonis, H., (1995), "The CHIP System and Its Applications", in Montanari, U., Rossi, F., (Eds.), *Principles and Practice of Constraint Programming*, proceedings of the First International Conference on the Principles and Practice of Constraint Programming, Lecture Notes in Computer Science Series, Springer Verlag, pp. 643-646.

22. J. M. Siskind, D. A. McAllester, (1993), "SCREAMER: A Portable Efficient Implementation of Nondeterministic Common LISP'", Technical Report IRCS-93-03, University of Pennsylvania Institute for Research in Cognitive Science.

23. J. M. Siskind, D. A. McAllester, (1993), "Nondeterministic LISP as a Substrate for Constraint Logic Programming", in proceedings of AAAI-93.

24. Sleeman, D., White, S., (1997), "A Toolbox for Goal-driven Knowledge Acquisition", in proceedings of the Nineteenth Annual Conference of the Cognitive Science Society, (COGSCI '97), Stanford, CA.

25. Turing, A. M., (1937), "On Computable Numbers, with an Application to the Entscheidungsproblem", in Proceedings of the London Mathematical Society, Vol. 42(ii), pp. 230-265; correction Vol. 43, pp. 544-546.

26. Wallace M. G., Novello, S. and Schimpf, J., (1997) "ECLIPSE : A Platform for Constraint Logic Programming", ICL Systems Journal, Vol 12, Issue 1, May 1997.

27. White, S., Sleeman, D., (1998), "Providing Advice on the Acquisition and Reuse of Knowledge Bases in Problem Solving", in proceedings of the Eleventh Banff Knowledge Acquisition for Knowledge-Based Systems Workshop (KAW98), Banff, Alberta, Canada.

28. White, S., Sleeman, D., (1998), "Constraint Handling in Common LISP", Technical Report AUCS/TR9805, Department of Computing Science, University of Aberdeen, Scotland, UK.

29. White, S., (forthcoming), "Enhancing Knowledge Acquisition with Constraint Technology", PhD Thesis, Department of Computing Science, University of Aberdeen, Scotland, UK.

30. Wielinga, B. J., Akkermans, J. M., Schreiber A. Th., (1998), "A Competence Theory Approach to Problem Solving Method Construction", International Journal of Human-Computer Studies, Vol. 49, No. 4.

Holism and Incremental Knowledge Acquisition

Ghassan Beydoun and Achim Hoffmann

School of Computer Sciences and Engineering
University of New South Wales
Sydney, NSW 2052, Australia
Email: {ghassan, achim}@cse.unsw.edu.au

Abstract. Human experts tend to introduce intermediate terms in giving their explanations. The expert's explanation of such terms is operational for the context that triggered the explanation, however term definitions remain often incomplete. Further, the expert's (re) use of these terms is hierarchical (similar to natural language). In this paper, we argue that a hierarchical incremental knowledge acquisition process that captures the expert terms and operationalises these terms while incompletely defined makes the KA task more effective. Towards this we present our knowledge representation formalism Nested Ripple Down Rules (NRDR) that is a substantial extension to the Ripple Down Rule (RDR) KA framework. It allows simultaneous incremental modelling and knowledge acquisition. In this paper we analyse the conditions under which RDR converges towards the target knowledge base (KB). We will also show that the extra maintenance cost of an NRDR KB is minimal, and that the maintenance of NRDR requires similar effort to maintaining RDR for most of the KB development cycle.

1 Introduction

In everyday use of language people use very complex processes. When a simple sentence: *"No smoking on planes"* is understood by a person, s/he has to know what *smoking* means, what *planes* are, and that a person must be flying on the plane for the sentence to cause him/her to alter his behaviour (which of course implies that s/he must know what *flying* is).

To explain that sentence to an extraterrestrial being of comparable intelligence, a human will have to introduce new terms. For example in explaining what a plane is he may proceed: *a plane is a vehicle used to transport people via air*. Then s/he will have to define what s/he means by *"vehicle"*, *"transport"*, *"air"*.. As s/he explains these terms s/he will have to consider the context of each term s/he chooses to use. For example, the alien may have previously heard the sentence *"he has certain air around him"* and wonders if this is the same *"air"* where plane travels. In both sentences the meaning of *"air"* is a function of the sentence, its structure and the epistemological links between all the constituent terms. In linguistic this is known as *semantic holism* which is supported by many contemporary philosophers like Quine [5] and Putnam [4].

Even in restricted domains, human expertise is believed to be holistic in nature. This causes experts to struggle to express themselves as they explain (justify) their expertise. This holism of expertise makes domain conceptualisation difficult. To ease this difficulty experts use intermediate abstractions that they (re) use in further explanations. For example in chess, experts introduce notions like *"centre development"* to justify some of their opening moves. When asked to explain such intermediate concepts, experts may oversee the definition of the concept in some contexts. They fail to provide a complete explanation that always covers their use, rather they provide an operational solution sufficient for the purpose of explaining the context on hand. Expert articulation of intermediate concepts may depend on his articulation of other concepts, which may not yet be made explicit or completely defined. Hence the incompleteness of these intermediate concepts is likely (if not often unavoidable).

Adapting the incremental knowledge acquisition process to match the expert's natural tendencies in giving his explanations will enable the expert to build an operational knowledge base more effectively. Towards this we present our knowledge representation formalism Nested Ripple Down Rules (NRDR), which allows the expert to give his explanations using his own terms. These terms are operational while still incomplete. To ease the maintenance of these terms, we use a Ripple Down Rule (RDR) tree for every term.

Any given concept in an NRDR knowledge base may depend on a number of other concepts. A change of one concept should ensure that the remaining concepts remain consistent with respect to this change. To maintain consistency of the knowledge base access to all past seen cases is required.

2. Presenting Nested RDR

An RDR tree is a collection of simple rules organised in a tree structure [2]. Every rule can have two branches to two other rules: A false and a true branch. Examples are shown in figure 2, where every block represents a simple RDR. When a rule fires a true branch is taken, otherwise a false branch is taken. If a 'true-branch' leads to a terminal node t and the condition of t is not fulfilled the conclusion of the rule in the parent node of t is taken, hence the inference is handled implicitly within the structure of the knowledge. If a 'false-branch' leads to a terminal node t and the condition of t is not fulfilled the KB is said to fail and requires modification. An important strength of RDRs is that they can be easily modified in order to become consistent with a new case without becoming inconsistent with previously classified cases .

Using NRDR [1], the expert can introduce his/her vocabulary, s/he has more freedom to express him/herself naturally than using normal RDRs. S/He uses RDR structure for allowing him/her to define a conceptual hierarchy during the KA process. Every concept is defined as a simple RDR tree. Conclusions of rules within a concept definition have a boolean value indicating whether the concept is satisfied by a case or not. Defined concepts can in turn be used as higher order attributes by the experts to define other concepts. The elementary level is the level of domain primitives. In the next section, we introduce technical issues in having holistic features in KA.

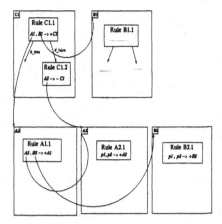

Fig2.1: An example of nested rules. An update in cocept A2 can cause changes in the meaning of rules in the KB.

3. Supporting KA of holistic expertise with NRDR

An NRDR KB requires modification if a 'false-branch' leads to a terminal node t and the condition of t is not fulfilled and the expert disagrees with the default conclusion returned by the knowledge base. The hierarchical structure of NRDR causes problems for keeping the entire KB consistent when a single concept definition needs to be altered (see figure 2.1). This is expected as after a concept definition is modified other concept definitions may be affected.

Given a case x that requires the KB to be modified, the modification can occur in a number of places. For example (figure 2.1) say case x satisfies conditions $A1$ and $B1$ in rule $C1.1$ but the expert thinks that case x is not $C1$, then the KB needs to be modified to reflect this. A rule can be added as an exception for the RDR tree describing $C1$, or alternatively, $A1$ can be changed by updating its definition, or $A2$ in rule $A1.1$ can be changed; and so forth. A more serious maintenance issue is dealing with *inconsistencies*[1] due to localised updates in the KB. For instance, if the expert updates $A1$ by updating $A2$ in rule $A1.1$, he may inadvertently change rule $C1.2$ that contains $A2$. Hence, the feature of local impact of refinement no longer holds. Dealing with inconsistencies requires access to all past seen cases correctly classified by the KB. In simple RDRs, a *corner stone case* is associated with every rule. In NRDR, every rule has a set of corner stone cases. This set contains all the cases that a rule classified correctly under the verification of an expert. These verified classifications must always hold. Cases may travel between sets because of the interactions within an NRDR KB. During check for inconsistencies, some of those sets of cases are classified again. Now, we give an example of a small KA session that produces inconsistencies. The KA task is to build a knowledge base to choose male models for an army scene in a Hollywood movie. The expert is an eccentric film producer who enjoys using expert systems in his work (see table 2.1). The KB starts with the default rule *"If True then*

---

[1] Given a case c classified by the KB, if this classification is inconsistent with respect to a correct past classification, then c is called an *inconsistency*.

Accept". After meeting the first case, the expert enters the rule "*If Too_heavy then Reject*", and explains the term "*too_Heavy*" with the rule "*If weight > 80 then too_Heavy*". The

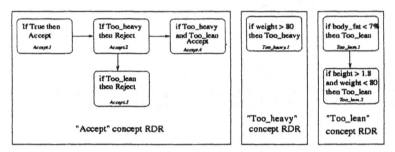

Fig2.3: Addition of "*If body fat > 9 % then Too heavy*" to account for case 5 causes case 4 to become an inconsistency.

expert also rejects case 2 as he finds the candidate too skinny. He enters a new rule to the highest level concept "*Accept*", the rule entered is "*If Too_lean then Reject*", it gets attached to the false link of rule Accept.2. He explains the new concept "*Too_lean*" : "*If body fat < 7% then Too_lean*". The expert accepts the third candidate although he's "*Too_heavy*" and "*Too_lean*", so he enters the exception rule "*If Too_heavy and Too_lean then Accept*", this rule is attached to the true link of rule Accept.2. See figure 2.3. Case 4 is rejected on the basis of rule Accept.3, the concept "*Too_lean*" is updated to cover this case, the expert enters a new rule "*If height > 1.8 and weight < 80 then Too_lean*". Finally, case 5 is rejected by the expert on the basis of rule Accept.2, he updates the concept "*Too_heavy*" to cover this case. He enters "*If body fat > 9% then Too_heavy*". This final rule also covers case 4. This makes it accepted by the KB (on the basis of rule Accept.4), note this case was rejected earlier by the expert, hence it becomes an inconsistency. To overcome this, the expert can rethink his change to concept "*Too_heavy*", or he may enter a new exception to rule Accept.4. In the next section, we will show that the inconsistencies problem has a small impact on the KB development cost.

Case number	Weight (Kg)	Height (m)	Body Fat %	Age (year)	Expert comment	Decision
1	90	1.75	40 %	21	Too Heavy	Reject
2	60	1.9	3 %	26	Too Lean	Reject
3	81	1.7	6 %	27	Too Heavy and too Lean	Accept
4	79	1.81	9.5 %	39	Too Lean	Reject
5	80	1.6	9.8 %	25	Too Heavy	Reject

Table2.1: The cases presented to the expert.

4. Theoretical Framework of RDR Structures

In this section we analyse the conditions under which a case becomes *inconsistent*. We then analyse the relation between the convergence of NRDR KBs and frequency of *inconsistencies*. The following definitions follow [6]:

Definition 1: The scope of a rule r, *scope(r)* is the set of objects that the rule fires for and no exception or preceding rule fired for.

Definition 2: The domain of a rule r, *dom(r)* is the set of objects that reach that rule and for which the condition of r is satisfied.

Definition 3: The context of a rule r, *context(r)* is the set of objects that reach that rule when being classified. In RDR, the context and domain of rules does not change during maintenance and extension of the KB. This is the reason behind RDRs'ease of maintenance. We extend the above set of definitions by the following notion:

Definition 4: The predictivity measure p of a rule r is the ratio of objects in its domain that are correctly classified, i.e. *pred (r) = | scope (r) | / | dom (r) |.*

Observation 1: Given a rule r_2 in a concept definition C_2, and r_2 uses a concept definition X that is modified by the addition of a rule r_1. A case becomes an *inconsistency* as a result of this update only if it falls simultaneously in the scope of the new rule r_1 and the context of r_2.

Clearly, not all objects in this intersection will become *inconsistencies*. Some cases may migrate to new rules where they are correctly classified, and furthermore not all cases within the intersection will migrate.

Observation 2: In an RDR tree for binary classification, rules within an exception level n have the same conclusion. Furthermore, these conclusions alternate within the exception hierarchy. This observation immediately follows:

Observation 3: Given a rule r_2 in a concept definition C_2, and *depth(r_2)* = n and r_2 uses a concept definition X that gets modified by the addition of a rule r_1 :A case c becomes an *inconsistency* as a result of this update only if it falls simultaneously in the domain of the new rule r_1 and the context of r_2, and c travels to a scope of a rule at depth n+ 2d + 1 within C_2 where d >0. This leads to the following theorem:

Theorem 1: The probability of a *travelling* case c becoming an *inconsistency* as a result of an update is < ½ as long the predictivity p is larger than 4/9 .

Proof: By observation 1, the total probability P_1 that a travelling case does not become an inconsistency:

$$P_1 = p + (1-p)^2 + (1-p)^4 + ...$$

Similarly, the total probability P_2 that a travelling case becomes an inconsistency:

$$P_2 = (1-p) + (1-p)^3 + (1-p)^5 ......$$

Every corresponding term in P_1 is larger than every corresponding term in P_2 except for the first term where the result of the comparison depends on the value of p. That is: p > 1- p iff p> ½ . However, including the second term in the comparison will give us 0.44 instead of ½, i.e :

$$p + (1-p)^2 > (1-p) + (1-p)^3 \quad if \ p > 0.44$$

and hence,

$$p + (1-p)^2 > (1-p) + (1-p)^3 \quad if \ p > 4/9$$

and finally, because $P_1 + P_2 = 1$ and $P_1 > P_2$ iff p > 4/9 Theorem 1 follows. QED##

Theorem 1 tells us that even when a case *travels* then most likely it will not become an *inconsistency*. So using observation 1 and theorem 1, given a rule r_2 in a concept definition C_2, and r_2 that uses a concept definition X that is modified by the addition of a rule r_1, the probability of an arbitrary case becoming inconsistent as a result of this update: ½ P (x ∈ dom(r_1)) P (x ∈ context(r_2))

Assuming uniform distribution, completion of rules on the first false link increases accuracy by p, completion of exception level n rules increases this accuracy by p^n. The addition of a rule at a level n-1 is 1/(1-p) more likely than the addition of a rule at level n because the former has 1/(1-p) times larger domain. So an RDR tree development occurs in a breadth first manner where false branches develop faster than true branches. Hence, plotting accuracy of the KB versus its size yields the graph in figure

3.3. In [3], this was empirically observed. As the RDR tree becomes more accurate, the number of cases required to cause an addition of a rule increases, hence changing the horizontal axis to number of cases instead of number of rules would yield an exponential function with a sharper rise and flatter top. Also, as the KB develops the domain size of newly added rules shrinks exponentially. So noting the above probability, we also expect the inconsistencies to decrease exponentially as shown in figure 3.3.

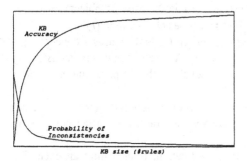

KB size (#rules)

Fig 3.3. Inconsistencies frequency versus KB correctness: As the KB gets larger, the incremental accuracy of the rules decreases. As the KB size increases the domain of the rules shrinks rapidly, taking down the probability of past cases becoming inconsistent close to 0. Hence, most of the inconsistencies occur in the early stages of developing an RDR concept.

5. Conclusion and future work

In this paper we have argued that KA can benefit from incorporating holistic features onto the knowledge base. Towards this, we presented our knowledge representation formalism, NRDRs, which is a substantial extension to RDRs. NRDR have a hierarchical structure that is a natural representation of the way humans give their explanations. It allows the expert to view the KB as a holistic model of his knowledge. Concepts are allowed to interact, but to ease the maintenance, additions are localised within a concept. We have shown that these interactions add very little burden on the expert.

References

1. Beydoun, G. and Hoffmann, A. *Acquisition of Search Knowledge.* in *the 10th European Knowledge Acquisition Workshop.* 1997.
2. Compton, P., Edwards, G., Kang, B., Lazarus, L., Malor, R., Menzies, T., Preston, P., Srinivasan, A., and Sammut, C. *Ripple Down Rules: Possibilities and Limitations.* in *6th Banff Knowledge Acquisition for Knowledge-Based Systems Workshop.* 1991. Canada.
3. Compton, P., Edwards, G., Kang, B., Lazarus, L., Malor, R., Preston, P., and Srinivasan, A., *Ripple down rules: Turning knowledge acquisition into knowledge maintenance.* Artificial Intelligence in Medicine, 1992. **4**: p. 463--475.
4. Putnam, H., *Representation and Reality.* 1988, London: MIT press.
5. Quine, W., *Two Dogmas of Empiricism.* Philosophical Review, 1951(1).
6. Scheffer, T. *Algebraic foundations and improved methods of induction or rippledown rules.* in *2nd Pacific Rim Knowledge Acquisition Workshop.* 1996.

Indexing Problem Solving Methods for Reuse

Joost Breuker

University of Amsterdam
breuker@swi.psy.uva.nl

Abstract. This paper is primarily meant as a position paper. After more than ten years of research on the nature of tasks, problem solving methods (PSMs) and ontologies, it appears to me that indexing PSMs by their function (task, goal, problem type) is not a good idea. The alternative – indexing by preconditions of their reuse – does not capture "what a PSM is about". A third approach is sketched in which not PSMs, but their major components – solution generators and solution testers – are indexed by (the explanation of) their operations.

1 Libraries of PSM and their indexing

There is a large consensus and experience that the two major components of a knowledge system – its domain knowledge and its task structure (reasoning) – can be abstracted into ontologies, respectively problem solving methods (PSM) to enable reuse. However, as the number of potentially reusable ontologies or PSMs grows, and are collected in libraries, such as the Ontolingua server [FFR97], or the *Common*KADSlibrary of PSM [BdV94], the problem of how these reusable components should be indexed becomes very serious. [vHSW97] and [VB96] have proposed to use "core" ontologies of fields of practice – *e.g.* medicine, law, electrical engineering — for covering and indexing large domain ontologies. These indexes are functional, abstract categories that represent "what a field or domain is about" are not only useful to obtain access to more domain specific terms, but also allow the indexing of (re)sources of knowledge in such a way as to enable management of knowledge. This may not come as a surprise, as abstract terminology, i.e. knowledge itself, has evolved just for this role. For instance the term 'disease' collects processes and organisms that interfere with normal biological processes. Human memory is highly organized and indexed by abstractions.

Problem solving methods (PSMs) do not belong to objects of knowledge with a long cultural history in mankind, and this may explain why the indexing of PSMs appears to be more complicated than our understanding and articulation of diseases. [1] Before discussing the indexing problem of PSMs, I should point out that more is involved than simply effective retrieval cues for a large collection of PSMs. Epistemologically adequate and ontologically valid indexing reflects an understanding of the key issues in a domain. The pivotal role of categories like 'disease' in medicine or 'norm' in law is evident. Moreover, these categories are related in such a way that they explain how a domain works. In medicine, an identification of a (kind of) disease is required to

---

[1] Disease is a far more complex and context dependent concept than problem solving method.

enable therapy selection; in law the observation or violation of a norm should be established before legal consequences are applied, and in engineering functional and structural models are the required input for mathematical modelling [BA97]. It is suggested that describing a core ontology for a domain or field of practice in terms of functional categories should be related by dependencies, rather than being molded into the default type hierarchies (taxonomies) [VB96,VBB99].

For PSMs it appeared that the most natural way to describe their roles is by reference to notions about the kinds of tasks or problems they should solve. Typologies of tasks were already proposed before the notion of PSM was explicit in knowledge acquisition [HRWL83], and they still are the predominant way to index PSMs in libraries for their reuse (for an overview see [VBV98, 410-412]). I will call this *indexing-by-function*, where typical terms are used like diagnosis, design, planning etc. If domain knowledge can be indexed by functional categories, it even looks more appropriate to view PSMs in these terms, as PSMs themselves can be viewed as functional (de)compositions. Usually, a secondary way of indexing is provided by the preconditions for (re)use of PSMs. Preconditions consist of requirements on domain knowledge (method ontology) and the task environment. The latter includes the task or goal itself (so we may see function as a major precondition for re-use), but here it is about the data and specific requirements for solutions (e.g. optimality, validity). As many of these preconditions may be implicit, the term *assumptions* is often used and covers a large part of these requirements [BFS96].

In this paper I will argue that these solutions are inadequate, and that a third type of solution which focuses on how PSMs operate may be more promising. It explains (makes understandable) how a PSM works, not by introducing operational terms, but by categorizing the components of PSMs into two major functions – generating solutions and testing solutions – in terms of inference operations and test methodology.

1.1 Functional indexing

That the use of task- or problem typologies for indexing PSM may not be such a good idea is a conclusion that was only recently suggested to me after more than a decade in coming to grips with the nature of this type of index itself. I will review in a nutshell the problems with these typologies. Although, builders of libraries for PSMs are careful not to propose a (new) typology, the belief that such a typology is needed is still unshaken (see *e.g.* articles in [BFE98]). Initially, the problems where related to terminological and ontological issues [Bre94a]. However, there is also a problem in the mapping of PSMs to these kinds of terms.

Ontology of tasks and problems The initial assumption in constructing an ontology for function terms in problem solving is that they concern terms like diagnosis, design, planning etc. These are the 'natural' terms used, and, the fact that one finds in AI fields of research completely (and almost exclusively) dedicated to these terms. Despite this apparent terminological consensus, the following problems have emerged (see [Bre94a] for more arguments.)

Typology of what? Diagnosis can be classified as a goal, a task, a problem, a solution, etc. In the context of problem solving methods it seems appropriate to see these terms as 'problem-types', as a task consists of a problem and a method to solve it [2](see also [Cla85]).

Ambiguity of terms Terms that are used have not unequivocal definitions or extensions. The definitions may have a large impact on the selection or construction of efficient PSM, *e.g.* [dKMR92], but one may object that this is not because of the notion of *e.g.* diagnosis itself, but because of specific preconditions on the solution (*e.g.* multiple *vs* single fault assumptions). However, the terms may refer to completely different kinds of problems. For instance, diagnosis is used for tracing causes of problems, but these causes may be faulty components (to explain malfunctioning), classes of abnormal states (to identify an explanation for an abnormal state), or histories of events (accident reconstruction). Each of these kinds of causes constitutes completely different kinds of problems: in this sense, medical diagnosis is an assessment problem, and accident reconstruction is largely a (backward chaining) planning problem. [3]

Not a taxonomy Typologies of something should contain preferably mutually exclusive types and and these types should cover the full scope of this something. Therefore, problem typologies have invariably been presented as taxonomies (see [Bre94b] for ten of such taxonomies.). They start with the distinction between synthetic and analytic problems. The next ply contains the familiar terms like diagnosis, planning etc., but may also have more idiosyncratic ones, like assessment, interpretation, debugging, or even terms which are hard to see as problem type (*e.g.* instruction). Whether they make up a complete set of mutually exclusive terms is hard to assess as there are no really hard, formal definitions (see above). However, the trouble with a taxonomic view becomes apparent at the next ply of such a taxonomy. At this layer, the terms used are always the same terms as in the previous layer, but modified with an adjective. This adjective either refers to some precondition or to a... PSM. Parametric design is a design problem in which the problem has been reduced to a set of given constraints that have to be resolved on the basis of the data from the case [MZ98] [4]. Worse, however, are the adjectives that refer to (families of) PSMs rather than to problem types, such as abductive diagnosis, systematic diagnosis, skeletal planning, refinement design etc. If the terms of the index and the terms for what they index overlap, this layer does not add any information in the refinement of searching for an adequate PSM. In fact, it hides what should have been explicit in the secondary criteria for selecting a PSM – the preconditions – and not as a choice of a PSM itself. How does one know that the diagnostic kinds of problem at hand require an abductive method?

As a remedy for all these problems I have proposed a typology consisting of a chain ("suite") that better reflects the a functional view on problem types than a taxonomy, by constructing a chain of dependencies between the types. Problem types are explicit

---

[2] We say that problems are solved; tasks are executed.

[3] I reserved the term diagnosis for trouble-shooting, as this is the core kind of problem addressed in the (model-based) diagnosis community in AI.

[4] In fact, here one would prefer the earlier term, configuration, which is not a design problem but a problem type of its own (assignment in the typology presented here.)

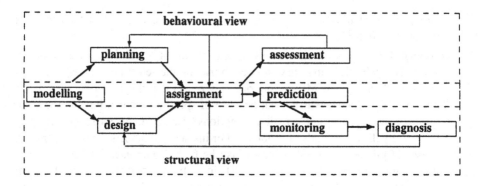

Fig. 1. A suite of dependent problem types and views

functions, *i.e.* terms with input and output arguments. The name of the function indicates the output argument; the output of a planning function is a plan; of a diagnosis function it is a diagnosis. A problem is defined by a discrepancy between an actual, input state and an intended, output state. The suite in Figure 1 makes also explicit what the required *input* is of a problem-type function. Diagnosis requires as an input state that some discrepancy between predicted (expected) and observed behaviour is identified: an error. This kind of discrepancy is the result of a monitoring which takes as its input a predicted state and compares it with an actual state. In its turn, prediction requires a behavioural model (plan; design) with assigned parameter values, etc. In this way, the suite indicates which kinds of already solved problems, either as instances or as generic knowledge is required to identify a certain problem type by regressing over this suite. For instance, diagnosis problems can only occur if all dependent problems have been solved, *i.e.* only for an actually working and known system. This suite is not fixed for a particular grain-size level, because these functions do not have a body; the body would consist of PSMs (which turn the problem type into a task). Therefore, these dependencies between also occur *within PSMs*. For instance, the test parts of PSMs can be all represented by the following chains of dependencies:

$$assignment \rightarrow assessment$$

$$assignment \rightarrow prediction \rightarrow monitoring$$

Does it help? This suite may be an improvement as an indexing tool over the loosely constructed taxonomies, but the question is still whether it works better. The answer is: not much, and the reason is that PSMs vary largely in specificity. The scope of reuse may range from almost the full set of problem types to a very specific version of a problem type. [MZ98] make the distinction between task dependent and task independent PSMs. The latter are PSMs that are good for almost anything: they have a large scope of reuse, but their use is rather limited, which coincides largely with what is conceived as "weak methods". Examples of these good-for-all methods are heuristic classification and cover and differentiate. Consistency based diagnosis is a good example of the other extreme, and it is debatable whether it completely solves the diagnosis problem as it returns only a faulty component, but not what the fault exactly is. There is no reason to belief that this is a real dichotomy. PSMs may differ in strength and scope ("use and reuse"), and they may even be scaled up or down in strength, trading off in scope [FS98,tTvHSW96]. Therefore, problem-types are not the kind of unit to indicate the scope of a PSM, in particular because this scope can even be manipulated.

1.2 Features, requirements, preconditions, assumptions and other creatures

If the use of assumptions has such an impact on the effectiveness of a PSM we may use these as a primary index, or, rather to make no longer a distinction between a primary indexing by function and a secondary by requirements. Fensel & Straatman [FS98] see the role of assumptions to increase the efficiency of PSM. In general, assumptions are not validated by the problem solver itself ("reasoning service"), but are the consequence of insights and experiences in the domain. Some of these may have become part of the domain knowledge (*e.g.* compiled out heuristics; taxonomies of solutions); others may constrain the solutions (*e.g.* multiple faults are so rare that we can work with a single fault assumption.). Indeed, assumptions make up a far richer indexing model, but, as the title of this subsection already indicates there is even far less consensus and insight of what these things are than for problem types. Moreover, the terms interact heavily. Multiple faults are typical for faults: they are not multiple solutions. Benjamins *et al* have presented some classification of assumptions that are inherent to PSMs for diagnosis, but the classification is rather flat and does not allow for easy refinement [BFS96].

2 Components of PSMs in context

The alternative to a functional view is an operational one. In *Common*KADSboth perspectives were used to describe PSM by inference structures. The problem types are functions that match PSM functions and the PSMs themselves bottom out in canonical inferences. These inferences are defined as operations on domain ontology representation categories, *i.e.* a kind of KL-ONE ontology. There is no reason that an operational view could not be applied to the higher levels as well. Beys *et al.* have proposed to use "task neutral" terms in describing PSM in an operational way [BBvH96]. They show that the scope of reuse may be extended in this way. By giving other names to roles in PSMs one does not change its effectivity, but the names are terms that have other ontological commitments. For instance, a causal network becomes an instance of a directed graph, so that also non-causal networks can fit the method ontology of a PSM. This result shows at least that the PSM (cover & differentiate, C&D) has a larger scope than originally foreseen; not necessarily that the PSM itself has changed. However, this kind of operational specification easily slips into a symbol level account of a knowledge level structure: knowledge structures become data structures. In this way, ontological distinctions may evaporate. This is possible because C&D does not have a real interpretation of causality. In fact, any chain of implications can be handled by C&D. If one codes a causal network by its inverse – is-the-result-of – a medical KBS may ask for diseases to find a common symptom. Viewing PSMs as algorithms applied to data structures may indeed work as an eye-opener to show that (knowledge level) prejudices about (weak) PSMs (see also [MZ98]). Even if a functional perspective is more natural for PSMs, there is certainly an advantage in indexing PSMs in what they are, rather than what they deliver, because this will better reflect similarities and distinctions between PSMs.

2.1 Contexts of discovery and of justification

An operational description of an artifact, like a PSM, invariably has to take into account how its components behave. However, these components are themselves the result of a functional decomposition. Therefore, it is unavoidable to take their architecture as a starting point. In (strong) PSMs two major components can be distinguished: those which generate solutions, and those which test these solutions. [5] One way to argue for this distinction is that it maps onto the explanation, respectively justification side of solutions to problems (see [Bre94a] for more arguments). The requirements to find solutions are completely different from those that are aimed at justifying them: in epistemology of science, the context of discovery and the context of justification are worlds apart.

Generating solutions There are two major ways by which solutions can be generated ([Cla85,dV88]): (1) by selecting from a prespecified set, *i.e.* by classification, or (2) by assembling them from available elements, *i.e.* by **construction**. This distinction suggests a direct mapping to the analytic vs synthetic problem types. However, many synthetic problems are solved by classification PSMs. For instance, the 'propose' subtask in propose & revise selects conclusions. Most synthetic problems are solved by some combination, as *e.g.* in skeletal planning or in refining solutions, where more specific components are added (assembly), and/or specific values are selected. Despite this combined category, the indexing by method that solutions are generated appears to provide a more clearcut indexing of PSMs by an operational perspective than by the functional perspective (see also [BFS96]).

Testing solutions A primary indexing of the testing parts of a PSM can be found in the nature of the arguments for supporting or rejecting a solution. Three major ways of generating argument can be distinguished:

- By verification: here it is the internal consistency of a solution that is at stake, *e.g.* via formal proof procedures.
- By validation: *i.e.* the testing whether the solution covers *empirical* data which are not explicitly included in the proposed or hypothesized solution. Two subtypes can be distinguished: (1) by satisfying external requirements (assessment) and (2) by prediction of observable behaviour. The latter, of course, refers to methodologies for empirical research: a world by itself.

---

[5] In (very) weak methods these two components may be intertwined: *e.g.* theorem proving, simple classification. It is somewhat paradoxal that the typical weak method 'generate & test' is the cleanest example of the distinction. Generate & test is rather a paradigm that covers almost all PSMs I know of.

– By debate *i.e.* by "dialogical" investigation of assumptions underlying solutions and tests.

These methods include one another successively. For debate, a KBS needs to know about the assumptions, underlying principles and some meaning of the concepts it uses. Although these competences are very expensive to terms of man and machine effort, in some fields (*e.g.* law) such a capability appears to be unavoidable for practical application.

2.2 Concluding

As efficiency is the key to problem solving [FS98], this distinction shows easily were efficiency can be gained. In many respects, testing by validation is certainly the most expensive part. It may involve complex planning of manipulations and observations (cf model based diagnosis). Data may be lacking, may be unreliable, etc. Therefore, much can be gained by assuming defaults, reliability of data, generality of concepts, etc. and relaxing requirements on justification. However, the costs can also be drastically cut if the solution generator focuses fast on a correct solution space. Here efficiency can be gained not so much by assumptions and heuristics but in particular by control regimes that exploit feed back from the testing components (refinement cycles) (see [MZ98] for a good example). In summary, I argue that (1) however natural, problem types are not a good primary index for PSMs, that (2) assumptions are too diversified to take such a role (now) and that they only tell part of the efficiency story, that (3) that PSMs should be indexed by the way their major components – generating and testing solutions – operate.

References

[BA97]   P. Borst and H. Akkermans. Engineering ontologies. *International Journal of Human-Computer Studies*, 46:365 – 408, 1997.

[BBvH96]   P. Beys, R. Benjamins, and G. van Heijst. Remedying the reusability-usability trade-off for problem solving methods. In B.R. Gaines and M. Mussen, editors, *Proceedings of the KAW-96*, Banff, Ca, 1996.

[BdV94]   Joost Breuker and Walter Van de Velde, editors. *The CommonKADS Library for Expertise Modeling*. IOS-Press, Amsterdam, 1994.

[BFE98]   R. Benjamins and D. Fensel-(Eds.). Special issue on Problem Solving Methods. *International Journal of Human-Computer Studies*, 49:305–649, 1998.

[BFS96]   V.R. Benjamins, D. Fensel, and R. Straatman. Assumptions of problem solving methods and their role in knowledge engineering. In W. Wahlster, editor, *Poceedings ECAI-96*, pages 408–412, 1996.

[Bre94a]   J. Breuker. Components of problem solving. In L. Steels, G. Schreiber, and W. Van de Velde, editors, *A Future for Knowledge Acquisition: proceedings of the EKAW-94, European Knowledge Acquisition Workshop*, pages 118 – 136, Berlin, 1994. Springer Verlag.

[Bre94b]   Joost Breuker. A suite of problem types. In Joost Breuker and Walter Van de Velde, editors, *The CommonKADS Library for Expertise Modeling*. IOS-Press, Amsterdam, 1994.

[Cla85]   W.J. Clancey. Heuristic classification. *Artificial Intelligence*, 27:289–350, 1985.

[dKMR92]   J. de Kleer, A.M. Mackworth, and R. Reiter. Characterizing diagnoses and systems. *Artificial Intelligence*, 56(2–3):197 – 222, 1992.

[dV88]   Walter Van de Velde. Inference structure as a basis for problem solving. In Y. Kodratoff, editor, *Proceedings of the 8th European Conference on AI*, pages 202 – 207, London, 1988. Pitman.

[FFR97]   A. Farquhar, R. Fikes, and J. Rice. The Ontolingua Server: a tool for collaborative ontology construction. *International Journal of Human-Computer Studies*, 46:707–728, 1997.

[FS98]   D. Fensel and R. Straatman. The essence of problem solving methods: making assumptions to gain efficiency. *International Journal of Human Computer Studies*, 48:181–216, 1998.

[HRWL83] F. Hayes-Roth, D.A. Waterman, and D.B. Lenat. *Building Expert Systems*. Addison-Wesley, New York, 1983.

[MZ98]   E. Motta and Z. Zdrahal. A library of problem solving components based on the integration of the search paradigm with task and method ontologies. *International Journal of Human Computer Studies*, 49:417–436, 1998. special issue on problem solving methods.

[tTvHSW96] A. ten Teije, F. van Harmelen, A. Th. Schreiber, and B. J. Wielinga. Construction of problem-solving methods as parametric design. In B. R. Gaines and M. A. Musen, editors, *Proceedings of the 10th Banff Knowledge Acquisition for Knowledge-Based Systems Workshop, Alberta, Canada, November 9-14*, volume 1, pages 12.1–12.21. SRDG Publications, University of Calgary, 1996.

[VB96]   A. Valente and J. Breuker. Towards principled core ontologies. In *Proceedings of the Knowledge Acquisition Workshop-96*, 1996. available also at ftp://ksi.cpsc.ucalgary.ca/KAW/KAW96/73valente.ps.Z.

[VBB99]   A. Valente, J. Breuker, and B. Brouwer. Legal modelling and automated reasoning with ON-LINE. *International Journal of Human Computer Studies*, 50, 1999. to appear in special issue on legal KBS.

[VBV98]   A. Valente, J. Breuker, and W. Van de Velde. The CommonKADS Library in perspective. *International Journal of Human Computer Studies*, 49:391–416, 1998. special issue on problem solving methods.

[vHSW97]   G. van Heijst, A.Th. Schreiber, and B.J. Wielinga. Using explicit ontologies in kbs development. *International Journal of Human-Computer Studies*, 46:183 – 291, 1997.

Software Methodologies at Risk[†]

Osvaldo Cairó[1], Julio Barreiro[2], and Francisco Solsona[2]

[1] Department of Computer Science
Instituto Tecnológico Autónomo de México (ITAM)
Río Hondo 1, 01000 México D.F.
cairo@lamport.rhon.itam.mx,
WWW home page: http://cannes.divcom.itam.mx/Osvaldo
[2] Universidad Nacional Autónoma de México (UNAM), 04510 México, D.F.
{barreiro,solsona}@mealy.fciencias.unam.mx

Abstract. We agree that even though technologies have been perfected during the last years and therefore performance of KBS has been improved, the crucial problem and bottleneck for the development of KBS remains the same: knowledge acquisition (KA), Why? In every project, experienced developers have in mind somehow a way to deal with knowledge and what steps they can follow. However, inexperienced developers want to know how to undertake the project. They need a number of good guidelines, preferably those that have proven to work well in practice. We will show it is extremely important to follow a software or knowledge engineering methodology. Nonetheless, at recent specialized conferences and workshops the following questions arise: Do we really need a methodology? Do you really believe methodologies work? We will try to offer some ideas, through the KAMET methodology, to clarify these points.

1 Introduction

We know thousands of Knowledge-Based Systems (KBS) have been applied worldwide in different knowledge domains. We agree that even though technologies have been perfected during last years and therefore performance of KBS has been improved, the crucial problem and bottleneck for the development of KBS remains the same: knowledge acquisition (KA). It is a fact. Even though last years have seen a rapid growth in capabilities in building KBS, knowledge acquisition remains the same. KA still constitutes the main factor that hamper a well controlled KBS life cycle. However, some considerations have changed since then.

First, problems in eliciting knowledge do not constitute the true bottleneck, since we do not know how to represent the implicit, detailed knowledge of a Human Expert (HE) [4]. The process whereby humans represent knowledge is not very clear yet [9]. Second, the knowledge elicited from multiple knowledge sources is in general extensive, inaccurate, incomplete, qualitative, and unordered, hence

[†] This project has been partially funded by CONACYT as project number D.A.J-J002-222-98-16-II-98 (REDII).

major problems of interpretation may arise [4]. Third, the transfer of knowledge directly from different knowledge sources to artificial machines is less organized, reliable, comprehensible, and effective than when it is represented in intermediate models. The knowledge is too rich to be transferred automatically from different knowledge sources to artificial machines. Therefore the main problem appears to be due to a lack of methods and tools for knowledge modeling [7].

1.1 Needing Methodologies

In every project, experienced developers have in mind somehow a way to deal with knowledge and what steps they can follow. However, inexperienced developers want to know how to undertake the project. They need a number of good guidelines, preferably those that have proven to work well in practice. However, at recent specialized conferences and workshops the following questions arise: Do we really need a methodology? Do you really believe methodologies work? We will try to offer some ideas to clarify these points.

Some professionals and graduate students appear to be confused regarding the necessity of using a methodology or not. Some interesting results surely confuse them. To do programs is fun for many people, someone can enjoy making things of her own design, even faster and cheaper than a large team, without following a methodology. As Boehm [3] says:

> Do not worry about that specification paperwork. We'd better hurry up and start coding, because we are going to have a whole lot of debugging to do.

Should we replace large professional teams by hackers? The answer is that we must always remember and look at what is being produced. We should take into account how much risk we are willing to take, and be aware that a failure in our decision can lead to utter chaos. Brooks [5] established the classification shown in table 1.

A programming system product can be achieved only through a methodology, is developed by a professional teamwork, and costs in most cases nine times more than a simple program. Risks are highly reduced, therefore, in the rest of the

Table 1. From a Program until a Programming System Product.

Program	Developed by hackers.
Programming Product	Developed by a professional teamwork, using a methodology.
Programming System	Collection of interacting programs, so that the assemble constitutes an entire facility for large tasks.
Programming System Product	It is a Programming System, and the intended product of most system programming efforts.

paper we will assume it is extremely important to follow a software or knowledge engineering methodology when developing a project.

2 Getting Deeper: More on Methodologies

You must invest time in selecting an appropriate methodology for the project, it is up to you how much risk you want to take. Un-commitment in taking these decisions might linger the project. On the other hand, by mastering the methodology, if it fails, you have the opportunity to adapt it. Always keep in mind the risk principle [8]:

If you do not actively attack the risks, they will actively attack you.

2.1 What Does Risk Mean?

A typical dictionary defines risk as the possibility of loss or injury. It implies that risk has two main components: the probability of some event occurring and the negative consequence if it occurs. Thus, to analyze risk we should be able to estimate these two factors. Boehm [1] translated this definition into the fundamental concept of risk management: the risk exposure, sometimes called risk impact.

$$RE = P(UO) \times L(UO) \tag{1}$$

Where RE means risk exposure, $P(UO)$ expresses the probability of an unsatisfactory outcome, and $L(UO)$ means the loss to the parties affected if the outcome is unsatisfactory.

Usually the perception of risk is higher for those items over which one have little or no control. However, the importance of the risk factors might be considered as some combination of risk frequency (that is, how likely it is that the risk will occur) and risk impact (such as, how serious a threat the risk represents if it does occur). In considering risks you must also consider their perceived level of control. This represents the degree to which the project manager perceived that their actions could prevent the risk from occurring.

Most of the probable risks or threats to projects can be reduced or avoided using an appropriate methodology. It can also be complemented with approximative methods, which can provide enough information to support risk management decisions.

2.2 Project Management Risks

Risk-reduction is a fundamental part of project management in software and knowledge engineering. Software risk management is important because it helps people to avoid disasters, rework, and overkill, it also stimulates win-win situations on software projects [1].

We should be aware that by avoiding or reducing the most significant risks, managers make more informed decisions, we obtain better outcomes, and hence the project will have a higher probability of success.

Boehm [2] suggests to use a software risk management plan, which consists of five steps:

- Identify the project's top risk items.
- Present a plan for resolving each risk item.
- Update list of top risk items, plan, and results monthly.
- Highlight risk-item status in monthly project reviews.
- Initiate appropriate corrective actions.

Successful management of a project leads to control. Control leads to quality. Quality leads to satisfied customers. And we know customers are the final arbiters of a product or service.

3   The KAMET Methodology

KBS today are still almost an art. The skillful integration of software technology, economic and human relations in the specific context of a knowledge engineering project is generally a difficult task. A KBS is a people-intensive effort that spans in most cases for a long period of time.

KA is a fundamental part of any KBS and it is considered to be a modeling activity, in which knowledge is defined as a cognitive process for which the problem to be solved becomes an artifact. As we mentioned above, KA still constitutes the main factor that hamper a well controlled KBS life cycle (see Section 1).

In this context the KAMET methodology was developed [6, 7]. It is a modeling methodology, designed to manage KA from multiple knowledge sources (KS). The method provides a strong mechanism to achieve KA in an incremental fashion, and in a cooperative environment. KAMET also integrates a variety of eliciting techniques in a coherent knowledge engineering framework.

Knowledge engineering projects need to simultaneously satisfy a variety of actors: human experts, fund sponsors, users, active knowledge sources, knowledge engineers, etc. We want to make winners of each of the parties involved in the knowledge engineering project.

3.1   Life-Cycle Model and Knowledge Integration

KAMET was inspired mainly in Boehm's spiral model [2]. It consists of four stages cyclically structured. We define models and refine them in the following stages. By the end of each stage, we have a set of models that represent the knowledge elicited from the different knowledge sources involved in the process. KAMET provides a cooperative framework that helps actors to gain deeper understanding of the models, and to mature the ideas behind them.

The project is strategically planned during the first stage. The project manager leads the team towards the construction of the initial model, in the second. A model must be built for every common working area or knowledge sub-domain, and the initial model is made of one or more of this models. This stage comprise the largest number of risks, which mainly arise because interviews involve knowledge introspection and verbal expression, resulting in a difficult task for experts. The knowledge elicitation may become monotonous and ineffective. The aforementioned problems lead to consider a certain degree of inaccuracy in the formulation of the initial model.

During the third stage of the methodology –development of the feedback model–, based on knowledge and experience, the initial model is analyzed and refined towards the creation of the feedback model. In the first round, with the aid of the DELPHI technique, the experts give their opinions, express their ideas, and solve problems about the initial models, writing mainly anonymous answers to questionnaires prepared by the knowledge engineers. KAMET does not enforce the use of any particular techniques, nonetheless for the second round, we have found useful in practice Larson's format to evaluate alternative solutions in search of the most effective and closest one to the ideal. Maier's technique is also adequate to evaluate two or more opposing ideas. This technique is very detailed and allows polarization to be diminished.

Through all the stages in the KAMET methodology, revision points are set which allow us to audit the project's current status. We must rely on metric's models developed before KA methodologies became widely-used, though. The idea behind the revision points is that all what can be measured can be improved, these also provides a strong indication that a stage is over.

3.2 Further Research

The KAMET methodology is going through a lot of changes lately. To keep the pace with today KBS, we have started modeling the stages of KAMET as building blocks, represented using the *Unified Modeling Language* (UML). This helps us measure the whole process, and provide us with useful indicators of software product quality: correctness, maintainability, and integrity.

We also encourage the use of a formal specification language during the first stage of KAMET. Because it should be noted that using a formally defined language (vocabulary, syntax and semantics) with mathematical basis, will help ensure that the software will execute within the system specification without resulting in unacceptable risk. In KAMET we use formal methods as a way to assured the program will satisfy its formal specifications, we measure the process, not the product, and this is why KAMET is also *process oriented*.

As yet, considerable work remains in adapting KAMET to new, ever-more complex environments. Clearly, more studies on metrics are called for, specially for KA methodologies.

4   General Conclusions

We have tried to show how important software methodologies are. Using a methodology is not an insurance of success, but a sign of competence and provides the means to reduce risks. Do we really need software methodologies? It is our experience developing the KAMET methodology, what leads us to strongly believe we certainly need them.

We also need and require urgently reaching an agreement concerning what should be measure and how should be measure. Knowledge engineering will remain an art while metrics and evaluation methods are not its backbone.

Concerning KAMET, the main objective is to improve the phase of knowledge acquisition and knowledge modeling process, making them more efficient and less error prone. The methodology provides a strong mechanism with which to achieve KA from multiple knowledge sources in an incremental fashion, and in a cooperative environment. KAMET is integrated with up-to-date literature, and seeks to be general.

Before making more detailed conclusions and recommendations, more studies should be perform to quantify the effects we have pointed out. Future work should examine KAMET in developing larger KBS. We also think that the principles illustrated here may have wider applicability, and should be generalized to give a deeper understanding of knowledge acquisition.

References

1. Boehm, B.: Software Risk Management. IEEE Computer Society Press. (1989)
2. Boehm, B.: A spiral model of software development and enhancement. IEEE Computers. (1988) 61-62
3. Boehm, B.: Verifying and Validating Software Requirements and Design Specification. IEEE Software. January (1984) 75-88
4. Breuker, J. and Wielinga, B.: Models of Expertise in Knowledge Acquisition. G. Guida and C. Tasso (eds). Topics in Expertise Systems Design: methodologies and tools. North Holland Publishing Company, Amsterdam. The Netherlands. (1989)
5. Brooks, F.: The Mythical Man-Month. Essays on Software Engineering Anniversary Edition. Addison-Wesley Publishing Company. (1995)
6. Cairó, O.: KAMET: A comprehensive methodology for knowledge acquisition from multiple knowledge sources. *Expert System with Applications*, 14, (1/2), (1998) 1-16
7. Cairó, O.: The KAMET Methodology: Content, Usage and Knowledge Modeling. In Gaines, B. and Mussen, M. (eds). *Proceedings of the 11th Banff Knowledge Acquisition for Knowledge-Based Systems Workshop (KAW'98)*. SRGD Publications, Department of Computer Science, University of Calgary, Proc-1, (1998) 1-20
8. Gilb, T.: Principles of Software Engineering Management. Chapter 6, Addison Wesley Publishing Company. (1998)
9. Vámos, T.: Expert Systems and the Ontology of Knowledge Representation. In Lee, J.; Liebowitz, J.& Chae, Y.(Eds). Critical Technology, Cognizant Communication Corporation, (1996) 3-12

Knowledge Acquisition of Predicate Argument Structures from Technical Texts Using Machine Learning: The System ASIUM

David Faure & Claire Nédellec

Laboratoire de Recherche en Informatique, UMR 86-23 du CNRS,
Équipe Inférence et Apprentissage,
Université Paris-Sud, bât 490, F-91405 Orsay,
{faure,cn}@lri.fr,
Tél {david, claire}: +33 (0)1.69.15.66.{07, 26}
Fax: +33 (0)1.69.15.65.86

Abstract. In this paper, we describe the Machine Learning system, ASIUM[1], which learns Subcaterorization Frames of verbs and ontologies from the syntactic parsing of technical texts in natural language. The restrictions of selection in the subcategorization frames are filled by the ontology's concepts. Applications requiring such knowledge are crucial and numerous. The most direct applications are semantic control of texts and syntactic parsing disambiguation.

This knowledge acquisition task cannot be fully automatically performed. Instead,we propose a cooperative ML method which provides the user with a global view of the acquisition task and also with acquisition tools like automatic concepts splitting, example generation, and an ontology view with attachments to the verbs. Validation steps using these features are intertwined with learning steps so that the user validates the concepts as they are learned. Experiments performed on two different corpora (cooking domain and patents) give very promising results.

Keywords: machine learning, natural language processing, ontology, predicate argument structure, corpus-based learning, clustering.

1 Introduction

Semantic knowledge acquisition from texts, such as predicate argument structures and ontologies is a crucial and difficult task and the manual acquisition is obviously long even in limited domains. New automatic methods involving both Natural Language Processing (NLP) and Machine Learning (ML) techniques ([Zelle93], among others) can give very good results in a short time. In this paper, we present ASIUM, a system that learns cooperatively from syntacticaly parsed texts without manual annotations, ontologies and subcategorization frames of verbs (*SF*) for specific domains following the principle of "domain dependence"[2] [Grefenstette92]. Subcategorization frames represent here a subcase of predicate argument structures where the predicate is restricted to a verb.

---

[1] Acquisition of SemantIc knowledge Using Machine learning methods.
[2] "*A semantic structure developed for one domain would not be applicable to another*".

ASIUM is based on an original unsupervised conceptual clustering method and, although the process cannot be fully automatized, provides interactive features in order to support the knowledge acquisition task.

We will show here how ASIUM is able to learn knowledge of good quality from possibly noisy texts and how ASIUM's cooperative features, together with its inductive capabilities, allow to acquire ontologies and *SF* in reasonable time[3].

2 Our approach

We attempt to acquire *SF* and ontologies from texts for texts control purposes for DASSAULT AVIATION company. Initially, we attempted to automatically revise and complete *SF* of a draft ontology manually acquired by a domain expert. This attemp failed for two main reasons: first the expert has too many a priori on the texts and second, he used incremental method to acquire the ontology. Revision of the acquired knowledge with respect to the training texts required profond reorganization of the ontology that incremental and even cooperative ML revision methods were not able to handle: it was locally consistent, but any revision leads to deeply restructuring it. This experiment illustrates one of the limitations of manual acquisition by domain experts without linguists and the need for knowledge acquisition tools.

Our aim is to *learn SF* and an ontology because no such bases were available. The few existing bases are too general and thus incomplete (EUROWORDNET or WORDNET). In a specific domain, the vocabulary as well as its possible usage are reduced, which makes such ontologies overly general. On the other hand, they may lack some specific terminology of the application domain.

As opposed to the approach consisting of completing and specializing general ontologies for specific domains as [Basili97] with WORDNET, the targeted approach we have chosen, even for English, is to learn suitable knowledge from a representative corpus of the domain, thus avoiding inconsistency risks.

3 Knowledge learned

ASIUM learns verb *SF* and *ontologies*. Here is an example of a *SF* for the verb to inject: `<to inject> <object: combustible> <in: furnace>`.

The two couples `<object: combustible>` and `<in: furnace>` are the *subcategories* of the verb to inject; object is a *syntactic role* and in is a preposition introducing an adjunct while combustible and furnace are their *restrictions of selection*. More generally a *SF* as ASIUM learns it, has the following form: `<verb> <syntactic role|preposition: concept*>*`.

The subcategories are arguments and adjuncts of the verb. In our framework, restrictions of selection (*RS*) can be filled with an exhaustive list of nouns (in canonical form) or by one or more *concepts* defined in

---

[3] About ten hours for the cooking domain of about 3 Mo of texts and 1120 verbs.

an ontology, where the meaning of the concepts is characterized by the *SF* they appear in. The ontology represents *generality relations* between concepts in the form of a directed acyclic graph. The axioms only express subsumption (IS-A) relationships between unary predicates or concepts. For instance, the ontology could define `fuel`, `gaz` and `carbon` as `combustible`, and `carbon` as both `combustible` and `burning wastes`. Our method learns such an ontology and *SF* in a cooperative and unsupervised (in the ML sense) manner from texts.

4 Overview of the method

The method implemented in the ASIUM system is included in a knowledge acquisition chain. It consists of the syntactic parser SYLEX [Constant95] providing ASIUM with all interpretations[4] of parsed sentences including attachments of noun phrases[5] to verbs and clauses, without any pre or postprocessing.

As a first step, ASIUM automatically extracts *instantiated subcategorization frames* from the syntactic parsing of clauses. The *instantiated SF* is similar to a *SF* but the *RS* are the actual head nouns occurring in the clause instead of concepts: `<verb> <prep. | syntactic role: head noun>*`.

Preliminary experiments show that instantiated *SF* are sufficient with respect to the learning task and that the ML method is robust with respect to parsing ambiguities or even failures.

The learning method relies on the observation of syntactic regularities in the context of words [Harris68]. We assume here that head nouns occuring with the same couple `verb+preposition/syntactic role` represent a so-called *basic class* and have a semantic similarity in the same line as [Grefenstette92], [Peat91] or others, but our method is based on a *double regularity model*: ASIUM gathers nouns together as representing a concept only if they share at least *two different* (`verb+preposition/syntactic role`) contexts as in [Grishman94]. Experiments show that it forms more reliable concepts, thus requiring less involvement from the user. Our similarity measure computes the overlap between two lists of nouns[6] (Details in [Faure98]). As usual in conceptual clustering, the validity of the concepts learned relies on the quality of the similarity measure between clusters which here increases with the size of their intersection.

Basic classes are then successively aggregated by a bottom-up breadth-first conceptual clustering method to form the concepts of the ontology level by level with expert validation and/or labelling at each level. Thus a given cluster cannot be used in a new construction before it has been validated. For complexity reasons, the number of clusters to be aggregated is restricted to two, but this does not affect the relevance of the learned concept as shown in [Faure98]. Verb *SF* are learned in

---

[4] In case of ambiguity, ASIUM takes all of them.

[5] Nouns phrases are reduced to head nouns (stopwords and adjectives are removed).

[6] $Sim(C_1, C_2) = 1$ for lists with the same nouns and $Sim(C_1, C_2) = 0$ for lists without any common nouns.

parallel so that each new concept fills the corresponding *RS* then resulting in the generalization of the initial synthetic frames which allows to cover examples which *did not occur* as such in texts. Thus, the clustering process does not only identify the lists of nouns occuring after the same `verb+preposition/function` but also augments this list by *induction*.

For example, from those instantiated *SF*, `<to travel> <subject: [father,neighbor,friend]><by:[car,train]>` and `<to drive> <subject: [friend,colleague]> <object: [car,motor-bike]>`, ASIUM learns both concepts `<Human>`, `<Motorized vehicle>` defined as `father,neighbor,friend,colleague` and `car,train,motor-bike` and both *SF*, `<to travel> <subject: Human> <by: Motorized vehicle>` and `<to drive> <subject: Human> <object: Motorized vehicle>`.

The risk of over-generalization is controlled both by a clustering threshold and the user. Concept learning could not be fully automated since the attachment of the concepts learned as *RS* of verbs must be validated by an expert in order to limit the risk of over-generality that the clustering threshold cannot completely avoid. Thus concept formation is intertwined with cooperative validation steps where the domain expert assesses and refines the learning results on line if needed, given acquisition tools like automatic concepts splitting, examples generation and ontology view with attachments to the verbs.

5 Experimentations

ASIUM has been applied first on a cooking recipe corpora in French with the aim of applying it to maintenance texts at DASSAULT AVIATION for language control purposes. Second, we have applied ASIUM on Oxy-fuel burner (a specific kind of burner using oxidants) patents for technical watch.

Evaluation of the unsupervised learned knowledge quality is a very difficult problem for which we have currently no solutions, but only highlights. First, ASIUM is included in a chain. Its efficiency could be partially measured by the utility and the improvement of the final task performance but once an error has been identified in the final output, locating the original faulty component is difficult in case an intermediate evaluation is not possible. Second, evaluating the cooperative system independently of the user is difficult. Third, the results of the learning process should be evaluated with respect to the quantity[7] and the nature of the user's work using counters on each type of action[8]. Counters will only give a partial view on the quality of the learned knowledge and the quality of the interaction tools and should be completed. Other evaluations of the quality of the results regarding redundancy of the corpora and of the induction effect in terms of completeness have been done in [Faure98]. They should be completed by correctness measures. As no negative example is available,

---

[7] Duration of the cooperative process regarding time needed in order to learn the same knowledge by hand.

[8] For instance, how many irrevelant inductions did the user refuse?

the measure of (verb+preposition/function+noun) induced from a training set and *not useful in a test set* could be a good indicator of correctness.

An evaluation of ASIUM results, done independently from a final application can not give a final answer to the evaluation question, only hits. For instance, the ontologies and *SF* learned could be compared to other lexicons but it would not only require the measurement of the similarity [Shaw89] but also the nature of the difference in case of a discrepancy.

6 Related Work

As proposed by [Hindle90] and [Pereira93], our method clusters nouns on the basis of syntactic regularities but without restricting the syntactic roles to be learned from subjects and objects. Our claim is that in technical domains the verbs are not only characterized by their arguments. Compared to [Grefenstette92], or [Bourigault96], ASIUM exploits two levels of regularities in the context instead of one. In ASIUM this would amount to learning basic classes as concepts which is obviously not suitable. [Brent91] learns the *SF* from large corpora from untagged texts with an automatic approach and focuses on learning five given *SF*. [Buchholz98] learns *SF* comparable to the ones learned by ASIUM with a supervised approach which is very time-consuming for the expert. In the same framework, WOLFIE [Thompson95] coupled with CHILL [Zelle93], learns case-roles and a lexicon from semantically annotated corpora by hand. Case-roles differ from *SF* as learned by ASIUM in that prepositions and syntactic roles are replaced by semantic roles such as agent or patient. Such information allows one to distinguish among the different semantic roles of given prepositions. As opposed to ASIUM ontology, the *RS* learned by WOLFIE are lists of attribute-values defining the concepts. Moreover WOLFIE requires that the input sentences parsed by CHILL are all annotated by semantic labels (roles and restrictions). Unsupervised learning, as in ASIUM, delays concept labeling after learning, thus reducing considerably the end-user task. In the same way, semantic roles could be labeled once ASIUM learns the *SF* by assuming that different restrictions (couples syntactic role/preposition+concept) reflect different semantic roles.

7 Conclusion

In this paper, we have presented a cooperative ML system, ASIUM, which is able to acquire subcategorization frames with restrictions of selection and ontology for specific domains from syntactically parsed technical texts in natural language. Texts and parsing may be noisy. The knowledge acquisition task is based on an original unsupervised clustering method. Needed expert validation and adjustment are supported by cooperative tools giving the expert a global and manageable view on the whole corpus helping him to integrate the needed domain knowledge that would not appear in the corpus.

Preliminary experiments on corpora of cooking recipes in French, and patents in English, have shown the applicability of the method to texts in restricted and technical domains and the usefulness of the cooperative approach for such knowledge acquisition.

Further work will address evaluation aspects and semantic classes of verb learning from *SF* and ontologies.

Acknowledgement: This work is partially supported by the CEC through the ESPRIT contract LTR 20237 (ILP 2).

References

[Basili97]   R. Basili and M. T. Pazienza. Lexical Acquisition for Information Extraction. In Maria Teresa Pazienza, editor, *Information Extraction: A Multidisciplinary Approach to an Emerging Information Technology*, pages 14–18, Frascati, Italy, July 1997. LNAI Tutorial, Springer.

[Bourigault96]   D. Bourigault, I. Gonzalez-Mullier, and C. Gros. LEXTER, a Natural Language Processing Tool for Terminology Extraction. In *7th EURALEX International Congress*, Göteborg, August 1996.

[Brent91]   M. R. Brent. Automatic acquisition of subcategorization frames from untagged text. In *Proceedings of the 29st annual meeting of the Association for Computational Linguistics, ACL*, pages 209–214, 1991.

[Buchholz98]   S. Buchholz. Distinguishing Complements from Adjuncts using Memory-Based Learning. In *Proceedings of the ESSLLI'98 workshop on Automated Acquisition of Syntax and Parsing*, 1998.

[Constant95]   P. Constant. L'analyseur Linguistique SYLEX. In *5ème École d'été du CNET*, 1995.

[Faure98]   D. Faure and C. Nédellec. A Corpus-based Conceptual Clustering Method for Verb Frames and Ontology Acquisition. In Paola Velardi, editor, *LREC workshop on Adapting lexical and corpus ressources to sublanguages and applications*, pages 5–12, Granada, Spain, May 1998.

[Grefenstette92]   G. Grefenstette. Sextant: exploring unexplored contexts for semantic extraction from syntactic analysis. In *Proceedings of the 30st annual meeting of the Association for Computational Linguistics, ACL*, 1992. 14-18.

[Grishman94]   R. Grishman and J. Sterling. Generalizing Automatically Generated Selectional Patterns. *Proceedings of COLING '94 15th International Conference on Computational Linguistics, Kyoto, Japan*, August 1994.

[Harris68]   Z. Harris. *Mathematical Structures of Language*. New York: Wiley, 1968.

[Hindle90]   D. Hindle. Noun classification from predicate-argument structures. In *Proceedings of the 28st annual meeting of the Association for Computational Linguistics, ACL, Pittsburgh, PA*, pages 1268–1275, 1990.

[Peat91]   H.J. Peat and P. Willet. The limitations of term co-occurrence data for query expansion in document retrieval systems. *Journal of the American Society for Information Science*, 42(5):378–383, 1991.

[Pereira93]   F. Pereira, N. Tishby, and L. Lee. Distributional Clustering of English Words. In *Proceedings of the 31st annual meeting of the Association for Computational Linguistics, ACL*, pages 183–190, 1993.

[Shaw89]   M.L.G. Shaw and B. R. Gaines. Comparing conceptual structures: consensus, conflict, correspondence and contrast. In *Knowledge Acquisition*, volume 1, pages 341–363, 1989.

[Thompson95]   C. A. Thompson. Acquisition of a Lexicon from Semantic Representations of Sentences. In *33rd Annual Meeting of the Association of Computational Linguistics, Boston, MA July, (ACL-95).*, pages 335–337, 1995.

[Zelle93]   J. M. Zelle and R. J. Mooney. Learning semantic grammars with constructive inductive logic programming. *Proceedings of the Eleventh National Conference on Artificial Intelligence*, pages 817–822, 1993.

An Interoperative Environment for Developing Expert Systems

Noriaki Izumi, Akira Maruyama,
Atsuyuki Suzuki, Takahira Yamaguchi

Shizuoka University
3-5-1 Johoku Hamamatsu Shizuoka 432-8011 Japan

Abstract. This paper proposes the interoperation environment which enables an expert system to get information available to improve its performance from others. First, we have given a method library of reusable templates in order to provide a correspondence between specification and implementation of inference structures. Next, a cooperation method has been presented, using the difference arising in the context of the correspondence between inference primitives of an originator and those of recipients. The wrapper with conversion facilities has been also provided, using a common domain ontology developed manually. After designing and implementing such an interoperation environment, experiments have been done among four heterogeneous expert systems. Furthermore, it has been shown that an expert system finds a way to perform a given task better by the interoperation with other three expert systems.

1 Introduction

As expert systems have been built up in many real fields over the past decade, the research on Cooperative Distributed Expert Systems (CDES) has emerged, integrating two kinds of technology from knowledge acquisition and software agents. The work in the field of CDES focuses on the cooperation among distributed expert systems but has not yet been getting into cooperation in real complex domains at a semantic level.

In order to develop a cooperative knowledge system as industrial applications in real and large scale, at present, few attentions are payed for knowledge level analysis and knowledge modeling. As seen in the fields of software agents and CDES, we are still in shallow interoperation just at a syntactic level among distributed heterogeneous expert systems. Even if useful information is acquired, there is a significant issue how the information is reflected in the implimentation-sturacture of knowledge systems. Thus, in this paper, we propose an environment for deep interoperation among four heterogeneous expert systems at a semantic level, modeling them at a proper level of granularity of knowledge, defining the relationship between models and implementations, using the difference arising in the context of the correspondence between the inference structure of an originator and the one of recipients, and presenting a wrapper with conversion facilities using a common domain ontology.

In the remainder of this paper, we first describe methods of modeling, operationalizing, cooperating and communicating (wrapping) heterogeneous expert systems. Next, we put the methods together into an interoperative environment, INDIES(an Interoperative eNvironment for Development and Improvement for Expert Systems) for them. The empirical results have shown us that a financial management expert system is supported by other three expert systems in finding a better solution.

2 Modeling and Implementing Expert Systems

In order for distributed expert systems to exchange useful information applicable to their better performance from others, the information about inference engines and knowledge bases, must be lifted from the implementation details to some proper conceptual details. In the field of knowledge engineering, the methodology has recently been developed to specify the semantics of expert systems free from implementation details.

Common KADS[1] is one of the well-organized knowledge libraries that provides inference primitives called canonical functions, such as Select, Compare, Merge and so on. We rebuild and extends canonical functions into "REPOSIT (REusable Pieces Of Specification-Implementation Templates)" which combines declarative semantics employed in Common KADS and procedural semantics like Prolog.

Each method of REPOSIT, as an inference primitive, has two types of expressions: one is the relationship among input, output and reference knowledge, which consists of a specification library, and the other is a prolog-based representation which consists of an implementation library. In REPOSIT framework, rectangles express methods corresponding to inference primitives and quarter-circles express knowledge as data used in the connected methods(Fig. 1. (a)).

To reflect a received information on their implementation, REPOSIT supports step by step operationalization of abstract models into detailed implementation descriptions from the following standpoint:

a) providing refinement policies,
b) standardizing the knowledge (data) management,
c) classifying the adding patterns of control structures.

In order to refine REPOSIT specifications, expressed as knowledge-flow-diagram (combination of methods and knowledge), we replace an abstract method with combinations of methods as follows:

1. dividing a method into data-type judgements and a function definition,
2. refining a method into combinations of fine-grained methods, and
3. replacing an operation for a set with the repetition of an operation for its element.

After applying the refinement rules described above, we augment a knowledge-flow-diagram with control structures, such as conditional branches, a distinction of deterministic and non-deterministic actions, and repetitions. To put it con-

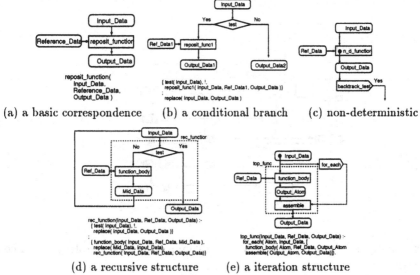

(a) a basic correspondence   (b) a conditional branch   (c) non-deterministic

(d) a recursive structure   (e) a iteration structure

Fig. 1. REPOSIT Expressions

crete, we replace an abstract method with fine-grained methods in the following procedure:

(a) adding conditional (Fig. 1. (b)),

(b) clarifying non-deterministic actions (Fig. 1. (c)), and

(c) developing loop structures (Fig. 1. (d)(e)).

After applying the above augmentation, we can get a prolog-based description corresponding to the augmented knowledge-flow-diagrams, which is available for implementation. To put the description executable, we give a data structre, consisting of atoms and lists as data primitives. In order to employ a name of knowledge in the specification directly, we define the primitive expressions of knowledge, which support a generic method of data-call-by-name as follows:

$$\text{atom}(\text{Atom\_id}, [\text{Cat}_1 : \text{Val}_1, ..., \text{Cat}_n : \text{Val}_n]), \tag{1}$$

$$\text{list}(\text{List\_id}, [\text{Atom}_1, \text{Atom}_2, ..., \text{Atom}_n]), \tag{2}$$

$$\text{alias}(\text{Alias\_name}, \text{Atom\_id\_or\_List\_id})). \tag{3}$$

In the above formulas, Atom_id and List_id represent entities consisting knowledge, and Alias_name corresponds the name of the entities

After given a data structure, a prolog-based description of specification can be refined into the prolog-implementation codes by using REPOSIT library for implementation, as in the same way of the specification-refinement.

3 Interoperating Distributed Expert Systems

3.1 Cooperation for Distributed Expert Systems

In order to interoperate expert systems, we employ a specification-sharing(SS)-based cooperation, called assisted coordination[2]. The shared specification comes

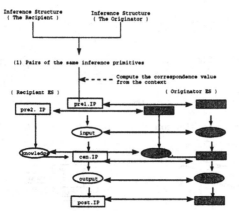

Fig. 2. A message generation facility

from REPOSIT library which serves as a common method ontology and a common domain ontology.

Although one expert system (originator) can get the information about capabilities of the other expert system (recipient) through the shared specification, it is important to identify the information available to (be able to) improve the originator. Because it costs too much to find out differences in extensive range to the whole inference structure, we adopt only the difference arising in the small context of correspondence between inference primitive of an originator and those of a recipient.

A method to find out the difference, arising between an originator and a recipient, is presented (Fig. 2) as follows:

1. Making a set of correspondence in which inference primitives are the same
2. computing a correspondence value by taking a look at the context of the inference primitive,
3. propagating the correspondence value to pre- and post- inference primitives,
4. completing propagation over all inference primitives,
5. picking up a difference with the values, which will be used as a reply message.

3.2 Communication between Expert Systems

When one expert system finds a fault in itself(for example, when its output was wrong or rejected by a user), it asks other expert systems to support it in changing for a better performance.

Because each expert system is modeled by its own vocabulary, it needs a conversion facility so that it can understand the messages sent from other expert systems. This paper calls a wrapper the module to convert one message from one expert system into another message that can be processed in the other expert system. When it is communicated between an originator and a recipient, originator's wrapper uses a common domain ontology to convert the reply messages from recipients.

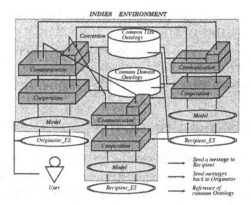

Fig. 3. An Overview of INDIES

Table 1. The Number of messages generated by interoperation

	Troubleshooting	Scheduling	EV-design	Total
1st	14	14	19	47
2nd	15	15	19	49

The originator tries to reflect a selected message on its own implementation. When it fails the reflection, the developers manually change the implementations of the originator based on the selected message. If the same fault still exists, or another fault comes up, when the modified originator's performance is tested, the above-mentioned interoperation process is repeated and another reply message is given to the originator until the originator's performance improves or the recipients send no reply message.

4 INDIES Implementation and Experimental Results

As the methods of modeling, operationalizing, cooperating and communicating (wrapping) distributed expert systems come up, we put them together into an interoperation environment for distributed expert systems INDIES(Fig. 3). INDIES has been implemented by SWI-Prolog ver. 2.9.6 with XPCE ver. 4.9.7.

Experiments have been done to how the financial management expert system FIMCOES[3](originator) is supported by a troubleshooting, an electric power management job scheduling and an elevator design expert systems through the interoperation in INDIES. Afterwards, the originator gets into INDIES, and sends its models and correspondence value desired (24 in this experiment) to the other three expert systems (recipients).

At the first interoperation, the originator received 47 reply messages from other three recipients(Table 1.). According to the selected message 'ADD "Propagate using an enterprise model" ', the new inference primitive of "propagate using an enterprise model" has been put just before "compare" primitive in FIMCOES inference structure. After implementing a new FIMCOES with the modification, we found that the modified FIMCOES had 4.7% performance gain compared to the original FIMCOES.

At the second interoperation, the originator received 49 reply messages from other three recipients (Table 1). Further examination showed that two messages, brought 11.1% performance gain to FIMCOES but other reply messages not.

5 Related Work and Discussions

In the field of CDES, much work focuses on strategies of unifying solutions that include uncertainty from multiple expert systems that use different representation of uncertainty. However, few systems try to deal with the management of semantics, at present.

On the other hand, R.Dieng's work [4] manages issues in cooperative knowledge-based systems. The specification to interoperate knowledge-based systems from the point of multi-agent systems has been analyzed, but not yet launched into full implementations and evaluation in real task-domains, as shown here.

As compared with our previous work[5] without REPOSIT, more than two weeks are needed as a cost of reflecting received messages in the originator's implementation, while REPOSIT reduces the cont into at most two days.

In the remainder of this paper, we have described the methods of modeling, operationalizing, cooperating and communicating distributed expert systems. Then, these methods have been put together into an interoperative environment INDIES. The experiment results have shown that the interoperation works on the four heterogeneous expert systems.

Message generation and selection facilities are still static. So, we are investigating various types of making correspondence and checking applicapabilities about the messages exchanged. Furthermore, we will pay much more attention to automatic construction of a common domain ontology.

References

1. Breuker, J., Van de Velde, W.: Common KADS Library for Expertise Modeling. IOS Press (1994)
2. Genesereth, M.R., Ketchpcl, S.P.: Software Agents. CACM.**37** (1994) 48–53
3. Garcia, P. V. D., Yamaguchi, T.: A Financial Management Consultation Expert System with Constraint Satisfaction and Knowledge Refinement. The Third Pacific Rim International Conference on Artificial Intelligence. (1994) 979-985
4. Dieng, R.: Agent-Based Method for Building a Cooperative Knowledge-Based System. Workshop on Heterogeneous Cooperative Knowledge-Bases.International Symposium on Fifth Generation Computer Systems (1994) 237–251
5. Yamaguchi, T.: DESIRE: An Interoperative Environment for Distributed Expert Systems. ECAI'98 Wrokshop on Applications of Ontologies and Problem-Solving Methods. (1998) 120-125

On the Use of Meaningful Names in Knowledge-Based Systems

M.G. Jansen and P. Beys

Department of Social Science Informatics, University of Amsterdam
Roetersstraat 15, 1018 WB Amsterdam, The Netherlands
Tel: +20 525 6795; Email: jansen@swi.psy.uva.nl

1 Introduction

In contemporary Knowledge Engineering (KE) the emphasis lies on the study of the description of two types of artefacts: Problem Solving Methods (PSMs) and ontologies. According to many authors (for example (Motta, 1998), (Schreiber *et al.*, 1999)) PSMs have a strong relation to a certain task or problem type. One reason for this is the recognition of what is known as the interaction problem (Bylander & Chandrasekaran, 1988). This states that a reasoning strategy cannot be described without knowing on what domain knowledge it will be applied, and, vice versa, that domain knowledge cannot be represented without knowing for what reasoning task it will be used.

Since the task always has some influence on the way knowledge is represented, a PSM is always related to a task and poses some requirements on the domain knowledge it uses. This is mirrored in the notion of *assumption* (Benjamins *et al.*, 1996). It is used to describe the interaction between a method, a task and domain knowledge in order to keep them separated as much as possible and so facilitate their potential for reuse.

Another way of describing PSMs is by describing their functionality. In such descriptions the requirements of a PSM on the domain knowledge it uses are strictly formal. In this sense the semantics of a PSM can be described much like a computer program.

However the relation a PSM has with the task it should be used for is often left implicit. The way this is often done is by using names in the description of the PSM which forces an interpretation upon humans but not machines. One of the disadvantages of such names is their lack of formal semantics which results in their being redundant in functional descriptions. From a formal point of view it is not clear that a method has a relation to a specific task. Indeed, one could ask whether a given method when considered abstractly could not be used for totally different tasks, at least in theory. (The notion of PSMs being task-neutral as put forward by Beys and van Someren (Beys *et al.*, 1996) reflects this idea.) Without the use of these names however it is often difficult to relate a method and the representation of domain knowledge to a task or problem type. It will be argued here to make this interpretation explicit by using ontologies. The practical implications of such an enterprise will not be elaborated upon and are in need of further study.

This paper is structured as follows: First, in section 2 the redundancy of meaningful names in abstract descriptions is discussed. They however play an important part in what is defined here as knowledge. Section 3 and 4 are used to describe the role of meaningful names in PSMs. Section 3 contains a sketchy introduction in describing the semantics of PSMs. It is followed by an example of a description of C&D in Section 4. The point here to be made is that meaningful names are redundant in the description of the semantics of the method. Section 5 contains a suggested solution which is about ontologies. Finally a conclusion, questions and answers are presented.

2 Meaningful names in knowledge representation

Let us first be clear what we mean by knowledge in this paper. Without going into a philosophical discussion knowledge is taken here to be any a posteriori contingency. This means that any statement which represents a possible state of affairs in the world, which is sometimes true and sometimes false is regarded as knowledge. Tautologies, such as *"it rains or it doesn't rain"* and contradictions do not fall under this definition. Note that mathematical and logical theorems which can be proved within an axiomatic system are tautologies. All axioms are tautologies by definition and any theorem derived from them is also a tautology. Of course such a viewpoint on the nature of knowledge is open for debate, but we will not elaborate upon it here.

A second assumption on the nature of knowledge is that a sentence must go with an interpretation. For example a proposition p which can be true or false doesn't suffice as knowledge. It must be knowledge of something, or to put it another way it must go together with some interpretation. It must be clear what p denotes.

In order to illustrate why these assumptions are important a small system is presented in Example 1. It consists of a number of facts which are of all the form isa(X, Y). In a very simple way it represents what is generally known as an *isa-hierarchy*. Under the header of FACTS a number of statements are listed followed by a very simple procedure which checks whether a statement of the form isa(X, Y) can be unified with an element from the transitive closure of the isa relationship.

```
FACTS:
isa(mammal, animal).
isa(bird, animal).
isa(reptile, animal).
isa(cat, mammal).
INFERENCE:
Input:  isa(X,Y).
Output: True or False.
Precondition: X or Y are variables or constants.
Postcondition: True iff the input can be unified with
an element of the transitive closure of the isa relation.
   False otherwise.
```

Example 1

An important point to make here is that nothing guarantees us that a fact like isa(mammal, animal) is indeed a representation of the knowledge that a mammal is an animal. To put it another way: it lacks semantics.

The implicit assumption when using such statements is that the reader, or the user of a system like the one in Example 1 is familiar with the intended meaning of the names being used. It is difficult to make this assumption explicit. Still, it may be of vital importance for the reuse and maintenance of knowledge represented in some form or other.

To appreciate this remark compare the system in Example 1 to an isomorphic copy in Example 2. From our assumptions regarding the nature of knowledge it follows that the system in Example 2 is devoid of knowledge about the world. We do not know what r(c1,c2) denotes but we have a pretty good idea about the denotation of isa(mammal, animal). Still, the systems are isomorphic which means that in a predicate logic they can not be distinguished. To put it another way: A computer doesn't matter whether it gets to execute system 1 or 2, they are just the same.

These two systems might be identical to a computer, they are not to us. What we see in Example 2 can be described as the skeleton, the *form without content*. In Example 1 the system has *content*: it contains knowledge about the world.

This problem is essential for what we would like to call knowledge-based systems. A system which has a list of facts which uses non-meaningful names does not represent any knowledge at all. At least not in the way we have defined knowledge here. It is concerned mainly with *form* not *content* (see (Sowa, 1997)).

```
FACTS:
r(c1, c2).
r(c3, c2).
r(c4, c2).
r(c5, c1).
INFERENCE:
Input:  r(X,Y).
Output: True or False.
Precondition:  X or Y are variables or constants.
Postcondition:  True iff the input can be unified with
an element of the transitive closure of the r relation.
 False otherwise.
```

Example 2

3 Semantics of PSMs

According to the CommonKADS methodology (Schreiber *et al.*, 1999) a PSM consists of a number of inferences with a control structure. The method aims at realizing the goal of a particular type of problem, like diagnosis, planning, assessment, etc. The inferences describe the lowest level of functional decomposition in the knowledge model. They each carry out a primitive reasoning step and as such can be considered as a program or procedure of which the internal structure is hidden.

Benjamins *et al* (Benjamins *et al.*, 1996) view the architecture of a PSM as consisting of functional specifications, requirements and operational specifications. Here *functional specification* means a declarative description of the in- output relation of the PSM. In general such a specification should describe what a software artefact does, independent from how this behaviour is achieved (Fensel, 1995). Here we'll follow this line of description with some minor modifications. Instead of input- output relations we use pre- and post-conditions as described by Dijkstra (Dijkstra, 1976). A very brief introduction into some main concepts is given here.

We assume that a PSM can be regarded as a program. It has input arguments and passes through a sequence of states. The first state the PSM is in is called the initial state, successful execution (termination) will leave the PSM in the so-called final state. The post-condition imposes (as its name says) a condition on the final state. It is just a predicate which describes what the final state should look like after computation. Assuming that a PSM is deterministic (every state has only one successor) and R is a post-condition there are three possibilities:

Activation of the PSM will lead to a state satisfying R.

Activation of the PSM will lead to a state satisfying non-R.

Activation of the PSM will not lead to a final state; it doesn't terminate.

The condition which characterizes all initial states such that activation of the PSM certainly results in a final state satisfying a given postcondition R is said to be the weakest pre-condition corresponding to that post-condition. The extension of the weakest pre-condition is thus the set of all initial states which are guaranteed to result to a desired final state after execution of the PSM.

In the next section the PSM Cover & Differentiate will be looked at.

4   A brief description of Cover & Differentiate

Cover & Differentiate is a PSM for diagnostic tasks. The reasoning part of the method consists, as the name indicates, of two main steps: A *cover* inference step in which potential explanations for symptoms are generated and a step called *differentiate* which confirms or rejects explanations. The main knowledge structure C&D works upon is called a *causal network*. In what follows the description of Schreiber et al (Schreiber *et al.*, 1993) will be used.

As said before C&D operates on a *causal network*. Each node in the network represents a *state* concept and is linked to others by a binary relation with the name *causes*. Initial nodes represent causes, final nodes symptoms and intermediate nodes denote internal states. The concept of *qualifier* is used to confirm or reject potential causes or states within the network. This is done by means of a binary relation called *manifestations*.

The inference structure which achieves the reasoning mechanism of C&D consists of two inference steps:

1. For each observed symptom, a set of potential explanations is generated, causally linked as specified in the causal network. This step is achieved by the so-called *cover* inference.

2. Each potential explanation resulting from the previous inference is analyzed and subsequently either confirmed or rejected by means of a *differentiate* step. This step consists of several inferences which will only be discussed briefly here. For more details about these the reader is referred to (Schreiber *et al.*, 1993).

Cover Inference

The cover inference is stated as follows: An explanation S_2 for a state S_1 is marked as considered when S_2 possibly causes S_1, i.e. when $causes(S_2, S_1)$.

Anticipate Inference

The anticipate inference is the first of a number of inferences that make up the differentiate step. It states that if a state S_1 is considered as an explanation for a state S_2 and S_1 always causes another state S_3 then S_3 should be true as well. In this case S_1 is accepted as explanation for S_2 and S_3, otherwise it is rejected.

Prefer & Rule Out

These inferences state that considered explanations which have a positive or negative qualifier attached to them are preferred, ruled out respectively, if the qualifier is observed. States which are preferred are being accepted as explanations, those which are ruled rejected.

In order to describe the post-condition for this method properly we have to introduce some vocabulary. The PSM will need two sorts of input which can simply be described as sets. A set O of observed symptoms (being a subset of a set off all possible symptoms) and a set Q of observed qualifiers. The causal network will be described as a graph $G = (R, V)$, where R represents the transitive causes relation and V the nodes in the network. (Actually we must make clear here which nodes are symptoms, states, explanations and qualifiers. Also note that there are two relations in the example causal network. We skip the technicalities which smoothen such details.)

The desired post-condition for $\text{PSM}_{c\&d}(O, Q)$ should look something like this:

There is a c which is an explanation of the observed symptoms O iff

c causes s

if *c causes s/* then *s/* $\in O$, for all *s/*.

if *c causes s* and *c/ causes s* and only is linked to an observed qualifier then *c/* does not explain *s*

About the pre-condition we can form some idea as well. For all input sets as described the PSM could give the result described in the post-condition. [1] Note that both the graph and the input are kept invariant; they do not change during the execution of the program and are true in every state.

Of course this description is far from being formal, but it is presented here just to give some idea what the pre- and post-condition should look like.

The reason for giving this expose here is to make a point about using meaningful names. Note that in the description of the post-condition *causes* is still being used, while we could have used any symbol. In fact from a formal point of view there is nothing causal to this relation. The same holds for what we have called symptoms, qualifiers etc. These are just names which could be replaced without loss of functionality by other names, provided that every occurrence of a name is replaced by its substitute.

---

[1] If there is no explanation for some observed symbols then both sides of the iff-statement in the post-condition are false.

But if we don't use the name *causes* how do we know it is a causal network? And if we don't know if we're dealing with a causal network how do we know if we can use the method for diagnosis? To generalize these questions: If you replace meaningful names describing a PSM (and since we have considered a PSM to be similar to a program or algorithm we have every right to do so) how do you know to which task it is related? Who tells us that the same PSM after substitution with other names can not be used for different tasks?

It is not difficult to show that the same $PSM_{c\&d}$ can be used for other purposes. If we replace *causes* by *has_feature*, *symptoms* by *descriptions of attributes* and *states* by *objects* and *attributes* we can use it for classification. By lack of space we must leave it to the reader to verify this claim, using the provisory pre- and post-conditions described above.

5 The need for ontologies

The problem described here is that any functional description only refers to logical *form*, not *content* and one can always find a different interpretation where the form is preserved but the content changed. If knowledge (in the sense it is defined above) is represented it always should come with an interpretation. This interpretation is almost always given *implicitly* by the use of meaningful names. What we have tried to make clear is that from a theoretical point of view this is not correct. The practical implication this might have is also hinted upon. By making use of meaningful names a PSM is related to a certain task, but the possibility of using it for other tasks not thought of remains totally obscure. By separating the interpretation of the PSM from what we called its abstract *form* this should be overcome.

A way of making such interpretations *explicit* should be looked for. The rudimentary answer proposed here is the use of ontologies.

The construction of ontologies should provide knowledge-based systems with content (Sowa, 1997). In fact ontologies can be used to make an intended interpretation for meaningful names more explicit. This can be done very similar to the way a sentence in first order logic is given semantics.

To illustrate this point consider an interpretation of the sentence isa(cat, mammal) in first order logic.

As domain we take the set $\{cat, mammal\}$.[2]

The characteristic function ϕ for isa will be as follows: $\phi(cat, mammal) = 1$, $\phi(cat, cat) = 1, \phi(mammal, mammal) = 1, \phi(mammal, cat) = 0$.

The denotation of cat: cat.

The denotation of mammal: mammal.

Similarly a functional description of a method and the data-structure it operates upon can be given semantics with the help of an ontology. The abstract non-logical symbols in the description of a method can be given an interpretation by linking them to an ontology. In this way the functional description is provided with content. And what

---

[2]Of course the elements of this domain set are not mere symbols but their denotation, the actual concept of cat and mammal. Note that one can easily give other interpretations of the constants cat and mammal and that a computer will not care which interpretation one chooses.

is even more important: The functional abstract description of the method is completely separated from the intended interpretation.

It is the primary purpose of an ontology to provide the semantics of the names in a knowledge-based system. In this sense ontologies can be seen as meta-level theories. They provide the interpretations or content of a knowledge-based system.

The description of a PSM should therefore consists of two parts. First a functional, formal description of the method is needed. This should not contain any meaningful names at all, for they are, as has been shown, redundant.

Second, the abstract symbolism of the functional description should be mapped onto an ontology, or to put it another way: The ontology should be mapped onto the functional description. This should give the structure its semantics by actually providing an intended interpretation. In a sense the empy structure can be regarded to be task-neutral, only when mapped to an ontology becomes a method related to a task.

6 Possible criticism and conclusion

Meaningful names play an important role in knowledge-based systems. They are mainly used to represent knowledge about the world. It has been argued here that the assumption that the meaning of such names is clear, is often left implicit. In the previous sections is has been argued that the implicit use of meaningful names should be made explicit by making the distinction between a purely functional description of a method or data-structure and an interpretation of it. By defining a mapping between a task-neutral description and an ontology such an interpretation can be explicitly defined.

There seems good reason to investigate the implicit assumptions which underlie both the specification of problem solving methods and knowledge representation in general. Anyway it seems helpful to increase the awareness of the importance of meaningful names in knowledge-based systems as they indicate assumptions which are still on a intuitive level.

Finally there is criticism. Here follow some questions, remarks and brief answers.

Criticism 1: *What's new? It all has been said and done.*

Answer: It is not our purpose to make a claim to originality here. Reading the literature and talking to people we came to the conclusion that the subject is not that trivial to most people and therefore worth writing down.

Criticism 2: *How do you use those mappings between PSM and ontologies? It will never work, it is too complicated.*

Answer: Well if you write a program using meaningful names you leave the mapping to the computer. The machine doesn't care whether you use *cat*, *C5678* or any other name. But we do care. It is true that we did not specify here how ontology mappings should work in practice, but the point we want to make is that the interpretation should be separated from the abstract method. That this is complicated in practice may very well be true. But so is life.

Criticism 3: *I would never use C&D for classification purposes. It is not efficient.*

Answer: You probably are right. Efficiency was not an issue here. The point of view here was computational and should be appreciated as such. We do not claim that you can use C&D for classification without problem. But from the specification without using meaningful names it is obscure why one shouldn't do so.

Critisism 4: *How could you say Example 2 has no knowledge? It is full of knowledge for example: r has no cycles.*

Answer: We limited the notion of knowledge to make clear that what is important is what r stands for. As long as that is not clear we say that is doesn't contain knowledge. Example 2 is a structure that can be used to describe many state of affairs in the world. That r doesn't contain cycles is an a priori truth from that perspective. Of course according to a more traditional definition of knowledge you are right. Our definition has no metaphysical pretensions. It was just put forward to make a point.

References

BENJAMINS, V. R., FENSEL, D., & STRAATMAN, R. (1996). Assumptions of problem-solving methods and their role in knowledge engineering. In Wahlster, W., editor, *Proc. ECAI-96*, pages 408–412. J. Wiley & Sons, Ltd.

BEYS, P., BENJAMINS, V. R., & VAN HEIJST, G. (1996). Remedying the reusability-usability tradeoff for problem-solving methods. In Gaines, B. R. & Musen, M. A., editors, *Proceedings of the 10th Banff Knowledge Acquisition for Knowledge-Based Systems Workshop*, pages 2.1–2.20, Alberta, Canada. SRDG Publications, University of Calgary. http://ksi.cpsc.ucalgary.ca:80/KAW/KAW96/KAW96Proc.html.

BYLANDER, T. & CHANDRASEKARAN, B. (1988). Generic tasks in knowledge-based reasoning: The right level of abstraction for knowledge acquisition. In Gaines, B. & Boose, J., editors, *Knowledge Acquisition for Knowledge Based Systems*, volume 1, pages 65–77. London, Academic Press.

DIJKSTRA, E. W. (1976). *A Discipline of Programming*. Englewood Cliffs, New Jersey, Prentice-Hall.

FENSEL, D. (1995). Formal specification languages in knowledge and software engineering. *The Knowledge Engineering Review*, 10(4).

MOTTA, E. (1998). *Reusable Components for Knowledge Modeling*. PhD thesis, The Open University, Milton Keynes, United Kingdom.

SCHREIBER, A. T., AKKERMANS, J. M., ANJEWIERDEN, A. A., DE HOOG, R., SHADBOLT, N. R., DE VELDE, W. V., & WIELINGA, B. J. (1999). *Engineering and Managing Knowledge, The CommonKADS methodology*. to appear.

SCHREIBER, A. T., WIELINGA, B. J., & AKKERMANS, J. M. (1993). Using KADS to analyse problem-solving methods. In Schreiber, A. T., Wielinga, B. J., & Breuker, J. A., editors, *KADS: A Principled Approach to Knowledge-Based System Development*, pages 415–430. London, Academic Press.

SOWA, J. F. (1997). *Knowledge Representation: Logical, Philosophical, and Computational Foundations*. Book draft.

FMR: An Incremental Knowledge Acquisition System for Fuzzy Domains

Rodrigo Martínez-Béjar[1], Francisca Ibáñez-Cruz[1], Thong Le-Gia[2], Tri M. Cao[2]
and Paul Compton[2]

[1] *Departmento de Inteligencia Artificial, Facultad de Informatica, Universidad de Murcia,*
Espinardo(Murcia) – C. P.30071, Spain.Phone: +34 9683 64634. Fax: +34 9683 64651.
E-mail: rodrigo@ dif.um.es

[2] *Department of Artificial Intelligence, School of Computer Science and Engineering, The*
University of New South Wales, Sydney, 2052 NSW, Australia. Phone: +61 2 9385 5518. Fax:
+61 2 9385 5995. Email : compton@cse.unsw.edu.au

Abstract: Ripple Down Rules (RDR) is an incremental Knowledge Acquisition (KA) technique that allows experts themselves to be in charge of performing the KA as well as the maintenance of the system. Although there are various real RDR approaches, fuzzy domain cannot be treated through RDR systems yet. The purpose of this work is to make use of the RDR advantages to construct fuzzy rule-based systems as well as to strengthen the utility of RDR in fuzzy domains. This aim has been achieved by introducing some assumptions relative to fuzzy domain modelling in combination with the construction of a new framework to manage and acquire (fuzzy) conclusions.

1   Introduction

Ripple down rules (RDR) was developed from the maintenance experience with an expert system (Compton *et al.*, 1989). The main motivation for developing RDR was the fact that experts could not explain how they had reached conclusions. For this reason, RDR uses the knowledge supplied by experts just in the context it was provided, that is, by following the sequence of evaluated rules. Moreover, if an expert does not agree with a conclusion, knowledge in the form of a new rule can be added. In this sense, rules are never removed or corrected, only added.

Multiple Classification Ripple Down Rules (MCRDR) (Kang, 1996) is an extension of the basic aspects of RDR for providing multiple independent conclusions for a case. However, current MCRDR approaches cannot be applied to fuzzy domains as such, since these systems operate with crisp values solely.

The aim of the work presented in this paper is to bring the advantages of MCRDR to developing fuzzy rule-based systems and to strengthen the utility of MCRDR in fuzzy domains, particularly in the early stages of development. Thus, by introducing some assumptions, a system for acquiring and managing knowledge in fuzzy contexts through MCRDR has been designed and implemented.

2   Fuzzy logic and ripple down rule systems

Fuzzy logic is a method that permits a gradual representation of likeness between two objects. It is based on Zadeh's theory of fuzzy sets (Zadeh, 1965). He defines a membership function to assign a grade of membership between 0 and 1 to each element in the range of all possible elements under consideration. This grade can be thought as a measure of compatibility between the element and the concept represented by the fuzzy set. Formally, the membership function for a fuzzy set A, written $\mu_A(x)$, is a real valued function defined as the application $\mu_A: X \rightarrow [0,1]$ for all x in a universal set X.

In Fuzzy Logic, there are a number of approaches that allow inference. We have used the so-called Generalised Modus Ponens (GMP).Through the GMP technique, the proposition *y is B* can be derived from the rule "if (*x is A*) then (*y is B*)" when the proposition *x is A* is true. The GMP can also be employed when the two propositions *x is A* and *y is B* are defined imprecisely. Thus, if a proposition *x is A'*, close to *x is A*, is true, the principle of the GMP is to derive another proposition, written *y is B'* close to *y is B*. This proposition is generated by taking into account both the underlying semantics of the implication of the rule and a measure of the likeness between A and A'. With all, the inference consists of defining a fuzzy set B', which is as close to B as A' is to A.

Many systems use the triple formed by the Z-function, the Π-function and the S-function (Zadeh, 1975) for defining fuzzy membership functions (i. e., fuzzy sets). Examples of this are <low, medium, high>, <short, medium, high>, etc. We will term to each component of T as T_l, T_m, and T_r, respectively.

In RDR rules are added by using the justification provided by the expert in the context of when the same wrong conclusion is reached. The new rules are only used in the context in which they were provided. The cases which had required new rules to be added are known as "cornerstone cases", which maintain the context of the KB. The system shows the differences between the old and the current case, to the expert and asks he or she to select some conditions from the list of differences which justify the new conclusion. These are used for conditions of a new rule and the system adds into the knowledge base.

With MCRDR, more general systems than those of single classification can be performed because it allows multiple refinements for a rule. When experts are maintaining a MCRDR system, they must construct a rule containing the differences between the case is entered to the system and the case associated to the last true rule in the KB. This process will be repeated until there is no case (associated to any rule) that satisfies the rule.

3   Applying RDR systems to fuzzy domains

By using classical RDR engines, fuzzy domains are not accessible, since RDR systems can only operate with crisp values for the attributes in their rules. Nevertheless, fuzzy domains are typically concerned with rules following the format IF (X_1 is V_1) and (X_2 is V_2) and .....and (X_n is V_n) then Y is A. By assuming that membership functions for fuzzy attributes follow the triple format $<T_l(x), T_m(x), T_r(x)>$ as indicated before, and that these can be defined as a function of α and γ, the following is proposed.

Definition 1: FMR system

Let R be a MCRDR system. R is said to be a *fuzzy multiple ripple down rule (FMR) system*, written *FMR system*, if its rules can be applied to fuzzy domains by modelling every fuzzy attribute, written A, as follows:

$$A = \begin{cases} attribute(\alpha, \gamma) \text{ is } \textit{fuzzy\_value} \\ \qquad \text{if A is intended to be a fuzzy attribute;} \\ attribute\textbf{R}(crisp\_value_1, \ crisp\_value_2,..,crisp\_value_n), \text{n} \geq 1 \\ \qquad \text{otherwise} \end{cases}$$

where *attribute* is the identifier used for A; α and γ are the parameters that define the membership functions for A according to the triple $<T_l(x), T_m(x), T_r(x)>$; *fuzzy_value* represents a fuzzy value given for A and defined by means of one of the elements of $<T_l(x), T_m(x), T_r(x)>$ (for example, $<$*high, medium, normal*$>$, $<$ *low, short, tall*$>$, etc.);

$\mathbf{R}$ represents a mathematical relationship (including equality, order and membership) between A and the elements of $\{crisp\_value_1, \ crisp\_value_2,.., \ crisp\_value_n\}$; $crisp\_value_i$, represents the ith non-fuzzy value for A, $1 \leq i \leq n$.

By considering the referred parameters, some compatibility criterion between two values of a fuzzy attribute can be defined. For it, we will keep the criterion that the values that a fuzzy attribute can possess are grouped into semantic compatibility classes by taking into account that the linguistic tags (i. e., the values) associated to $T_l(x)$ and $T_r(x)$, respectively, should not overlap. Thus, given a triple, written $< T_1, T_2, T_3>$, containing three different linguistic tags associated to the elements of the triple $< T_l(x), T_m(x), T_r(x)>$; and given two elements, written V_1 and V_2, belonging to the union set $\bigcup\limits_{i=1}^{3}\{T_i\}$, V_1 and V_2 are defined as being two compatible fuzzy tags, written compatible_tags (V_1, V_2), if $\bigvee\limits_{k=1}^{2}\left(V_{12} \subseteq (\{T_k\}\cup\{T_{k+1}\})\right)$ where $V_{12} = \{V_1\}\cup \{V_2\}$.

To analyse compatibility between two (eventually) different fuzzy attributes the relative position of the two sets of parameters defining their respective membership functions should also be considered. Based on this premise, the following can be written.

Definition 2: compatible fuzzy attributes

Let F_1 and F_2 be two fuzzy attributes belonging to a FMR system represented, according to definition 1, as "$c_i.a_i(p_i)$ is v_i" respectively, where $p_i = (\alpha_i, \gamma_i)$, $i = 1, 2$. F_1 and F_2 are said to be two *compatible fuzzy attributes*, written *compatible_fuzzy_atts* (F_1, F_2), if $[(F_1 = F_2)$ or $((c_1.a_1 = c_2.a_2)$ and (compatible_parameters$(p_1,p_2))]$ holds where, compatible_parameters(p_1,p_2) = [compatible_tags (v_1,v_2)) and (within_compatible_ranges $(p_1, p_2))$ and (sufficient_distance$(p_1, p_2))]$ where

$$within\_compatible\_ranges(p_i,p_j)= \bigvee\limits_{i \neq j=1}^{2}\left[(\alpha_i \in PCR(\alpha_j,p_j)) \text{ and } (\gamma_i \in PCR(\gamma_j,p_j))\right];$$

$$PCR(x, p_k) = [x - MPCD(p_k), x + MPCD(p_k)]; \qquad MPCD(p_k) = \frac{\gamma_k - \alpha_k}{2};$$

sufficient_distance$(p_i,p_j)=$

$$\overset{2}{\underset{i\neq j=1}{V}}\left[(\alpha_j \geq \alpha_i) \text{ and } (\gamma_j \geq \gamma_i) \rightarrow (MPCD(p_j) \geq K_j * MPCD_i(p_i))\right];$$

$K_j = \min\{\beta_j - 0.5, 0.5 - \beta_j\}$

Now, let us consider the hypothesis where a fuzzy attribute must be confronted to a crisp one. The crisp attributes can respond to various formats, namely, the alphabetical one and the numeric interval-based one. These two possibilities are considered for the following definitions.

Definition 3: alphabetical compatibility

Let F_1 and A_2 be a fuzzy attribute and a non-numerical, crisp attribute in a FMR system and represented, respectively, as "concept$_1$.attribute$_1$(p$_1$) is v_1" and "concept$_2$.attribute$_2$ = v_2" where $p_1 = (\alpha_1, \gamma_1)$. F_1 and A_2 are said to be alphabetically compatible, written a-*compatible(F$_1$, C$_2$)*, if (concept$_1$.attribute$_1$ = concept$_2$.attribute$_2$) and (compatible_tags(v_1,v_2)).

The counterpart of the above definition is the following:

Definition 4: numerical compatibility

Let F_1 and N_2 be a fuzzy attribute and a numerical, crisp attribute in a FMR system and represented, respectively, as "concept$_1$.attribute$_1$(p) is v_1" and "concept$_2$.attribute$_2 \in (v_{inf}, v_{sup})$" where $p_1 = (\alpha,\gamma)$. F_1 and N_2 are said to be numerically compatible, written n-*compatible(F$_1$, N$_2$)*, if (concept$_1$.attribute$_1$ = (concept$_2$.attribute$_2$) and the following holds

$$[v_{inf}, v_{sup}] \subseteq \begin{cases} \left(-\infty, \dfrac{\alpha + \gamma}{2}\right] & \text{if } v_1 = T_1; \\[2mm] [\alpha, \gamma] & \text{if } v_1 = T_2; \\[2mm] [\gamma, \infty) & \text{if } v_1 = T_3 \end{cases}$$

Then, the condition for a given rule in a FMR system to be fired by an input case, can be established as follows:

Definition 5: fuzzy ripple down rule setting

Let CR_i be a condition of a rule, written R; let CI_j be a condition for an input case, written I; and let CR_i and CI_j be respectively represented (according to the representation format adopted here) as follows:

$$C_k = \begin{cases} c_k.a_k(p_k) \text{ is } v_k & \text{if } a_k \text{ is a fuzzy attribute} \\ c_k.a_k R(v'_1, v'_2 ,.., v'_{n_k}) & \text{otherwise} \end{cases}$$

Where $C_k \in \{CR_k, CI_k\}$; $k \in \{i, j\}$; $p_k = (\alpha_k, \gamma_k)$; n_k = number of values involved in $c_k.a_k$

R is said to be set by I, written *set (R, I)* if $\forall CR_i \in R, \exists CI_j \in I$, such that compatible_ attributes(CR_i, CI_j) holds where compatible_valued_attributes (CR_i, CI_j)
=

$$\begin{cases} \text{compatible\_fuzzy\_atts}(CR_i, CI_j) \text{ if both } CR_i \text{ and } CI_j \text{ are fuzzy attributes;} \\ a\text{-compatible}(CR_i, CI_j) \text{ if one of the arguments is a fuzzy attribute and} \\ \qquad\qquad \text{the other is a non-numerical, crisp one;} \\ n\text{-compatible}(CR_i, CI_j) \text{ if one of the arguments is a fuzzy attribute and} \\ \qquad\qquad \text{the other is a numerical, crisp one;} \\ \text{match}(CR_i, CI_j) \text{ if both } CR_i \text{ and } CI_j \text{ are crisp attributes;} \end{cases}$$

$$\text{match}(CR_i, CI_j) = \begin{cases} true \text{ if } CR_i \text{ and } CI_j \text{ are in accordance with their values} \\ false \text{ otherwise} \end{cases}$$

$$R = \bigcup_{i=1}^{Card(R)} CR_i \; ; I = \bigcup_{j=1}^{Card(I)} CI_j \; .$$

4 Conclusion management and rule condition acquisition in FMR systems

In FMR , the standard GMP approach is used. So, given a fuzzy rule IF x is A THEN y is B, we firstly generate a matrix (termed Fuzzy Associative Memory in Kosko (1992)) M for storing the association (A, B). Given $x \subseteq X$ and $y \subseteq Y$, we are defining the matrix M (Bouchon-Meunier (1992)) using the Rescher-Gaines implication, namely, $M^{(4)}(x,y) = 1$ if $f_A(x) \le f_B(y)$ and 0 otherwise (Rescher-Gaines implication).

On the other hand, semantic conflicts among attributes can arise when experts are shown a set of conclusions after running an input case. Therefore, the system should have a mechanism to face to the situation where multiple conclusions about the same attributes and concepts are produced by the system. In FMR, the criteria adopted to eliminate the (possible) presence of replicate conclusions in semantic terms are the following. Firstly, the system groups all the conclusions generated for an input case into compatibility classes according to the criteria indicated before in this article. Secondly, for every conclusion included in all the so-obtained classes, we make use of certainty theory.

Although certainty factors for rules are usually supplied by experts in rule-based systems, in FMR this factor (for each rule) is calculated automatically. For it, the root node of the FMR tree is supposed to have a certainty factor equals to 1 by default. For the rest of rules, the certainty factor depends on the *correction curve* of the rule, that is, the curve identifying the relation between the number of corrections made from R and the number of cases seen for R.

In order to get the "best" of the replicate conclusions, given a fuzzy rule condition, the distance between the parameters defining the attributes of the rule conditions is considered. Thus, the imprecision factor associated to a fuzzy condition in a FMR system is defined as being directly proportional to the length of the segment where the fuzzy membership function for one element of a certain universe can take several values. In particular, such a factor will depend on the distance between the two fuzzy boundaries (i. e., α and γ), so that the larger the length of the fuzzy interval, the larger the imprecision factor of the rule. As α approaches to γ, the imprecision factor approaches to 0. Also, the value of the (fuzzy) attribute is considered to determine such a segment.

If one expert wants to correct a conclusion of the KB, the rule providing the right conclusion is added at the end of the path going to the rule that produced the wrong conclusion. If the approximate conclusion is incorrect from the expert's perspective, we use a kind of propose and revise method to adjust the output. With all, the rule added, if any, should be compatible with and have a less associated imprecision than the rule that produced the wrong conclusion. Moreover, the new rule will be added at the end of the path going to the rule that produced the less precise conclusion. Only fuzzy rules producing new fuzzy conclusions are added at the top of the FMR knowledge tree.

5 Conclusions

Ripple down rules (RDR) aim at using the knowledge only in the context provided by the expert, this context being the sequence of rules evaluated to give a certain conclusion. MCRDR is a RDR-based approach that allows experts to have multiple conclusions for a given input case

In real life, there are many problems involving fuzzy terminology. However, current RDR systems cannot be applied to those. Although fuzzy logic is normally used to deal with fuzzy domains, RDR systems obligate to assign crisp values to fuzzy-by-nature attributes.

In this article, a new methodology, based on a set of compatibility criteria between valued attributes for running cases has been proposed. By considering the nature of MCRDR systems and some properties relative to fuzzy processing, in this new approach, experts can be helped to make their choice when they are shown several conclusions alluding to the same feature. For it, we make use of certainty factor theory. In our approach, experts do not have to give any certainty factor value for each condition in a rule. Moreover, given a condition, the system generates a certainty factor value for this condition from the uncertainty underlying the context of the rule under question in the KB structure.

The system proposed here is also capable of generating inferred conclusions, that is, conclusions that are not in the KB. For it, we make use of fuzzy inference by using the Generalised Modus Ponens approach. Besides, in order to reduce the (possible) presence of replicate conclusions, the system generates an imprecision-based factor for each conclusion.

References

Bouchon-Meunier B., (1992). Inferences with imprecisions and Uncertainties in Expert Systems, *Fuzzy Expert Systems Theory,* CRC Press.

Compton, P., Horn, R., Quinlan, R. and Lazarus, L. (1989). Maintaining an expert system, In J. R. Quinlan (Eds.), *Applications of Expert Systems*, 366-385, London, Addison Wesley.

Kosko, B., (1992). Neural Networks and Fuzzy Systems. *Prentice-Hall, Englewood Cliffs*, N.J.

Zadeh, L. A. (1965). Fuzzy sets, *Information and Control*, **8**: 338-353.

Zadeh, L. A. (1975). The Concept of Linguistic Variable and Its Application to Approximate Reasoning, *Information Sciences*, **8**: 199-248, 301-357; **9**: 43-80.

Applying SeSKA to Sisyphus III

Päivikki Parpola
Hauenkalliontie 2 B 54
FIN-02170 Espoo
Finland
Phone: +358 9 420 8482

Helsinki University of Technology
Department of Computer Science and Engineering

Abstract. *SeSKA* (Seamless Structured Knowledge Acquisition) is a methodology for constructing and maintaining *knowledge bases* (KB). The iterative sequence of development stages creates a series of *object-oriented* models, connected by *seamless transformations*.

Principles of applying SeSKA to the *Sisyphus III* rock classification problem are described. Extended semantics of input schemes for SeSKA are presented. Also conversions from schemes in Sisyphus III material are sketched. The Sisyphus projects are often used as test benches for different KA methodologies. A proper evaluation of SeSKA can be made only after a complete KB has been constructed using it.

1 Introduction

The Sisyphus III Project. The Sisyphus experiments [5] are attempts to compare and evaluate different *knowledge acquisition* (KA) methods and techniques [4]. The Sisyphus III project involves classification of rocks based on realistic interview transcripts and other material.

The SeSKA Methodology. Seamless Structured Knowledge Acquisition (SeSKA) [1, 2] is a methodology for development and maintenance of knowledge bases (KB). During KB construction, a series of OO models (fig. 1) is created and part of them are modified during the development process. *Seamless transformations* are defined between sequential models. Seamless transformations define the principles according to which a certain model can be constructed and modified based on another model. Different models in the chain are described below.

- *Domain model* (DM) contains domain or abstract *concepts* and *relations*. Concepts are described by a number of *features*.
- Initial *dependency graphs* (DG) acquired from different sources. DGs present inferential dependencies between features of DM concepts. Descriptions can be attached to different dependencies.
- The actual DG is a combination of initial DGs.

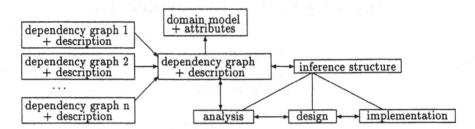

Fig. 1. The chain of models created in order to build a KB. Seamless transformations are illustrated with arrows.

- *Inference structure* (IS) presents the structure of possible inference sequences performed. The IS is shared among three sets of descriptions.
- Collections of *analysis, design and implementation* descriptions are attached to inferences in the IS.

Contents of this Paper. Section 2 describes the basic and extended forms of DM and DG, as well as conversions from other formalisms. Section 3 explains combining DGs. Section 4 describes the remaining phases of SeSKA. Section 5 contains discussion and conclusions.

2 Information Used as Input

2.1 The Basic DM and DG

DM. Concepts and relations are presented as object classes. *Features* (properties or parts) of concepts are presented as attributes of concept classes. The DM is acquired from knowledge sources but restricted to the essential based on dependency graphs (see below).

DG. Domain concept features and dependencies between them are presented as object classes. Features are simultaneously attributes of DM concepts.

DGs can be illustrated using graphical networks or text indentations. A feature of a concept is presented in the form *'Concept.feature'* (or *'Class.attribute'*).

The DG is usually formed based on (inferential) dependencies between features of concepts, preferably with attached descriptions.

2.2 Possible Extensions and Modifications of the DM and DG

Sisyphus III material cannot be presented in basic DM and DG form. A number of extensions will be made to the basic DM and DG in order to enable transformations from schemes used in Sisyphus III material.

Abstract Concepts. Groups of objects with some common property (with a common value) can be represented with an abstract concept that can be inherited by the concepts in the group. Abstract concepts can form an inheritance hierarchy or lattice of several layers.

Nodes in Initial DGs. The following notations are useful when coding knowledge into the DGs. Node names can be extended with an attribute value: *'Concept.attribute=value'*. The forms *'attribute.value'* and *'Concept.value'* can be used as shortcuts for the presentation as long as they do not cause ambiguities or confusion. Other shortcuts can also be used, as long as they can be converted to the form 'Concept.attribute=value'.

Presentation of Protocols through Dependencies. In addition to presenting plain inferential dependencies (contents of the KB) in the DG, protocols too can be presented: each step of a protocol is presented as a DG item, depending on both the previous step of the protocol and the contents of the current step.

A Wider View of Attributes. In addition to properties and components, attributes of concepts (possibly appearing as nodes of the DG) can also be (results of) events, etc. In classification problems like Sisyphus III, dependencies will be created between the 'identity' features (i.e. identification) of concepts and their other features.

2.3 Utilizing Results of Different KE Interviews

The Sisyphus material contains transcripts of KE interviews. In order to be usable, KE transcripts have to be either (1) converted to formalisms understood by SeSKA, or (2) used as knowledge sources for extraction of useful knowledge.

Transcripts of item sorts (card sorts) and repertory grid analysis are suitable for direct conversion due to their formal nature.

Transcripts of structured interviews, self reports and and laddered grid interviews can be used as knowledge sources for manual extraction. The following kinds of knowledge can be elicited:

- *Features of concepts* affecting both DM and DG.
- *General dependencies between features* of abstract or concrete concepts. If these dependencies (rules) apply only to a certain group of concepts, the result depends also of the restriction.
- *Protocols* for performing the task (only structured interviews and self reports). Protocols can be presented in the DGs, as described in section 2.2.
- *Groups of concepts with a common property.* Also criteria for differentiating individuals in the group were presented in self reports and laddered grid interviews.

- Do some of the experts say they are not sure?
- Does the majority agree? Could someone with a different opinion be wrong?
- Is there a two-way division of opinions? Could this be a question of a borderline?
- Could different samples of the same rock vary in this respect?

Based on the answers either a single or alternative values can be given to the attribute in question.

There may be alternative protocols to be used. If the protocols differ only by an insignificant order of steps to be taken, they can be considered the same protocol. There may remain several separate DGs from combining dependencies that can be integrated with the help of protocols.

4 Developing the KB

4.1 Forming the Initial Inference Structure

The IS presents the structure of possible inferences, just as in CommonKADS [3]. The components of the IS are called *roles* and *inferences*, and are presented by objects. Roles in the IS are formed using some suitable heuristics, e.g. "all attributes that some attribute directly depends on form a role".

The same mechanism is also extended to protocols presented in the form of dependencies. Protocol skeletons are filled in with inferential dependencies.

The descriptions associated with dependencies form the initial analysis descriptions, associated with the corresponding inferences of the IS formed.

4.2 Development and Maintenance of the KB

The three kinds of descriptions, attached to each inference, form three sets of descriptions, sharing the IS. These sets can be considered to form three models. Different descriptions of inferences can contain a different number of blocks.

Whenever need for change appears (in e.g. the implementation model) the corresponding part of the analysis model is traced using the shared IS. Necessary changes are made in the analysis model, and then propagated to the design and implementation models. Development is thus cyclic, with information flowing forward and backward between the three models sharing the IS.

5 Discussion and Conclusions

SeSKA (Seamless Structured Knowledge Acquisition) is a methodology for developing and maintaining of knowledge bases (KB). During the iterative process, a series of object-oriented (OO) models, connected with seamless transformations, is created.

The Sisyphus III problem involves creating a KB for rock classification. The Sisyphus projects are used as test benches for different KA methodologies. A

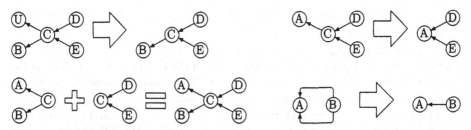

Fig. 2. DG combination: An unnecessary result node (upper left) or an intermediate node (upper right) can be removed. Two DGs can be joined (lower left). One of two duplicate dependencies may be removed (lower right). Text descriptions of both of the duplicate dependencies have to be preserved, however.

The terminology of the interviews should be maintained when information is first coded to the DM and the DG.

The Sisyphus III material also contains colour photos and micrographs of rocks. These may be associated with descriptions of dependencies (for identification), or as attributes of concepts in the DM.

3 Combining Different DGs Produced

The DGs contain dependencies, acquired from different sources (experts) and different types of interviews. The terminology of the initial DGs may vary and has to be harmonized, before or after forming the DGs. Different dependencies acquired through interviews of a certain type should first be combined, then the combined results of different techniques can be combined.

3.1 Combining Complementary DGs

DGs containing complementary material can be combined using simplification and combination rules [1]. These rules may allow bringing together different fragments of knowledge, even before building a KB. The context of validity has to be determined for each DG. Two rules for 'remove', and rules for 'join' and 'simplify' are illustrated in fig. 2. There will almost certainly be overlapping information left, not removed by the rules. This should be analyzed and edited carefully, in order to keep the KB manageable.

3.2 Combining Contradicting DGs

Contradicting material is more difficult. There are no absolute rules for these situations, but common sense can be used. If different experts give different values for the same attribute, e.g. grain size, of a certain rock, the following alternatives should be checked:

proper evaluation of SeSKA can be made only after a complete KB has been constructed using it.

Acquired knowledge in SeSKA is presented in two kinds of models — the domain model (DM) and the dependency graph (DG). The DM and DG can be modified and extended in a number of ways. Conversions from other presentations, made possible by the extensions, are presented.

Fragments of converted material are combined, applying formal rules or principles based on common sense. An initial description of the KB can be formed based on both inferential and protocol dependencies. The KB is developed utilizing the shared inference structure, guaranteeing traceability.

SeSKA provides a rather thin approach, concerned only with KB development, but not with, e.g. user interface (UI) development. This, however, makes the process uncomplicated and suitable for quick prototyping. When real systems are built, SeSKA has to be combined with other methods.

The main contributions of this paper are to present the extensions to SeSKA input and to present principles for combining contradictory knowledge (in addition to complementary). Current trends of research involve building a rock classification KB, and applying problem-solving methods to models built using SeSKA.

SeSKA has been tested manually, as the tool supporting SeSKA is still under development, using the programming language Java.

Acknowledgments

I thank professor Markku Syrjänen for his advice and encouragement, and Pekka Jussila, MSc. (tech.), for his comments. I also thank Mr. Michael Vollar for proofreading my English.

References

1. Parpola, P.: Seamless Development of Structured Knowledge Bases. In Proceedings of KAW98, Eleventh Workshop on Knowledge Acquisition, Modeling and Management. Banff, Alberta, Canada, 18th-23rd April, 1998. http://ksi.cpsc.ucalgary.ca/KAW/KAW98/parpola/.
2. Parpola, P.: Development and inference in integrated OO models. Proceedings of CIMCA'99 - The international conference on computational intelligence for modelling, control and automation. Vienna, Austria, 17-19 February, 1999. IOS Press.
3. Schreiber, G., Wielinga, B., de Hoog, R., Akkermans, H., van de Velde, W.: CommonKADS, a Comprehensive Methodology for KBS Development. IEEE Expert Vol. 9 (1994) No. 6, pp. 28-37.
4. Schweickert, R., Burton, A. M., Taylor, N. K., Corlett, E. N., Shadbolt, N. R., Hedgecock, A. P.: Comparing knowledge elicitation techniques: a case study. Artificial Intelligence Review (1987) No. 1 (January), pp. 245-253.
5. Shadbolt, N., Crow, L., Tennison, J., Cupit, J.: Sisyphus III Phase 1 Release. November 1996. http://www.psychology.nottingham.ac.uk/research/ai/sisyphus/.

Describing Similar Control Flows for Families of Problem-Solving Methods

Rainer Perkuhn

Institute AIFB
University of Karlsruhe (TH)
D-76128 Karlsruhe, Germany
e-mail: perkuhn@aifb.uni-karlsruhe.de

Abstract

A library of software components should be essentially more than just a juxtaposition of its items. For problem-solving methods the notion of a family is suggested as means to cluster the items and to provide partially a structure of the library. This paper especially investigates how the similar control flows of the members of such a family can be described in one framework.

Keywords: Problem Solving Methods, Reuse, Similarities, Categories of PSMs, Software Architectures, Meta Modeling

1 Introduction

The notion of a problem-solving method (PSM) was inspired by a lot of different approaches (Generic Tasks [Chandrasekaran, Johnson, and Smith, 1992], CommonKADS [Schreiber et al., 1994], Method-to-Task Approach [Eriksson et al., 1995], Components of Expertise [Steels, 1990], GDM [Terpstra et al., 1993], MIKE [Angele, Fensel, and Studer, 1996]). PSMs describe the reasoning behaviour of an intelligent agent. Though, suitable models are especially conceptual ones and "platform-independent" by providing modeling primitives on the knowledge level ([Newell, 1982]). Up to now the competing modeling frameworks converged and reached consensus on the fundamental issues a common ("unified") theory has to cover. [Angele et al., 1996], [Perkuhn, 1997] summarize the synthesis of this development, the new proposal for UPML ([Fensel et al., 1999]) tries to capture the result in a unified modeling language.

Reuse of PSMs promises time, cost, and quality improvement in the development process of a knowledge-based system, incl. maintenance, and a more reasonable assessment of the quality of the resulting product. Mainly, investigations on the reuse of PSMs focus on the development of libraries ([Motta, 1997], [Breuker and van de Velde, 1994]) but from a reuse process point of view these are useful only to a limited extent. Either they offer only a collection of items with no real support of how to select an appropriate one. Or they attempt to cover a more generalized structure, e.g. task-method-decomposition trees ([Benjamins, 1993]), but are very poor in showing up the relations between the possible specializations. The latter approach seems more promising but evaluations have shown their deficiencies ([Orsvärn, 1996]). The main critics is that the designer of the library did not consider (and is not able to represent) in his models of how to adapt the generalized structure to a special application. The tower-of-adapter approach ([Fensel, 1997]) is derived from the necessity to adapt general models, like e.g. basic search schemes, to more specialized circumstances, e.g. special PSMs like propose&revise. In principle, the approach is a constructive one but up to now it neither offers models that contain the information of the overall structure of the resulting system in a communicable form - as the conceptual models do - nor offers construction plans of how to combine the basic templates with some adapters to come to a certain overall conceptual structure. Of course, adapters might improve the reusability of a system like any other design pattern ([Gamma et al., 1994]) can do. But especially conceptual models of PSMs contain information that is closer to an architectural description ([Shaw and Garlan, 1996]) of the general structure of the target system. Nevertheless the approach is an interesting alternative rsp. completion to indexing the library with simple keywords or logical formulae-based pre-/post-condition annotations. Actually, it is not far away from object-orientation - another view on reuse that claims that the inheritance hierarchy provides a reasonable structure of the reuse components and, thus, solves a good deal of the indexing problem. But a PSM cannot be captured completely by the notion of an object in this sense since it e.g. contains an explicit specification of the control flow. [Perkuhn, 1997] suggested the concept of a family of PSMs that describes the overall architecture for a class of similar methods. In the same fashion as in object-orientation it is intended to structure a part of the library. Thus, only a family has to be retrieved from the library by an additional mechanism. Afterwards the selection of a PSM corresponds to systematic browsing through the family. [Perkuhn, 1997] focussed on inference structures while this paper especially investigates how to describe similar control flows for a range of closely related PSMs.

2 Families of PSMs

Most aspects of a PSM that can be represented in a specific part of the model (layer rsp. view) can be distinguished between elements like concepts or roles and steps in the problem solving process on the one hand and relations between them on the other hand. [Perkuhn, 1997] introduced colouring as a means to express that they are not necessarily parts of the model. All elements in the same colour form a region. A coloured region possibly has to be omitted if certain conditions are not fulfilled. In the example of [Perkuhn, 1997] (a family for assignment tasks that covers generate-and-test, propose-and-exchange, and propose-and-revise) different regions depend on the availability of the knowledge for static roles namely propose, exchange, and revise. The former two are illustrated in figure 1. The revise region is part of the refinement of the exchange step that

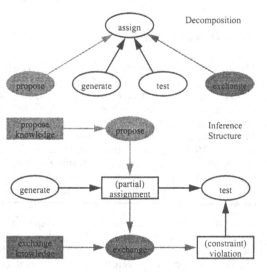

Figure 1. Coloured task decomposition and inference structure for the assignment family (cf. [Perkuhn, 1997])

is not shown here. If one of these static roles cannot be filled, i.e. the knowledge is not available or cannot be acquired either, the corresponding region has to be removed from the model. For these cases it seems to be appropriate to colour and remove all related connections, too. But in other cases the resulting model has to be kept consistent rsp. coherent. E.g. to restore the coherence of a taxonomy or a sequential control flow the gap in the model has to be bridged with the transitive closure of the adjacent relations (cf. figure 2) - if possible and reasonable. Colouring is a creative modeling act and expresses as an epistemological primitive on a cross-model level that the

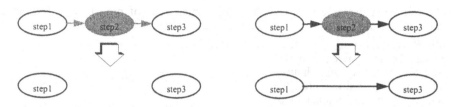

Figure 2. Optional connections vs. transitive closure of adjacent connections

model should still make sense in all variations with or without the regions in every context.

Capturing similar control flows imposes additional requirements on the modeling framework. The control flow specification has to prescribe which steps are performed in which order. If the reasoning process reaches a state where it can follow different succeeding paths, the control flow has to specify how to go on. In the ordinary PSM scenario the decision depends on boolean expressions - normally expressing an internal state during computation. Resembling the manner of procedural programming languages if- or case-statement-like expressions evaluate these boolean expressions and according to their truth value decide for one path. Overlaying different control flows introduces a new aspect that has to be distinguished from these internal states.

In the example family some variants begin with a propose step, others with a generate step. Some other variants use the generate step as a fallback action if for a certain variable ("parameter") no propose knowledge is applicable. Since in most cases - if propose is realized - generate is not taken into consideration at all it is not appropriate to put these two steps into a sequential order. Rather they should be treated as alternatives. An additional mechanism is necessary to handle the fallback variant, but, actually, this distinction exactly reflects the difference of ordinary inter-process communication via return values and extra-ordinary exception handling. This new form of alternative does not depend on an internal state of the computation. It is a kind of non-deterministic decision point to be resolved with respect to the possible variants.

At the decision point the problem-solving process is in a state similar to a person that wants to get from one place to another one. When the person reaches a point where the path splits and he/she can decide how to go on - assuming that both paths still lead to the target place -, normally, the selection is not arbitrary but depends on some properties of the alternatives. In this framework these are annotated as features to the different paths. The next step is then determined by an external strategy that weighs up the different properties. In the example of the assignment family the alternative paths can be annotated as "founded" on the one hand, and "random" on the other hand. A usual default strategy (cf. table 1) would reflect the superiority and prefer the founded alternative over the random one.

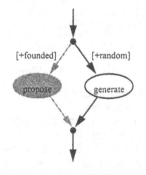

Figure 3. Decision criteria annotated as features

| strategy "founded" | prefer a [+founded] path over any other |
| strategy "not random" | prefer any path over a [+random] one |

Table 1 - Two default strategies

The following example illustrates how the combination of properties and internal states is annotated as feature-conditioned boolean expression.

All PSMs of the assignment family can be categorized into two groups: those that work holistically, i.e. they first complete the system model (in an inner loop) before they test and revise it, and those that work incrementally, i.e. they already test and revise incomplete models (partial assignments) and extend them in an outer loop. Executing propose or generate once yields one value for one variable. So, afterwards the control flow has the option to repeat this first step or to test the system model built up so far. This general property is expressed by the feature [+holistic] for completing first, and [-holistic] for the interleaving tests. The logical complement is used here to express the mutual exclusiveness of the two alternatives. The path back to the beginning (the inner loop) is only considered if the strategy prefers "holis-

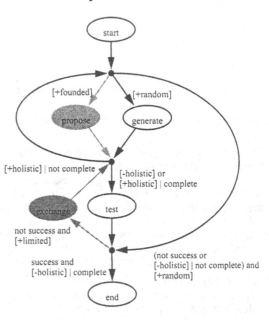

Figure 4. A coloured non-deterministic control flow for the assignment family

tic ways". The path related to the test is considered if "incremental ways" are preferred but also at least finally in the holistic case. So, deciding for an incremental strategy has trivially the following effect: The loop can be ignored but the connection to test has to be realized as an unconditioned path. The holistic strategy still prefers both paths. But

strategy "holistic"	`prefer [+holistic] over [-holistic]`
strategy "incremental"	`prefer [-holistic] over [+holistic]`

Table 2 - Two complementary strategies to be selected by the user

it is clear that the inner loop should not be repeated infinitely but only until the model is complete. This is what may be expressed by an ordinary boolean expression like "complete" or "not complete". Thus, the feature-conditioned boolean expression has to be read as: Even if the strategy preferred the path due to the feature, solely the evaluation of the boolean expression determines which path to follow. It is worth while to mention that the completeness of the model has to be checked only once - either before or after the test. Thus, this framework is able to cope with different strategies that cause different global effects on the control flow.

By introducing two modeling primitives, namely *features* in a somehow non-deterministic control flow on the one hand and *strategies* apart from the control flow on a "strategy layer" to resolve the non-determinism on the other hand the two different concerns what alternatives are available and which one should be selected could be modelled separately. Thus, a family is a parametrized representation of several PMSs with respect to the optional components and the strategies that can be chosen. This framework offers the advantage in contrast to other approaches ([ten Teije, 1997]) that the parameters are very closely attached to the conceptual models and, by this, can be exploited in a communicative situation. All parameters can be expressed in a way that can be understood by an expert but they are also useful for the knowledge engineer. After selecting a family the parameters can be checked systematically, e.g. with a questionnaire, to provide actual parameters for an instantiation of the generic family.

3 Conclusion and Related Work

The ambition to make reuse of knowledge (level) models more flexible is not new ([Geldof, 1994]). In the first version KADS ([Schreiber, Wielinga, and Breuker, 1993]) suggested a strategy layer for this purpose. But both only consider the possibility to chose between different methods with the same competence for one task. Similarly GDM ([Terpstra et al., 1993]) allows the application of alternative rewrite rules that may cause comparable effects to the graph transformation rules in the approach presented here. But none of these three frameworks allows to model explicitly decision criteria or resolution strategies. There is no flexibility related directly to the conceptual models and there is no way to capture global effects on different strategies. GDM claims that meta knowledge helps them to cope with some of these problems. But similar to task features ([Aamodt et al., 1993]) there is no direct relation to the respective part of the model so that it could be explained and justified from its context.

Other approaches focus more on strategic aspects. TASK+ ([Pierret-Golbreich and Talon, 1997]) tries to describe these with abstract data types; DESIRE ([Brazier et al. 1997]) allows to specify multi agent systems. But both are only loosely coupled to the conceptual models in the sense presented here and they are not able to separate the concerns on different layers. DESIRE e.g. uses ordinary if-statements for activating agents, i.e. for selecting the control flow. Thus, the difference between ordinary control flow and strategic aspects is not obvious in these models.

Very close in spirit is the idea of configuring PSMs via parametric design ([ten Teije et al., 1996], [ten Teije, 1997]) that is investigated for diagnosis. But the suggested parameters are only hardly to understand as underpinned by the conceptual model. The major weakness of the models is the insufficient expressiveness for specifying control flow especially for capturing alternatives.

The work presented in this paper is the only one that combines the strict relation to the conceptual models with an explicit layer to capture and specify alternatives and their resolution.

References

[Aamodt et al., 1993] A. Aamodt, B. Benus, C. Duursma, C. Tomlinson, R. Schrooten, and W. van der Velde: *Task Features and their Use in CommonKADS*. Deliverable 1.5. Version 1.0, Consortium, University of Amsterdam, 1993.

[Angele et al., 1996] J. Angele, S. Decker, R. Perkuhn, and R. Studer: Modeling Problem Solving Methods in New KARL. In: [KAW, 1996], 1-1 - 1-18.

[Angele, Fensel, and Studer, 1996] J. Angele, D. Fensel, and R. Studer: Domain and Task Modeling in MIKE. In: A. Sutcliffe, D. Benyon, F. van Assche (eds.): *Domain Knowledge for Interactive System Design*, Chapman & Hall, 1996, 149-163.

[Benjamins, 1993] R. Benjamins: *Problem Solving Methods for Diagnosis*. Ph.D. Thesis, University of Amsterdam, Amsterdam, 1993.

[Brazier et al. 1997] F.M.T. Brazier, B.M. Dunin-Keplicz, N.R. Jennings, and J. Treur: DESIRE: Modeling Multi-Agent Systems in a Compositional Framework. *International Journal of Cooperative Information Systems: Multiagent Systems*. 6 (1), 1997, 67-94.

[Breuker and van de Velde, 1994] J.A. Breuker and W. van de Velde (eds.): *The CommonKADS Library for Expertise Modeling*. IOS Press, Amsterdam, 1994.

[Chandrasekaran, Johnson, and Smith, 1992] B. Chandrasekaran, T.R. Johnson, and J.W. Smith: Task-Structure Analysis for Knowledge Modeling. *Communications of the ACM*, 35(9), 1992, 124-137.

[Eriksson et al., 1995] H. Eriksson, Y. Shahar, S.W. Tu, A.R. Puerta, and M.A. Musen: Task Modeling with Reusable Problem-Solving Methods. *Artificial Intelligence, 79*, 2, 1995, 293-326.

[Fensel, 1997] D. Fensel: The Tower-of-Adapter Method for Developing and Reusing Problem-Solving Methods. In: [Plaza and Benjamins, 1997], 97- 112.

[Fensel et al., 1999] D. Fensel, R. Benjamins, S. Decker, M. Gaspari, R. Groenboom, W. Grosso, M. Musen, E. Motta, E. Plaza, G. Schreiber, R. Studer, and B. Wielinga: The Component Model of UPML in a Nutshell. To appear in: *Proceedings of the 1st Working IFIP Conference on Software Architecture (WICSAI)*, San Antonio Texas, USA, February 22-24, 1999.

[Gamma et al., 1994] E. Gamma, R. Helm, R. Johnson, and J. Vlissides: *Design Patterns. Elements of Reusable Object-Oriented Software*. Addison-Wesley, Reading/Mass. 1994.

[Geldof, 1994] S. Geldof: Towards More Flexibility in Reuse. In: *Proceedings of the 14th International Conference in Artificial Intelligence, KBS, Expert Systems, Natural Language of Avignon*. Paris, 1994, 65-75.

[Gennari et al., 1994] J.H. Gennari, S. Tu, Th.E. Rothenfluh, and M.A. Musen: Mapping Domains to Methods in Support of Reuse. *International Journal of Human-Computer Studies (IJHCS)*, 41, 1994, 399-424.

[KAW, 1996] *Proceedings of the 10th Banff Knowledge Acquisition for Knowledge Based Systems Workshop (KAW'96)*, Banff, Canada, November 1996.

[Motta, 1997] E. Motta: *Reusable Components for Knowledge Modeling*. Ph.D. Thesis, Knowledge Media Institute, Open University, Milton Keynes, UK, 1997.

[Newell, 1982] A. Newell: The Knowledge Level. *Artificial Intelligence*, 18, 1982, 87-127.

[Orsvärn, 1996] K. Orsvärn: Principles for Libraries of Task Decomposition Methdos - Conclusions from a Case Study. In: N. Shadbolt, K. O'Hara, G. Schreiber (eds.): *Advances in Knowledge Acquisition. Proceedings of the 10th European Knowledge Acquisition Workshop (EKAW'96)*, Nottingham, England, May 1996, Lecture Notes in Artificial Intelligence (LNAI), vol. 1076, Springer, Berlin, 1996, 48-65.

[Perkuhn, 1997] R. Perkuhn: Reuse of Problem-Solving Methods and Family Resemblances. In: [Plaza and Benjamins, 1997], 174-189.

[Pierret-Golbreich and Talon, 1997] C. Pierret-Golbreich, X. Talon: Specification of Flexible Knowledge-Based Systems. In: [Plaza and Benjamins, 1997], 190-204.

[Plaza and Benjamins, 1997] E. Plaza, R. Benjamins (eds.): *Knowledge Acquisition, Modeling and Management. Proceedings of the 10th European Workshop (EKAW'97)*, Sant Feliu de Guixols, Catalonia, Spain, October 1997, Lecture Notes in Artificial Intelligence (LNAI), vol. 1319, Springer, Berlin, 1997.

[Puerta et al., 1992] A. R. Puerta, J. W. Egar, S. W. Tu, and M. A. Musen: A Multiple-Method Knowledge Acquisition Shell for the Automatic Generation of Knowledge Acquisition Tools. *Knowledge Acquisition*, 4, 1992, 171-196.

[Schreiber, Wielinga, and Breuker, 1993] G. Schreiber, B. Wielinga, and J. Breuker (eds.): *KADS. A Principled Approach to Knowledge-Based System Development*. Knowledge-Based Systems, vol. 11, Academic Press, London, 1993.

[Schreiber et al., 1994] A.Th. Schreiber, B.J. Wielinga, R. de Hoog, H. Akkermans, and W. van de Velde: CommonKADS: A Comprehensive Methodology for KBS Development. *IEEE Expert*, December 1994, 28-37.

[Shaw and Garlan, 1996] M. Shaw, D. Garlan: *Software Architectures. Perspectives on an Emerging Discipline*. Prentice Hall, Upper Saddle River, NJ, 1996.

[Steels, 1990] L. Steels: Components of Expertise. *AI Magazine*, 11(2), 1990, 29-49.

[ten Teije, 1997] A. ten Teije: *Automated Configuration of Problem Solving Methods in Diagnosis*. Ph.D. Thesis, University of Amsterdam, Amsterdam, 1997.

[ten Teije et al., 1996] A. ten Teije, F. van Harmelen, G. Schreiber, and B. Wielinga: Construction of Problem Solving Methods as Parametric Design. In: [KAW, 1996], 12-1 - 12-20

[Terpstra et al., 1993] P. Terpstra, G. van Heijst, B. Wielinga, and N. Shadbolt: Knowledge Acquisition Support Through Generalized Directive Models. In: J.-M. David, J.-P. Krivine, and R. Simmons (eds.): *Second Generation Expert Systems*, Springer, Berlin, 1993, 428-455.

Meta Knowledge for Extending Diagnostic Consultation to Critiquing Systems[1]

Frank Puppe

Institute for Artificial Intelligence and Applied Informatics,
Würzburg University, Am Hubland, D-97074 Würzburg, Germany

Abstract. Critiquing systems check for weaknesses in the user's solution and may suggest corrections. Although their usefulness was first emphasized in diagnostic domains [6], the main success of knowledge based critiquing systems have been in design applications [4, 13]. While in the latter a deep understanding is often not necessary for critiquing purposes, in complex diagnostic domains the capability to solve the problems is critical for critiquing systems. However, they need additional knowledge to adjust to the user's solution instead of merely inferring solutions by themselves. We analyze that knowledge and propose a minimal model for extending a diagnostic consultation to a critiquing shell.

1. Introduction

A critiquing system has been defined as a "decision support system that allows the user to make the decision first; the system then gives its advice when the user requests it or when the user's decision is out of the system's permissible range" [2]. They are particularly useful in domains, where knowledge based systems are unable to take legal or economic responsibility for the adequacy of their solutions. For example, developers of medical consultation systems would not accept, that they - as legal proxies of their systems - are responsible for its diagnoses and therapy recommendations in the same way physicians are. In such situations human experts need the full knowledge to solve problems by themselves. Therefore they cannot profit very much from knowledge based systems offering the same capability, unless there is some synergy effect. This holds not only for medicine, but for all applications where human experts are still better than knowledge systems and where wrong decisions might be very dangerous or expensive. While the potential for synergy between human experts and machine intelligence is large due to their different strengths and weaknesses, it is not easy to exploit, because someone has to decide, under what circumstances whose solutions are better. Few knowledge based systems have faced this challenge, but usually left it to expert users, at best with the support of good explanation components. A major exception are critiquing systems [13], which were popularized by Perry Miller [6] in the eighties due to his frustration with acceptance problems of knowledge based systems in medicine.

Fischer et al. [91] distinguish between two general approaches of critiquing:
- Analytical critiquing: The system checks products with respect to predefined features and effects. This approach does not need a complete domain model and is particularly suited for many design problems (e.g. JANUS [3] for kitchen design).
- Differential critiquing: The system generates its own solution, compares it with the user's solution and points out relevant differences. Many critiquing systems e.g. HYPERCRITIC [7], a ship damage control system [11] or the electronic cockpit assistant CASSY [5] have a component which represents an ideal expert as yardstick for

---

[1] This work has been supported by the Deutsche Forschungsgemeinschaft (DFG; grant Pu 129/2 1).

the correctness of the user's decision. However, if the user's solution is radically different from the system's solution, a direct comparison might be not very helpful. This can be avoided to some degree by evaluating the user's solution step by step in his/her context.

The main success of critiquing systems lies in the design domain [4, 13]. When an artifact has to be constructed meeting certain requirements, it is quite easy to check, whether the solution meets the requirements, even if there is no knowledge how to configure the artifact from primitive elements in the first place. Under these circumstances, critiquing systems are often easier to build than problem solvers, and they might be very useful to assess the quality of an offered solution, even if they are unable to repair detected problems. For example, grammar and style checkers in text editors are much easier to build than generators of well readable sentences. In diagnostic domains, similar situations exist, e.g., when a hypothesis can be questioned if certain conditions do not hold. In general however, to criticize a hypothesis requires knowledge to reconstruct the inference process and the ability to find better hypotheses. The reason is the inherent probabilistic nature of most diagnostic domains. If an expert suggests a diagnostic or therapeutic decision s/he usually has good arguments in favor for it – and as well against it. The problem is the weighing of both. Since the weight of the arguments depends on the peculiarities of the case, a critiquing system needs lots of detailed knowledge. This is probably an important reason, why diagnostic critiquing systems in vague domains did not proceed much beyond the prototype stage initiated by the pioneering work of Perry Miller.

Therefore we propose a reuse approach: Add additional knowledge for critiquing to the knowledge of a standard diagnostic problem solver without overburdening the knowledge provider. It aims at a synthesis between differential and analytic critics [12], the latter supplementing the differential approach by checking for a minimal performance standard and by making sure, that the user's solution contains no obvious mistakes stored in a library.

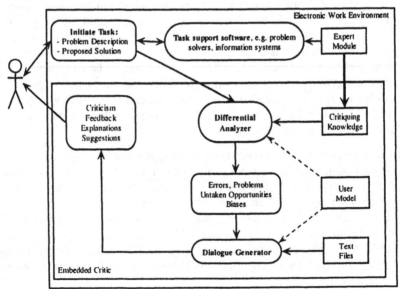

Fig. 1: General architecture of critiquing systems, with emphasis on the reuse of the expert module.

An architecture for critiquing systems is shown in fig. 1 (adapted from [13]). The user enters a problem description together with a solution. In the problem solving process, s/he may be supported by task support software, e.g. information or knowledge systems based on an expert module. The embedded critique consists of a differential analyzer detecting errors, problems, untaken opportunities or biases in the proposed solution. Based on a user model, the dialogue generator then decides on what information to present to the user in what form (criticism, feedback, explanations, suggestions). The difference to the model from [13] is, that the expert module of the task support software is reused by the critiquing system and enriched by additional "critiquing knowledge".

Critiquing systems are quite similar to intelligent tutoring systems [14] and in particular to training systems (e.g. [10]) presenting a problem to the user and providing feedback in the solution process. The main difference is, that training systems have total control over the characteristics of the presented problems. Therefore they do not have to question their problem solving capabilities and face much less uncertainty about the correctness of their generated feedback than critiquing systems.

Designing a critiquing system depends on an analysis of what can go wrong in diagnostics. It relates to the quality of the input data, the data gathering process and the solution. Accordingly, a diagnostic critiquing system can pursue different goals:

- Check for a *minimal performance standard*. This includes the avoidance of well known errors as well as the conformity with positive guidelines.
- Check whether the *cost/benefit relation* for problem solving is acceptable. In many diagnostic domains expensive tests for checking everything exist, but there might be a limit for the total costs refundable in a given case.
- Check the *reliability of the input data*. This includes, whether sufficient data for problem solving are available and how reliable the data items are. The latter is particularly important, if the solution depends on a few critical observations.
- Check, whether *better solutions* (e.g. more probable) than the proposed one exist and rate the difference.
- Check, whether *plausible alternatives* to the proposed solution exist. They need not necessarily be more probable, but should take the importance of diagnoses into account, e.g. in medicine, whether they are dangerous, treatable or urgent.

2. Additional critiquing knowledge and inference strategy

To achieve these goals, critiquing systems need additional knowledge besides a knowledge base for solving problems:

A *minimal performance standard* can be expressed with positive and negative categorical rules or constraints, which might be qualified with a weight and an informal explanation, e.g. if granites, then glimmer with high weight. This partial knowledge is used in the way of the analytical critiquing approach. Although a good knowledge base should implicitly include such knowledge, a critiquing system greatly profits from representing it explicitly as a different knowledge type. This has several advantages during knowledge acquisition, which compensate for the redundancy: First, partial knowledge for avoiding severe mistakes can be seen as a second level of competence, which lessen the severity of break-downs in the full knowledge base. Second, it is easy to check the adequacy of categorical knowledge, but much more difficult to decide, whether such knowledge is implicitly encoded in cases or probabilities of a full knowledge base. Third, changes in full knowledge bases might have unforeseen side effects, especially if the developer of the knowledge base is not available. Adding "safety constraints" to a body of existing knowledge is much less error-prone. The usefulness of this kind of "safety net" in complex domains is also demonstrated in the medical literature, where so called guidelines [8] for ensuring a minimal performance standard in well-circumscribed situations are gaining popularity. In complex domains, guidelines cannot be complete and there remains considerable room for decisions not covered by the minimal performance standard. Therefore we classify such guidelines as partial knowledge.

A check of the *cost/benefit relation* needs knowledge about the costs and benefits of the diagnostic tests and therapies. While the costs and risks can be easily represented for each action, the benefits are context-sensitive. There are two strategies: a local strategy, where each test is justified in terms of the hypotheses it helps to clarify, and a global strategy, where a threshold for the cumulated costs of all tests is precomputed based on general parameters of the case (e.g. the diagnostic costs for an old car should not exceed x percent of its current value). While the knowledge for the local strategy is usually contained in a standard knowledge base and its usefulness depends on its overall quality, the global strategy requires additional knowledge about such thresholds.

Due to our experience, *unreliable input data* is responsible for most of the errors of an interactive diagnostic system in routine use. Therefore, some consistency checking is necessary even in the consultation mode (e.g. for relations like the systolic blood pressure being higher than the diastolic one). However most of the possible errors with input data cannot be detected by consistency checking. A possible solution would be to request the user to enter the degree of reliability for every observation. This would be very time-consuming and therefore lower user acceptance of the whole system. Instead, default values can be used for the typical reliability of observations (e.g. laboratory data is usually more reliable than history information). Only in critical instances, the user is requested to overwrite the default value. They arise if an important conclusion depends on the existence of a typically uncertain symptom. For example, the density of a rock can be assessed or measured by weighing the clean rock and its water displacement. If assessing is used as default, the user should overwrite the low default reliability value when measuring. Another situation where one should be cautious about the validity of conclusions is, if not enough input data is available, either because the respective tests have not been performed or the user answers important questions with "unknown". Therefore, for each conclusion the minimal input data requirements should be defined explicitly, e.g. for classifying igneous rocks, one should always be sure about the presence or absence of the key minerals quartz, feldspar, pyroxene, olivine.

In diagnostics, finding *better solutions* than the user's proposal requires the availability of a fully developed problem solver able to compute and compare the probability of the user's solution with its own. However, differences between the system's and the user's solution can be due to many causes. Even if the data seems reliable and not too incomplete, the system might err for lots of other potential reasons, e.g. its knowledge base might contain errors, the case might be very untypical, there might be different schools of opinions which are not necessarily better or worse. There are several complementary solutions to this problem: The system should be critical about the quality of its own solution. Since this depends on the quality of the knowledge base as a whole or for inferring each diagnosis, the latter should be specified. This might be done by self-assessment of the expert who built the knowledge base or by evaluation with cases. Several knowledge bases for the same domain might improve the assessment, e.g. if all of them agree on the same diagnosis, but disagree with the user's proposal, there is more justification to criticize the user than if knowledge bases dissent. The different knowledge bases might use different representations (e.g. heuristic, causal, case-based or statistic knowledge), and/or might be developed by different experts. Finally, the system can perform a differential analysis, i.e. analyze whether different expectations of the user's and its own solution for certain observations exist and compare these expectations with the actual observations. If some of them are yet unknown, it might suggest to explore them.

Checking for *plausible alternatives* to the user's solution is in principle similar to checking for better solutions, but uses different criteria for making suggestions. The system might focus on important diagnoses, either specified by the user or by standard criteria like treatability, danger and urgency. For example, it often makes sense to suggest therapeutic actions for a treatable diagnosis, which is dangerous without therapy - even if the diagnosis is not the most probable one. An alternative might be to suggest additional tests, but the corresponding time delay should be taken into account. If the treatment is risky in itself, the various outcomes with and without therapy and their probabilities must be weighed. If all parameters can be quantified, decision theory is the best choice.

The inference strategy of the critiquing system is straightforward. It infers its own solution and tries to reconstruct the user's solution based on the problem description. Besides it checks with its additional knowledge, whether there is some reason for critiquing the user's actions (i.e. tests, diagnoses, therapies) in a particular case. The result is a list of potential critiquing items (in the following summarized as "containers").

1. Check whether a negative critiquing constraint is violated. Since they represent typical errors of the user, they are noted in a container named "standard-errors".
2. Check of the explicit positive critiquing rules. If such a rule recommends an action which the user has not chosen, this is noted in a container "guideline-ignorance".
3. Check of the importance of the system's and the user's diagnoses and the costs and risks of their tests and therapies. Diagnoses with high importance values are listed in a container "important-diagnoses" and costly tests and therapies in "high-costs".
4. Reliability check of the input data for the items in the critiquing containers from the first two steps and for the user's as well as the system's actions. If they depend on single data items being marked as unreliable, the system notes these action/data pairs in a container "increase-reliability".
5. Completeness check of the input data with respect to both the system's and the user's actions. If important data is missing, the data together with the respective action is recorded in a container "increase-completeness".
6. Check the reliability of the system's actions. Actions are listed in a container "high-rated-system-actions", if the numerical score of their certainty combined with the general reliability in the respective part of the knowledge base is rather high.
7. Check for different expectations for observations based on the assumption, that the system's resp. the user's solution is correct. Record these observations with their respective values and their actual value in a container "differential-analysis".

If there are several knowledge bases, the steps 4-7 are done for each knowledge base independently. All critiques are rated with a severity number according to importance.

The user feedback is generated from these critiquing containers based on the severity of the items and the user model with preferences concerning the priorities and the different critiquing types. The user model acts in essence as a filter on the items. There are many interdependencies between the item in the critiquing containers: The ratings of standard errors, guideline-ignorance, high-rated-system-diagnoses and differential-analysis depend strongly on the reliability check of the respective input data, and high-rated-system-diagnoses also depend strongly on the degree of completeness of the necessary input data. If the system's action list contains important diagnoses not taken into account by the user, their critiquing priority is increased. Besides presenting potential problems on the critiquing list, the system also tries to offer remedies, in particular requests for additional data or for increasing their reliability.

3. Conclusions and Outlook

Diagnostic critiquing systems help the diagnostician in the decision making process indirectly, commenting the user's decisions only if they seem to be suboptimal. They can reuse the knowledge base of a well structured diagnostic consultation system needing relatively little additional knowledge as outlined in this paper. Currently we are working on implementing and evaluating these concepts in various medical domains based within our diagnostic shell kit D3 [9].

Critiquing systems can also extend the capabilities of intelligent training systems by enabling them to deal with more realistic cases without clear solutions. A high potential lies in the promising field of diagnostic multiagent systems [1], where different agents work together to diagnose complex cases. For example, one agent might critique the results of another agent if both agents have similar competence profiles.

4. References

[1] Bamberger, S. (1997): Cooperating Diagnostic Expert Systems to Solve Complex Diagnosis Tasks, in: Proc. of German Conference on AI (KI-97), Springer, LNAI 1303, 325-336.

[2] van Bemmel, J. and Musen, M. (1997): Handbook of Medical Informatics, Springer.

[3] Fischer, G., McCall, R. and Morch, A. (1989): Design Environments for Constructive and Argumentative Design, in: Human Factor in Computing Systems, Proc. of CHI'89, ACM, 269-275.

[4] Fischer, G., Lemke, A., Mastaglio, T., and Morch, A. (1991): The Role of Critiquing in Cooperative Problem Solving, ACM Transactions on Information Systems 9/3, 123-151.

[5] Gerlach, M. and Onken, R. (1994): CASSY – The Electronic Part of a Human-Electronic Crew, in: 3rd International Workshop on Human-Computer-Teamwork, Cambridge, UK.

[6] Miller, P. (1986): Expert Critiquing Systems, Springer.

[7] Mosseveld, B. and van der Lei, J. (1990): HYPERCRITIC: A Critiquing System for Hypertension, in: O'Moore et al.: Medical Informatics, Europe '90, Springer.

[8] Ohmann, C. (1997): Was ist Qualitätsmanagement? [What is Quality Management], in: Scheibe (Hrsg.): Qualitätsmanagement in der Medizin - Handbuch für Klinik und Praxis, ecomed.

[9] Puppe, F. (1998): Knowledge Reuse among Diagnostic Problem Solving Methods in the Shell-Kit D3, in: International Journal of Human-Computer Studies 49, 627-649.

[10] Puppe, F. and Reinhardt, B. (1995): Generating Case-Oriented Training from Diagnostic Expert Systems, Machine Mediated Learning 5, No. 3&4, 199-219.

[11] Ramachandran, S. and Wilkins, D. (1996): Temporal Control Structures in Expert Critiquing Systems, in: TIME-96, Workshop of the FLAIRS 96, Florida.

[12] Rhein-Desel, U. and Puppe, F. (1998): Concepts for a Diagnostic Critiquing Systems in Vague Domains, Proc. of German Conference on AI (KI-98), Springer, LNAI 1504, 201-212.

[13] Silverman, B. (1992): Survey of Expert Critiquing Systems; Practical and Theoretical Frontiers, CACM 35, No.4, 106-127.

[14] Wenger, E. (1987): Artificial Intelligence and Tutoring Systems, Morgan Kaufman,

Exploitation of XML for Corporate Knowledge Management

Auguste Rabarijoana, Rose Dieng , Olivier Corby

INRIA, ACACIA Project, 2004 Route des Lucioles, BP 93,

06902 Sophia-Antipolis Cedex, France

E-mail:{Rose.Dieng, Olivier.Corby}@sophia.inria.fr,

Tel: 33 - 4 92 38 48 10 or 33 - 4 92 38 78 71, Fax: 33 - 4 92 38 77 83

Abstract. This paper emphasizes the interest of XML meta-language for corporate knowledge management and presents an experiment of enterprise-ontology-guided search in XML documents constituting a part of a corporate memory.

1 Introduction

Extending the definition proposed by [14], we define a corporate memory (CM) as an *«explicit, disembodied, persistent representation of knowledge and information in an organization, in order to facilitate their access and reuse by members of the organization, for their tasks»*. Several techniques can be adopted for building the CM [6]: it may be non computational, database-based, document-based, knowledge-based, case-based, Web-based... The Web can serve as a basis for information and knowledge distribution in a uniform way. Ontologies can be exploited for guiding information search on the Web, as in Ontobroker [7], SHOE [10], and WebCokace [3].

Our work is situated in the context of a *document-based corporate memory, distributed through the Web*. After showing the interest of XML meta-language for corporate knowledge management, we will describe an experiment of enterprise ontology-guided search in XML documents.

2 XML and Knowledge Management

HTML, the most popular language for Web documents, has some drawbacks: lack of extensibility, of structure and of validation [1]. As HTML is used as a presentation-oriented markup language, it is very difficult to process information embodied in HTML. In order to obviate these drawbacks, a working group of W3C created XML (eXtensible Markup Language) intended to be a standard for creation of markup languages [8]. XML has been designed for *distributing structured documents on the Web*. It is a kind of light SGML (Standard General Markup Language), simplified to meet Web requirements.

The specification of XML can be found in [2]. Contrarily to HTML, XML allows the users [1]: (a) to define their own tags and attributes; (b) to define data structures, and to nest document structures at any level of complexity; (c) to make applications allowing to test the structural validity of a document; (d) to extract data from a XML document. As such, the new standard XML has some major advantages for CM management, mixing SGML and Web advantages.

Many Views on the Same Data. XML enables to manage information and knowledge in a unique structured way and enables several different processings. Knowledge servers retrieve information while clients are in charge of presenting it to users through adapted interfaces. It is then possible to take users and context into account and to present different views of the same data: it may be possible to generate graphic views, table of contents or to show the data themselves. Furthermore, data are loaded into the client (the browser) and can be processed locally: e.g. XML data can be processed by Java applets [1]. Hence, XML may represent for data what Java represents for programs: transparent portability through machines and operating systems.

Documents Built from Heterogenous Data. XML enables to manage structured documents and structured data in a uniform way. The XML format has been designed to enable document description as well as arbitrary data description. It is hence possible to mix data and documents in order to build *virtual documents issued from several sources*. Data may come from a technical data base while text may come from a document management environment. Furthermore, it is possible to annotate documents with modeled knowledge, so-called ontologies.

Standard for Information Exchange. In order to facilitate communication and information exchange, a community (i.e. a department, a company, a group of companies of the same domain, a company and its related providers and clients, etc) may define a standard domain-oriented or application-oriented vocabulary by means of a DTD (Document Type Definition). A DTD is a syntactic specification being used as model for XML documents. A document is considered as valid if it respects the DTD with which it is associated. Documents or data can then be expressed with the defined XML markups and then be exchanged using these markups [1].

Document Formatting . XML has a companion formalism called XSL (Extensible Stylesheet Language), to define document-oriented presentation format. XSL may present a document in HTML, PDF, etc. It may also generate a generic format, that may be postprocessed to generate a standard output format. XSL also enables elementary document processing such as sorting, generating table of contents, tables, reorganizing the document structure. Using XSL, it is hence possible to define several output formats for the same document structure: XSL is a document transformation and formatting language. It is possible to write once and to publish many times, from the same source, to different media: digital and paper-based ones. This is very interesting for CM management.

Hypertext. XML will also offer tools to build powerful hypertext documents by means of XLL (XML Linking Language), and XPointer, the language that enables navigation in documents according to their structure. XLL will implement the major hypertext functionality that can be found in dedicated tools: links between more than two documents, external links, links with semantics, etc. With external links, documents can be annotated from the outside, without modifying the source.

Information Search. XML facilitates information search because documents are structured and, hence, can be considered as a database. It is possible to rely on standardized markups to search information in a structured way. Moreover, the database community is currently integrating XML with database technology and search languages (cf. XML-QL [5]).

XML and Memory Management. XML as a structured document open standard may be a good candidate to facilitate migration to new systems or software through long time period: XML documents exist by themselves, independently of processing tools.

3 Enterprise model - guided search in XML documents

Taking into account those interesting features of XML, we developed the system OSI-RIX (*Ontology-guided Search for Information Retrieval In XML-documents*), based on techniques of *enterprise-model-guided search in XML documents*.

3.1 Information Search Guided by Knowledge Models

Our main objective is to perform information search in documents on the Web, guided by knowledge models. The result should include only relevant answers i.e. Web documents which «correspond semantically» to the request. Instead of developing a specific extension of HTML, we choose to handle XML documents. The knowledge models that will guide the search will be CommonKADS expertise models, represented in standard CML language [13]. Two main phases are necessary: (a) the *creation of XML documents* containing structured, semantic information, so that they can be found later on as answers to requests. This document creation is performed by the document author or by the CM builder; (b) and *search for information in the XML documents*. It is carried out by the OSIRIX system, after a request of the CM user.

Creation of Documents. The documents must be annotated by ontological information in order to have a «semantical value» enabling their retrieval.

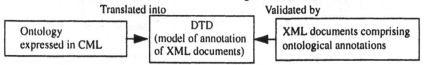

Fig. 1: Link between CML and XML

This ontological information can stem from an ontology developed by the company or imported from external world, and upon which the company members agree. From this ontology, a DTD will be generated by our system OSIRIX: then the documents of the CM must respect this DTD that indicates the (optional) elements that can be used as ontological annotations in the documents. We could also require the company members to agree directly on a given DTD. But, as a DTD is rather difficult to read, we prefer to require the company members to agree on the ontology supposed represented in CML. Then, in order to enable to annotate semantically the documents by this ontology, the OSIRIX system generates automatically a DTD based on this ontology.

Search for Information. In order to answer the user's requests, the system seeks in the ontological part of the documents, if an ontological answer is present there or not. The ontological filtering engine finds the documents answers among the candidate documents. If the system does not find exact answers, it can exploit the ontology to seek approximate answers: it can exploit the concept hierarchy to find an answer corresponding to subconcepts of the concept appearing in the initial request. A scenario of information retrieval is shown in figure 2.

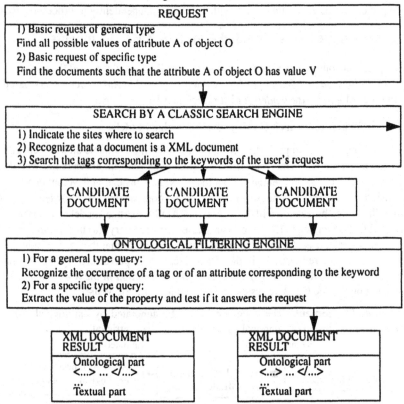

Fig. 2: Scenario of the information search in XML documents

Example: for the request «Find all the reports written by any company for the project named GENIE», OSIRIX will find documents having ontological information such as :

```
<project>
    <name> GENIE</name>
    <report> Rapport final du projet Genie, Thème 3, Lot L3.3.2.1
        <authors> Nada Matta, Olivier Corby</authors>
        <company>INRIA</company>
        <title>Description de modèles de coopération et gestion de conflits</
title>
        <date>Juin 1996</date>
    </report>
</project>
```

3.2   Implementation of the OSIRIX System

Translation Engine from CML into a DTD. The translator of CML to DTD, detailed in [12], is implemented using the tool PPML (Pretty Printer Minicomputer-Language) of CENTAUR generator [4], and a manager of object inheritance mechanism. PPML allows to generate a textual representation starting from a tree of objects. Here is a part of the translator of the concepts in CML into DTD:

```
concept(*name, con_body(*descr, *super, *prop_list, *axioms)) ->
    [<v>
    [<h 1> «<!ELEMENT» *name «(» inhslotvrg(*name) *prop_list «)>»]
    [<h 1> «<!ATTLIST» *name «name_id» «ID #IMPLIED>»]
    def_child::*prop_list];
```

Example : from the following concept of an ontology in CML:

```
concept report
    properties: title: universal
                authors: universal
                date: universal
                company: universal
end concept report
```

the following DTD will be generated automatically:

```
<!ELEMENT report (title?, authors?, date?, company?)>
<!ATTLIST report name_id ID #IMPLIED>
<!ELEMENT title(#PCDATA)>
<!ELEMENT authors (#PCDATA)>
<!ELEMENT date(#PCDATA)>
<!ELEMENT company (#PCDATA)>
```

Once the DTD obtained, the authors create their XML documents, by respecting the specifications of the DTD.

Validation engine. The purpose of the validation engine is to check if the syntax specified in the DTD is well followed by the documents of the company [2]. We chose the parser «XML for JAVA» of IBM [9]. The validation of a document allows the company to make sure that this document can later constitute an answer.

Ontological filtering engine. The ontological filtering engine [12] aims at determining all the XML elements that are present in a given XML document, and to test the semantic presence of a concept (or any other entity) in the XML document. We call «semantic presence» of an attribute (resp. concept) in a XML document, the fact that this attribute (resp. concept) appears in the XML document as a tag in the ontological part. Ontological information can be regarded as meta-information and need not be visible through a browser. The test on the two kinds of basic requests relies on this «semantic presence».

We used SAX, an event-based application programming interface [11]: it sends back events to the application, each time that it meets an element, an attribute, a document, etc. The type of event depends on the type of data encountered.

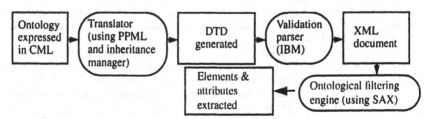

Fig. 3: Internal architecture of OSIRIX

Implementation. We used WebCokace [3] to implement in CML an extension of the AIAI>s enterprise ontology [14] that was translated into a DTD (using PPML). We exploited the IBM validation parser «XML for JAVA», in order to validate the XML documents w.r.t. the DTD. We implemented the ontological filtering engine. It remains to implement the query interface and to integrate the ontological filtering engine in a browser (once browsers for XML will be available).

4   Conclusions

The paper stressed the advantages of XML for corporate knowledge management and presented OSIRIX that offers enterprise ontology-guided search in XML documents. As WebCokace [3], it relies on CommonKADS method and CML language: the extension of AIAI Enterprise ontology was implemented in WebCokace and the translator was implemented using PPML. The exploitation of XML instead of HTML and a lack of exploitation of axioms are the main differences between OSIRIX and WebCokace, Ontobroker [7] or SHOE [10]. Compared to classic search engines, information search is still keyword-based in OSIRIX, but there, the keywords have a semantics. As a further work, we will exploit the CML axioms, we will implement the request interface, and once XML browsers will be available, we will integrate OSIRIX in them.

References

1. Bosak, J. XML, Java, and the Future of the Web. March 1997. http://sunsite.unc.edu/pub/sun-info/standards/xml/why/xmlapps.htm
2. Bray, T. , Paoli, J., Sperberg-McQueen, C. M. Extensible Markup Language (XML) 1.0 W3C Recommendation. http://www.w3.org/TR/REC-xml
3. Corby, O., Dieng, R. A CommonKADS Expertise Model Web Server, Proc. of ISMICK'97, Compiègne, (1997).
4. Projet Croap INRIA. The PPML Manual.. Manuel de référence du Pretty Printer Mini-language I et II.
5. Deutsch, A., Fernandez, M., Florescu, D., Levy, A. Suciu, D. XML-QL: A Query Language for XML. Submission to the World Wide Web Consortium, (1998).
6. Dieng, R., Corby, O., Giboin, A., Ribière, M. Methods and Tools for Corporate Knowledge Management. Proc. of KAW'98, Banff, Alberta, Canada, (1998).
7. Fensel, D., Decker, S., Erdmann, M. and Studer, R. Ontobroker: Or How to Enable Intelligent Access to the WWW. In B. Gaines, M. Musen eds, Proc of KAW'98, Banff, Canada, (1998).
8. Garshol, L. M. Introduction to XML. http://www.stud.ifi.uio.no/~larsga/download/xml/xml_eng.html
9. Hiroshi, M., Kent, T. Parser IBM XML for JAVA. http ://www.alphaworks.ibm.com/formula/xml. World Wide Web Journal
10. Luke, S. , Spector, L., Rager, D., Hendler, J. Ontology-based Web Agents. In Proc. of the First Int. Conference on Autonomous Agents, (1997).
11. Megginson Technologies Ltd. SAX 1.0 The Simple API for XML. http://www.megginson.com/SAX/
12. Rabarijoana, A. Aide à la recherche d'informations sur le Web guidée par des modèles de connaissances. DEA Report, INRIA-Sophia-Antipolis, (1998).
13. Schreiber, G., Wielinga, B., Akkermans, H., van de Velde, W., Anjewierden, A. CML: The Common-KADS Conceptual Modelling Language. In L. Steels & al, eds, A Future for Knowl. Acqu.: Proc. of EKAW'94,Hoegaarden, Belgium, (1994) 1–25. Springer-Verlag, LNAI n. 867.
14. Uschold, M., King, M., Moralee, S., Zorgios, Y. The Enterprise Ontology. The Knowledge Engineering Review , Vol. 13, Special Issue on Putting Ontologies to Use (1996).
15. Van Heijst, G, Van der Spek, R., and Kruizinga, E. Organizing Corporate Memories. In B. Gaines, M. Musen eds, Proc. of KAW'96, Banff, Canada, (1996) 42-1 42-17.

An Oligo-Agents System with Shared Responsibilities for Knowledge Management

Franz Schmalhofer and Ludger van Elst

German Research Center for Artificial Intelligence (DFKI),
University Bldg. 57, Erwin-Schroedinger-Str., D-67663 Kaiserlautern
{schmalho,elst}@dfki.uni-kl.de

1 Introduction

Management and information sciences as well as everyday practice in organizations have shown that in the modern information age, knowledge is the most important asset for any business enterprise [1]. However, many employees of companies frequently complain that important and interesting information is not forwarded to them. Simultaneously they sigh about being swamped with useless information that is arriving at their desktops. Their complaints of obtaining too much and too little information is a clear indication that they are not getting the information which is right for their specific interests and the particular tasks which were assigned to them. This is specifically true for the modern information age and the knowledge society where the available information increases dramatically from year to year and the potential speed of distribution appears to be almost unlimited.

In this paper, we propose a possible solution of the knowledge management problem with particular regard to the responsibilities that result from different users cooperating in such systems. In section 2, we present a brief analysis of knowledge management techniques that are often in use nowadays. Section 3 introduces the structure of an oligo-agents system for knowledge management in organizations. In section 4, the cornerstones of proposed system are summarized. Section 5 finishes the paper with a short disussion.

2 Knowledge Management in Multi-User Environments

The problem of getting the *right information* to the *right people* at the *right time* is the central issue of any practical knowledge management endeavor. Although it is not exclusively a technical problem, the new intranet-based technologies can very well help to develop a more complete solution to the distribution and comprehension of information in organizations.

The technologies which are most frequently used these days for the management of information in intranets are *corporate and organizational memories*, *e-mail* (including the possibility of defining *alias lists*), *news systems* and *search engines*. Hierarchical browsing and search engines are used for retrieving some desired information from the organizational memory (information pull). Similar to a traditional newspaper, electronic news systems are used to distribute timely information (categorized according some existing areas of interest, e.g. "rec.music.makers.percussion"). List servers provide similar functionalities for a more local community. Similar to traditional mail, electronic mail is used for sending out individual or bulk letters by alias lists (information push).

Each of these tools has explicitly or implicitly built in certain categorizations or representations about groups of people or groups of documents. For example, the categories of a news system represent the different document classes which are shared between the providers and the consumers of the information in the news system. Other relevant categorizations, e.g. which persons may be interested in obtaining some news are, however, neither explicitly nor implicitly represented in such news systems. E-mail distribution lists in the form of aliases, on the other hand, are typically organized so that the aliases represent groups of people who are interested in obtaining similar information. For the knowledge management task in which the different functionalities are combined, all these different representations are important, even when they are not explicitly or implicitly represented in the specific tool.

In a more technical description, having the right documents at the right people at the right time means that within some given timeframe one achieves 100% recall with regard to a given information base and 100% precision with respect to the particular information consumer. As there is of course the well-known trade-off between precision and recall, this is obviously already a difficult problem for a single user query of an information base and . For multi-user domains it does not become any easier, especially because users may independently have control over one of the parameters as well as different interests whether precision or recall values should be optimized. Although the forementioned information tools (e-mail lists, news systems, etc.) may provide important components for the desired solution, a unifying view which is focused on the concept of time and information responsibility is needed for achieving some significant progress.

3 The Distribution and Comprehension of Documents within an Organization

Because in a multi-user environment different people may have separate control over the recall and precision parameters, not only the technical aspects but also social entities like responsibilities, contracts and agreements are of central importance for successful knowledge management. We therefore need to consider the different *social roles* of the people participating in such a system.

When an intranet is used as an organizational memory, one usually distinguishes between the *authors* (or *information providers*) who supply the various documents, the *administrators* who maintain the memory system (i.e. they serve the function of librarians) and the *information consumers* who read some of the stored documents. Because the distribution of documents is a separate task in its own right, it requires responsible action. This role is taken by a so-called *distributor* who is equipped with the required privileges.

The core task of the proposed system involves assigning groups of *information consumers* to *groups of documents*. As mentioned above, the functions of news systems and alias lists should be combined with a representation of the structure and contents of the organizational memory. These functions will be implemented as an oligo-agents system with *two types of agents*, namely the *global agents* (a global manager GloMa and comprehension assistant) and *individual agents* (termed ConPersonA, ConPersonB, ... for each information consumer and ProPersonA, ProPersonB, ... for each information provider, respectively). These agents live in a three-tier client/server architecture. The global agents are located at an *application server* and have access to the organizational memory. The individual agents are located at the *clients* and communicate with the organizational memory via GloMa by using the standard intranet protocols.

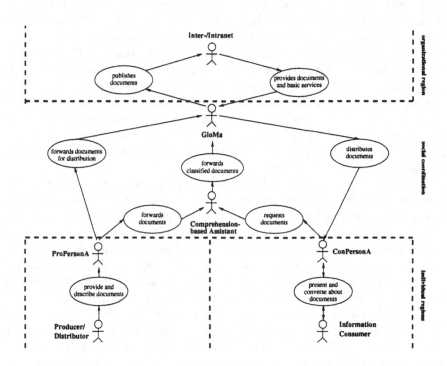

Fig. 1. Structure of the oligo-agents system for distribution and comprehension assistance within an organization

As shown in Figure 1, the issue of individual and social responsibilities is adressed by deviding the system into three regions: The first region embodies the *organizational needs*, e.g. the requirements of the underlying intranet or corporate memory. Individual regions embody the *personal interests* of the different individuals who are involved (information providers, distributors and consumers). A social coodination region serves as a *negotiation space* for discussing conflicting as well as consonant interests. The agents located in this region have access to global knowledge (e.g. about all documents) as well as to different portions of knowledge that belong to individual agents (provided that the individual agents enable them, e.g. in the case of a user query).

In the next section, we give a comprehensive overview of the pivotal properties of the oligo-agents system to accomplish the task of information dissemination.

4 The Oligo-Agents System in a Nutshell

The central data structures of the proposed system are *distribution lists* and *interest lists* which are conceived as relations between information consumer groups and document groups. The lists can be described at *abstract levels* (intensional descriptions) which are based on *concrete descriptions*. These concrete descriptions can easily be matched with the information base and thereby the extensions of the consumer-document relations can be obtained. The **distribution and interest lists** are defined by a) the *attributes* that are already used in the organizational memory for describing the documents (e.g. document type, language, version, brief summary, etc.), b)*structural properties* with respect to the location where the document is stored in the organizational memory and the site where an information consumer is organizationally located (e.g. in the organigram) and c) *automatic contents analysis techniques* that allow a three-level representation of each document.

The content descriptions of the documents are generated by a **comprehension assistant**[2]. This assistant generates word-oriented representations (*surface level*) as well as more abstract representations in discrete (*propositional level*) and continuous (*situational level*) representation spaces.[1] The comprehension assistant coordinates a negotiation process between the different users so that the representation spaces can be specified in a way that they are useful and understandable for the various users. Thereby a mutual understanding may be shared among increasingly more people and increasingly more documents.

The **global manager** GloMa *keeps and maintains repositories* that are used for the definition of user profiles (information consumers), document groups and distribution and interest lists. Thereby it is possible to use the available information, consisting of document attributes, document contents and organizational structures as a whole. Furthermore, GloMa maintains a *continually updated representation of the organizational memory*. Each document that is newly published, updated or translated in the organizational memory must thus be reported to GloMa. Unlike the openess of the world-wide web, an organizational memory allows the formation of a relatively complete representation,

---

[1] Whereas the propositional level's abstraction are more local (by the application of ontologies and thesauri), the situational level forms abstractions of entire documents by *latent semantic analysis* [3].

because the relevant actions of the various users can in principle all be reported to GloMa.

Documents of the organizational memory that *participate* in the distribution and comprehension assistant are *marked* and can thus be distinguised from those documents that are solely stored (and not to be distributed). Thereby, it is possible to *introduce the assistant function to an increasingly larger set of documents* and the functions of information distribution and storage can be combined in a gradual manner. Since the responsibilities of authors, administrators and distributors are clearly defined, the consequences of the various distribution list are kept under control.

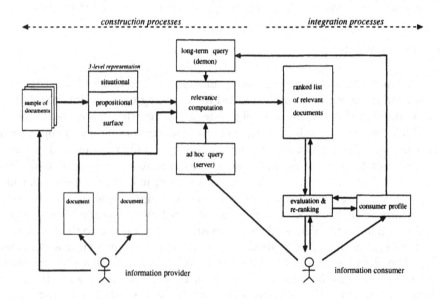

Fig. 2. Knowledge construction and knowledge integration processes for three-level representations as a means for accomplishing mutual understanding among information providers and information consumers

Decoupling of *definition time, information-identification time* and *presentation time* (through assisting each of these activities by a specialized agent with an appropriate time concept) allows distribution to be determined either by the individual or as a common responsibility of administrator, author, distributors and information consumers. These responsibilities may concern one-shot distributions as well as periodical repetitions of some general distribution specification.

Figure 2 shows how the document providers and information consumers of the organizational memory can employ the distribution and comprehension assistant to improve their consensual understanding of documents in the organizational memory. An *initial coordination of individual and global concerns* (at the definition time of potential communications in the intranet) is achieved by a more or less representative sample of documents from which a three-level representation. Information-identification is initiated by long-term queries as well as ad hoc queries. The most relevant information (i.e. the right documents) become explicitely specified (information identification time). As in most information retrieval systems, a rather local and simple relevance measure is used, namely the similarity of a particular document and the user query. Integration processes enable an information consumer to converse with the oligo-agents about his individual relevance rankings of the various selected documents on the basis of the three-level representation. Such individual re-rankings can be based on more complex relevance metrics that might consider the whole set of selected documents and therefore allow for more global aspects like the *information gain.*

5 Discussion

In this paper, the problem of knowledge management, especially knowledge dissemination in an organization, is tackled by proposing the coordination of individual and global concerns in an oligo-agents system with shared responsibilities. This system is embedded in an organizational memory. From an application point of view, the functions that are provided by the distribution and comprehension assistant enable the information consumer to get a personalized view of the organizational memory. This view consists of individual aspects that are based upon a semantic document analysis as well as upon organizational aspects in the form of distribution lists in which a distributor determines the portion of information that is delivered to the consumer. Beyond the concept of a personal newspaper, this personalized view is supplemented by a clear assignment of individual and joint responsibilities for different facets of the knowledge management task, including spacial (location of information and users), temporal (decoupling time for the different users) and content-oriented (document comprehension) aspects. The combination of these elements leads to a flexible tool for handling information distribution and information gathering, two of the core problems of knowledge management.

References

1. Nonaka, I., Takeuchi, H.: *The Knowledge-Creating Company.* Oxford:University Press, 1995.
2. van Elst, L.: Ein kooperativer Informationsassistent zum gemeinsamen Verstehen von Textdokumenten (*An information assistant for the cooperative comprehension of text documents*). Master Thesis, Department of Computer Science, University of Kaiserslautern, 1998.
3. Deerwester, S., Dumais, S., Furnas, G., Landauer, T., Harshmann, R.: Indexing by Latent Semantic Analysis. *Journal of the American Society for Information Science,* 41(6), 391–407, 1990.

Veri-KoMoD: Verification of Knowledge Models in the Mechanical Design Field

Florence SELLINI*·**, Pierre-Alain YVARS**

* PSA Peugeot Citroën, Knowledge Engineering
DTII/IMTI/CCIC/Charlebourg/LG, 18 rue des Fauvelles,
92256 La Garenne Colombes Cedex, France.
** ISMCM-CESTI, GRIIEM Research Team
3 rue Fernand Hainaut, 93407 St Ouen, France.
Florence.Sellini@wanadoo.fr

Abstract.

Our research takes place in the field of Design Aid Systems for mechanical sets. The aim of work is to make " right " knowledge model with know-how capitalisation. We present in this article, our approach to validate a priori conceptual models. We have made the choice of an explicit representation to give more efficiency to the verification mechanisms defined. We focus on Model structure used for product class representation.

1. Introduction

Our research concerns the mechanical design aided field within systems based on knowledge. Our problem is to acquire the design know-how in order to describe a product class, and is to model this know-how in order to reuse it inside a design aided system connected to a geometric modeller.

After reminding of the main important reasons which lead us to validate knowledge models constructed during KBS application design, we detail our methodological approach **Veri-KoMoD**[1] of Model verifying [6]. In the following sections, we are focused to the Meta-Models used to describe a product class.

2. Design methodology for the verification of Models

The work presented is based on three axes as follows : "Verification Mechanism uses References to verify the Knowledge Representation".

---

[1] **Veri**fication of **K**nowledge **Mo**dels for **D**esign

2.1 KoMoD[2] : a formalism for knowledge representation structure

The structure type used for knowledge modelling is fundamental for the validation process. If knowledge is not structured enough, then the validation is almost impossible [4]. For the Know-How knowledge representation on the product design to be validated (product description and design rules), we need to clearly identify the used modelling structures. Out of DEKLARE[3]'s models, we defined entities of the used Meta-Models. Keeping our goal of validating them, we improved these models, bringing more declarativity to ease the complex knowledge expression.

2.2 The Model of references for verification

The *Model of references for verification*, also called the *C-Model* by [1], contains all the knowledge required to undertake a verification of the conceptual Models that we use. This Model corresponds to the explicit, detailed description of the Meta-Models. This knowledge could be classified in three different categories. Firstly, there is the knowledge which relates to the construction of the Model, the writing formalism. Then, there is the knowledge which allows the Model to be simplified during construction, thus preventing any unnecessary overload. Finally, there is the knowledge concerning Model consistency. It is principally relative to the presence of relations on connectors. Depending on the case, this knowledge is expressed in the form of definitions (« what must be»), or rules (« it is prohibited to.. »).

2.3 Definition of verification mechanisms

A differentiation has to be made between two types of verification : macro-verification and micro-verification.

Macro-verification or verification of the macroscopic structure of the diagram, involves the consistency of the representation of concepts from a structure viewpoint and the consistency of interaction between objects. This verification is performed in reference to the syntax. We will first of all describe the verification of the structure of the diagram in the sense of relations between concepts, then turn to the verification of the integrity of the connected diagram with the presence of relations over connectors and, finally, we will address the overall necessary verification of the diagram.

Micro-verification particularly affects knowledge supported by the concepts. This is professional knowledge. This verification is performed in consistency with the syntax of each object defined at Meta-Model level and with the characteristics of the domain of expertise concerned. It involves considering why it is impossible to cover professional knowledge as a whole on an overall basis and how to generate the contexts into which the sets of concepts participating in the same design solution will be isolated. The distinction made between these two types of verification is not absolutely linked to a temporal approach, according to which one verification ought to be made before another.

---

[2] Knowledge Modelling for Design
[3] European Esprit Project n°6522

3. Focus on knowledge representation structure

In the DEKLARE approach, the result of modelling task, is, on one hand, the class product model to be design (the WHO), and on the other hand, the model of the mechanical design process (the HOW).

3.2 A multi viewpoints product representation

The description of the product is made from three basic viewpoints : structural, functional and geometric. The mechanical parts designer may thus use different approaches in his design task : specification of functions to be fulfilled, the choice of structure and the dimensions of a mechanical set that he is not going to reinvent ; he also has at his disposal a complete geometric representation. A detailed presentation of this modelling structure is given in [7].

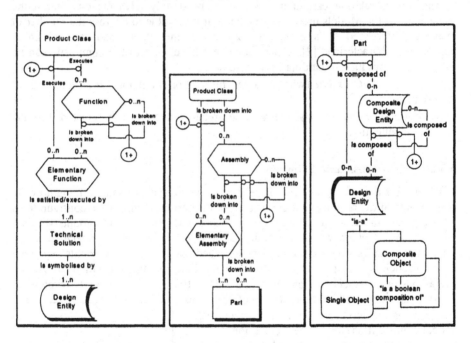

Figure 1. Product Meta-Model : functional (1), structural (2) and geometrical (3) points of view.

The functional Meta-Model describes the various functions which the entire product class must fulfil. This is a functional breakdown diagram. A structural Meta-Model is a structural breakdown diagram of the product which comprises the different variants existing in the product class. Unlike other views, which are diagrams describing the overall product, the geometric viewpoint is used to construct the geometric representation of each component part of the product (parts defined in the structural view) by using Design Entities (functional surfaces defined in the functional view (cf. *Figure 1*). Structural and functional views are related to the geometric views by "link" elements. The link between the structural view and the geometric view is made via the *Part* entity which thus has a dual viewpoint. For the functional and geometric views, it is the Design Entity which serves as the interface.

3.3 Making quite explicit structure relations using declarative knowledge

This paragraph relates to the principal enhancements made to the Models in [5] which contribute to a more extensive expressivity of knowledge. In order to improve verification of Models, the explicit nature of the knowledge represented must be consolidated. To do this, we have integrated cardinalities and meta-constraints called *relation connectors* to make structure relations explicit (composition hierarchy structure). This concept is similar to that of the association constraints in UML [3] or other entity/association formalisms.

3.3.1 Cardinalities

The use of relation cardinalities seems to be doubly advantageous within the framework of the Models used. On one hand, it is possible to express the number of instances referenced to a composite object; on the other hand, an existential dependence characteristic [2] of the component in relation to the composite can be expressed. Utilisation of cardinalities expresses :

- *the statement of possible* (whole) values (discreet or continuous) for the number of instances,
- *the optional or mandatory nature* of the relation, therefore the existence of the component entity.

3.3.2 Meta-constraint definition

To describe a product class, certain relations have to be expressed, defining how the components of the product are put together, or the various composition configurations for a product. In particular, to make this knowledge of the different variants within a *Product* class explicit, we have introduced the notion of *relation connectors*. These relation connectors are *meta-constraints*, managed like the other constraints expressed in the Model, by the propagation driver at the time of implementation. These are **meta**-constraints since they are constraints that affect other constraints (profession constraints expressed in the form of relations between parameters). In fact, since they affect Model composition links, they condition whether certain entities exist or not and the association between other entities which themselves contain constraints.

Four basic connectors have been defined for our needs :

- AND_Equivalent: (+)
- « At least one » : (1+)
- Mutual exclusion: (X)
- Implication: (→)

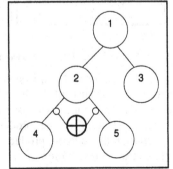

Figure 2. Presence of the connectors

These are not logic connectors but are rather similar to constraints. Their behaviour is governed by their semantics. The connectors have two possible statuses in the implementation: *true* and *violation* : The *true* status *(1)* corresponds to a *success,* and indicates that the constraint imposed by the presence of the connector is respected. *Violation (0)* corresponds to a *failure,* and indicates that the connector has not been respected and this therefore corresponds to choices prohibited due to the presence of this connector. For example, let us look at the table (cf. *Table 1*) summarising the behaviour of the AND_Equivalent (+) connector (cf. *Figure 2*). *Table 1* is not a truth table (or Karnaugh table) in the sense of Boolean algebra. It is a table summarising the couples of nodes allowed if the AND Equivalent connector is present.

node[4] 4	node 5	case in Figure 2
0	0	Violation
0	1	Violation[5]
1	0	Violation
1	1	true

Table 1. Behaviour of the AND-Equivalent connector

3.3.3 Making the different variants within the product class explicit

The example in *Figure 3*, represents the Connecting Rod-Piston assembly (structural viewpoint). The various assembly possibilities must appear on the Model. The connectors and cardinalities allow this to be expressed clearly.

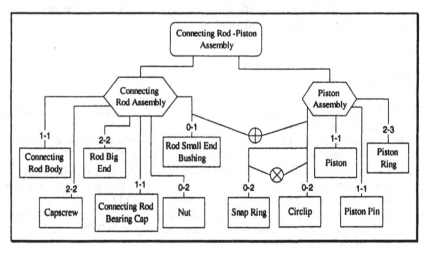

Figure 3. Structural Model of the connecting rod - piston assembly

On the Model in *Figure 3*, an AND Equivalent (+) connector has been added between the "Rod small end bushing" and "Snap ring" or "Circlips" elements so that choice and definition of these is dependent.

---

[4] The value 0 corresponds to the non-active status of the node (value 1 represents the active status).

[5] The term violation indicates that the connector does not allow the choice of this configuration.

The use of cardinalities also allows part of the knowledge to be expressed. In the case of the parts of the Connecting Rod-Piston assembly, the cardinality (1) for the "Connecting Rod Body" gives information on the mandatory nature of this element. In the same way, the "Nut" part has as cardinality of (0-2), therefore it is optional. The notation used indicates a restriction to only 2 choices : 0 or 2 Nut instances. The integration of connectors on relations and cardinalities allows a maximum of information to be made explicit, which, in itself, contributes to the removal of ambiguity and makes verification when reviewed by the specialist that much easier.

Conclusion

In this article, we have presented a contribution to *a priori* verification of product models in mechanical design. Three principal areas have been covered in detail: concepts and tools for the declarative modelling of product classes, specifically using connector or meta-constraint ideas, the Model of References for Verification, adapted to our requirements, as well as the mechanisms to be implemented to put this approach into operation. The entire set of verification mechanisms demonstrated is in the process of implementation in the GRIIEM's KoMoD (KnOwledge MOdelling for Design) design-aid application development. The Model of References for Verification has been formalised into a set of production rules, interpreted by a first order object-oriented inference engine. The representation of product knowledge is performed by the cognitive scientist using KoMoD. The detection of inconsistency is done automatically in real time for each modelling action the scientist undertakes. The perspectives given to this work particularly concern integration of the entire set of verification mechanisms into one software environment.

References

[1] **M. Ayel & M.-C. Rousset** - *La cohérence dans les bases de connaissances* pages. Paris, Cépadues Eds. (1990).

[2] **C. Djeraba, G.-T. Nguyen et D. Rieu** - Objets composites et liens de dépendance dans un système à base de connaissance, *INFORSID'93* , Lille, p. 353-372 (1993).

[3] **P.-A. Muller** - *Modélisation Objet avec UML.* Eyrolles ed, 421 pages. PARIS(1997).

[4] **C. Pierret-Golbreicht** - *TASK, un environnement pour le développement de systèmes flexibles*, Rapport de Recherche, report n° RR n°1056, LRI Orsay(1996).

[5] **A. Saucier** - *Un modèle multi-vues du produit pour le développement et l'utilisation de systèmes d'aide à la conception en ingénierie mécanique*, PhD Thesis in Mécanique, ENS de Cachan(1997).

[6] **F. Sellini** - *Contribution à la représentation et à la vérification de Modèles de connaissances produit en ingénierie d'ensembles mécaniques.*, PhD Thesis in génie industriel & informatique, Ecole Centrale de Paris(1999).

[7] **F. Sellini & P.-A. Yvars** - Méta Modèle déclaratif pour la représentation du produit en conception mécanique, *IDMME'98* , Compiègne(1998).

A Flexible Framework for Uncertain Expertise

Heiner Stuckenschmidt and K. Christoph Ranze

Center for Computing Technologies,
Bremen University
P.O.B. 330440, 28334 Bremen, Germany
{*heiner,kcr*}*@tzi.de*

Abstract. In this paper we argue that the development of knowledge-based systems built to work in partially uncertain domains benefit from the use of different conceptualisations for certain and uncertain parts of the knowledge. We present conceptualisations that have proven to be useful, namely the KADS model of expertise and a causal model of uncertainty that reflects well known approaches to uncertain reasoning like Bayesian belief nets. After a brief introduction to these conceptualisations we propose a translation approach that aims at an integration of these conceptualisations in a common knowledge model that can be used in a knowledge engineering process.

1 Introduction

Model-based approaches are the leading technology in knowledge-based systems development. All of these approaches are conceived to guide users to a (formal) model of the problem-solving process and the underlying domain knowledge. In real-world applications adjectives like 'probable, 'possible' or 'incomplete' are attached to domain knowledge and data. We summarize these phenomena of non-categorical knowledge as *uncertainty*. Having recognized that uncertainty plays an important role in the development of knowledge-based systems we have to find ways to deal with this kind of uncertainty when building knowledge models. Investigating different KADS-based knowledge engineering approaches we found no sophisticated formalism for explicit representation of uncertainty.

The problem is not that there are no ways to deal with uncertain knowledge. There there is a huge amount of elaborated (numerical) calculi representing and processing uncertain knowledge in application systems. One of the most prominent approaches are belief nets using subjective probabilities to determine the value of different random variables.

So what is the real problem that prevents notions of uncertainty to be integrated in existing knowledge engineering approaches? We think that the problem is that existing approaches for handling uncertainty follow a conceptualisation used to describe a knowledge domain that is completely different from the one used in common knowledge engineering approaches.

We argue that if it is neccessary to deal with uncertainty in complex domains one has to bridge the gap between these different conceptualisations. On one hand we need rather simple conceptualisation of models of uncertainty to enable uncertain reasoning. On the other hand we are not willing to give up the more elaborate conceptualisation of models of expertise that has been proved to be useful for analysis, model building, and reuse.

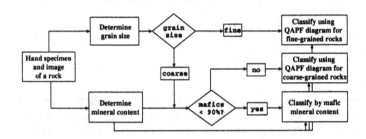

Fig. 1. Rock classification

Figure 1 shows a snapshot of the classification task from the Sisyphus III domain [1] which serves as an example for the need of such a combined approach within this paper. A rock class of a hand specimen is determined through a classification scheme of mineral contents. The selection of a certain scheme depends on the grainsize of the specimen which can be computed through image analysis.

In the following we describe the different conceptualisations of expertise and uncertainty model and present a translation approach to integrate these conceptualisations.

2 A Conceptualisation of Expertise

Conceptualisations of expertise are typically subdivided into three kinds of knowledge: *domain, inference, and task knowledge* as defined in the KADS model of expertise [6]. In the following we describe this conceptualisation on an abstract level. Those parts of the real world relevant to the given task are described with their properties within the domain model. The formal specification of this knowledge is realized by a set of ontological primitives enabling the user to define complex structures: *concepts, instances* of these concepts, *attributes* of and *relations* between concepts. Based on the modeled elements there are *inference actions* performing single steps of the problem-solving process. Inference actions operate on elements from the domain layer. These elements are described through *input-, output-* and *static roles* which are placeholders determining the role the element plays in the problem-solving process and the type of domain objects that can play this role. The task layer contains knowledge about how the elementary inference steps can be combined and executed to achieve a certain goal. This knowledge is organized in *tasks* which are compositions of *subtasks* including control knowledge about their execution in order to achieve the *goal* of the main task. Primitive tasks which do not have subtasks show a one-to-one correspondence to *knowledge sources* within the inference layer. Together these three layers form a model of expertise that claims to capture all aspects of expert reasoning relevant to the development of knowledge-based systems. A common model is achieved by connecting the different layers in the sense that the roles of inferences are filled with domain knowledge and tasks are executed by applying inferences which produce a result corresponding to the task's goal.

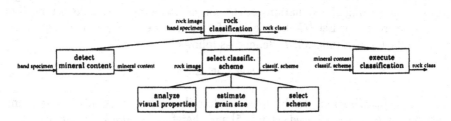

Fig. 2. Task model for rock classification

Figure 2 shows a task model of the given classification problem as an example of the flavor of expertise models. Further investigations show that the estimation of the grainsize of a rock through an image analysis produces uncertain results and might be realized e.g. with a Bayes net. Based on the grainsize a certain classification scheme has to be selected. The classification of the rock class itself takes no uncertainty into account, because the classification schemes are based on clear data and certain information.

3 A Conceptualisation of Uncertainty

In this section we review a conceptualisation of uncertain expertise knowledge proposed in [4]. The conceptualisation consists of three basic concepts:

A set of hypotheses is a variable, whose values denote different hypotheses concerning the same assertion. The hypotheses are assumed to be conflicting in the sense that only one of the hypotheses can be true at a time. Variables are denoted by small letters. If v is a variable then W_v represents the set of all possible values for v.

A valuation function [7] attaches a degree of certainty taken from a set of truth values to configurations of hypotheses. In the following, sets of truth values are always denoted as Ψ. Valuation functions are denoted by capitals corresponding to a valuated variable:

$$V : W_v \rightarrow \Psi \tag{1}$$

A set of hypotheses and a valuation function over this set form a basic modeling element for uncertain domain knowledge which is denoted as *phenomenon of uncertainty*. A simple phenomenon of uncertainty UP is a pair consisting of a set W_v of hypotheses and a valuation function V on this set.

$$UP = (W_v, V) \tag{2}$$

Causal relations [3] are special valuation functions defined on different phenomena of uncertainty mapping one or more phenomena of uncertainty and a special value set indicating the strength of the causal influence on a target phenomenon. Such a causal relation determines the valuation function of the target phenomenon using the valuations of the source phenomena and the strength of the causal relation. Let UP be the set of all phenomena of uncertainty, then a causal relation is a function F defined as follows:

$$F : UP^n \times \Psi \to UP \tag{3}$$

This conceptualisation can be used to describe different calculi for handling uncertainty in a graph-based setting [5] and therefore provides a useful approach to the specification of uncertain knowledge.

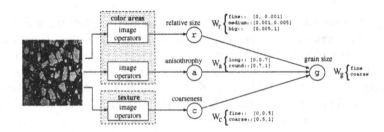

Fig. 3. Detection of grainsize through image analysis

Figure 3 shows the details of the detection of grainsize through image analysis. There are four variables with their hypothesis sets which are connected via causal relations. The concrete configuration of the variables r, a and c for a given specimen is computed through image operators which induce the uncertainty into the model.

4   Mapping the Conceptualisations

The descriptions of common conceptualisations of expertise knowledge on one hand and knowledge for uncertain reasoning on the other hand reveal significant differences. While the conceptualisation of models of expertise try to capture all aspects of the problem-solving process using a variety of different interconnected modeling primitives, the conceptualisation of uncertain knowledge uses only a few simple primitives thus enabling efficient processing of uncertainty. Due to these differences an integration of the conceptualisations raises severe problems. We propose a different approach using translation mappings between models of expertise and models of uncertain knowledge. These mappings can be used to make uncertain inference within the conceptualisation of uncertainty possible while keeping the advantages of the conceptualisation used in models of expertise. The use of translation mappings imply the following three-step process:

Determination of the language for the model of uncertainty is the first step. For this purpose, variables and relations of a causal model of uncertainty are explicitly connected to the terminology in the model of expertise.

Uncertain inference is executed within the model of expertise deriving valuations of previously unknown phenomena.

Determination of assertional knowledge is the last step. It uses the results of uncertain inferences to state axioms about knowledge to be used in the problem-solving process within the model of expertise.

During this process two kinds of translation mappings are used. The first one is a reference mapping that is used to translate the terminology of the model of expertise into the one used in the model of uncertainty. This means, that different modeling primitives from the model of expertise (e.g. attributes and relations) are mapped onto the primitives used for uncertain inference, namely phenomena of uncertainty. The same holds for inference actions that are translated into causal relations between in- and output roles that are also described using phenomena of uncertainty. To establish a complete connection between the conceptualisations not only the terminology, but also the assertions have to be translated. This step mentioned above as 'determination of assertional knowledge' is performed by a semantical mapping. This mapping translates valuation functions into logical axioms that follow the terminology of the model of expertise. Doing this, it transfers the results of uncertain inference (which is essentially a definition of the different valuation functions) into assertions that can be handled within the conceptualisation of expertise.

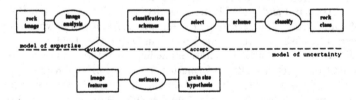

Fig. 4. Detail of an abstract inference scheme for rock classification

Using this connection between the different conceptualisations it becomes possible to formalize the complete problem-solving process as shown in figure 4. The uncertain part of the inference is embedded in the certain model. The uncertain part is triggered by an evidence that determines a valuation function over the image features. The result of uncertain reasoning, which in our case is the grain size of the specimen, is incorporated in the certain model using an acceptance criterion [2] which selects one hypothesis on the basis of the valuation function over the whole hypotheses set.

5 Discussion

In this paper we showed how different conceptualisations of certain and uncertain knowledge can be integrated into a common problem-solving model. This enables us to perform a complete analysis of a problem statement containing uncertainty using elaborated knowledge modeling approaches. Therefore we can profit from advantages connected with these approaches but we don't have to force uncertain knowledge into a complex conceptualisation which is hard to handle. In our example this leads to the possibility to process uncertain input from image data and at the same time to use existing classification schemes. If we had used the conceptualisation of expertise for the whole model it would have been hard to integrate the image data into the problem-solving process due to its uncertainty. Using the conceptualisation of uncertainty for the whole model we would have had to re-specify the classification schemes into an unnatural form. Beside these simplifications of the analysis and modeling process our approach implies further possibilities. Existing conceptualisations of expertise can be reused and incorporated into a common model with conceptualisations of uncertainty (e.g. belief nets) that have been learned from data using machine learning techniques not applicable to more complex conceptualisations.

References

1. U. Gappa and F. Puppe. A study of knowledge acquisition - experiences from the sisyphus III experiment for rock classification. In *Proceedings of the 11th Workshop Knowlegde Acquisition for Knowledge-Based Systems*, Banff, Alberta Canada, 1998.
2. H. E. Kyburg. Probabilistic acceptance. In Dan Geiger and Prakash Shenoy, editors, *Proceedings of the Thirteenth Conference on Uncertainty in Artificial Intelligence*, San Francisco, 1997. Morgan Kaufmann Publishers.
3. J. Pearl. Structural and probabilistic causality. In D.R. Shanks, K.J. Holyoak, and D.L. Medin, editors, *The Psychology of Learning and Motivation*, volume 34: Causal Learning, pages 393–435. Academic Press, San Diego, CA, 1996.
4. K. C. Ranze and H. Stuckenschmidt. Modelling uncertainty in expertise. In Jose Cuena, editor, *IT & KNOWS Information Technologies and Knowledge Systems, Proceedings of the XV. IFIP World Computer Congress*, Serial Publication of the Austrian Computer Society, pages 105–118, Vienna/Budapest, September 1998.
5. A. Saffiotti and E. Umkehrer. PULCINELLA - a general tool for propagating uncertainty in valuation networks. In *Proceedings of the 7th Conference on Uncertainty in AI*, pages 323 – 331, Los Angeles, CA, 1991.
6. Guus Schreiber, Bob Wielinga, and Joost Breuker, editors. *KADS: A Principled Approach to Knowledge-Based Systems Development*, volume 11 of *Knowledge-Based Systems*. Academic Press, 1993.
7. P.P. Shenoy. Valuation-based systems: A framework for managing uncertainty in expert systems. In L.A. Zadeh and J. Kacprzyk, editors, *Fuzzy Logic for the Management of Uncertainty*. Wiley and Sons, 1989.

Elicitation of Operational Track Grids

Randy P. Wolf

1006 Woods Cove Rd,Scottsboro, AL 35768 USA

rwolf@worldisp1.net/(256) 574-3686

No Affiliation

Abstract. Acquisition of operational knowledge is integral to the general process of knowledge acquisition and is particularly pertinent to the process of analyzing problems and their associated domains. A type of repertory grid known as a track grid can be used to aid such acquisition and analysis. Track grids can be elicited using track grid analysis but track grid analysis does not focus on eliciting operational knowledge. A version of track grid analysis which is specifically tailored to elicit operational knowledge will be presented.

1 Introduction

Knowledge acquisition (KA) systems are intrinsically concerned with acquiring operational knowledge[1] because real-world knowledge is usually concerned with entities which exist in a state of flux and less so with static Platonic entities. KA systems which focus on problem-solving methods [2, 3] have an even stronger association with operational knowledge. Such systems are primarily concerned with problems which typically require a change of state of the problem from being 'unsolved' to being 'solved.'

The ubiquitous nature of coexistant, essential operational (subsequently abbreviated as 'O') knowledge in both general and problem-solving contexts in conjunction with the assumed value of KA in these contexts provides sufficient motivation to seek to develop an elicitation technique for acquiring O knowledge. Additional motivation is provided by the presumptive utility of an ability to acquire such O knowledge in sufficient fidelity to permit the performance of acquired algorithms. The approach will use a repertory grid form known as track grids [10–13] to acquire O knowledge. Track grids provide a general KA capability based on personal construct theory [6] and repertory grids [1, 4, 9]. Track grid analysis (TGA) can acquire O knowledge while acquiring general track grids but the technique is not designed to focus on eliciting this type of knowledge.

The major contribution of this paper is to develop an elicitation technique specific to O track grids because no such technique previously existed. It will be

---

[1] This paper considers operational knowledge to be knowledge which describes action: knowledge about change of state. There are other, somewhat different definitions of operational knowledge such as defining operational knowledge to be 'knowing what to do when' [8]. A related type of knowledge is strategic knowledge which is defined to be 'knowing what to do next' [5].

shown that TGA may be modified so that O knowledge is specifically elicited while the basic nature of track grid analysis is retained.

2   Background

A track grid is formed by realizing that a conventional repertory grid can be considered to be equivalent to asking a question and by allowing differing questions to be asked. Figure 1 shows a known conventional repertory grid:

5	1	1	5	5	Symbolic / Numeric
5	5	5	2	1	Widely available / Not widely available
1	1	1	5	1	Scientific / Business

ADA LISP PROLOG COBOL FORTRAN

Fig. 1. Conventional Repertory Grid.

A grid functions as a question with elements serving as subject(s) of the question and with constructs/poles serving as answer(s). The implicit question for a conventional grid is always the same: 'what are the constructs which describe the elements?' If a repertory grid does not act as a question, does not answer this question, then the listed 'constructs' are not constructs at all according to personal construct theory [6]. Laddering questions have been used to elicit new grid information so there is a precedent for using questions to define grids [1].

Figure 2 reformulates Figure 1 into a track grid form. Allowing explicit questions means that it should be possible to ask any relevant question which produces a useful answer. Ergo, the question for one grid might ask about some portion of another grid or about another grid as a whole. The lower grid in Figure 2 asks about who uses certain languages (an important characteristic of high level languages). A good basic set of types of questions would be questions about *who, what, when, where, why,* and *how.*

TGA assumes that if a grid is a question then a group of related grids is a group of related questions. Hence, elicitation is naturally structured as a conversation with the grid questions being asked in an appropriate order. Restating: elicitation is best accomplished by *asking the right person the right questions at the right time.* TGA determines the right questions to ask, the right order in which to ask the questions, and then asks the questions. To date, groups of related grids which define an executable procedure have always been created manually This established the basic feasibility of acquiring grids which contain sufficient detail to allow a procedure or algorithm to actually be performed but it did not determine whether it is basically feasible to *elicit* such groups of grids.

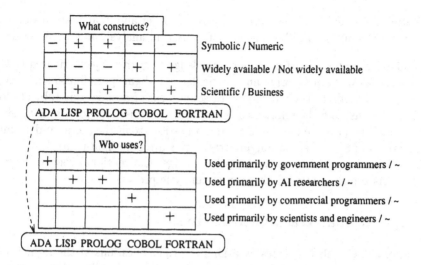

Fig. 2. Track Grids for High Level Languages.

It will be shown that judicious elicitation of appropriate questions and question order allows the acquisition of groups of grids that can be performed (O grid sets). TGA not intended to produce this result is non-O track grid analysis.

3 Non-operational Track Grid Analysis

TGA exists within a framework of track grid analysis and synthesis. TGA is concerned with asking the right questions at the right time to acquire some body of knowledge. Questioning results can be used to drive a synthesis production system: this is track grid synthesis. If the actual results of this synthesis production system match the expected results then this is reason to believe that the right questions are being asked at the right time. Figure 3 shows the process.

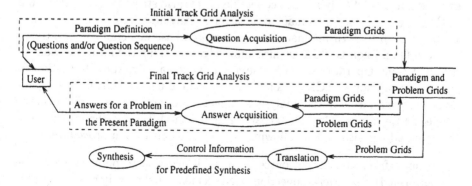

Fig. 3. Overall Track Grid Analysis and Synthesis.

Initial TGA gets the questions and question order and final analysis obtains answers to the questions. Two benefits of track grid analysis and synthesis are:

Provides for acquisition of paradigm knowledge (e.g. the object-oriented (OO) paradigm) without favoring any particular paradigm (paradigm-neutrality). A given paradigm is concerned with some form of atomic unit (objects for OO analysis) and the relations of these units (e.g. methods for OO analysis). It should be possible to tailor a series of questions to fit the atoms and atomic relations of any given paradigm. Track grids are paradigm-neutral.

Provides for acquisition of synthesis knowledge. Conventional repertory grid systems typically assume usage in an analytic process.

4 Operational Track Grid Analysis

Operational TGA also operates by asking the right questions at the right time. Because O grid sets must conform to certain guidelines, the elicitation questions seek to acquire a group of grids that have a certain structure. In general, non-O TGA does not seek to acquire groups of grids that have a certain structure.

An O grid set must meet standards similar to those that a computational procedure must meet. There must be some overall process that is to be performed which is composed of divisible steps that can actually be performed. There must be some sequence in which the steps are to be performed. In terms of track grids, these standards translate to a network structure of grids (although a tree structure is more common) with some single grid acting as the 'start' grid: the first grid to be executed. This start grid is decomposed into a number of subordinate grids which act as a definition of the steps to be taken by the start grid. Each of these subordinate grids may in turn be decomposed. Eventually, subordinate grids are decomposed into defined primitives which can actually be performed. Operational TGA acquires this structure.

This particular grid structure is not the only way to arrange O knowledge in track grids such that the result is performable, is equivalent to a computational procedure. This is one way to achieve that result, however. Just as track grids in general are paradigm-neutral, track grids which support execution are also paradigm-neutral. Studying the acquisition of this grid structure is advantageous in that it can be shown to map to a universal language[7, 13] which in turn is known to map to a Turing machine, the accepted base model of computation.

Both O and non-O TGA acquire knowledge by asking the right questions at the right time. Operational TGA assumes a particular structure of questions is needed, overall non-O TGA does not. However, final non-O TGA uses the questions acquired during initial analysis and hence does assume a specific sequence of specific questions. The counterpart of final non-O TGA is the execution of the acquired algorithm. The following describes the elicitation procedure:

1. Acquire from knowledge source the overall question to be answered(to be performed):This overall question is an element of the grid(the start grid if this is the initial call). Conceptually, this technique exploits the equivalency

between performing an action (e.g. 'add 2 numbers') and answering a parallel question (e.g. 'what is the sum of 2 numbers?').

2. Acquire which subsidiary questions must be answered before the overall question can be answered:These subsidiary questions act as poles which apply to the overall question. These subsidiary questions will also eventually become the track questions for individual, subsidiary grids.

3. Acquire the sequence for answering these subsidiary questions:Ask 'what order' with the subsidiary questions acting as subject(s).

4. Acquire whether answering each subsidiary question involves a primitive or further, decompositional questions. In the case of a primitive, a shell script which can actually be executed is mapped to be a pole which applies to the subsidiary question. In the case of decomposition, additional subsidiary grid structure is formed by recursively applying this elicitation procedure.

The short term goal has been to determine the basic feasibility of eliciting O knowledge. To date, a limited number of processes have been acquired. One such acquired procedure demonstrated execution, alternation, and iteration: the characteristics of a universal language. Although this establishes basic feasibility, capabilities beyond basic feasibility are of interest. Future work will include using O elicitation to acquire grids sets that heretofor have only been acquired manually: dyadic elicitation, PCCG [12], and non-O TGA. Also, it would be useful to elicit operational TGA itself (an ability for self-compilation validates a compiler so self-elicitation is a worthwhile validation goal) and the track grid prototype itself. Eventually, other validation tests such as those offered by Sisyphus problems will need to be performed.

5 Results and Conclusion

The specific results of this research are the elicitation technique itself and the characteristics of the resulting acquired operational grids. The elicitation process is fully automatic in that a single session with a user answering natural language questions is all that is needed to create an operational grid set. However, if a primitive is needed which is not already defined, the knowledge source must enter a definition of the primitive. Assuming no intervention by a knowledge engineer, this requires programming skill on the part of the user.

The characteristics of a grid set elicited by operational TGA differs in two ways from manually-created sets. One difference is that no information acquired that is superfluous to the targeted algorithm. An advantages of track grids is that not only can 'how' a procedure is performed be acquired but also explanatory information such as questions about 'why' or 'where' is also typically acquired. Also, the automatically generated grids of the O grid set contain a fair amount of automatically generated elements and poles. Every subitem of a manually-created grid is personally meaningful to some knowledge source. A similar result is observable when assembler code created by a human is compared to that created by a compiler. Overall, the result is that operational TGA elicited grid sets do not seem to be as information rich as manually created sets.

The pervasive nature of operational knowledge in general and problem-solving KA environments indicates a need for an ability to elicit and acquire such knowledge. The application of track grids and particularly of operational track grids is potentially one way to support this need. The demonstrable basic feasibility of elicitation of operational knowledge is a positive indicator which encourages further investigation. However, there is a very real need for further validation before any judgement can be passed concerning the eventual pragmatic value of this type of elicitation.

References

[1] Boose, J.H., and Bradshaw, J.M., "Expertise transfer and complex problems: using AQUINAS as a knowledge-acquisition workbench for knowledge-based systems," Boose, J., and Gaines, B. (Eds.), *Knowledge Acquisition Tools for Expert Systems*, Academic Press, NY, NY, 1988.

[2] Chandrasekaran, B., "Generic Tasks in knowledge-based reasoning: High level building blocks for expert system design," *IEEE Expert*, 1., 23-30, Fall 1986.

[3] Eriksson, H., Shahar, Y., Tu, S.W., Puerta, A.R., and Musen, M.A., "Task Modeling with reusable problem-solving methods," *Artificial Intelligence*, 79, 293-326, 1995.

[4] Gaines, B.R., and Shaw, M.L.G., "Knowledge Acquisition Tools Based on Personal Construct Psychology," *Knowledge Engineering Review*, 8(1), 49-85, 1993.

[5] Gruber, T.R., *The Acquisition of Strategic Knowledge*, Academic Press, San Diego, 1989.

[6] Kelly, G.A, *The Psychology of Personal Constructs*, W. W. Norton, NY, NY, 1955.

[7] Pratt, T.W., *Programming Languages: Design and Implementation*, 2nd Edition, Prentice-Hall, Englewood Cliffs, New Jersey, 1984.

[8] Rich. E. and Knight, K., *Artificial Intelligence*, McGraw-Hill NY, NY, 1991.

[9] Shaw, M.L.G. and Gaines, B.R., "KITTEN: Knowledge Initiation and Transfer Tools for Experts and Novices," *Knowledge Acquisition Tools for Expert Systems*, Boose, J. and Gaines, B. (Eds.), Academic Press, Harcourt Brace Jovanovich, San Diego, 1988.

[10] R. P. Wolf and H. S. Delugach, "Knowledge Acquisition via the Integration of Repertory Grids and Conceptual Graphs", in *Auxiliary Proceedings, 4th International Conference on Conceptual Structures*, (pp. 108-120), P.W. Eklund, G. Ellis and G. Mann, eds., 1996, University of New South Wales, Sydney, Australia, Aug. 19-23 1996. ISBN 0 7334 1387 0

[11] R. P. Wolf and H. S. Delugach, "Knowledge Acquisition Via Tracked Repertory Grids", Technical Report No. TR-UAH-CS-1996-02, Computer Science Department, Univ. of Alabama in Huntsville, 1996, ftp://ftp.cs.uah.edu/pub/techreports/TR-UAH-CS-1996-02

[12] Wolf, R.P., and Delugach, H.S., "PCCG: An Operational Tracked Grid for Creating Conceptual Graphs," Lukose, D., Delugach, H. Keeler, M. and Searle, L. and Sowa, J. (Eds.), *Conceptual Structures: Fulfilling Peirce"s Dream, Fifth International Conference on Conceptual Structures, ICCS 1997*, 617-620, Seattle, Washington, USA, Aug. 3-8, 1997.

[13] R. P. Wolf *Knowledge Acquisition via Integration of Personal Constructs and Conceptual Graphs* Ph.D. Dissertation, University of Alabama at Huntsville, Huntsville, AL, USA, http://www.umi.com

Author Index

Springer
and the
environment

At Springer we firmly believe that an
international science publisher has a
special obligation to the environment,
and our corporate policies consistently
reflect this conviction.
We also expect our business partners –
paper mills, printers, packaging
manufacturers, etc. – to commit
themselves to using materials and
production processes that do not harm
the environment. The paper in this
book is made from low- or no-chlorine
pulp and is acid free, in conformance
with international standards for paper
permanency.

 Springer

Lecture Notes in Artificial Intelligence (LNAI)

Lecture Notes in Computer Science